SERPENT IN EDEN

SERPENT IN EDEN

FOREIGN MEDDLING AND PARTISAN POLITICS IN JAMES MADISON'S AMERICA

TYSON REEDER

OXFORD
UNIVERSITY PRESS

OXFORD
UNIVERSITY PRESS

Oxford University Press is a department of the University of Oxford. It furthers
the University's objective of excellence in research, scholarship, and education
by publishing worldwide. Oxford is a registered trade mark of Oxford University
Press in the UK and certain other countries.

Published in the United States of America by Oxford University Press
198 Madison Avenue, New York, NY 10016, United States of America.

CIP data is on file at the Library of Congress

ISBN 978–0–19–762859–1

DOI: 10.1093/oso/9780197628591.001.0001

Printed by Sheridan Books, Inc., United States of America

For Matthew, TC, Cody, and Adelaide

CONTENTS

ACKNOWLEDGMENTS

―――⬦∘⬦∘⬦――

I HAD THE GOOD FORTUNE of writing this book while affiliated with three departments across two universities (well, technically one unit and two departments). I started this project while a member of the Papers of James Madison (my home unit) and the Corcoran Department of History at the University of Virginia. I finished it at my current position in the History Department at Brigham Young University. Many kind colleagues in both institutions helped bring this book to fruition. John Stagg, editor-in-chief of the Papers of James Madison, has forgotten more than most of us know not only about James Madison but about the history of the early republic. His expertise proved invaluable. I also thank my other colleagues at the Madison Papers, Armin Mattes, Angela Kreider, Anne Colony, Ellen Goldlust, and Mary Wigge for their expertise that improved this book. I had the unique and fortunate experience of being Alan Taylor's student at UC Davis and then his colleague in the History Department at UVA. He was just as generous a colleague as he was an adviser, imparting his time and knowledge to improve this project. Max Edelson and Christa Dierksheide asked penetrating questions and gave valuable insight to better the book. Sara Meyers from UVA's Classics Department also lent me her expertise to decipher some Latin. The faculty and staff at BYU have been very supportive of my research, and I especially thank Matt Mason, Jeff Shumway, and Andy Johns for their feedback. Christopher Blythe of BYU's English department and charter member of the JSP ambulatory society has strengthened the project, and I, of course, always feel the support of the rest of the friends and members in that society. Jen Nelson, BYU

History Department Manager, has gone above and beyond in making sure I have had the resources I needed to complete this project.

This book has benefited from the sharp eyes and minds of good friends and scholars who reviewed the manuscript in full or in part. Lindsay Chervinsky, John Stagg, and Matt Mason all read it in its entirety. Lige Gould, Kathleen Duvall, Steffanie Reeder, and Frank Cogliano read significant portions. I appreciate the time they gave and the knowledge they imparted. Several roundtables and workshops improved this book. I presented a paper on James Madison and foreign intrusion to a Madison Scholars Roundtable at Montpelier in 2018, when this book was a vague thought in the recesses of my mind. The scholars there were generous with their input. It was there I first met Akhil Reed Amar, whose scholarly achievements are only surpassed by his personal generosity, and I thank him for his engagement with my research. I'm grateful to have presented some early ideas for this book to the faculty and graduate students at UVA's Early American Seminar and to have received their important feedback. This would have been a very different book without their help. With the sponsorship of the Omohundro Institute, and in the depths of a global pandemic, a panel of scholars at a virtual writing table workshopped a chapter for me. Those scholars included Rebecca Brannon, Daniel Ackermann, Katlyn Carter, Robert Colby, Alexi Garrett, Cassandra Good, Donald Johnson, Linda Killian, Timothy Leech, Laura Macaluso, Christopher Minty, Rachel Shelden, Duangkamol Tantirungkij, and Helena Yoo Roth. They helped me improve not only that chapter but the entire book. I especially thank the guest presenters to the table, Alexis Coe and David Head. I also had the good fortune to present an early chapter of this book at an Omohundro Institute Colloquium, where Karin Wulf, Paul Mapp, Cathy Kelly, Joshua Piker, Fabrício Prado, and Nick Popper helped me refine my ideas.

I am indebted to many other institutions and individuals who improved this book by providing research funds, offering translation suggestions, and helping me procure research material. I enjoyed a fellowship with the Fundação Luso-Americana Para o Desenvolvimento and Direção-Geral do Livro, Arquivos e Bibliotecas, which allowed me to conduct productive research in Portugal's Torre do Tombo. The Washington Library provided helpful support, allowing my research to continue in the midst of a pandemic. I thank the American Philosophical Society for a Franklin Research Grant that funded vital research in European archives. Funding from UVA and BYU supplemented the support of those institutions. Elizabeth Chew and the Staff at James Madison's Montpelier have been vital partners in my study of Madison's life and career. Brett Rushforth, Heather Harman, and Martin Bonny helped me work through sticky French translations. Jim Ambuske and José M. Guerrero Acosta helped me track down a private image of Diego de Gardoqui. Andrew Fagal of the Papers of Thomas Jefferson and Sara Georgini of the Adams Family Papers helped me procure research documents. Portions of this book were published in the *Journal of the Early Republic* and *The Routledge History of U.S. Foreign Relations* (2022).

My agent, Carolyn Savarese helped me connect with Tim Bent of Oxford University Press, and their help has been invaluable. Tim is a meticulous editor, whose revisions enriched the writing and sharpened the analysis in this book. I'm grateful to Alex Rouch, Rachel Ruisard, Amy Whitmer, Patterson Lamb, and the production team at OUP for helping *Serpent in Eden* move from a thought to a book. I also thank Sam Freedman of Columbia University, who gave helpful advice to usher the book into light.

As has ever been the case, I have had an incredible network of family and friends, without whom I could not have written this book. My parents, Doug and Laura Reeder, continue to offer their unwavering support, as do my parents-in-law, Lynn and Jeanne Taylor. Ryan, Jill, Burke, Traci, Cody, Andra, Steffanie, Kammi, Rick, Beej, and Meg gave suggestions about cover design and feedback on the writing. My children, Matthew, TC, Cody, and Adelaide, have kept my life in perspective and focused on things that matter most. As always, my wife, Karen, has been a rock of support, allowing me to bounce ideas off her, offering suggestions, and in myriad ways shouldering loads that allowed me to write this book. Like most good things in my life, this wouldn't have been possible without her.

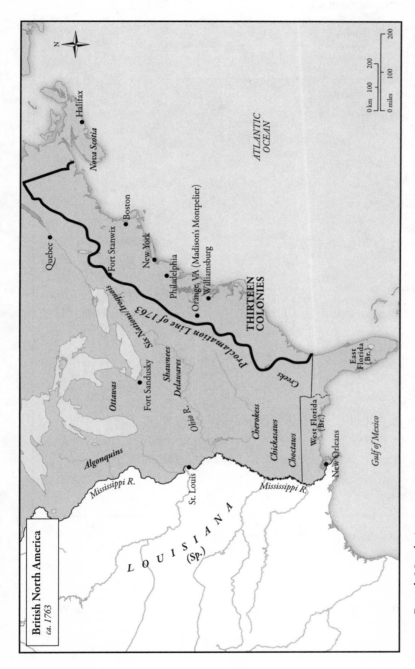

MAP 1 British North America, 1763

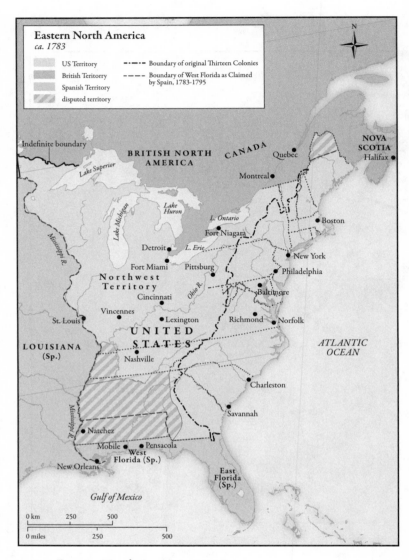

Eastern North America
ca. 1783

US Territory
British Teritorry
Spanish Territory
disputed territory

——·—· Boundary of original Thirteen Colonies
—— —— Boundary of West Florida as Claimed
by Spain, 1783-1795

N

Indefinite boundary

BRITISH NORTH
AMERICA

CANADA

Quebec

NOVA
SCOTIA
Halifax •

Lake Superior

Montreal •

Lake
Huron

Lake Michigan

L. Ontario

Fort Niagara

Boston •

Detroit •

L. Erie

Mississippi R.

Fort Miami

Pittsburg

New York •

**Northwest
Territory**

Ohio R.

Philadelphia •

Cincinnati

Baltimore •

Vincennes

St. Louis •

Lexington •

Richmond •

Norfolk •

**UNITED
STATES**

ATLANTIC
OCEAN

LOUISIANA
(Sp.)

Nashville •

Charleston •

Mississippi R.

Savannah •

Natchez •

Mobile •

Pensacola •

**West
Florida (Sp.)**

New Orleans •

East
Florida
(Sp.)

Gulf of Mexico

0 km   250   500

0 miles   250   500

MAP 2 Eastern North America, ca. 1783

MAP 3 Western Europe, ca. 1763

INTRODUCTION

———◦◦◦◦———

The Spy and the Con Artist

IN LATE NOVEMBER OR EARLY DECEMBER 1811, Paul-Émile Soubiran wandered the deck of the Boston-bound *New Galen*. Years of shady escapades and double-dealing had finally caught up with the French con artist, and Napoleon Bonaparte's police had chased him out of Europe. Fleeing first to Britain, he had boarded the *New Galen* for Boston in November. Among the other passengers, he masqueraded as the Count Edouard de Crillon. Meanwhile, he schemed for a way back into Napoleon's good graces.[1]

While he strolled through the night air on the ship's deck, Soubiran happened to encounter a man named John Henry, another dejected traveler and, unbeknown to Soubiran, a former British spy. He had met Henry before and noticed that the Irishman usually dined alone and shot pistols on deck to while away the voyage.[2]

As the pair talked in the darkness, Henry confided in Soubiran. Two years earlier, Governor General James Craig of British Canada had employed Henry as a secret agent in America. He had commissioned Henry to determine whether President James Madison's political opponents—the Federalists—might consider severing their stronghold of New England and seceding from the United States. Federalist New England might then become a British ally in the war against Napoleon's France—an idea the staunchly anti-British Madison would never entertain. Henry had felt slighted when in exchange for his work he received a paltry compensation.

I

The former spy traveled to Britain to seek a more substantial sum or at least a government appointment for his services. He failed. Embittered and impoverished, he boarded the *New Galen* for his return to America.[3]

Henry told Soubiran about some documents he had retained from his secret mission. Soubiran recognized a chance at redemption in France and formulated a plan. Still acting as the Count de Crillon, he proposed that they cooperate with the French government to sell the papers to the Madison administration. He guessed that the president would pay handsomely for documents that detailed a secret British mission to conspire with his political opponents. Henry could exact revenge on the British, Soubiran could impress French officials, and they both could swindle the US government.[4]

Though anything involving Soubiran exists in the realm of a John le Carré novel, that seems a probable reconstruction of what happened aboard the *New Galen*. Once in the United States, Soubiran and Henry related their plan to Louis Sérurier, the French envoy in Washington. Sérurier cautiously advanced the scheme in hope that it would alert Madison to Governor Craig's intrigues and push the United States closer to war with Britain. Careful not to dirty his own hands, he used Soubiran as his proxy.[5]

Soubiran and Henry managed to see President Madison and convinced him that the documents in their possession would prove a conspiracy between Federalists and Britain. Intrigued, the president purchased the stash for $50,000 of public money, an incredible expense. He could have built a warship for about the same amount. To his own embarrassment, he learned that although the papers revealed British connivance, they contained no incriminating information about his political opposition.[6]

Once it all became public, Federalists riddled Madison with charges of misconduct for using public funds to purchase documents meant to discredit their party. Madison countered that the British had employed Henry to subvert the US government and dismember the union. It was an act of war.[7]

All the players in this tawdry episode—John Henry, Paul-Émile Soubiran, James Craig, Louis Sérurier, and even President Madison—participated in a destructive cycle that plagued the early republic: Foreign powers meddled in US politics; US partisans accused each other of colluding with foreign powers; those accusations deepened party animosity; that animosity made it easier for foreign powers to meddle in US politics. Though not indisputably the early republic's most egregious scandal of the kind, the Henry-Soubiran incident crystallizes the malicious harmony between foreign meddling and partisan hostility. To Federalists, Soubiran was a French serpent who had beguiled the administration, while Republicans—Madison's party—described Henry as a British serpent who tempted their opponents to treachery. Each side was convinced that the other imperiled their republican paradise.[8]

Yet the United States was no Eden. After independence, it was a wartorn land with a floundering economy and an uncertain future. The new republic didn't leap onto the world stage as a major player; it limped on as a European pawn. The expansive nation boasted the "trunk and limbs of a Giant," quipped one foreigner, but the "muscles of an infant." Unlike their grandchildren, who would embrace Uncle Sam as a symbol of American virility, early Americans usually represented their republic as a fair woman—precious but vulnerable.[9]

Since the late seventeenth century, North America had played a strategic role in the European balance of power. European wars extended across the Atlantic, most starkly during the Seven Years' War that ended in 1763 and shifted half of North America from French to British control—or at least nominal control. Native American nations retained significant power throughout the continent, and they forced concessions and alliances from empires that competed for the land. Early Americans imagined Indians as a composite of subdued subjects who owed them allegiance and foreign actors who might side with their enemies. Their Native American neighbors seemed a threat from the inside and the outside. American colonists inevitably were entangled in the global power struggles of their European homelands.[10]

By 1776, many colonists hoped that independence would rid them of European politics. As Thomas Paine put it in *Common Sense*, "It is the true interest of America to steer clear of European contentions, which she can never do, while, by her dependance on Britain, she is made the makeweight in the scale of British politics." Despite Paine's optimism, European powers sought to manipulate US politics to their own geostrategic benefit. Convinced that they lay at the mercy of rapacious foreign powers, Americans believed that they needed to unite against foreign danger. They disagreed, however, about which foreign empire presented the gravest danger. Those debates grew more polarized as Britain and France warred in Europe for over two decades, each pressuring Americans for support.[11]

As a party system developed in the United States, dominated by British-backing Federalists on the one hand and French-favoring Republicans on the other, policy disagreements descended into factional tribalism. Distrust led each side to accuse the other of foreign collusion. Partisans sometimes indulged in the very behavior they denounced, recruiting foreigners to counter the purportedly corrupt, foreign-backed ambitions of their political opponents. The path was well trodden by the time Madison paid Henry and Soubiran. As early as 1789, when Alexander Hamilton feared that the French stoked Madison's anti-British legislation, he opened secretive, unauthorized backchannels with a British agent to counter the effort. Across more than two decades, the nation spiraled into a destructive symbiosis between foreign meddling and partisan politics.

Through it all, nobody claimed a more central role than James Madison. As a leading delegate at the Constitutional Convention, Republican congressional leader, secretary of state, and president, Madison grappled with foreign meddling across three decades. At the same time, as a party leader, he fed the partisanship that bred it. His career epitomized the calamitous barrage of accusations and counteraccusations of foreign collusion that culminated in the War of 1812.

Madison initiated his public career in the 1780s as a resolute adversary of foreign manipulation. As partisan strife intensified over the years, Republicans and Federalists interpreted the foreign policy opinions of their opponents as aid and comfort to America's enemies. With confidence in the superiority of their own ideologies, they arrived at the certainty that their detractors must possess sinister motives. The mutual distrust accelerated, culminating in the Henry-Soubiran scandal.

As that affair reveals, most early American leaders, including Madison, worried less about foreign meddling than about the *wrong kind* of foreign meddling—the kind that harmed their political objectives. Madison colluded with foreign nationals to prove that Federalists colluded with foreign nationals. Foreign rulers knew they could count on American political partisans as unwitting tools so long as Americans distrusted each other more than they feared foreign intrusion.

After victory in the Revolutionary War eliminated the immediate threat of British armies, Americans learned that little else united them. Even among the limited enfranchised white male population, they differed in heritage, regional origin, religion, occupations, financial interests, customs, and even languages. New Yorker John Jay subscribed to a fantasy when he called Americans "a people descended from the same ancestors, speaking the same language, professing the same religion, attached to the same principles of government." He was writing in 1787 to plead with skeptical Americans to ratify the Constitution and unite into a more cohesive nation—an unnecessary task if his vision of American homogeneity had reflected reality.[12]

Less rhapsodic, Madison acknowledged that, like people of all societies, Americans were "divided into different Sects, Factions, & interests," as he put it at the Constitutional Convention. If most Americans agreed that they wanted a republic, they failed to agree on what that meant. They debated the size, shape, scope, and functions of their republic until the term signified, as John Adams moaned, "any thing, every thing, or nothing." They feuded over state and federal powers, taxes, slavery, commerce, and foreign policy.[13]

Only a few years after Americans secured their independence, foreign agents, such as Alexander McGillivray of the Creek Nation and Diego de Gardoqui of Spain, observed and relished American political discord. They reasoned that if the people held political sovereignty but disagreed about the national direction, the whole experiment must collapse. Spain, France, Britain, and Indian nations could then retake the territory they lost during the prior three decades due to the Seven Years' and Revolutionary wars.[14]

Rather than lament domestic political divisions, Madison embraced them as a healthy sign. "Liberty is to faction what air is to fire," he reminded his compatriots in *Federalist* no. 10. He worried about political discord insofar as it tempted foreign powers. In 1787, Madison spearheaded the Constitutional Convention to address the dilemma of foreign meddling and internal division. If the framers could construct a union powerful enough to withstand foreign incursion, Americans could welcome social and political diversity. He envisioned a nation that accommodated an abundance of political factions—so many, in fact, that no single party could gain a majority and cudgel minority parties.[15]

Frustrating his expectations, the Constitution fostered a two-party system, the very kind he had intended it to deter. After the implementation of the new government in 1789, Americans generally gravitated to two conflicting visions for their republic. They also oscillated between despair that their republican experiment would crumble and faith that it would endure innumerable generations. With so much at stake, partisans dueled— sometimes literally—over their competing views.[16]

When revolutionary France declared war on Britain in 1793, Americans split their sympathy between the two nations. Madison and his friend Thomas Jefferson, then at the head of the State Department, mustered Republicans against secretary of the treasury Alexander Hamilton's Federalists—Republicans sympathizing with France, Federalists with

Britain. The parties remained fluid and ill-defined but provided a platform for opposition politics.[17]

In 1794 and 1795, Republicans and Federalists cemented their animosity as they debated the Jay Treaty, which attempted to resolve lingering territorial and commercial disputes between Britain and its former colonies. With Madison leading the charge, Republicans decried the Federalist-backed accord, arguing that it subjected the United States to British economic dominance. During the political feud, British officials uncovered alleged proof of corrupt dealings between the French diplomat in the United States and the Republican-leaning secretary of state, Edmund Randolph. They sent the intelligence to Timothy Pickering and Oliver Wolcott, both Federalists in President George Washington's cabinet, who wanted to sideline Randolph and save the Jay Treaty from his misgivings about it. The pair used the information to accuse Randolph of conspiring with France, ignoring the irony that they had coordinated clandestinely with the British government to obtain the evidence.[18]

French diplomat Pierre-Auguste Adet added fuel to the fire of party competition during the election of 1796, when he promoted Jefferson's Republicans against John Adams's Federalists. By 1798, the United States was edging toward war with France, with Federalists accusing the European nation of violating American neutrality. In response, French officials assured Republicans that Federalists had thwarted peace negotiations for political purposes. Convinced that Republicans were cooperating with France to undermine the Adams administration, Federalists passed the Sedition Act, proscribing slander against the president. Republicans reviled the act as a ploy to criminalize political dissent. By the end of the 1790s, foreign meddling had blurred the line between partisan opposition and criminal sedition.[19]

By pitting Americans against each other, foreign agents exposed unresolved tensions about where sovereignty resided in a republic. Modern legal theorists may draw tidy distinctions between the people who possess sovereignty and politicians who exercise power, but American partisans rarely belabored such technical niceties as they tried to fashion a functional government from a novel political theory. Most Americans shared Madison's opinion—advanced in a report published in 1800—that "the people, not the government, possess the absolute sovereignty" in the United States. Early Americans usually conceived of "the people," or enfranchised citizens, as white males with at least some property. It was a constricted definition yet still one more liberal than most Europeans would have recognized.[20]

Americans contrasted their system against European monarchies. In monarchies, as one Pennsylvania politician put it during a ratification debate in 1787, "supreme power is lodged in the king and not in the people." Because the monarch was the government, the people could not subvert the monarch without subverting the government. By contrast, US officials— including presidents—were expendable caretakers of the government. As the Portuguese diplomat José Corrêa da Serra wrote in 1819, "Those that govern do not have any power and force besides the parties which elect them for a short while, and can get rid of them at the end of it. They are dependent administrators rather than sovereign lords." Corrêa da Serra succinctly summarized what foreign diplomats and operatives had recognized for decades: If they hoped to influence American policy, they needed to influence party politics.[21]

Given that the US government exposed its representatives to lawful overthrow every election cycle, foreign agents reasoned that they could legitimately incite the people against government leaders. The Spanish diplomat Carlos Martínez de Yrujo used that logic in 1804, when he published pseudonymous essays in Federalist newspapers to rally opposition to Madison and Jefferson's aggressive grabs at the disputed territory of West Florida. Yrujo used the press better than any other foreign agent of the time to mold public opinion, or "the true sovereign of a democracy" as he called it.[22]

Americans never determined conclusively whether the people or the government possessed ultimate sovereignty. They frequently changed their minds depending on whether their favored party held power, especially executive power. When their party controlled the presidency, they often reverted to European notions that sovereignty resided with the government and that the people should defer to it. When out of power, they tended to insist on their right to dissent. As one satirist quipped in the mid-1780s, "When we had other rulers, committees and conventions of the people were lawful . . . but since I *myself* became a ruler, they cease to be lawful." Foreign agents raised the stakes of the debate as they provoked disaffected partisans against government representatives and their policies.[23]

Anxious to discredit their political foes, those out of power frequently accused the party in power of bowing to foreign influence to maintain political control. Parties in power indicted the opposition for recruiting foreign nations to undermine the government. Foreign agents recognized that American partisans would turn their ire against each other before they would train it on foreign governments. When they wanted to exert their influence on US policy, they could stoke the flames of political discontent and let party politics do the rest.

Foreign agents found especially fertile ground for tampering in the western regions between the Appalachians and the Mississippi. Americans brawled over US policy in the West, convinced that it lay most vulnerable to foreign aggression. Western territories had changed hands multiple times between the 1760s and the 1803 Louisiana Purchase. As secretary of state, Madison believed he had scored a coup against foreign intrigues by securing Louisiana for the United States, but foreign governments continued to jostle for power in the region.

In late 1806, France, Britain, and Spain took interest in a cryptic scheme hatched by former vice president Aaron Burr, whose plans may have been as heinous as treason or as innocent as a land purchase. His ambitions were murky at the time and remain so today, probably forever unintelligible to all but himself. Still, theories abounded. Republicans charged that the British wanted to help Burr sever western states from the union, while Federalists saw the French behind his plot. Each party raced to prove that the other had aided the suspected traitor. Partisan politics mired the investigation, and Burr walked free, benefiting from Americans' inability to distinguish legitimate conspiracies from petty politics.[24]

Indians of the Great Lakes and Ohio River regions exacerbated party tension as they allied with Britain to protect their land. After the anti-British Madison became president in 1809, Britain's rulers anticipated war, and they armed and provisioned Native Americans in return for protecting Canada. Like their European counterparts, Indians made strategic alliances that they believed would promote their prosperity.[25]

When bloodshed erupted between Native and US forces in 1811, Republicans accused the British of instigating the violence. Anxious to disgrace the president, Federalists blamed the fighting on Madison's misguided policies in the West. Madison's defenders recast those accusations as sympathy for the British and their Indian allies who had murdered Americans. The dispute convinced Madison that Britain, Indians, and Federalists posed a joint threat to US security—a dangerous cabal of foreign agents testing the loyalty of domestic dissidents.[26]

As far as Madison could see, Britain stood at the center of that threat. For several years, tension had mounted as the Royal Navy harassed US ships that traded with France. Madison especially despised the British practice of impressment—stopping US vessels and seizing sailors suspected as British subjects liable to conscription in the Royal Navy.

Madison's opponents reviled his anti-British policies, prompting British rulers to deploy secret agents such as John Henry to survey Federalist opposition. They counted on Federalists to boot Republicans from power and to steer the nation toward friendlier relations with Britain. Republicans had long suspected that Federalists favored a reunion with the British Empire. Madison thought that Henry's documents would finally unveil the conspiracy. All they unveiled was the damaging relationship between party malice and foreign intervention. Madison helped materialize his own worst fears when he started a war with Britain that left the capital in ashes by the end of summer in 1814. Party strife and foreign meddling left American political institutions in crisis and the republic teetering on the brink of disaster.[27]

I

"Guile in the Garden"

The *Dolus in Horte* [guile in the garden] ought ever to be before us, &
guard us like a friendly Beacon against hidden & dangerous Designs.
—The Reverend James Madison to James Madison Jr.,
September 18, 1782

ON SEPTEMBER 6, 1783, STORM clouds gathered over the British outpost
of Sandusky on the southern shore of Lake Erie, where Alexander McKee
addressed a diverse conclave of warriors: Isidore Chêne, a British agent
who coordinated Indian attacks against American rebels; Simon Girty,
an Irish-descended interpreter who had lived with the Seneca since youth
and gained a reputation as a venomous enemy of American revolutionaries;
T'Sindatton, a Huron chief who had strengthened his people by absorbing
American prisoners of war into his community. Eminent among the group
was Joseph Brant, a Mohawk known as a zealous British ally and defender
of Indian sovereignty.[1]

A handful of other prominent chiefs and warriors joined them around
the council fire—a solemn venue for deliberation. They represented thirty-
five Indian nations from the Great Lakes region to Florida. These nations
had little in common except that they had been allied with the British
during the Revolutionary War.[2]

McKee bore news that matched the dismal weather. It was time to stop
the fight. As deputy Indian agent for the British, McKee reminded his
hearers that his government had decided to end the "long, bloody, expen-
sive and unnatural war" against revolutionary America. He urged them to
cease fighting and release American prisoners.[3]

Born to a Pennsylvania frontier trader, McKee felt a strong kinship with western Indians. He had married a Shawnee woman who bore their son. He had watched Indians suffer, kill, and die for their land. He knew that those who gathered with him feared what the American victory meant for them all.[4]

Before the war, King George III had tried to keep peace with western Indians by restraining the westward movement of his American subjects. In 1763, the British Crown had gained vast dominions between the Appalachian Mountains and the Mississippi River when it defeated France in war. The court established what became known as the Proclamation Line of 1763, beyond which Anglo-Americans could not settle. British Americans itched to acquire the land, inhabited mostly by Native nations. Many Indians expected that Americans would overrun their territory if the colonists managed to discard their imperial government.[5]

Once the Revolutionary War erupted, Indians across the continent calculated risks and chose sides. The Catawba of the Southeast and the Oneida near the Great Lakes allied with the rebel colonists. They hoped that Americans would respect their land and sovereignty in return. In the lower Mississippi Valley, some Chickasaw, Choctaw, and Cherokee groups managed a precarious neutrality. Many powerful contingents of Iroquois, Delawares, Shawnees, Creeks, and Cherokees allied with the British and fought Americans in the Ohio and Mississippi valleys. The Indians had continued hostilities long after the main British army had surrendered to George Washington at Yorktown two years earlier. They and others assembled at Sandusky to confer with their defeated ally and chart a path forward.[6]

The fight must end, McKee declared. He tried to reassure those assembled that the king would continue to protect their trade and that they would remain British allies. Most important, he affirmed that the British government would not cede Indian land to Americans as part of the recent peace. He uttered a half-truth at best. In the peace treaty negotiated in Paris, the British surrendered territory to the newly independent Americans from the Atlantic coast to the Mississippi River. The agreement said nothing about what would become of the land that belonged to Britain's Indian allies. Americans presumed it belonged to them. When one Creek chief learned that the British had surrendered Indian land to Americans, he called it a lie propagated by the rebels. "An Englishman will never turn his back & betray his friend." British Indian agents could only bemoan the "situation of our poor unfortunate allies." McKee did his best to convince his audience that they should lay down their weapons and bear their losses "with manly fortitude." If the Indians hoped to protect their lands during peacetime, they would need to confederate with each other and with British officials in Canada.[7]

To press that idea, McKee yielded the floor to Joseph Brant, who represented (at least, claimed to represent) a loose coalition of six Indian nations called the Iroquois confederacy from the region of western New York. Brant reflected a mixture of identities: born a Mohawk, baptized a Christian, Indian raised, British educated. He was a Native warrior and a British gentleman. During the 1750s, he had fought for the British–Mohawk alliance against the French in the Seven Years' War. The British and Mohawks routed the French from the continent, and Brant learned the importance of choosing the right ally. In his late teens at the time, he enjoyed the favor of the influential British Indian agent William Johnson and gained a reputation as a precocious student at an Indian school in Connecticut. He studied British culture and diplomacy to enhance Mohawk negotiating power. During the decade before the Revolutionary War, Brant and Johnson maintained the firm alliance between the British and Mohawks—the "Covenant Chain," as they called it. When war erupted between Britain and the upstart American colonists, Brant again gambled on the British. This time, he lost.[8]

Brant stood before the council fire at Sandusky as the Mohawk's chief sachem and a captain in the British military. He wielded a ceremonial wampum belt—a brilliant display of beads and shells. "We the Six Nations with this belt bind your Hearts and minds with ours," he said, "that there may be never hereafter a separation between us, let there be Peace or War, it shall never disunite us." The rest of the chiefs assented. The agreement produced a formidable but fragile confederacy of thirty-five Indian nations and the British Empire.[9]

The council fire at Sandusky represented an ominous threat to Americans. Revolutionaries may have eked out victory in the late war, but they remained surrounded by hostile nations. Plagued by political uncertainty, social unrest, and economic suffering, many Americans fretted that foreign powers would carve apart their country. At Sandusky, Brant and McKee had formed only an unstable confederacy, but the American union boasted nothing better. Their governing charter, the Articles of Confederation, bound the states as a shaky alliance rather than a single nation. Congress possessed powers to wage war and conduct diplomacy but little else. Deprived of the power to exact taxes, regulate foreign or domestic commerce, or effectively recruit soldiers, it remained but a "diplomatic assembly," as John Adams called it. Without a more united government, the United States might fall. No one felt that alarm as keenly as James Madison.[10]

The Politician

Just over five feet tall, James Madison cached his sharp intellect within a diffident façade and a frail body. Though charming and pleasant in private, he cultivated a public image of inscrutable sobriety. "This is a man who must be studied for a long time to form a just opinion of him," recounted one acquaintance. The scion of his father's plantation, Montpelier, he enjoyed deep roots in the elite Virginia planter class. He had inherited his first slave at the age of eight.[11]

Like other elite young Virginians, Madison had received a gentleman's education. At a boarding school in Virginia's coastal Tidewater region, he learned mathematics, literature, and geography. Most important for a top-class education, he studied classic Roman and Greek antiquity. At boarding school, he developed "an appetite for knowledge," as he remembered in a short autobiography. Beginning in 1769, he fed that appetite with education at the College of New Jersey, now Princeton. He devoured information. He lost sleep and damaged his health by studying all night and into the early mornings. The voracious student completed two years of college in one. By the end of his studies in 1771, he knew Latin, Greek, and more French than most young men of his class. He could decipher some Italian and Spanish, and he dabbled in Hebrew.[12]

Madison's studies infused him with a passion for civil liberty, especially religious liberty. While in New Jersey, he discovered religious diversity he had never encountered in Virginia, where the government-supported Church of England—or Anglican Church—dominated. Although he remained nominally Anglican the rest of his life, he returned home from college a fierce advocate of religious freedom. He "squabbled and scolded abused and ridiculed," as he worded it to a friend, the "diabolical Hell conceived principle of persecution" against religious minorities in Virginia. As much as anything, the Church of England turned him against the British government in the early 1770s.[13]

Despite his commitment to civil liberty, Madison valued conformity over diversity by mid-1774. That summer, he felt besieged, he bristled, by "War blood and plunder on the one Hand and the Threats of Slavery and Oppression on the Other." He referred to retaliatory attacks from western Indians and Britain's Coercive Acts. The Coercive Acts punished Boston radicals for throwing East India Company tea into the harbor. Although directed at Massachusetts, the acts seemed to promise the subjugation of all British America. Madison began to panic about his security. He feared that minorities would aid external powers in destroying the gentry's liberty—which he equated with Virginian liberty.[14]

The American Revolution threw Madison into a lifelong struggle to square civil liberty with national security. He warned that "the Scotch and some interested Merchants" were conspiring to counter anti-British colonial boycotts. Like other elite Virginians, he believed Scottish merchant immigrants had usurped the tobacco trade, driving planters into debt. When Madison's uncle failed to pay a debt to a Scottish trader, the sheriff confiscated the planter's enslaved laborers and horses, and his uncle stormed the Martinsburg jailhouse to recover them. Along with Indians and the British government, Scots provoked the ire of an increasingly frantic Virginia gentry.[15]

In December 1774, Madison accepted an appointment as the youngest member of the Orange County Committee of Safety—the county's revolutionary government. As a councilor, he amplified his zeal against supposedly insidious Scots. In 1775, James Herdman of the Bromfield Parish, a "Scotch Parson" as Madison derisively called him, refused to observe a fast day designated by the Continental Congress. Madison exulted that the local committee of safety "ordered his Church doors to be shut." He hinted that the clergyman deserved tar and feathers. Reverend John Wingate, a local Orange County minister, was "of the same Kidney" as Herdman. Hardly an ardent Tory, Wingate had pledged to participate in colonial boycotts against Britain. But the minister kept poor company. He boarded with a Scot named Andrew Shepherd who had to apologize at one point for criticizing the Virginia Convention. In early 1775, the rector received pamphlets critical of the Continental Congress from a Scottish merchant. By March, Madison's committee had confiscated and burned the offending pamphlets. Madison gloated that with public pressure Herdman had become very "supple & obsequious."[16]

Like Scots, Quakers elicited little sympathy from Madison during the turmoil of revolution. Madison complained that most refused to join revolutionary boycotts. He assumed that Pennsylvania Quakers opposed the boycott because of their commercial ties to London rather than for moral or ethical reasons. They possessed "sinister or secret Views," he hinted, and they infected the "honest and simple" Quakers of Virginia. Everywhere he looked, Madison found evidence that external powers and domestic traitors plotted against American liberty and security.[17]

Madison counted the enslaved among the internal enemies. In 1775, Virginian revolutionaries exiled their royal governor, Lord Dunmore, to a warship off the coast. In November, Dunmore proclaimed freedom for any young enslaved or indentured servant who joined his ranks against the rebels. Hundreds fled their plantations and hastened to Dunmore's service. Sensible that enslaved men and women detested bondage, the planter class had conjured awful images of their slaves murdering them in their sleep long before Dunmore's proclamation. The governor's new "Ethiopian regiment" redoubled their fears. Madison had anticipated the proclamation as early as June. He felt confident that the mighty Virginia commonwealth could stand against the British—unless the enslaved fought for the empire. "If we should be subdued," he warned, "we shall fall like Achilles by the hand of one that knows that secret." Alone, external enemies posed little threat. Combined with subversive internal populations, however, they could destroy nations. Madison carried those lessons with him as a legislator.[18]

Just twenty-five years old in 1776, Madison had earned a reputation as one of the "most fit and able men" in the county. His prestige earned him a spot at the Virginia Convention, which had directed the colony's affairs since Dunmore's exile. Madison headed to the capital in Williamsburg that May and sat among giants of Virginia politics. The gathering featured the handsome and gracious Edmund Pendleton, who had served in colonial government since Madison rocked in a cradle. It boasted Patrick Henry, already famous for his biting oratory and blistering attacks against the home country. It included the wealthy and sharp-witted George Mason. Sitting quietly among his distinguished peers, Madison internalized lessons about the fragile balance between civil liberty and national security.[19]

On the third day of the convention, Madison received an appointment to the Committee of Privileges and Elections. The committee enjoyed the power to punish people deemed "inimical to the rights and liberties of America." The mandate gave the members broad latitude. For example, they ordered temporary confinements for Ralph Wormley and John Tayloe Corbin who expressed sentiments "unfriendly and dangerous" to Virginia.

The young delegate from Orange silently observed a committee that tried to preserve security by restricting individual liberty.[20]

He soon received the chance to try to reconcile these dueling ideals. By late spring of 1776, the Virginia Convention anticipated independence from Britain and began to forge a new state constitution. George Mason took the lead. By June, he had produced a draft of a state constitution and a Declaration of Rights, which outlined twelve broad principles of free government. The ninth on the list stated that "all men should enjoy the fullest toleration in the exercise of religion." Fearing that the language offered inadequate protection to religious dissenters, Madison broke his deferential silence. He countered with an amendment that allowed "full and free exercise" of religion. By striking the word "toleration," he cast religious freedom as a right inherent with life, not a privilege conceded by the government. His amendment also prohibited special "emoluments or privileges" for any religion. Madison wanted to dispel any possibility that Virginia would favor one faith above another. Mason's provision would have allowed the government to regulate religion if it threatened "the peace, the happiness, or safety of society." Madison left the clause unaltered in his amendment.[21]

Despite the overture to religious conservatives, Anglican elites abhorred his swipe at established religion. The convention rejected the amendment. Undeterred, Madison revised his wording, scrapping the "emoluments or privileges" clause to make the amendment more attractive to conservatives. At the same time, he narrowed Mason's exception for state security. Madison feared that Anglican elites would use any pretext to persecute religious minorities, including "the peace, the happiness, or safety of society." He proposed that the government could only restrain religious freedom if it threatened "the preservation of equal liberty, and the existence of the State."[22]

Madison's proposal won the support of the convention, and he struck a blow against the established church. Mason had once derided the "useless Members" of the Declaration committee who would smother his work with "a thousand ridiculous and impracticable proposals." If he counted the youthful, soft-spoken Madison among them, he changed his mind after working with him. Mason supported Madison's amendment, Madison adopted Mason as a mentor, and the pair cultivated a vital partnership in Virginia politics.[23]

In the fight over the language of religious freedom, Madison grappled with a paradox that would badger the rest of his career: Government power imperiled individual liberty, but individual liberty could enfeeble the very government that protected it. The American Revolution nurtured Madison's devotion to civil liberty, and it launched his struggle to harmonize it with national security.

The Council

In April 1777, Madison stood for election to the newly created Virginia Assembly. For the first time in his career, he faced an opponent in an open election. Virginians drank heavily, and they expected candidates to offer liquor at the polls. Conventional wisdom correlated the amount of whiskey a candidate served with the number of votes he received. A self-disciplined, republican purist, Madison expected deliberation to trump inebriation. He refused to serve his constituents alcohol. He miscalculated. His tavern keeper opponent offered hardy libations to the electorate and won the election. At least that is how Madison told the story. He may have found comfort in the belief that his only unsuccessful election came down to booze rather than ideas. Regardless, Madison walked away with the same lesson: One must win power before one can wield power. Even in a republic, passion might still rule reason, and a candidate must embrace it to win elections. He loathed the idea, but he made peace with it.[24]

Madison may have lacked the common touch, but he compensated with elite connections. In November, the Virginia Assembly elevated him to a prestigious position as one of eight members on the governor's council. The council advised Governor Patrick Henry.[25]

Executive power taught Madison that weak republics struggle to defend their sovereignty. In his first session at the council, he received what he called "alarming Accounts of the Distresses of the American Army." British troops had captured Philadelphia and displaced Congress to York, Pennsylvania. Some senior officers wavered in their faith in George Washington. The commander-in-chief decided against an assault on Philadelphia and withdrew his beleaguered army twenty miles away to the wooded protection of Valley Forge. Soldiers trod the shoddy encampment barefoot and starving, and disease killed 2,500 of them. Fifteen hundred men fled either to save their skins or to save their families from poverty.[26]

The government lacked money. Washington lacked men. Troops lacked supplies. To remedy the problems, Congress could only request states to send money and men, but state governments already drowned in debt and struggled to recruit soldiers.

Virginia suffered with the rest. The governor's office contended with draft riots, failing public credit, and a militia "ill armed, half clad" and "ignorant of Discipline," as Madison and his fellow councilors put it in a report. Even if Virginia could scrounge enough men and supplies to send northward, Madison dreaded that Congress's disarray would impede the supplies from reaching the troops. He helped Henry craft a letter to Virginia's delegates in Congress that complained of the "uncertainty & Confusion" in the supply chain and criticized Congress's lack of oversight. The council lamented the "mismanagement in which have flowed Evils threatening the Existence of american Liberty." Liberty required a government weak enough to respect it but strong enough to protect it.[27]

Like many other Americans, Madison equated security with control of their western frontier. Most whites nominally acknowledged Native sovereignty, but they insisted that Indian nations owed some form of allegiance to white governments. Madison called them a "perfidious people" for attacking Virginian settlements in the West, implying that Indians somehow owed loyalty to people threatening their land. In the Declaration of Independence, Thomas Jefferson addressed Indian attacks in tandem with "domestic insurrections" that the British excited among the enslaved. Slaves and Indians remained simultaneously a part of and apart from the American body politic.[28]

The year before he had joined the governor's council, Madison had tasted personal loss from British-allied Indians. In 1776, Cherokees killed Madison's jailhouse-raiding uncle in South Carolina. A British Indian agent had organized the attack. The Cherokees kidnapped Madison's aunt and the couple's two daughters. Militiamen found the aunt's body in the South Carolina mountains over a month later. They never found the sisters. Rebel Americans believed they saw a ruthless combination in the British–Indian alliance.[29]

Most revolutionaries failed to see that Indians who allied with the British fought of their own accord. Those nations may have needed Britain as an ally, but they hardly needed prodding to protect their land. By portraying Indians as British tools, revolutionary Americans imagined them as more dangerous, not less. They believed the alliance combined the might of the British with the supposedly irrational "savagery" of Indians. If the American rebels could defeat the British, they hoped that the Native allies would lay down their arms. As the Virginia frontier commander George

Rogers Clark informed Governor Patrick Henry, "There can be no peace expected from many [Indian] nations, while the English are at Detroit."[30]

In Williamsburg, Madison helped oversee Clark's expedition to demolish the British–Indian alliance in the Ohio Valley, which Virginia claimed as its land. With a personality as fiery as his red hair, Clark collected 150 men and advanced toward Illinois country. In mid-1779, he seized British outposts at Cahokia, Kaskaskia, and Vincennes.[31]

At Vincennes, Clark captured Canada's lieutenant governor, Major Henry Hamilton. To frontier Americans, Hamilton embodied a bloodsoaked pact between British troops and western Indians. They called him the "scalp-buyer" for coordinating Indian attacks against Americans. Not the merciful sort, Clark retaliated by tomahawking several unarmed Indians to death at Vincennes. He then sent Hamilton in chains to Williamsburg. The major became a prize prisoner of Virginia's new governor, Thomas Jefferson. Jefferson reinforced Madison's belief that Virginians must strip the British and Indians of their power in the West. In the heat of war, Jefferson made no secret of his desire to drive Indian "wretches" beyond the Mississippi. In the Declaration of Independence, he accused George III of exciting "the merciless Indian savages" against frontier Americans.[32]

Jefferson, Madison, and the rest of the council locked Hamilton in irons and cast him into a Williamsburg dungeon in solitary confinement. They refused to allow him even pen and paper. In eighteenth-century convention, high-ranking prisoners normally could expect respectful treatment. Some might even rent nearby estates and socialize with the local gentry. To Jefferson and Madison, however, Hamilton represented the most dangerous aspect of the British military—its alliance with Indians. They would not risk clemency for the man who "gave standing rewards for scalps."[33]

Meanwhile, Madison helped oversee a secret mission for the Irishborn frontiersman David Rogers to reconnoiter British strength on the Mississippi and purchase materiel from Spanish-held New Orleans. Spain had not yet declared war against their common enemy Britain, but the court at Madrid secretly slipped funds and supplies to Americans. Rogers led a company of about sixty-five men to New Orleans. He procured the supplies, conferred with the Spanish governor about the war effort, and started his return east.[34]

Traveling in harsh conditions, on October 4, 1779, his force arrived with three keelboats at the confluence of the Licking and Ohio rivers near present-day Cincinnati. They spied a party of seven Indians crossing the mouth of the Licking to the Kentucky side—the American side as they fancied it. Discretion advised that Rogers ignore them and continue up the river. Instead, he ordered his troops to dock their keelboats. He charged into the woods with his men to kill the outnumbered Indians.[35]

One hundred seventy Shawnees sprang on the hapless Americans. Rogers collapsed dying. Blood cascaded from his abdomen as his men fell dead and maimed. Some men dashed for the boats but were tailed and tomahawked. A few scrambled onto a boat and raced away. Shawnees captured the other boats and cut off their retreat. Within minutes they killed nearly fifty Americans. Several Americans fled into the woods, some wounded and fainting from loss of blood. Rogers clawed through the forest to safety but was beyond help. He survived the night under the care of his companion John Knotts. Knotts abandoned his doomed commander the next morning. Rogers was never seen again. Americans would not seize the West without a price.[36]

Madison likely learned in late November that the council had sent Rogers and his men to their deaths. Before he had directed Rogers west, then-governor Patrick Henry predicted danger for Rogers's return trip but considered the mission "of the greatest concern to the State." Virginians could not imagine security without control of the West.[37]

Control remained elusive. The few survivors of Rogers's expedition delivered their single remaining supply boat to Clark. It did him little good. He wanted to take Detroit as a final blow against the British in the Northwest but could never raise the men or money for the assault. By January 1780, Clark could only foresee "depredations from Many Nations of Indians" that operated with support from Detroit. He found it futile to attack Indians when the British compensated their losses "four fold." Not even Hamilton's capture stemmed the danger, Clark lamented.[38]

British Indian agent James Colbert had sent word of Hamilton's surrender to British officers in the southern department at Pensacola. Originally from Scotland, Colbert began trading among the Chickasaws soon after he arrived in Georgia in the 1730s. He married a Chickasaw woman from an influential clan. Like Joseph Brant in the North, he became a vital link between the British and Indians during the Seven Years' War and the Revolutionary War. As a Scottish loyalist who nurtured a British–Indian alliance, he represented everything Madison feared for the United States in its war against internal dissenters and foreign powers.[39]

Colbert promised his colleagues that he would rally western Indians to counter future attacks. British commanders backed his efforts, urging their Native allies to repel American assaults along the Ohio River. By March 1780, Clark witnessed "the English Regaining the Interest of Many Tribes of Indians," a development that would "prove Fatal to Kentucky and the Total loss of the Western Cuntrey on the Mississippi." Americans incessantly feared that the West would slip from their grasp, an event that would spell calamity.[40]

Allies

While Colbert raced along the Cherokee River to muster support for the British, a fellow Chickasaw leader countered his efforts during a visit to New Orleans. Payamataha and his delegation likely arrived at the city by traveling the Mississippi River from Mississippi's upland ridge and hills. They arrived in December 1779 and would have docked at the city front. The capital of Spanish Louisiana lay nestled between Lake Pontchartrain and the river. Modest stockades hugged the city's approximately 800 residences along a river bend. Most residents had been French subjects until 1763, when magistrates stunned them with news that the empire had transferred New Orleans to Spain. Fort towers on either end of the city reminded passing vessels that Spain controlled access to the Gulf of Mexico.[41]

Looking northwest toward the city, Payamataha would have observed a large parade ground called the Plaza de Armas, flanked on the east by an artillery yard and the king's storehouse. Behind the square teetered a decrepit wood-framed church and a dilapidated presbytery. One hundred yards west along the quay stood the stately official residence of Governor Bernardo de Gálvez, the thirty-three-year-old governor whom Payamataha had come to meet.[42]

Almost sixty years old, Payamataha remembered those years when he had fought with the British against the French during the Seven Years' War. The chief hated the "artful and covetous French," with their "forked tongues." In 1756, he had assured his British allies that "we look upon your enemies as ours." But times had changed.[43]

Now Payamataha met Britain's Spanish enemies to discuss Chickasaw neutrality or even an alliance with Spain. Earlier in the summer, Spain had followed France into war against Britain. Benjamin Franklin and other American diplomats had courted the support of France and Spain since early 1776, even before Americans had declared independence. At first, the European nations sent arms and ammunition. After the Continental Army won a decisive victory at Saratoga in upstate New York in late 1777, France allied with the United States and joined the war. As a Catholic monarch with colonial dominions, King Charles III of Spain hesitated to ally with the predominantly Protestant, anti-imperial republicans in America. He refused to sign an official alliance with Congress, but Spain nonetheless entered the war as an ally of France. For several years, Payamataha had promoted neutrality against Colbert's preference for the British. Once his Spanish neighbors entered the war, he acquired greater leverage to persuade fellow Chickasaws to his side.[44]

Payamataha made a stir in New Orleans. Governor Gálvez showered him with ceremonial pomp, gifts, and a medal. Gálvez had prepared for such an occasion for over a year. He had complained to his superiors in Madrid that Spain's small medals offended Native leaders and couldn't compete with those that the British distributed. An order of acceptably large medals arrived in 1778. After years of fighting Apaches in the viceroyalty of New Spain, Gálvez found it easier to understand and befriend Indians than to defeat them. He knew that southern Indians demanded reliable arms and goods from European empires in exchange for their support. They also required gifts out of respect for a long-established diplomatic custom to cement bonds between a more powerful ally and a weaker partner.[45]

Gálvez coveted the territories of East and West Florida—usually referred to as the Floridas. West Florida covered a narrow strip of land along the Gulf Coast that extended from Baton Rouge to Pensacola. It possessed the important waterway of the Mobile River and the strategic fort at Pensacola. Britain created the colony after it won the territory from France at the end of the Seven Years' War. As part of the same peace, Spain had ceded the Florida Peninsula to Britain, which governed it as East Florida. Anxious to reclaim the Floridas, Gálvez pleaded with Payamataha and other gulf Indians to ally with Spain against Britain.[46]

As Gálvez tried to outpace the British with his gifts, Indians exploited the competition for their loyalty. British general John Campbell complained that southern Indians expected deerskins, wages, and double the provisions of British soldiers besides "extraordinary Rewards" for their chiefs. He conceded, though, that "the present is no time" to quarrel about expenses. After the war stalled in the North, the British had invaded Georgia and South Carolina in 1779. They hoped that loyalists and Indians would help secure victory there. Starved for men, Campbell retained a contingent of Indians even after the Natives sold their provisions for rum, got drunk, and became "insolent and obstreperous." The British could not lose Native support to the Spanish, but they could barely afford to keep the Indians as allies.[47]

While he maneuvered against the British in the Gulf region, Gálvez created as much fear as relief among Americans who intended to annex the West. When Gálvez had received David Rogers in New Orleans, the American delivered a letter from Patrick Henry. The Virginia governor suggested that if Spain helped the United States capture West Florida and add it to their union, Spain could rid the Mississippi Valley of its dangerous British enemies. The audacious proposal must have amused Gálvez. If he helped take West Florida, he would claim it for Spain, not the United States. Americans worried that Spain would simply replace Britain as a European foe in the West.[48]

By making alliances with southern Indians, Gálvez could toss the British out of the Gulf region and keep Americans away from the Mississippi River. The Spanish minister of state, Count Floridablanca, had contemplated the plan in Madrid since 1778. He insisted that Spanish magistrates must obtain the friendship of Native Americans so that "they became friends of their friends and enemies of their enemies."[49]

Floridablanca ordered Gálvez and the governor of Spanish Cuba to send spies to Philadelphia, where the Continental Congress met. The agents would report on disputes between factions within Congress and any schemes that would injure Spain. The spies were also to hint that Congress should make no peace terms without "the protection of Great Powers," meaning France and Spain. Otherwise, they would suffer "fatal consequences." Floridablanca expected the United States to play the junior partner in the war.[50]

In June 1778, Juan de Miralles arrived in Philadelphia to report on British troop movements, act as an unofficial emissary to Congress for Spain, and observe American leadership. At sixty-five, Miralles had spent a lifetime constructing trade networks around the Atlantic. Affable and extravagant with a taste for high-priced silk suits and luxurious houses, he charmed his way into elite American society under cover as a merchant. He partnered with American financier Robert Morris. He wined and dined George and Martha Washington. He gave massive personal loans to Congress. At the same time, he reported on American ambitions to annex the Floridas and other western territory that Spain coveted.[51]

Washington knew how to flatter Miralles in return. The commander-in-chief wanted Spanish support as the war opened in the South. In May 1779, he invited Miralles to participate in a military parade, troop review, and extravagant feast. He received Miralles in the camp with a ceremonial blast of thirteen cannons. During the parade, Miralles rode prominently near the front, just two places behind Washington. Reveling in the ovations, Miralles rode his horse in a crimson suit draped with a golden aiguillette. Impressed by Washington, Miralles praised the revolutionaries and pressed his government to fight Britain.[52]

However sincere their friendship, Washington and Miralles needed to secure Spain and America's fragile bond. Washington knew Miralles's opinions would carry weight in Madrid, and Miralles needed to convince Americans to discard their pretensions to the Floridas and drop demands to navigate the Mississippi River. The Spanish agent confided to the French minister that he foresaw a day when Spain and the United States would become enemies. He fretted that Americans might flood the West, unite with British Canada, and threaten Spanish territory. Given the risks, Spain refused to ally with the United States even as they fought a war together against a common foe. Even at their most cordial, US-Spanish relations suffered from uncertainty and suspicion.[53]

A member of Congress by 1780, Madison perceived that Spain's demands might tear apart the United States. Most members of Congress agreed to yield the Floridas to the Spanish if they recognized US independence and allowed Americans to navigate the Mississippi. That resolution rankled the minority who complained about the "Villains" who forfeited the territory to Spain. Southerners and westerners feared that Congress would sacrifice the West to win concessions that benefited the Northeast.[54]

Late in the year, Congress contemplated ceasing its demands for the Mississippi to keep Spain in the war. The suggestion exasperated Madison, who had led the charge to secure US navigation on the river. He warned that if northeasterners "will not support other States in their rights, they cannot expect to be supported themselves when theirs come into question." He recognized that unless the United States conducted foreign affairs with "unanimity & decision," foreign powers could manipulate political and sectional interests to their advantage.[55]

In Paris, the French minister of foreign relations, the Count de Vergennes, labored to unite his bickering Spanish and American allies. Vergennes had worked in French diplomacy since 1739. He needed his entire arsenal of diplomatic experience to marry the United States and Spain to the same cause. When France declared war against Britain in 1778, Americans' colonial rebellion became a world war. For France and Spain, the ramifications transcended American independence. They wanted to rewrite imperial maps in America, the Caribbean, Europe, the Mediterranean, and Asia. Vergennes viewed the United States as a minor player on a large international stage. To exact revenge on Britain for France's losses in the Seven Years' War, he needed his longtime Spanish ally more than he needed insurgent Americans.[56]

Like Spain, France seemed a mismatched ally for the United States. As British subjects until 1776, most Americans had learned to despise the French and their Catholicism. Many American soldiers—including Washington—had fought as British soldiers during the Seven Years' War to oust the French from the continent. Pro-British Chickasaws reminded Americans of the ancient hatred and protested, "We are very much surprised that you would cry for assistance to people who sometime ago would roast you and Even Eat you."[57]

Vergennes wanted to hurt the British more than he wanted to help the United States. He hoped to keep the new nation as a French pawn against Britain in North America, not unleash it to expand across the continent. The minister expected that any peace deal would confine Britain to Canada and hand the Floridas to his junior ally, Spain. He assured the Spanish that the redrawn map "will be a sufficient hindrance to prevent the Americans from trying to be dangerous neighbors and excessively enterprising." Vergennes pressured Congress to abandon the Floridas and navigation on the Mississippi. In 1780, as John Jay negotiated with France and Spain in Europe, he suspected "that France is determined . . . to make us debtors to their influence."[58]

By 1781, Gálvez and his Indian allies had captured British forts at Baton Rouge, Mobile, and Pensacola, giving the Spanish leverage to bargain for territory along the Gulf. Madison had sensed the shifting winds early in the year and abandoned his fight for the Mississippi. Gálvez secured the Floridas for Spain, and Spanish ministers outmaneuvered the United States for control of the river. Madison detested the empire the rest of his career.[59]

Many Americans feared that their allies would prove as troublesome as their enemies. Loyalist John Randolph reminded Jefferson that "France is perfidious, Spain insignificant, and Great Britain formidable." Jefferson had entertained the fear since 1776, when some of his fellow congressmen warned that France, its subordinate ally Spain, and Great Britain "would agree to a partition of our territories" among themselves. Britain allied with Indians. France fought Britain. Spain sided with France. Indians aided Spain. All seemed to threaten the United States.[60]

Peace

In a small, fashionable community just west of Paris, a courier arrived at the Hôtel de Valentinois close to midnight on November 19, 1781. The elegant hôtel boasted a large wing on either side of an opulent parterre. Fine belvederes with Tuscan columns topped the two buildings to over-look the River Seine toward Paris. In the darkness, the courier approached the slightly smaller wing bearing an urgent message from Vergennes for the hôtel's esteemed resident, US emissary Benjamin Franklin. After he read Vergennes's note, the experienced printer used his home press to make copies of the letter and broadcast it to Paris: British commander Lord Cornwallis had surrendered his army to combined French and American forces at Yorktown, Virginia.[61]

The next morning, Franklin penned his response to Vergennes. France's aid had "riveted the Affections" of Americans, he assured the French minister. "Indeed the King appears to me . . . to be *le plus grand Faiseur d'heureux* [the greatest maker of happiness] that this World affords."[62]

Franklin's fellow emissaries in Europe disagreed. New Yorker John Jay and New Englander John Adams sidelined Franklin from the peace talks once they commenced in Paris in 1782. Adams anticipated that Vergennes intended "to keep us down if he can—to keep his Hand under our Chin to prevent Us from drowning, but not to lift our Heads out of [the] Water." Old and ill, Franklin could not contest the ascendancy of Jay and Adams in the discussions.[63]

In America, Congress replicated the disagreements among the emissaries. Madison predicted that Britain would practice "the arts of se-duction & division in the U. States" to pry sweeping concessions from the US commissioners. French ministers had worried that the British would foment discord among the states, pry them away from the union one at a time, and unravel the alliance with France. The new British prime minister, the Earl of Shelburne, assumed that if Britain could keep America in its commercial orbit, the former colonies would eventually reunite with the homeland. Northeasterners would benefit most from that arrange-ment, given their economic reliance on British trade. Madison feared that northeasterners would cede to temptation, discard their French allies, sacrifice western and southern interests, and maybe even stop short of full independence to acquire trade privileges.[64]

Vergennes reinforced Madison's fears. The minister warned that British negotiators might not agree to US independence. He cautioned that Shelburne intended "to deceive all parties, and above all to incite the Americans to acts of perfidy." Vergennes wanted to extinguish all hope that Americans would sign a separate peace with Britain. Madison and his fellow Virginia delegates warned that Congress must maintain "a scrupulous fidelity" to France and "a vigorous preparation for expelling the [British] enemy from our Country." With the United States caught between potential British and French puppet masters, one minister invoked biblical imagery to caution Madison: "The *Dolus in Horte* [guile in the garden] ought ever to be before us, & guard us like a friendly Beacon against hidden & dangerous Designs."[65]

Meanwhile, Madison combated the anti-French contingent. John Jay warned Congress that Vergennes would oppose US land claims west of the Appalachians to protect his Spanish allies. Congress also learned that French negotiators had considered surrendering America's right to Canadian fisheries. In mid-1782, anti-French congressmen proposed that they violate their 1778 treaty with France and instruct the emissaries in Europe to negotiate a separate peace with Great Britain. Madison distrusted the French, but he believed that the United States still needed them to counter British negotiators and to tame their Spanish allies. He finagled his way onto key committees to resolve the dispute.[66]

The debates convinced Madison that the thirteen states must approach foreign policy with a united front. With Madison as chair, one committee insisted that the emissaries fight for US boundaries that extended to the Mississippi and Americans' right to navigate the river. But smaller states refused to sacrifice other peace terms that they considered imperative just so Madison's Virginia could claim its land in the West. To win their votes, Madison conceded that Virginia and other states with western claims might relinquish the land to Congress. To bring New Englanders on board, the committee recommended that America's peace commissioners demand the use of Newfoundland fisheries. Madison served on another committee that resolved that the commissioners should continue to cooperate with France. If the United States hoped to survive, Madison realized, the separate states needed to unify their efforts to repel enemies and win friends. His deft maneuvers won the support of previously anti-French zealots.[67]

Madison may have carried the day in Congress, but in Paris, Adams and Jay still distrusted France. Jay bristled that Vergennes and his superiors wanted to keep the United States "under their direction" and limit their claims to the Mississippi. Vergennes had secretly sent an agent to Britain to discuss US independence. The agent convinced Shelburne that France would try to limit America's territorial claims after the British recognized US independence.[68]

British agents aggravated the distrust between the allies. They intercepted negative French correspondence and fed it to the already suspicious Jay. In one note, a member of the French legation in America derided the republic's claims to Newfoundland fisheries. Britain and France may have agreed that the peace would include US independence, but they hardly viewed Americans as independent.[69]

Fueled by suspicion, the American peace commissioners decided, in Jay's words, to "cut the cord that ties us to France." Even Franklin endorsed the move. In Paris, they collaborated in secret with Shelburne's pick as chief negotiator, Richard Oswald. Knowing that they had disobeyed Congress, Jay pleaded, "Had I not violated the instructions of Congress their dignity would have been in the Dust" due to French intrigues.[70]

To conclude peace before Vergennes could intervene, Shelburne and Oswald offered generous terms to Jay, Adams, Franklin, and Henry Laurens. The commissioners secured the Mississippi as the western boundary from the Great Lakes to the Spanish Floridas, along with rights to use Newfoundland fisheries. The British abandoned their Native American allies. None of the European powers invited Indians to the table. The treaty remained silent on Indian land, leaving Americans to assume it belonged to them.[71]

France and Britain preferred to see the West in the hands of Americans rather than their enemy, fearing each other more than they feared the new republic. That reality served Americans during peace negotiations, but it also exposed them as pawns. They could have what Europe decided they could have. As Madison conceded by December 1782, Vergennes had tried to make America "sensible of her own weakness," though Madison still believed America "more in danger of being seduced by Britain than sacrificed by France." With enemies and friends blurred, Americans quarreled over whom to trust.[72]

Congress

On September 14, 1783, John Thaxter—John Adams's private secretary— sped in a carriage along the post road from Paris to L'Orient, France. He carried an urgent dispatch from Adams, Jay, Franklin, and Laurens: the signed peace treaty with Britain. After four days of hard riding and little sleep, he arrived in L'Orient with exhausted horses and to the bitter news that he had missed his ship. Contrary winds trapped him in L'Orient for another week. Thaxter did not arrive in Philadelphia until November 22, the same day that Madison left the city to return home. His congressional term had ended on November 2.[73]

Madison departed before he saw the definitive treaty, but he had seen enough of the negotiations to worry that Congress could not function as a federal government. While Thaxter lingered in L'Orient, Madison had seethed to Jefferson that the British enjoyed an upper hand in negotiations due to disunity among the states "and the impotence of the fœderal Govt." The peace commissioners had tried to insert commercial agreements into the treaty with Britain. The British refused the proposals because they knew that Americans could never unite sufficiently to retaliate against the trade restrictions on US commerce.[74]

Madison summarized Congress's dysfunction for Jefferson. The Department of Foreign Affairs languished without a secretary. The Marine Department had sold almost all US naval vessels. The Department of Finance "is an object of almost daily attack" and would soon "be reduced to its crisis."[75]

Thaxter brought welcome news of peace, but that news also meant that the army would now dissolve. Most members of Congress insisted that the Articles of Confederation prohibited a peacetime military establishment. They resolved to disband the military once the definitive treaty arrived. Madison rejected the logic of discharging the military when the United States would remain surrounded by potential enemies. He preferred a strong revenue system that would keep military forts garrisoned.[76]

Even had Congress wanted to employ a peacetime military, the Articles of Confederation hamstrung its ability to raise money to sustain it. Congress could request money from the states, but it could not raise its own revenue. In the summer, Madison had fled with Congress to Princeton, driven there by mutinous Philadelphia soldiers who demanded promised pay that Congress couldn't deliver. States threatened to withhold funds and compensate their soldiers directly but for less than what

Congress had promised. Madison warned that if Congress failed to stabilize its finances, a "dissolution of the union will be inevitable," each region becoming a petty confederacy.[77]

Madison labored to bring national cohesion to Congress with little success. Under the Articles of Confederation, individual states could veto revenue proposals. Stymied by state differences—a "paroxism of jealousy," as Madison called it—Congress failed to enact a revenue system to meet its urgent needs and pay its war debt. The failure threatened to sink the republic's domestic and international credit. Nonetheless, the unflinching Articles of Confederation required unanimous consent from the states to amend them, making sweeping changes nearly impossible. The demand for unanimity ironically threatened to sunder the union.[78]

Madison linked America's domestic discord with its international weakness. If disagreements persisted, the confederacy might dissolve. If the confederacy dissolved, quarrels might arise and invite foreign "intrusion into American disputes." Americans would surrender the sovereignty they had just won.[79]

Confederacies

While Madison contemplated the dissolution of his confederacy, Joseph Brant traveled to the British Fort Niagara to ensure the survival of his. At the September council fire at Sandusky, the gathered nations had agreed to send representatives to Niagara with Brant to solemnize their friendship. Overlooking the Niagara River as it emptied into Lake Ontario, the fort had boasted British might after they had captured it from the French in 1759. The Indian representatives convened there in early October and reaffirmed the confederacy.[80]

Brant sought protection and vindication in the British–Indian confederation. He had journeyed along Lake Erie toward Fort Niagara at the same time Thaxter was crossing the Atlantic with the peace treaty. Western Indians may have "laid the Hatchet aside" after the war, as Brant had declared at Sandusky, but they would wield it again should Americans give them "just cause to use it."[81]

At the close of 1783, neither Madison nor Brant knew which of their respective confederacies would outlast the other. To Madison, foreign powers prowled the borders of the union. The British–Indian coalition lurked in the North, met by Spanish–Indian alliances to the Southwest. After the British surrendered at Yorktown, Madison grew more skeptical that his confederacy would endure, not less. "The present union," he had predicted to Jefferson in November 1781, "will but little survive the present war." Without a war, Americans had little to unite them.[82]

Far from making a grand debut, the United States barely managed a timid entrance. Languishing with internal divisions and a frail government, the republic lay exposed to hostile enemies and slightly less hostile allies. With the war over, foreign powers awaited the day when the union would collapse and they could seize the pieces.

In December 1783, Madison departed for home. He left convinced that Congress needed fundamental changes if the union hoped to withstand foreign antagonism. The Articles of Confederation sacrificed national security to safeguard liberty; Madison aimed to protect both. As he journeyed home in freezing, torrential December rains, he pondered "the proper means of preserving the confederacy."[83]

2

"Calamities from Abroad"

As a weak government . . . is ever agitated by internal dissentions; so
these never fail to bring on fresh calamities from abroad.
—JAMES MADISON, 1788

WHILE MADISON SLOGGED HOME TO Montpelier through the rain-
drenched roads of Virginia, Creek leader Alexander McGillivray pondered
his own society's future. McGillivray owned a splendid plantation in the
Indian town of Little Tallassee, in the rolling hills south of the Tennessee
River Valley. His estate nestled against the Coosa River, where he
commanded what one observer called "a small village" of enslaved blacks
and white overseers. The plantation boasted orchards and livestock that
most white southerners would have envied.[1]

Madison and McGillivray shared more in common than either would
care to admit. Each hailed from elite families in their communities. One
year older than Madison, McGillivray descended from a Scottish father
and prominent Creek mother—an advantage in the Creek's matrilineal society. Madison and McGillivray each left home at a young age to receive a
gentleman's education from a Scottish tutor. Like Madison, McGillivray
had a "delicate and feeble" constitution, prone to ill health. They burnished
their reputations more as political organizers than as military heroes, and
both possessed a placid temperament that belied their steely tenacity. Each
was *a* leader—though not *the* leader—among a disunited population.
After the war, each labored to mobilize his community into a united political body.[2]

McGillivray had sided with Britain against Spain and the Americans
during the war. After their surrender at Yorktown, the British had offered

to resettle him with loyalists—perhaps in the West Indies or Canada. He preferred to stay with his family and land. But Georgians assumed that their western boundary now extended west to the Mississippi. The region included more than 100,000 square miles from the Tennessee River to the thirty-first parallel near the Gulf. Spain and the United States each claimed the land based on differing interpretations of the recent peace treaties.[3]

McGillivray and other Indians cared little about the terms of the peace. No Americans or Europeans had asked their opinion about the settlement, and they would yield their land neither to Spain nor America. Southern Indians feared, however, that the more numerous Americans would invade "like a plague of locusts," as a council of prominent chiefs complained to Spanish authorities. Former enemies, McGillivray and Spain now needed each other to keep Americans from overrunning the disputed territory.[4]

On the same day that Madison likely trudged into Montpelier— December 5, 1783—McGillivray sat in his plantation house to write the Spanish military governor of Pensacola, Arturo O'Neill. McGillivray had not yet received word of the finalized peace, so he wrote cautiously, but he was angling to become Spain's Indian agent among the Creeks. He made no explicit bids, though he derided a competitor for the position and reassured the governor that he would not welcome British loyalists to his land. McGillivray wasn't sure what the future would bring, but he expected that the Spanish would replace the British as his most valuable European ally.[5]

McGillivray assured O'Neill that their alliance could build on the ruins of a weak, divided United States. He reminded the governor that frontier Americans detested the taxes that Congress tried to collect to pay its war debt. They would soon move farther west "out of the reach of the Authority of Congress." McGillivray preferred to entrust his future to "a great Monarch" rather than the "distracted Republic." The United States could not last long in its divided state. He predicted that Britain, France, and Spain would soon "settle the matter by dividing America between them."[6]

In May, McGillivray headed to Pensacola to meet with O'Neill and Esteban Miró, the new Spanish governor of Louisiana. Creeks tended to negotiate treaties as a large community, with dozens of leaders signing the parchment on behalf of their clans and towns. With his European-style education, McGillivray ignored the Creek tradition and met the Spaniards as the sole, self-appointed representative of the nation. On May 31 and June

1, he negotiated and signed a treaty that solidified friendship between the Creeks and Spain. They contracted with a company of British loyalists to provide the Creeks supplies and ammunition. The agreement spawned many Americans' worst fears for their republic—"a dangerous confederacy," as one report called it, "between the several Indian Nations, the Spaniards and British agents."[7]

It is now common to take for granted that white Americans eventually would divide and usurp Indian land. In the 1780s, however, most Americans worried that Europeans and Indians would divide and usurp American land. Madison worried with the rest, and he began to conceive a constitutional structure that would repel that future.

The Journey

Madison could not remember a worse winter than the early months of 1784. As deep snow blanketed Montpelier, he sheltered in the comfortable plantation house with his parents, attended by enslaved men and women who endured the winter in frigid slave quarters. Due to icy, impassable roads, the Madison family entertained few visitors. Madison rejoiced in the isolation. The "winter blockade," as he called it, left him alone to study and ponder governments, history, constitutions, and international law. No mere academic exercise, his study regimen began to yield a vision of a nation that could protect its citizens' liberty from their own government and from foreign incursion.[8]

He needed books. A lot of books. As the roads improved in March, he pleaded with his friend Jefferson to purchase the necessary volumes while in Congress up north and to send them to Montpelier. He didn't care if Jefferson inadvertently sent duplicates. He just needed books on anything that shed light on the constitutions and laws of confederacies throughout history. He wanted to study from the brightest minds on law and diplomacy—Cornelius van Bynkershoek, Emer de Vattel, Edward Coke, Hugo Grotius, Abraham de Wicquefort, and Christian Wolff, among others. The more Madison studied, the more he became convinced that the United States needed a stronger federal government to command respect from Europe.[9]

Spring gifted Madison the chance to turn his thoughts into legislation. He won election to the Virginia Assembly, which by then convened in Richmond. He sponsored resolutions and drafted bills that would cede more power to the federal government to regulate the confederacy's foreign affairs. Although his efforts succeeded in Virginia, they would remain fruitless unless the other states went along. Congress languished in exasperating "impotency."[10]

To pass the time between legislative sessions, Madison planned a "ramble" into the Northeast in September. His trip became an excursion after he encountered the Marquis de Lafayette and his entourage at Baltimore. The French aristocrat had come to Washington's aid during some of the darkest days of the Revolution. As a result, he commanded the love of Americans, who rendered him, as Madison observed, "the most flattering tokens of sincere affection."[11]

The marquis convinced Madison to travel with him to New York to observe treaty negotiations between US commissioners and Joseph Brant's Iroquois confederacy at Fort Stanwix. Americans, Britons, and Indians hoped that the treaty would finally settle the question of Indian land in the Great Lakes region as well as who had jurisdiction to effect such an agreement. New York political elites cast Indians as "Dependants on this State" and argued that state officials should decide their fate. Congressional authorities declared the Indians independent, defeated nations. Unable to decide whether Indians were internal dissenters or external threats, Americans began to imagine them as a dangerous combination of both.[12]

When Madison and his companions reached Philadelphia in early September, they boarded for several days at the residence of Mary House, where Madison had stayed while in Congress. As he caught up with his old friend, they discussed the plight of House's daughter, Eliza Trist. The young mother had traveled down the Mississippi to Louisiana to join her husband, only to find him dead. Compounding her misery, she was stuck there until the spring because Spain meanwhile had closed the Mississippi to American travelers.[13]

Beyond eliciting Madison's sympathy for his friend, the tale inflamed his ire over a brewing geopolitical conflict. Spain had allowed Americans to use the Mississippi as a wartime necessity without guaranteeing its use after peace. In 1784, the monarchy decided to protect its commerce and prevent smuggling along the river by denying the United States navigation rights. The maneuver threatened Madison's wish that Americans would populate the West and use the river to export their agricultural goods.[14]

He saw more at stake than commerce. With other Virginia elites, Madison worried that many westerners would lend their allegiance to whichever nation protected their financial interests. If frontier folk doubted the American confederacy's ability to do that, they would be, as George Washington remarked, "driven into the arms of . . . foreigners." America, Spain, and British Canada clamored for their loyalty. They "stand as it were upon a pivot," Washington declared. "The touch of a feather, would turn them any way." Washington worried less about the Mississippi and wanted to connect the West to the United States through canals from Chesapeake Bay to the Ohio River. Madison, however, thought the Mississippi vital.[15]

In Philadelphia, he unburdened his thoughts to Lafayette. "The ideas of America and Spain irreconcilably clash," he explained to his travel companion. France needed to convince Spain to correct course, he pleaded. Otherwise, "an actual rupture is near at hand." He warned Lafayette that if France failed to help the United States secure the Mississippi, anti-French Americans might invite Great Britain to help them. Lafayette promised to address the issue with Vergennes.[16]

Not content with Lafayette's promise, Madison sat alone in his boarding room to confide his fears by letter to Jefferson, who had traveled to France. Madison reviled Spain's "impolitic & perverse attempt to shut" the Mississippi to Americans. He leveled his best legal and diplomatic arguments against Spain's decision to deny Americans access to the river. If Spain persisted, it would "sow the seeds of inevitable hostility" with the United States. For decades, Spain's power had waned in Europe despite its vast domains in North and South America. Madison argued that Spain underestimated the United States at its own peril. He foresaw a day when the security of Spain's American dominions would "depend more on our peaceableness, than her own power." For the present, Madison admitted that the United States posed no threat to Spain due to "the Complexity of our fœderal Govt. and the diversity of interests among the members of it." Disunity bred weakness, and weakness made a poor bargaining chip.[17]

As Madison, Lafayette, and their company moved on to New York, the Mississippi still tortured Madison's mind. Lafayette showed him a letter he had written to Vergennes about the issue. It was less forceful that Madison would have liked, and the Frenchman promised to press the subject further when he had more time.[18]

In New York, the travel party boarded barges that carried them up the Hudson toward the Mohawk River. The region still wore the scars of battle, with homes surrounded by stockades built to protect Americans from Indian and British attacks. "Everything recalled the war to us," one party member reported. The sights no doubt reinforced Madison's hostility to British–Indian alliances.[19]

On September 29, the group spilled into Fort Stanwix, greeted by a patchwork of Indian shelters scattered around a miserable tangle of cabins that fire had nearly destroyed in 1781. Heavy rains had rotted what the fire hadn't scorched. One cabin housed cheap trinkets that the cash-strapped Americans hoped would pass as diplomatic gifts. Madison's company lodged at the fort for several days while Indian representatives, US commissioners, New York officials, and 150 troops meandered in.[20]

Madison observed the negotiations, mortified by the evident weakness of his confederacy. With congressional and state commissioners all clamoring for authority, Indians had no idea who was in charge. Joseph Brant complained that Americans had sent "two separate Bodies to manage these Affairs." The proceedings unveiled the United States as a bickering assembly of thirteen bodies with no national power. By attempting to supersede congressional commissioners, New York's representatives had "violated both duty & decorum," Madison griped. Only Lafayette impressed the Indians. The European "eclipsed" the bungling American commissioners.[21]

While the Americans maintained shacks and offered knickknacks at Fort Stanwix, the British gifted arms and land at the imposing Fort Niagara. Compared to the British, Madison wrote Jefferson with an evident sigh, Americans "are not likely to make a figure otherwise that will impress a high idea of our power or opulence."[22]

After Madison returned to Virginia and his seat in the assembly, the situation continued to fester. From Congress, fellow Virginian John Mercer warned Madison that Britain's western presence and "intrigues with the Indians" evinced "a settled plan, unfriendly, if not hostile to the United States." Americans faced the threat with "internal Weakness & total want of resource." Mercer lamented that with the war over "discordant manners & sentiments of the different States, have produc'd great heats & animosities in Congress." Meanwhile, Madison scowled, the Spanish were "spurring on" Indians south of the Ohio River, and Congress needed to make treaties with southern Indians and with Spain to access the Mississippi. Congress remained too inept even to convene a full quorum for business. Mercer forecast that the machinery of government "will not be long kept in motion, unless great & effectual repairs are made."[23]

From Trenton—Congress's fourth home in three years—Madison heard rumblings about a convention to revise the Articles of Confederation. After twirling the subject in his mind on Christmas day, 1784, he concluded that "the Union of the States is essential to their safety against foreign danger, & internal contention." Americans could not rely on "the perpetuity & efficacy of the present system." Madison hoped the states would soon approve the convention.[24]

By late winter 1785, Madison returned to his books at Montpelier, reading law, politics, and diplomacy. As he read, he began to envision a government that could balance power and liberty. He imagined a constitution that could embrace political dissent but mitigate the danger of internal divisions. Such a government could protect its citizens from foreign hostility without threatening their freedom. That vision became more important as the United States began to negotiate for access to the Mississippi River.[25]

The River

On October 1, 1785, Sarah Livingston Jay received a surprise—boxes of valuable gifts from Diego de Gardoqui. One of the wealthiest women in New York, Jay lived at her brother-in-law's Manhattan house while she awaited completion of a stone mansion among other opulent homes on Broadway. Gardoqui had met her in Spain while her husband, John Jay, had served as a diplomat in Madrid. Now Gardoqui had come to the United States as a Spanish representative to negotiate western borders with John, the recently appointed US secretary of foreign affairs. While Sarah had resided in Spain, Gardoqui came to know her as a vain woman who delighted in flattery and gifts. More important, Gardoqui believed she dominated her husband, who loved her "blindly" and did "nothing without her knowledge." However fair or unfair his description, Gardoqui concluded that "with a little skill" and some well-timed "lavishments" he could secure the friendship of the power couple.[26]

Fifty years old, Gardoqui had used his command of English to aid negotiations with Americans since 1777. Educated in Britain, the son of wealthy Bilbao merchants, he was a natural pick as the minister to negotiate with the United States. Gardoqui may have justifiably expected to arrive as a hero to Americans. He had smuggled arms to colonial arsenals before fighting had even begun during the Revolution. He armed the rebels throughout the bleak early days of the war, risking his personal fortune. Few Americans knew of his clandestine heroics, though. Even if they did, the Mississippi clash tarnished any former goodwill with Spain.[27]

Gardoqui had arrived in New York earlier in the year with instructions to settle the border problems and resist American pleas to use the Mississippi River. The Spanish government allocated him secret funds to charm not only the Jays but also other prominent Americans, such as George Washington and his fellow Virginian Henry Lee. As he told his superiors, "There are many needy in the government body," and he calculated that feasts, "good wines," and bribes would win him the favor of Americans he needed. He masked bribes as loans, giving Lee at least two loans of 5,000 pesos from his official account. "He is very much mine," Gardoqui boasted to Madrid. The Jays returned the initial gifts to avoid compromising their positions as "public characters," but John did accept a fine horse with the permission of Congress.[28]

To complement his strategy of bribery and flattery, Gardoqui intended to use Americans' divisions against them, knowing that they would never pursue a united policy in the West. Although Americans had split into many factions, Gardoqui believed the North held the most power, unified by their commercial interests. The Spaniard felt confident that he could persuade northerners to abandon the Mississippi issue if he promised enticing trade benefits with Spain. The war had left the US economy in tatters, and many northerners hoped that a healthy Spanish trade would solve the crisis. They agreed with Massachusetts delegate Rufus King that the westward migration would syphon citizens from the East until "entire separation" occurred. Gardoqui assumed he could convince at least half the states to drop the Mississippi demands.[29]

At first, his plan seemed to work. He agreed to yield disputed land to Americans and grant the confederacy trade privileges if they dropped their demand for access to the Mississippi. Admitting defeat, Jay tried to maneuver congressmen to concede the Mississippi issue. Incensed southerners refused. They insisted that any agreement needed approval from nine states, yet Gardoqui and Jay could secure only seven. Jay's opponents worried, as James Monroe warned Madison, that the agreement would separate westerners "from the federal government & perhaps throw them into the hands eventually of a foreign power." As Gardoqui reported to his government, his opponents panicked that the confederacy would split and westerners would ally with Great Britain.[30]

When negotiations stalled in late summer 1786, some northerners threatened to separate from the confederacy. They arranged secret meetings with Gardoqui to negotiate independently, but the talks went nowhere.

Gardoqui needed Congress to restrain westerners from encroaching on Spanish dominions, something that northerners could not do if they broke from the union. Gardoqui summoned "an infinity of guises and talents to barter with both parties and bolster the majority."[31]

In February 1787, Madison returned to Congress convinced that Gardoqui intended to divide the East and West and to "foment jealousy" between the North and South. He fretted that America's internal divisions benefited Spain and Britain, who waited "to seize an opportunity of embroiling our affairs." Britain retained western forts on land it had officially ceded to the United States and obstructed vital trade to the British West Indies that Americans had enjoyed as British subjects. The British exploited "the want of fœderal spirit" to cause "a breach in our confederacy," Madison repined. If northerners sacrificed the river to Spain, he warned, westerners would "court" Great Britain to protect their "betrayed rights," the worst calamity Madison could imagine. He needed to convince Spain to change course.[32]

The Mansion

On March 13, Madison and his colleague William Bingham strode by New York's Bowling Green and approached Gardoqui's lavish mansion at the head of Broadway. Believing it necessary to live "on a first class footing," Gardoqui had purchased "the finest house in the city." To court favor, he hosted elegant entertainment in the home, situated just a few blocks from New York's city hall, where Congress met. This meeting with Madison and Bingham was more subdued. Gardoqui considered Madison a friend, but Madison distrusted the Spaniard's government.[33]

The Americans warned Gardoqui that the British would seduce westerners from the union and foment dissension among them against Spain if Spain barred them from the Mississippi. Gardoqui dismissed their arguments. "Spain could make her own terms . . . with Britain" and even make it "bend to her views," he assured Madison and Bingham. Madison thought he was bluffing, but Gardoqui knew that Spain had the upper hand with control of the Mississippi. It possessed what westerners needed.[34]

The Spaniard "hinted" that westerners "would make good Spanish subjects" and that Spain might use the river to entice them to join the empire. Madison wondered if he was joking. He wasn't, at least, not entirely.[35]

FIGURE 2.1 Detail of a View of the Kennedy, Watts, Livingston, and Stevens Mansions, Bowling Green, NY. Gardoqui occupied what was known as the Kennedy Mansion (*farthest left*) at the head of Broadway across from New York's Bowling Green. Courtesy New York Public Library Digital Collections.

About five months before Madison visited Gardoqui's mansion, Congressman James White of western North Carolina had called there as well. Conceding that Spain would never grant Americans access to the Mississippi, White predicted that his constituents "will consider themselves abandoned by the Confederation." Spain could "win them forever."[36]

North Carolinians and Virginians had poured across the Appalachians and established the settlements of Kentucky, Franklin, and Cumberland in the eastern Tennessee River Valley. The regions agitated for independent statehood. Eastern elites worried that their "states will crumble to atoms," as Jefferson put it, if they allowed "every little canton" to form a separate state. After Congress refused their petitions for statehood, some westerners began to deliberate independence from the United States and an alliance with Spain.[37]

White hailed from Pennsylvania, but he had made his fortune in land speculation in the western reaches of North Carolina. Born in the North, educated in Europe, and invested in the West, he made an ideal ambassador for those who wanted to strike a deal with Spain. Like other westerners, he considered the Mississippi vital to his interests.[38]

As superintendent of Indian affairs in the South, White grasped the importance of Spain's alliance with southern Indians. In 1785, Georgians had unilaterally tried to usurp territory disputed by Spain, Indians, and the United States. The next year, Spain secretly supplied McGillivray's Creeks with ammunition to combat the Georgians. Westerners such as White believed that independent, friendly relations with Spain could win them the Mississippi and peace with Indians.[39]

"Every state fears its neighbor, differs in its principles, is split into do-mestic parties and has no private or public credit," Gardoqui explained to Floridablanca in Madrid. Northern independence would have done little for Gardoqui, but western independence intrigued him. If westerners declared independence and allied or united with Spain, his government would enjoy a buffer between the encroaching United States and Spanish territory.[40]

Still hoping to reach an agreement with Congress, Gardoqui listened to White but made no promises. Over the following months, he cajoled and schemed to counter Virginians' demands for access to the Mississippi. He published anonymous arguments to persuade Americans to his view. By the time he met with Madison that spring, his efforts had foundered. He, too, began to envision an alliance with westerners that would integrate them into Spanish dominions or adopt the region as a client state.[41]

When he met with Madison five months later, Gardoqui told him nothing about his meeting with White. As Madison and Bingham stood to depart, Gardoqui reiterated "the inflexibility of Spain." He warned the Americans against pursuing the issue, and they left. On March 29, Madison met Gardoqui again, joined by the other Virginia delegates. They rehashed the same points they had discussed two weeks earlier. Mixing frankness with flattery, Gardoqui predicted the demise of the union but insisted that he hoped it would flourish, "which was more than *France* or any other Nation in Europe did."[42]

Madison doubted the sincerity of Gardoqui's good wishes and suspected that the Spaniard was trying to alienate him from France. Gardoqui indeed wanted to convince the delegates that France wouldn't support their claims to the Mississippi, something the Spaniard feared in fact was untrue. He had heard rumors that France was an "enemy" to his mission. Gardoqui considered Madison "France's creature" and suspected that the Virginian worked with Lafayette to defeat Spain's objectives. Madison believed that French officials shared his alarm that westerners would return to the British orbit, and he welcomed Lafayette's support as evidence that France would back US claims to the river. He saw Gardoqui's warning about France as a bluff—bluster that exposed the Spaniard's fear that the French court sided with Americans.[43]

Bluffing or not, Gardoqui assessed France more accurately than either he or Madison realized. The French court had no interest in aiding the United States against its Spanish ally. As he often did, Madison overestimated France's friendship to the United States. Jay's assessment came closer to reality: "France will invariably . . . prefer the good will of Spain to the good will of America." Later that year, French officials reminded their diplomat in the United States, "We have never pretended to make of America a useful ally; we have had no other object than to deprive Britain of that vast continent." The new republic probably would collapse, they shrugged. The United States had no friends on the continent.[44]

Gardoqui repeated his half-joke that westerners might join the Spanish empire. Then, his smile faded, and he intimated that "some person connected with the Western Country" had proposed the idea, divulging nothing more about White's visit months earlier. He assured Madison that the king would never consider such a scheme, but he meant the intelligence as a soft threat. Spain held all the cards. If the United States failed to restrain land-hungry Americans from moving west and threatening Spanish land, Spain could lure them from the republic.[45]

In Congress the next day, Madison and his allies demanded that Jay report on his negotiations with Gardoqui. When Jay admitted that he was considering a treaty that would surrender use of the Mississippi, Madison led the charge to block the potential deal. He even suggested that Congress send Jefferson from Paris to Madrid to reset talks, a prospect Jefferson disliked even more than Jay did. By the end of April, Madison convinced Congress to abandon Jay's negotiation with Gardoqui.[46]

The fight convinced Madison, as he wrote Jefferson after his first meeting with Gardoqui, that Americans had allowed Spain to "foment distrusts" among them. He heard rumors that "British partisans are already feeling the pulse" of frontier settlements to see if westerners would be willing to reunite with the empire. In Madison's view, Congress could have thwarted the disaster had they acted with "harmony and confidence" to demand the Mississippi. Instead, he lamented, "the intemperance of party" had betrayed America to foreign interference.[47]

Madison meant that the *wrong* party had betrayed America to the *wrong* foreign power. To counter Spanish and British designs, he desired France to mediate negotiations for the river. Virginia delegates had been negotiating secretly with France since the fall. Madison gladly tried to recruit a foreign government to advocate his own sectional interests. When Madison pleaded for "harmony" in Congress, he meant that he wanted northerners to agree with him.[48]

However blind to his own partisanship, Madison recognized that foreign governments could exploit political differences to weaken the United States. Amid the Mississippi fight, he began to devise a system that would unify the states under a national government. That government would legislate according to the national interest rather than the interests of a squabbling party that cobbled together a slim congressional majority manipulated by a foreign power. He set out for Philadelphia, where he hoped to cure the "*mortal* diseases of the Confederacy." Otherwise, he expected "general chaos or at least partition of the Union."[49]

The Convention

Madison had been advocating changes in the Articles of Confederation since the early 1780s, and in the summer of 1786, had turned his advocacy into a crusade. In September of that year, he traveled to Annapolis to attend a convention intended to recommend additional powers to Congress, especially commercial powers.[50]

Madison bemoaned Congress's inability to tax imports. He believed the tax vital to retaliate against Britain's import taxes and trade restrictions in the West Indies. He preferred "perfect freedom" of trade, but the United States could not achieve that so long as Britain and other nations imposed restrictions. Starved for revenue and powerless to collect taxes effectively, Congress possessed no leverage over Spain on the Mississippi issue, unable to threaten war. Madison brooded to James Monroe, "Must we remain passive victims to foreign politics?"[51]

To combat British "machinations," the states needed to act with "harmony," Madison pressed. If one state passed duties against Britain and another state refused, the United States could exert no pressure. If Congress couldn't manage the task, he griped, the "fœderal system should be amended." People "can not long respect a Government which is too feeble to protect their interest." Madison demanded a trade war, and he hoped the Annapolis delegates would grant Congress the ability to wage it.[52]

True to Madison's somber predictions, the Annapolis convention failed before it began. Only three states sent enough delegates to act. Even so, a young, brash New York lawyer with a fierce pen refused to waste the meeting.[53]

Alexander Hamilton had advocated longer and harder than anybody to revamp the government. His brazenness contrasted with Madison's reticence, just as his impoverished childhood on an obscure Caribbean island contrasted with Madison's elite upbringing in Virginia. But Hamilton's poverty had steeled him with purpose. He migrated to New York, gained an education, shone in the Revolutionary War, earned Washington's trust, married into a wealthy family, and met Madison in Congress in 1783. Madison welcomed him as an ally in the fight for a stronger federal government.[54]

Hamilton insisted that the convention meet again and repair all the "defects" of the Articles of Confederation, not just those involving commercial issues. On behalf of the Annapolis delegates, he composed a message to the states, calling on them to send delegates to Philadelphia in May 1787. Shaken from his pessimism, Madison signed the message, stirred the Virginia Assembly to endorse the meeting, and pleaded with Washington to attend, prevailing one month before the delegates gathered.[55]

As the Philadelphia convention approached, Madison shut himself in his New York boarding room to organize the theories he had been formulating for years. In the spring of 1786, he had plunged into history, making a systematic list of past confederacies—their constitutions, characteristics, strengths, and defects. As far as he could see, the United States was trying to accomplish the unprecedented: create a stable, viable republican entity. The Swiss confederacy divided into Protestant and Catholic cantons, and each bloc allied with opposing foreign powers. Internal religious wars bloodied German states during the 1600s until the Peace of Westphalia allowed foreign nations to dictate a new German constitution. Foreign ministers usurped Belgian sovereignty "by tampering with the provinces & cities" to foment disunion. Romans "seduced" members of the Achaean League, and Macedonians fostered "dissensions" among them. History abounded with examples of mighty powers inciting internal divisions.[56]

One confederacy especially vexed Madison. In Temple Stanyan's *Graecian History*, Madison read about the Sacred War, which began as a religious dispute between the Phocians and Amphictyons but expanded across the Greek peninsulas. Stanyan described how one party recruited the assistance of Philip of Macedon, who exploited religious division to endear him to Greek factions. Philip "fomented divisions in Greece" and acquired a seat in the council of the Amphictyons. Masking "artifice and hypocrisy" as "zeal for religion," Philip eventually upended Greek sovereignty.[57]

The example jolted Madison, who had wrestled with the line between religious freedom and national security during the Revolution. He had revisited the subject in the mid-1780s when he fought for religious liberty in Virginia. After reading Fortuné Barthélemy de Félice's interpretation of the Sacred War, he concluded that had Greece strengthened its union "she would never have yielded to Macedon."[58]

Madison sounded the alarm to his colleagues. He warned Washington that foreign nations might "imitate" Philip and exploit American divisions to exacerbate disunity. He reminded Jefferson that the United States stood in "danger of having the same game played on our confederacy by which Philip managed that of the Grecian state." He fretted that some Americans would serve as "fit instruments of foreign machinations."[59]

In late 1786, riots had erupted in Massachusetts as the state government tried to collect taxes in a depressed economy. The protestors advocated debt relief through inflationary measures that Madison feared would ruin the economy and credit of the confederation. Rather than see cash-strapped farmers in financial straits, Madison saw "adversaries . . . secretly stimulated by British influence." Foreign intrusion and domestic discord harmonized in a toxic rhythm.[60]

Convinced that Americans could embrace diverse opinions without allowing foreign powers to exploit their divisions, Madison recorded his solution in his New York boarding room. They needed to unify under a stronger central government and relinquish "every concession in favor of stable Government" that did not infringe on fundamental rights. Unlike most republican theorists of his time, Madison rejected the assumption that governments naturally craved power. Instead, he imagined an ill-defined power benchmark. If governments acquired too much of it, they would pursue more until they overthrew liberty. If a government's power fell below that benchmark, "the direct tendency is to further degrees of re-laxation, until the abuses of liberty beget a sudden transition to an undue degree of power." A weak government could not protect liberty against internal strife or external pressure.[61]

Madison also countered conventional wisdom that republics thrived only as small, homogenous communities. From his fight for religious li-berty in Virginia, he determined that "the majority may trespass on the rights of the minority" too easily in a small republic. He began to envision an expansive republic with so many factions that no single group could form a majority and threaten minority rights. At the same time, a strong federal government could neutralize the hazards of diversity. It would bind the factions into a common interest, dissuading them from entertaining foreign alliances. Convinced that the national government could better protect liberty than state governments, Madison concluded that Congress should possess veto power over state laws. It took Madison months to ar-ticulate his ideas. By the time he departed New York for Philadelphia, though, he believed that he had found a way to square liberty with national security.[62]

He faced a Herculean task trying to convince others. In the weeks be-fore convention delegates descended on Philadelphia, Gardoqui had met secretly with some of them, and they confided their doubts that they could reach any agreement. They admitted to Gardoqui that it could take years to contrive a new constitution because of the "disunity of spirits," to use Gardoqui's phrase, that prevailed. Americans could call them-selves a confederation all they wished, Gardoqui quipped, but "there is no confederation."[63]

Madison left New York for Philadelphia on May 3, 1787. After the other Virginia delegates straggled into the city through poor weather, he began to shepherd his theories into a body of fifteen resolutions. Rather than amend the Articles of Confederation, the resolutions outlined a completely new government system. The Virginians presented the plan to the other delegates on the first day of debate. Over the swel-tering summer, crammed into an upper room of the Pennsylvania state house, the convention members debated, harangued, tinkered, clarified, and changed the plan. But Madison had made his theories the basis of debate.[64]

Foreign intrusion hung like Damocles's sword over the proceedings. In every major discussion, Madison weighed the likelihood that proposals would invite or repel it. When tensions peaked, some delegates weaponized the fear. In mid-June, John Dickinson of Delaware accused Madison of trying to coerce an agreement that would subordinate smaller states to the larger. He warned Madison, "We would sooner to submit to France or any other foreign power" than to a plan that would throw them "under the domination of the large States." Madison argued that the small states' counterproposal would fail to "secure the Union against the influence of foreign powers over its members." After another Delaware delegate suggested the same as Dickinson in open debate, Madison condemned their "rash policy of courting foreign support." He wanted to call Delaware's bluff, but Elbridge Gerry of Massachusetts worried that "if we do not come to some agreement among ourselves, some foreign sword will probably do the work for us." Gerry endorsed compromise with the small states and chaired the committee that forged it, narrowly avoiding a dissolution of the convention in its first weeks.[65]

For four months, Madison teamed with others to turn the United States from a loose confederacy into a nation. The new Constitution allowed the federal government to coerce taxes from individuals rather than request them from states. It created a presidency that could more efficiently meet foreign threats and negotiate treaties. It authorized the national government to raise an army and navy. It stripped states of their power to create currency and regulate interstate commerce, granting those responsibilities to Congress. It invested Congress with the ability to coerce states to respect federal treaties. Madison didn't get everything he wanted, especially the federal veto on state laws. Still, when the delegates signed their handiwork on September 17, he hoped they had granted the government "proper stability & energy."[66]

By its own terms, the Constitution required nine states to ratify it before it became operative, and Americans split into broad factions for and against the charter. George Mason disappointed Madison when he huffed out of Philadelphia without signing. Most Americans who opposed this stronger union believed, like Mason, that the national government would descend into "a corrupt, tyrannical aristocracy" and trample the states. Those who supported ratification identified as Federalists and called their opponents Antifederalists. The terms belied the complexity of the debate. Many Antifederalists admired certain aspects of the Constitution and many Federalists despised parts of it. Still, supporters of ratification cast detractors as adversaries of national unity.[67]

Gardoqui delighted in "the disgust over the new government, which if not adopted may result in confusion, or, what is better, in two confederations." He knew that many westerners feared that a distant national government would ignore their pleas for the Mississippi. Westerners also assumed that the North would not allow them to form new states. Under the new Constitution, each state would receive two senators, and northerners worried that new western states would ally with the South to dilute northern power. To Gardoqui, the time seemed ripe to make the West a client state of Spain.[68]

The General

On September 5, 1787, while Madison helped add final touches to the Constitution in Philadelphia, James Wilkinson strutted through New Orleans to meet Governor Miró. He cut an unintimidating figure but possessed a sharp mind and unbounded ambition. A general by the age of twenty, Wilkinson had earned an admirable reputation during the Revolutionary War. Egotistical and bombastic, he headed west after the fighting, determined to serve any master that would advance his interests. That September, he slipped Miró a secret proposal.[69]

Wilkinson foresaw a day when the West "will be a distinct confederation" from the East. He advised Miró to allow westerners of "real influence," meaning himself, to access the Mississippi. They would then separate the West from the United States and deliver their allegiance to Spain. If Spain refused, he assured Miró, westerners would embrace the help of British Canada. The American had overstated westerners' desire to ally with Spain to inflate his own usefulness. His project pivoted on Kentucky's uncertain independence, but most Kentuckians preferred to remain in the union as an independent state.[70]

Still, Miró refused to dismiss the scheme. The British threat badgered his mind. If he refused westerners artillery, gunpowder, and ammunition, they would resort to Britain, destroying Spain's chance to win their loyalty. Even if Kentuckians never gained independence from the United States, he might attract them to Louisiana and make Spanish subjects of them. Westerners would enter Spanish dominions grateful to abandon "a precarious government" unable to protect their commerce or defend them against Indians. Apparently, Miró assumed they would overlook Spain's having restricted their access to the Mississippi and its having previously armed Indians against them.[71]

Some did. In April 1788, Creek leader Alexander McGillivray received two deputies from the western Virginia regions at his Little Tallassee plantation. The pair sued for peace from recurring hostilities with Creeks. They assured McGillivray that westerners "were determined to free themselves from a dependence on Congress, as that body coud or woud not protect" them. They would cede their loyalty to Spain in return for use of the Mississippi and peace with the Creek nation.[72]

In May 1788, Wilkinson encouraged Miró to pursue their measures while quarrels "distract and divide" eastern states. He warned the governor that Spain's French allies secretly operated against Gardoqui in Congress. France yearned for Louisiana, and French authorities hoped that Americans could acquire the territory and barter it to them. Gardoqui suspected the same thing. Everybody saw, he claimed, how the French minister tried to charm Virginia's congressional delegates.[73]

Like Wilkinson, Gardoqui insisted that Spain should never cede the river, because "on it depends the union of the states." So long as the Spanish held the Mississippi, they could divide westerners against the East. If, however, the United States "unites as it grows," Gardoqui warned Madrid, it would become a "fearsome" nation.[74]

Federalists

In mid-November 1787, Hamilton recruited Madison to help convince his fellow New Yorkers to ratify the Constitution. Madison had witnessed the city's opposition to a stronger union since he returned to Manhattan from Philadelphia on September 24. Like Hamilton, he considered New York's support vital.[75]

Before approaching Madison, Hamilton and John Jay had produced seven essays supporting the Constitution and splashed them into New York newspapers. They called them *The Federalist* and wrote under the pseudonym "Publius"—patterning themselves after a key founder of the Roman Republic. After Hamilton wrote the introductory essay, John Jay opened *The Federalist* with what he knew best—foreign affairs. He warned that America must unite under a firm national government or split "into three or four independent and probably discordant republics or confederacies, one inclining to Britain, another to France, and a third to Spain." America would make "a poor, pitiful figure" in the eyes of foreign nations. After Jay finished the fifth essay, Hamilton addressed internal dissensions. Unless united by a national government, the states would descend into "violent contests with each other." Powerful states would exact tribute from weaker neighbors. So divided, the states would "become a prey to the artifices and machinations" of foreign powers. Jay addressed foreign intervention, and Hamilton discussed domestic strife, but neither resolved what Madison saw as the fundamental problem: Foreign powers might intentionally promote internal disputes to perpetuate what he termed "anarchy and weakness."[76]

With his first essay—the tenth in the series—Madison lifted *The Federalist* from an influential defense of the Constitution to a timeless piece of political theory. In it, he formalized his ideas about factions and parties—groups that, as he defined them, acted on "some common impulse of passion." Governments could not extinguish political factions without extinguishing liberty, he theorized, but perhaps they could control the worst tendencies of factions. He articulated his unconventional theory that many parties would compete for power in a large national republic, prohibiting the rise of an oppressive majority. Americans could live peaceably not because they respected each other's opinions, but because no single faction could control political power.[77]

If liberty inflamed factions, the government needed to ensure that foreign agents could not exploit factionalism to shatter the union. Madison found the solution in increased federal power. In the following essay, he argued that a robust union created a "bulwark against foreign danger," with more susceptible states bolstered by the "strength and resources" of a central government.[78]

In his next three essays, all published by mid-December, Madison hastened to teach Americans what he had learned from his study of ancient confederacies. Weak governments invited "internal dissensions," which inevitably bred "fresh calamities from abroad." Just look, he argued, at the religious disputes of the Greeks and at Philip who "secretly fostered the contest" to infiltrate Greek councils. When "dissensions broke out" among the Achaeans, Romans promoted chaos to entice its members from the league. "By these arts," Madison lamented, "the last hope of ancient liberty, was torn into pieces." The Germans, Swiss, Belgians, and others all proved the same thing. Without a strong union, "surrounding powers" would "nourish" the discord within a confederacy to keep it "always at their mercy."[79]

Madison reasoned, "Security against foreign danger . . . is an avowed and essential object of the American union. The powers requisite for attaining it, must be effectually confided to the federal councils." His message resounded: Strengthen the central government or let foreign powers exploit internal divisions to usurp US sovereignty. The Constitution synchronized Madison's ambitious vision of a politically diverse nation with a strong central government that would protect liberty without succumbing to foreign scheming.[80]

In March, Madison finished his twenty-ninth and final *Federalist* essay days before he departed for Montpelier. Having done what he could in New York, he now needed to convince skeptical Virginians at their ratifying convention in Richmond the coming June. Madison had hesitated to return to Virginia, believing that the ratifying conventions should consist of men who had not framed the charter in Philadelphia. He also wished to avoid attacks on his reputation and disputes with Antifederalists whom he considered friends, probably especially George Mason. Washington repaid Madison for the earlier pressure to attend the convention in Philadelphia, urging Madison to run for election to the ratifying convention. He insisted that nobody could defend the charter "with more precision." Others echoed Washington, and Madison relented.[81]

On March 23, Madison stood atop an outdoor rostrum in Orange, Virginia, and stared at a large crowd. The wind blew strong, a formidable foe for his weak voice. For the first time in his life, he would deliver an open air stump speech. He despised the spectacle, but, as he phrased it, countless "absurd and groundless prejudices against the fœderal Constitution" forced him to campaign for a seat at the convention. He may have remembered the time that he failed to electioneer and suffered the only popular election loss of his political career. Overcoming his discomfort, he launched "a harangue of some length" in defense of the Constitution. At the end of the day, he and a fellow Federalist received nearly four times as many votes as their Antifederalist opponents. He would go to Richmond to fight for his work.[82]

In Richmond, Madison brawled with his by-then political rival, Patrick Henry, who derided the Constitution as a national invasion of state sovereignty. With others, Madison suspected that Henry, irked by the Mississippi controversy, preferred disunion. Madison saw more bluster than brains in Henry. For much of the decade, he had wrangled with the eminent orator in the Virginia Assembly, especially over religious liberty. He likely chuckled at Jefferson's quip that they devoutly "pray for his death."[83]

Madison pitted his intellect against Henry's eloquence. During his first speech, he stood before the convention in the main hall of Richmond's

Academy of Sciences and Fine Arts. Suffering an illness, and speaking almost in a whisper, Madison reminded the delegates that "internal dissentions" had "more frequently demolished civil liberty, than a tenacious disposition in rulers." The next day, he elaborated, repeating his favorite examples of ancient confederacies and the foreigners who subverted their liberties. If Virginians wanted to combat foreign intrigue, they needed the Constitution.[84]

On June 25, the convention ratified the document. Unbeknownst to Madison, New Hampshire had become the ninth state to ratify days before, making the Constitution operative. With the vote of Virginia—the most powerful state in the union—the Constitution became not only official but viable. Madison sped back to Congress in New York to aid the transition and to keep Antifederalists from diluting the new charter with debilitating amendments. He was confident that if he succeeded, the United States could secure the West and the Mississippi.[85]

But Gardoqui hadn't given up.

Separatists

For months, Gardoqui had been grooming his friendship with John Brown, the congressman who represented Virginia's Kentucky region. In July, Congress denied Kentucky statehood, and Gardoqui sensed that Brown's fury at the decision made him ripe for manipulation. After "artfully insinuating" that Kentuckians would enjoy Spanish support if they split from the union, Gardoqui hosted Brown at his mansion to talk details. Brown promised the minister that he would soon return to Kentucky, promote the plan, and keep the Spaniard apprised of developments.[86]

Brown and Madison boarded at the same Manhattan house, and Brown confided to Madison about his meetings with Gardoqui. Madison convinced him to stop reporting Gardoqui's overtures to Kentuckians. Then he wrote Jefferson—swearing him to secrecy and shielding Brown's identity—informing him that Spain might exploit the rampant "disgust" in Kentucky "to seduce them from the union."[87]

After he went home, Brown wrote to Madison, admitting that he had still not decided what to do about Gardoqui's proposal. Madison shot a reply, warning Brown of the "political calamity" that would result from the "hazardous" plan. He assured the Kentuckian that Congress would never forsake westerners in their fight for the Mississippi. Gardoqui waited impatiently for an update from Brown and finally wrote him in October for information. In December, Brown responded that their plan wouldn't work; Kentuckians would stick with the United States for the time. Gardoqui would have to look elsewhere for American allies.[88]

Young James Sevier seemed an ideal candidate when he appeared at Gardoqui's mansion that fall bearing secret letters from his father, John. The elder Sevier governed the rogue state of Franklin in western North Carolina. Since 1785, Franklinites had battled with word and pistol for independence from the parent state. By 1788, they suffered from internal conflict, pressure from North Carolina, and Indian attacks, so the desperate governor sent his son to plead with Gardoqui for Spanish support.[89]

To aid the Franklinites, Gardoqui recruited James White, the separatist who had first sparked his interest in western independence. Cautious to conceal his own involvement, Gardoqui sent White to Cuba as a secret agent under the alias Jacques Dubois. In Havana, White convinced Captain General José de Ezpeleta to support Franklin as a client state. White then sailed for New Orleans to meet Miró, who knew more than Ezpeleta about Franklin's internal dysfunction.[90]

By the time White met Miró in spring 1789, the Spanish governor had received orders from Madrid to abandon support for western independence, whether in White's Franklin or Wilkinson's Kentucky. Among other issues, Spanish authorities couldn't reconcile aiding Americans who coveted the land of their Indian allies. Instead, they pursued the more cautious plan of enticing Americans to Spanish dominions. Better to invite them and integrate them than allow them to encroach unsolicited, went the logic. Even had Miró wanted to help White, Franklin had already collapsed. In February, Sevier and other leaders had sworn allegiance to North Carolina and placed their bets on the United States rather than on Spain.[91]

That same month, the citizens of Madison's district voted to send him to New York as a member of the House of Representatives in the First Congress of the new government. Like other republicans who believed that candidates should not appear too anxious for political power, Madison despised the indignity of "electioneering." During the Revolution, however, he had learned that campaigning worked (even if it meant liquoring up voters), and he needed to be elected to Congress if he wanted to steer the government toward his vision. Madison already had the backing of Federalists, but to win Antifederalists, he assured them he would support their demands for a bill of rights in the Constitution.[92]

On his way to New York, Madison stopped at Mount Vernon to confer with Washington, who would soon make his own trip to the city as the first president of the United States. Washington shared alarming news. He had received reports that a former loyalist operated as a British secret agent in the West, trying to incite westerners to unite with Britain against Spain. Unaware that the news had little substance, Madison paired it with reports that Spain had been syphoning Americans across the Mississippi to Spanish territory, sapping the region of its population.[93]

The revelations reinforced Madison's conviction that the new Congress must combat foreign schemes. As he continued to New York, he pondered the looming "contentions first between federal & antifederal parties, and then between Northern & Southern parties." Those divisions would soon test whether he and his fellow Framers had constructed a nation that could accommodate political conflict and yet repel foreign danger.[94]

3

"The Epoch of Party Formation"

This time . . . will probably be the epoch of party formation and differentiation.
— Count de Moustier, French minister to the United States

IN THE MID-AFTERNOON OF APRIL 23, 1789, New Yorkers thronged the streets to watch what seemed like, to one observer, "an infinite number of ships and long boats" festooned with flags and banners parade through the harbor's Upper Bay. The city swelled with excitement as the nearby battery discharged celebratory shots and music rang from the ships as they fired cannons. Not outdone by the nautical display, city folk had immersed New York in satin and wreaths. Bells tolled; people cheered. The cortege of ships neared Murray's Wharf at the mouth of the East River, and all eyes trained on an elegant barge with an open awning draped in red curtains.[1]

In a buff and blue suit, George Washington stood on the barge amid a coterie of sailors who wore matching white uniforms and black caps. He stepped out of the craft to a welcome committee composed of the governor of New York, congressmen, troops, the city mayor, and other luminaries. The party formed a procession that marched about a half mile down Queen Street to escort Washington to his new executive mansion. Crowds stampeded the streets and threw flowers from windows to greet the first president to the nation's capital. Washington came as close to the embodiment of national unity as anything they could grasp.[2]

Count de Moustier rode in a carriage at the rear of the parade, representing France at the festivities. As Washington's retinue waded through a sea of spectators, with city officers wielding staves to manage the crowds, Moustier advanced to the middle of the bustle until he saw the president.

He clambered out of the carriage, congratulated Washington amid the din, and accompanied him on foot toward the executive mansion.[3]

After Moustier departed the crowd, storm clouds gathered over the city. Rain waited mercifully for most to find shelter. Moustier would have just reached his elegant residence, not far down Broadway from Gardoqui's. New Yorkers bathed the city in candlelight in Washington's honor that evening, but a torrent punished anyone who braved the streets to witness the brilliant scene.[4]

As far as Moustier could see, the weather could have served as a metaphor for the tempests that awaited the nation. "Here are these Americans," he had ruminated weeks earlier, "launched onto this great sea. . . . These pilots, accustomed to steering small boats with some success on water seldom and little disturbed, will have another notion of the art of governing when they will have weathered the same storms and encountered the same perils that prove formidable even for men more able and experienced than the great politicians of America." No matter how much Americans celebrated their new government, they remained a divided, vulnerable people.[5]

The Constitution had consolidated the nation "in language" only, Moustier observed. If Americans failed to cooperate, "this consolidation will be even less complete." For weeks, he had watched the new Congress struggle to convene enough members to begin business. It was beset by protracted, contentious elections and dilatory representatives. Moustier scarce could fathom "how a body, whose members do not have the same understanding" might captain the ship of state in unison.[6]

Americans couldn't even agree on what to call their president, amusing Moustier with their debates. "The most zealous federalists," to use his description, seized the frenzy of Washington's inauguration to argue for king-flavored titles such as "Serene Highness" or "Majesty." Their opponents, such as Madison, denounced such monarchical trappings and argued for the more modest, more republican, title of "president."[7]

No extraneous debate, the argument reflected two opposing views of the American republic. Many Federalists hoped to remake their nation in the British image, only with more protections for their liberties. Alarmed by the chaos and weakness they thought they saw under the Articles of Confederation, a small radical element even pined for a monarchy. They hoped that by replicating Britain's government they could replicate its industrial prosperity. Other Americans welcomed a more democratic character, at least for white men. Madison gravitated toward that camp, parting company with some of his previous allies in the fight for the Constitution. He and others envisioned a nation graced by republican simplicity, which would spurn the supposedly corrupting influences of industrialization and draw strength from the land and agriculture. Hardly the stuff of national glory, ardent Federalists thought.[8]

Crisis in France festered the differences. The French government had exhausted its treasury fighting the British alongside Americans. The crown lacked money, and the people lacked bread—a recipe for revolution. That spring, reports trickled to the United States that French masses had constrained the king to convene the nation's governing assembly for the first time since 1614. The unrest pitted Americans who favored a strong government modeled after Britain against those such as Madison who favored France and its budding revolution.[9]

As Moustier contemplated the "infant state" of America, he prophesied that the coming years would "be the epoch of party formation and differentiation." If quarreling Americans hoped to make anything of their new nation, he concluded, they would need France. The French king had helped them clear their enemies from "the ground they wanted to occupy," and only the king could help them cultivate that ground into a nation. If France didn't pull the strings in the new government, Britain or Spain surely would, Moustier predicted. Moreover, Indians remained "disquieting" if not "dangerous neighbors," who were making alliances with Europe to harass Americans in the West. The dire picture spelled foreign trouble for the new government as it prepared to face the storms the Frenchman forecast.[10]

The Cabinet

On May 13, Washington stepped into Moustier's mansion. One of the grandest residences in the city, it boasted a great hall, where the count had lately hosted resplendent parties. Washington arrived for a tea party with about 150 other guests. French and American officers and ladies danced a quadrille, arranged specially for the president. Moustier organized the event as part of a campaign—as carefully choreographed as the quadrille—to rehabilitate his reputation. He had slipped into disfavor among New York's elite, as rumors swirled of an illicit relationship between the minister and his sister-in-law. Madison considered the Frenchman "unsocial, proud, and niggardly" besides promiscuous.[11]

The minister almost certainly invited Madison to the tea party. He saw that Washington had begun to depend on his fellow Virginian almost as a sort of prime minister. The congressman had helped the president write key addresses, including the inaugural speech. Since their meeting at Mount Vernon, Washington had relied on Madison for advice about the transition to the new government and the precedents he would set as president.[12]

Moustier needed his reputation intact, for Congress had begun to deliberate legislation vital to French interests—legislation proposed by Madison. After hosting a series of balls and fêtes, he began "to rise in popularity," as a fellow Frenchman in America observed. "Everyone who used to speak against him finds themselves charmed." Even Madison had to admit, "Moustier begins to make himself acceptable," or at least less obnoxious. Madison's reassessment would have pleased the minister, for he described the Virginian as "the Representative most renowned for his knowledge, his activity, and his integrity."[13]

Moustier impressed Madison more with his "commercial ideas" than with his parties. The Frenchman had begun to lobby congressmen to pass Madison's anti-British trade agenda. In his first speech in the new Congress, Madison had proposed that the body finally pass an impost, a tax on imports. He wanted moderate taxes on goods from countries that had a commercial treaty with the United States and more onerous rates on countries that refused to respect US sovereignty and commercial rights.[14]

Madison made no secret that the legislation targeted Great Britain. Americans staggered under debts to British creditors and remained leashed to British manufactures. Madison wagered that Britain needed "essential" foodstuff from the United States more than Americans needed "superfluities" from Britain. If Congress united, they could pressure Britain to allow more US goods and to grant Americans access to the British West Indies. More important for Madison, the legislation would encourage more commerce with friendlier nations. "The real object" of the plan, as one discerning Briton put it, "is to throw the trade of the States into the hands of France."[15]

Moustier exerted "all his influence," according to one of his critics, to aid the legislation. The count assured his government that "French merchants could replace the English profitably both in selling and buying" if Americans entangled Britain in commercial warfare. He proposed a scheme for France to exploit the "propitious circumstance" and penetrate US trade.[16]

The Senate rejected Madison's plan, diluting the proposal until it was useless. Madison may have viewed Moustier as a political asset, but his detractors detested the foreign interference. Alexander Hamilton derided it as a ploy "to promote coldness and animosity between" Britain and America.[17]

Moustier was unimpressed when Washington appointed Hamilton as treasury secretary that September. "I do not believe him very well disposed toward France." Hamilton "would like nothing better," the count groused, "than to completely disengage" the United States from France and draw it closer to Britain and its allies.[18]

The minister read the new secretary right. Jefferson recalled that Hamilton once described the British political system as "the most perfect government which ever existed." Jefferson may have twisted Hamilton's words, but the memory captured Hamilton's views accurately enough. Madison had heard Hamilton say something similar during the Constitutional Convention: "In his private opinion he had no scruple in declaring . . . that the British Government was the best in the world." The treasury secretary and like-minded Federalists believed that Britain had denied American colonists their rights, but they thought the British government struck the right balance between freedom and national might.[19]

Hamilton wanted to infuse the presidency with power even the British king lacked. During his service as Washington's aide-de-camp at Valley Forge, he saw the war effort suffer from congressional mismanagement. During the 1780s, he soured on Congress even more as he witnessed the same shortcomings that Madison had seen. A "feeble executive" means "a bad government," he concluded. As a cabinet member, he planned to use executive power to nourish ties with Britain and to refashion US finances in the British image.[20]

Before the first session of Congress, Madison almost certainly counted on Hamilton's support for his anti-British imposts. In one *Federalist* essay, Hamilton had insisted that the Constitution would unite Americans enough to force Britain to the bargaining table. With his appointment as treasury secretary, however, Hamilton descended from the clouds of theory to the mire of practice. He may have dreamed of a day when the United States could command international respect by economic coercion. For the time, however, he believed the young country needed Britain. Hamilton yearned to improve America's faltering public credit, and he could ill-afford a trade war. Americans received most of their foreign goods from Britain. If they axed those imports, the treasury would lack money to pay its debt. To save his plan, Hamilton needed to defeat Madison's.[21]

Moustier rejoiced when the Senate confirmed Thomas Jefferson as secretary of state in late September, while the Virginian was still in France. Moustier considered Jefferson "the man whom we could most hope to see at the head of this department." From France, Jefferson applauded Madison's agenda. Britain had "moved heaven, earth & hell to exterminate us," he railed from Paris, while France "spent her blood & money to save us." How dare Congress place both nations on the same footing?[22]

Hamilton's allies considered Jefferson "greatly too democratic"—"a republican and a frenchman," as one derided him. With foreign affairs in Jefferson's hands, Moustier hoped US diplomacy would favor France. The minister left the United States in October 1789 before Jefferson returned. During his short time in New York, however, he had observed and aided a breach in American politics along French and British fault lines—a breach that future agents could exploit.[23]

Partners

On October 8, 1789, Madison sat in Washington's three-story executive mansion. He had tarried in New York more than a week after the first session of Congress closed, waiting for Jefferson, whose return he expected any time. He and Jefferson planned to travel to Virginia together, but Jefferson hadn't arrived, and Madison could wait no longer. He visited the president to bid farewell until Congress reconvened early the next year.[24]

Washington solicited Madison's advice a final time before their parting. He asked him if he thought the executive branch should send Gouverneur Morris as an unofficial emissary to London to smooth differences with Britain. Madison disliked the idea, partly because of Morris's reputation as a philandering rake. Madison had worked closely with Morris at the Constitutional Convention. He appreciated the native New Yorker's "superior talents," but he knew that the man's egotism sometimes clouded his judgment. He worried that Morris would botch the mission by spending more time angling for a permanent ambassadorship than tending America's interests. More important, Madison worried that an unsuccessful mission would foil his congressional agenda.[25]

Madison preferred economic coercion to what he considered diplomatic kowtowing. Britain had yet to send an emissary—official or otherwise—to the United States, and Americans would betray weakness if they made the first move. He wanted to force Britain's compliance with his impost bill.

Without that pressure, Morris's mission would look more like a cry for pity than a demand for justice.[26]

Madison objected to Morris's appointment for the same reason Hamilton supported it: Both men viewed Morris as pro-British. Washington may have told Madison that Hamilton had recommended Morris in the first place. Whatever he knew about Hamilton's role, Madison saw forces combining to undermine his plan to exact British respect.[27]

He advised Washington to delay his decision about Morris until the president consulted Jefferson. For good measure, Madison sent the president a follow-up memorandum with the same advice. He knew Washington favored his impost plan, and he needed to persuade him to give it another chance in Congress before he sent Morris on an ill-advised mission. With more time, Madison pleaded, he could muster enough support to pass the legislation.[28]

After he left the executive mansion, Madison wrote to Jefferson from his boarding room on Maiden Lane in lower Manhattan. He needed to convince Jefferson to dispel thoughts of retirement, accept the secretary of state position, and help him derail Morris's appointment. "I wish to see you as soon as possible after you become informed of the new destination provided for you," he wrote, aware that Jefferson remained ignorant of his appointment as secretary of state. "It is of infinite importance that you should not disappoint the public wish on this subject. . . . Drop me a line the moment you get on shore." He scribbled so fast he failed to notice he had misdated the letter by two years. He folded it, sealed it, and left it in New York for Jefferson to collect on his arrival.[29]

Madison had no idea that Jefferson still lingered in Havre, France, tormented by wind and rain while he waited for decent weather to sail. He didn't arrive in the United States until November 23, and he didn't receive Washington's official request to serve as secretary of state until December 11. The last week of the year, Madison rode to Monticello to discuss the appointment in person and convince Jefferson to accept it. He returned to New York confident he had succeeded. Jefferson arrived in the city to assume the office on March 21, 1790. Four days later, he received Madison's urgent but, by then, obsolete letter.[30]

Number 7

The delay gave Hamilton nearly six months to steer US foreign policy with an ally of his own—a British intelligence agent named George

Beckwith. While in the British army, Beckwith was a primary contact for Benedict Arnold, the American hero of Saratoga turned traitor, during the Revolutionary War. Beckwith's wiry frame appeared unassuming, but his keen mind and charm commanded respect. He spent the war years nourishing contacts with loyalists across New England. His adroit intelligence operations earned him the rank of major soon after the Battle of Yorktown. He spent the final months of the war helping loyalists evacuate to friendlier regions.[31]

In 1787, the governor general of British Canada, Lord Dorchester, recruited Beckwith to ascertain whether some Americans might fancy a reunion with Britain. For all his intelligence-gathering talents, the major failed to scrutinize his sources adequately, privileging information that confirmed his biases. Pro-British contacts such as Philip Schuyler convinced him that "there is not a gentleman in the States from New Hampshire to Georgia, who does not view the present Government with contempt . . . and who is not desirous of changing it for a Monarchy." Even after the states ratified the Constitution, Beckwith expected the eventual collapse of the republic.[32]

Beckwith traveled to Britain by the spring of 1789 and conferred with the home secretary, Lord Grenville, about American affairs. That summer, Grenville learned of Madison's anti-British proposals in Congress. He sent Beckwith to New York to array pro-British officials against the legislation. Beckwith carried a warning to his American contacts: Britain would not yield. The ministry would retaliate and wreak havoc on American commerce if Madison's plan passed.[33]

Beckwith appeared in New York in late September, his status somewhere between an unofficial emissary and a secret agent, a "petty spy" as one associate described him. He arrived after the Senate had already blunted Madison's plan, but he decided to deliver his warning anyway to deter future attempts. On September 30, he sat with Senator William Samuel Johnson of Connecticut whom he considered an "undeviating" friend of Britain. The senator dismissed Madison as "an Eleve"—a student or follower—of Jefferson, who harbored a "French bias." He assured Beckwith that "enlightened" senators would foil the pro-French pair.[34]

The British agent worked through five more contacts before he met the man he most wanted to see, Alexander Hamilton. Beckwith assigned each contact a code number, listing Hamilton as "No. 7." He had warned

Hamilton's father-in-law, Philip Schuyler ("No. 2"), of retaliation if Congress passed punitive measures against Britain.[35]

When Hamilton learned about Beckwith's private talk with Schuyler, he requested a meeting with Beckwith, desperate to avoid a trade war. They needed privacy, likely meeting at Hamilton's house on Wall Street near the beginning of October. Their conversation wasn't illegal, but Hamilton hosted Beckwith without the knowledge or sanction of the president. He met the agent not as a representative of the executive branch but as a private individual who exploited Jefferson's absence to advance his own foreign policy.[36]

Hamilton opened the conversation. "I have requested to see you . . . to suggest a measure, which I conceive to be both for the interest of Great Britain, and of this Country." The United States now had a government strong enough to honor treaties, and "I have always preferred a Connexion with you, to that of any other Country," he assured Beckwith. "We think in English, and have a similarity of prejudices, and of predilections."[37]

Hamilton proposed an accord that would have infuriated Madison had he known about it. Americans would benefit from "strong ties" with Britain and preferred to consume British rather than French goods, Hamilton told Beckwith. He divulged that the president might send an unofficial emissary to Britain, though the president had not yet decided about the Morris mission. The treasury secretary affirmed Britain's right to retaliate against the new American imposts even though the tariffs didn't discriminate against the empire. He pretended that Washington endorsed his views. Hamilton assumed the exact conciliatory stance that Madison feared would project American weakness. Madison would have contested nearly every point of the conversation.[38]

In fact, the discussion soon turned to Madison. "I was much surprized," Beckwith admitted, to find Madison "amongst the gentlemen, who were so decidedly hostile to us." Obviously, he knew little about the congressman.[39]

"I confess," Hamilton returned, "I was likewise rather surprised at it. . . . The truth is," he continued, "that although this gentleman is a clever man, he is very little Acquainted with the world. That he is Uncorrupted And incorruptible I have not a doubt; he has the same End in view that I have, And so have those gentlemen, who Act with him, but their mode of attaining it is very different."[40]

Hamilton revealed how little he understood Madison. Although the two shared the goal of stabilizing national credit, they agreed on almost nothing else. Believing that he and Madison wanted the same thing from

Britain, Hamilton thought he was playing the good cop to Madison's bad cop. He pressed Beckwith to consider a treaty before Madison returned to Congress with even stronger anti-British plans.[41]

Madison wanted to wrench the United States from Britain's commercial grasp, not sign a treaty that would make Americans more dependent on British goods. He intended to force Britain to yield and favor French trade. Hamilton believed that France could never furnish the trade the United States needed to strengthen its national credit.[42]

Hamilton permitted Beckwith to communicate their conversation to Lord Dorchester and London, but he wanted to conceal it in America. He was treading where he had no authority, pushing the country closer to Britain without the knowledge of the president or the confirmed secretary of state. With Washington considering Morris's appointment, however, he hoped to smooth the way and assure Britain of America's desire to cooperate.[43]

With Jefferson stuck in Europe, Madison lost his chance to thwart Morris's appointment. On October 13, 1789, Washington selected Morris, who was in France on business. Dorchester forwarded Beckwith's intelligence to Grenville, and Whitehall knew about the possible mission before Morris did. By stepping into Jefferson's void, Hamilton committed the United States to diplomacy rather than commercial warfare. In the process, he undermined America's bargaining position just as Madison feared. As far as Dorchester understood Beckwith's report, Hamilton had conceded that Britain held all the cards. After learning that the pro-British Senate would never pass Madison's legislation, London saw no reason to budge. Morris met a cold reception when he arrived there the following March.[44]

Hamilton may have inadvertently injured his own plan for a treaty, but at least he and the Senate reined America back from the brink of economic suicide, as he saw it. He and his allies who consorted with Beckwith assumed that they countered Madison and Moustier's schemes to inflict a crippling trade war on America. Hamilton may have considered his antics bareknuckle politics but hardly subversion.

Backchannels

On March 21, 1790, Madison took advantage of his Sunday break from Congress to write his long-time associate Edmund Randolph. "Mr. Jefferson is not yet here," he informed their mutual friend. Word had traveled ahead that Jefferson waded through deep snow and miserable roads.

Almost the instant Madison put down his pen, however, a messenger brought him welcome news: The new secretary of state had arrived.[45]

Jefferson's appearance in New York increased Hamilton's anxiety about a commercial treaty with Britain. The next day, he warned Beckwith that Jefferson believed France's young revolution would succeed and improve commerce between France and America. To counter that future, he urged Beckwith to promote a treaty with the United States, again falsely assuring him that Washington favored an official exchange of ministers. Beckwith reported Hamilton's continued desire "to cultivate a connexion" with Britain, then returned to Canada.[46]

Almost as soon as Beckwith arrived in Quebec, a crisis sent him sprinting back to New York. Britain and Spain were threatening to go to war with each other over a territorial dispute on the West Coast of North America. Each country wanted to ensure that the United States would not ally with the enemy if hostilities erupted on the continent. On the morning of July 8, Beckwith sat with Hamilton in New York again. He showed the secretary a letter from Dorchester, expressing hope that the potential war would not alter America's desire "to establish a firm friendship and Alliance with Great Britain." In reality, Britain had no interest in a treaty or alliance with the United States. In fact, Whitehall officials were pondering how to pry Kentucky and Vermont from the union for Britain's benefit, though probably not even Beckwith knew that. Hamilton interpreted the conversation in its best light, assuming that Britain stood ready to negotiate.[47]

Hamilton welcomed the possibility, because Morris had reported from London that British officials likely would refuse to sign a treaty. If Britain rejected diplomacy, it would reignite calls for commercial warfare, an issue Madison had already reintroduced in Congress. Hamilton hoped Beckwith's message would counter Morris's pessimistic reports.[48]

Hamilton wanted to share the news with Washington, but the meeting with Beckwith had put him in a bind. In London, Morris had proposed a commercial treaty with Britain, but nothing like an alliance. Hamilton alone had hinted at that possibility during his earlier meeting with Beckwith about which Washington still knew nothing. He needed to disclose Beckwith's communications without revealing that he was the reason British officials supposed the administration might want an alliance. Around noon, he went to Washington's new Broadway mansion— Moustier's former residence, which the president had purchased when the minister departed—for a meeting with the president and Jefferson. While Hamilton had been talking with Beckwith that morning, Washington had been posing for a portrait by painter John Trumbull. The session had finished shortly before Hamilton walked in, accompanied by Jefferson.[49]

Hamilton recounted his meeting with Beckwith and delivered the president a memorandum describing it, but he altered significant details. He reported that Britain might wish an alliance with the United States, fudging the actual language of Dorchester, who inquired whether the United States still desired such an alliance. If reported accurately, Dorchester's inquiry would have befuddled Washington. The president had never instructed Morris to propose an alliance and had no idea that it was Hamilton who had given British leaders the impression that the United States might consider one. Hamilton couldn't faithfully report Dorchester's message without admitting that he had had an undisclosed meeting with Beckwith.[50]

Jefferson saw the intelligence as British "tamperings" to entice the administration with illusions, and Washington shared his skepticism. The president directed Hamilton to gather additional information from Beckwith and report back. Hamilton must have breathed a sigh of relief that Washington didn't assign the task to Jefferson, who might have learned that he had previously negotiated without the president's authority. During his subsequent meetings with Beckwith, Hamilton talked to him as if the United States had proposed the alliance and reported to Washington as if the British suggested it. While Jefferson, Washington, and Madison hoped that conflict between Britain and Spain would give the United States leverage with both, Hamilton secretly undermined their efforts, trying to throw the nation into the British scale. So much for his argument in the *Federalist* that "unity" is the first ingredient in an effective executive branch.[51]

Debt

The war crisis fizzled over the autumn, dissipating talks of an alliance but not Hamilton's desire for a commercial treaty. Hamilton needed the treaty to sustain a sweeping economic plan he had proposed to Congress. A treaty would invite British imports, which would increase revenue, that would pay down America's debt and thus improve its credit, which would allow it to borrow at lower interest rates. Wealthy investors would lend the government money, giving them a stake in its success. Credit-worthy government securities could act as cash, a boon to America's cash-strapped economy.[52]

To Madison, the plan reeked—a corrupt partnership between a bloated federal government and greedy speculators. Hamilton was as surprised to learn that Madison rejected his plan as Madison was to learn that Hamilton denounced his anti-British imposts. Madison had supported elements of Hamilton's proposal several years earlier and had offered no strong opinions about national finances when Hamilton had solicited his thoughts just months before.[53]

By 1790, wealthy financiers had purchased a mass of government IOUs from impoverished Revolutionary War veterans, who had received the notes as payment for their military service. The soldiers sold them to speculators at deep discounts in the 1780s, when the spiraling economy and poor government credit made them almost worthless. Now Hamilton wanted to reimburse the speculators for the full value of the notes, awarding investors handsome profits at the expense of veterans. However unfortunate for the soldiers and their families, he argued, America's credit would continue to sink if it failed to honor its commitment to the note holders.[54]

Madison protested that the system would perpetuate a moneyed aristocracy and impoverished underclass, exactly what he believed had corroded Britain's government. Reversing his position from years earlier, he wanted the government to split the payout between the original holders and the speculators. The notes had increased in value so much as to make any other option unconscionable, he argued. Congress rejected that impracticable idea and passed Hamilton's plan.[55]

After the initial defeat, Madison attacked Hamilton's idea for the federal government to bail the states out of nearly $25 million of debt. The treasury secretary wanted to assume the debt to make creditors more beholden to the federal government. Along with other southern states, Virginia had paid most of its public debt, but Hamilton's plan would compel Virginians to help pay for Massachusetts's rampant arrears. Madison saw a contest between responsible landholders of the South and vile moneymen of the North.[56]

Madison battled the bill all spring, but he restrained his attacks after northerners agreed to move the national capital closer to Virginia in exchange for its passage. He considered the bill bad policy but not unconstitutional, so he yielded to "a spirit of accommodation." That spirit fled when Hamilton introduced the next leg of his finance program.[57]

In December, the treasury secretary submitted a plan to Congress for a national bank. "You will not be in love with some of its features," Madison wryly understated to his like-minded political mentor, Edmund Pendleton. Private investors would support and run the institution but reserve one-fifth of the stock for the federal government. With the backing of the government, the bank would infuse the economy with ready money and spur industry. It would also provide emergency loans to the national treasury. Hamilton volunteered that he wanted to marry the *"monied interest"* of the country with the federal government.[58]

Madison had seen the same sort of marriage between Parliament and the Bank of England, and he detested it. As far as he could see, it would subject landholders great and small to the caprice of New England bankers and moneygrubbers. If Hamilton's earlier policies benefited commercial tyrants unfairly, this one would give them control over the government. In every point, seethed Madison, the plan reflected a corrupt British model.[59]

The congressman prepared for political combat in his usual way—painstaking study. By early 1791, he had relocated to Philadelphia, a new temporary home for Congress while engineers constructed the District of Columbia. Back in the familiar boarding place of Mary House, Madison conjured his assault on the bank bill. On February 2, he strode one block south to the large Philadelphia courthouse where Congress met and delivered one of his longest speeches yet.[60]

Madison assailed the bill not just as bad practice, but as an unconstitutional and disastrous policy, one that would fundamentally alter the character of the republic. He tutored his hearers on the history of banks, from the high Middle Ages through the Bank of England, focusing on their defects. He rejected arguments that Congress possessed implied power to pass the law. If Congress could incorporate a bank, he warned, they could establish monopoly companies like the South Sea Company or the East India Company, British institutions Americans had abhorred since their colonial days. He unfolded a theory of strict constitutional interpretation, allowing Congress no other powers than those specifically identified in the Constitution. He expounded a formula for interpreting passages that were unclear about Congress's power. The bank bill failed all of his constitutional tests.[61]

Despite Madison's diatribe, Congress approved the bank less than a week later. In an ominous sign, the vote split directly along sectional lines, with the South voting against it and the North favoring it. Congress had begun to split into two broad blocs, exactly the kind of party system Madison had intended the Constitution to deter. Now he stood as leader of one of the emerging factions.[62]

Like most partisans, Madison blamed partisanship on his opponents. He reviled the "partizans" of the bank bill as "speculators and Tories," evoking the long-maligned British party most hostile to the American Revolution. Focused on the faults of the opposition, he failed to recognize his own contribution to partisan hostility in which belligerents conflated political rivals and foreign enemies.[63]

Boarders

In mid-March 1791, papers and books were spread about Madison's small boarding room at Mary House's establishment. Madison had started to revise his notes on the Constitutional Convention and to prepare a blitz against Hamilton's national blueprint. Congress had adjourned, and his congressional colleagues had evacuated House's residence. The exodus gave him the study sanctuary he desired, but it also freed room for a new, potentially awkward boarding companion—George Beckwith.[64]

By then, most government insiders knew that Beckwith was Dorchester's informal eyes and ears in America, and Madison knew he nurtured no love for either him or Jefferson. To save his friend from discomfort, Jefferson invited Madison to join him a few blocks away to "take a bed and plate with me." Madison declined, not wanting to insult Beckwith by leaving just as the agent arrived.[65]

Jefferson finessed the situation to his advantage. Hostilities had erupted in the West as Americans advanced on Indian land. British officials used the conflict as a proxy war to keep American hands off western forts that Americans believed Britain should have relinquished after the Revolution. At the same time, Dorchester worried that hostilities would threaten Canada. He preached peace but armed his Native allies for defense. As Washington prepared a military expedition against the Native nations, he learned that British Canada supplied Indians with materiel. Beckwith seemed the quickest route of protest to Dorchester. As the chief diplomat, Jefferson refused to meet with Beckwith personally, reluctant to accord the informal agent official attention. He asked Madison to talk unofficially to Beckwith.[66]

In mid-April, Madison approached Beckwith, who denied British interference. The US government couldn't prove whether the British had sold Indians arms for war or merely hunting, he argued. Maybe not, Madison countered, but any reasonable person could see that the large quantities could be intended only for war.[67]

Madison departed with no idea that Beckwith had been communicating with Hamilton in secret for months about the conflict. The treasury secretary sought to temper passions in the West to salvage cordial relations with Britain, especially as Morris's mission faltered in London. Madison was gaining momentum in Congress for his anti-British imposts, and most Americans suspected British involvement in the dispute with Indians. Hamilton needed evidence of Britain's good faith.[68]

Back in January 1791, Hamilton had secretly suggested to Beckwith that Canada mediate peace between the United States and the western Indians. Dorchester relished the chance to advance British interests in the West, but he needed the request to come from Washington. By the time Hamilton received Dorchester's positive response through Beckwith in March, the president had trained his fury against the Native nations and concluded that Morris's mission had failed. It was no time for Hamilton to suggest British mediation, and he couldn't admit to Washington that he had initiated the idea behind his back.[69]

The treasury secretary hoped circumstances would improve over the summer, when he planned to revisit British mediation with Beckwith. Instead, Washington grew more belligerent and organized an invading force to subdue the Native combatants.[70]

That fall, US commanders led troops into the heart of Indian country in the Ohio River Valley. Untrained and ill-clad, they marched in misery but confident they would soon subdue their enemies. On November 3, they set up camp along the Wabash River. The night passed quietly enough. At dawn, they fell in for parade, completed their drills, and were dismissed as usual.[71]

Then shots and terror echoed from ahead as an advance unit of Kentucky militiamen tore through the trees toward the main army, pursued by a combined force of Indians, who had lurked in the woods all night. Terrorized soldiers fumbled weapons as Shawnees, Delawares, Miamis, Iroquois, and others spilled over a creek into battle. After a short, baffled resistance, Americans abandoned arms and careened in retreat. When they regrouped days later, they counted 630 casualties compared to a couple dozen for Indians.[72]

By mid-December, Beckwith learned of the defeat and sent the news to John Graves Simcoe, the lieutenant governor of the recently formed province of Upper Canada in the Great Lakes region. Simcoe detested US independence. During the Revolutionary War, he had led a ragtag regiment of loyalists to distinction and earned promotion to lieutenant colonel. He lamented the loss of the colonies and longed to resubjugate America to the British crown. The lieutenant governor appreciated loyalists' service during the war and considered pro-British Americans a key to reunification.[73]

With news of the American disaster at the Wabash, Simcoe anticipated good news for Britain. He had already dispatched Captain Charles Stevenson to New York as a spy to gauge old loyalist sentiment and ascertain how to deploy it against the United States. "You cannot conceive the terror the last victory of the Savages has spread over the country," Stevenson reported. Amid rumors Americans would seek peace, he advised, "A peace must if possible be prevented." If war continued, the belligerents might request Upper Canada to mediate, allowing Britain to strip western forts from America for good.[74]

In March 1792, Washington learned from an informant that Stevenson had been advocating British mediation. Hamilton knew by then that Washington would never go that route, and he feared that British interference would only worsen their relationship. When the cabinet agreed on March 9 to reject British overtures, Hamilton concurred.[75]

Despite Hamilton's reversal, Stevenson still fed Simcoe visions of British reconquest. "The ruin of America appears unavoidable," he exulted in May. New York's economy was sinking, and the state would "look up to us for support," he predicted. New England was "dissatisfied with Congress," and the "Southern and Eastern States" were "dissatisfied with each other." "Surely on the breaking up of this vast machine an able Minister with full powers may from the wreck collect materials enough to form an Empire."[76]

Stevenson hadn't given up on Hamilton, either. "As he is not a declared enemy," he suggested to Simcoe, "there may be means of making him a secret friend." Britain enjoyed "a very strong and declared party" in Hamilton's home state. If New York joined Canada, Vermont would follow. Britain could then seize West Point, where the reconquest of America would commence.[77]

Simcoe lost faith in Hamilton that summer, despite Stevenson's optimism. The new British minister, George Hammond, had tried to convince the New Yorker to reconsider his stance on mediation, but he refused. Thereafter, Simcoe counted Hamilton among the "determined enemies of Great Britain." A magistrate has rarely uttered a poorer character assessment.[78]

Hamilton had aligned with his colleagues, but they knew nothing of his counteractive backchannel diplomacy. When Washington heard a hint from London that the United States had requested British intervention, the indignant president rejoined, "Such mediation *never* was asked . . . it not only never *will* be asked but would be rejected if offered. The United States will never have occasion, I hope, to ask for the interposition of that power or any other." He protested unaware that Hamilton had tried to surrender the sovereignty he safeguarded. With Washington's subordinates pulling in different directions, foreign nations poised to exploit the breaches. The president needed all his gravitas to keep his administration from fracturing.[79]

Parties

Washington was tired. He had served his country for almost two decades without a pause. His compatriots expected him to epitomize republican simplicity and executive glamour, individual freedom and national vigor, the common citizen and the exalted statesman. Forever measured against the conflicting ideals of the new nation, he spent his life on guard against missteps. By 1792, his most trusted counselors waged political war against each other, and Americans expected him to arbitrate their differences. He wanted to retire, and he wanted somebody to whom he could unburden his mind.

On May 5, 1792, he asked Madison to visit him at his new Philadelphia residence. That same day, Madison trekked one block eastward to Washington's house on Sixth and Market. Once inside, he may have headed upstairs to Washington's private study, where the president tended to conduct official business. Washington confided to Madison his plan to retire after his first term, something he had only revealed to his cabinet secretaries. Aware that everything he did set a precedent, he wanted Madison's advice about how to disclose the decision to the public. At first, Washington remained coy about his reasons, explaining only that he considered his presence unnecessary to stabilize the government. Like Washington's cabinet, Madison disagreed and urged him to stay.[80]

Then Washington opened up. The president wearied not only from public life and health issues but with "the spirit of party" that had infiltrated the government, especially between Jefferson and Hamilton. Hamilton's enemies castigated recent government policies, and Washington worried that their attacks would sully his honor, a precious asset in the eighteenth century. The war hero was a great leader but no scholar. He admitted that he felt unequipped to settle the constitutional and legal disputes that rankled his cabinet.[81]

To temper Washington's doubts, Madison recounted what he considered an even-handed analysis of the parties. Some antifederalists still harbored discontent for the new government while Hamilton's allies despised republicanism and wanted a mixed monarchy. Neither extreme could gain ascendancy, he reassured Washington, especially if the president's "conciliating influence" persisted another four years.[82]

Madison proceeded to reveal the very biases that agitated Washington in the first place. If Washington stepped down, he said, nobody else could assume the mantle. Maybe Jefferson, but the secretary of state was also tired of public life, and "local prejudices in the Northern States" might militate against him. That left only Vice President John Adams and Chief Justice John Jay. Adams's "monarchical principles" would repulse "republicans every where." Jay clandestinely shared Adams's values and had a bad habit of selling out Americans to Britain and Spain in his foreign negotiations. Madison refused even to mention Hamilton. Washington wanted impartial advice; he received partisan criticism. He soured on the conversation and changed the subject.[83]

By late August, Washington could no longer reconcile his principal secretaries through indirect gestures. He wrote Jefferson and Hamilton, pleading for "mutual forbearances and temporising yieldings *on all sides*." Otherwise, "our enemies will triumph," he augured. Their divisions would invite foreign powers to throw their "weight into the disaffected Scale" and expedite "the ruin" of the nation.[84]

His warnings solicited venom-laced responses. Hamilton wanted "a king and house of lords," Jefferson fumed. The man's entire history "is a tissue of machinations against the liberty of the country." Hamilton told Washington that he hoped to reconcile with Jefferson in the future, but he couldn't "*for the present*." For months, he had waged an anonymous newspaper war with Jefferson and Madison, and he refused to surrender. To counter the Hamilton-friendly *Gazette of the United States*, the Virginians had recruited Madison's old classmate Philip Freneau to create the *National Gazette*. Jefferson supplemented the newspaperman's salary by employing him as a clerk in the State Department, where Freneau secured anti-British and pro-French material to publish. For nearly a year, Madison had published anti-Hamilton essays in the newspaper.[85]

Hamilton admitted to Washington that he had attacked Jefferson in the *Gazette of the United States*, but he pleaded necessity. He had refrained until he was convinced "that there was a formed party deliberately bent upon the subversion" of his program, which he equated with the subversion of the government. Within the week, he renewed his newspaper assault on his fellow cabinet member.[86]

Madison returned the vitriol days later. Hamilton's "antirepublican" party "debauched themselves" into thinking they could govern "by the pageantry of rank, the influence of money and emoluments, and the terror of military force." Money "is the most active and insinuating influence" in that party, he charged, and its adherents would divide Americans against each other to secure their power. Madison assumed that he preached truth while his opponents played politics.[87]

Madison no longer trusted the "checks of power" he thought that he and the other Framers had embedded into the Constitution. He had hoped the new government structure would promote a variety of political parties, which would compete and deny preeminence to any one faction. He expected the same to happen between the executive, legislative, and judicial branches. Hamilton seemed to obliterate both forms of competition as he gained more influence among congressmen and usurped more power for the presidency. The treasury secretary reminded his detractors of British cabinet members who revolutionaries believed had hoodwinked the king and controlled Parliament to oppress the colonies.[88]

To meet the peril, Madison promoted a new kind of competition between an elite ruling party and the people's opposition party. "The people" formed the last line of defense against an aggressive government and manipulative elites. He intended to mobilize the "Republican party" against Hamilton's "British partisans." Madison meant the phrase "Republican party" as a description of his side's values rather than a title for his party (in any case different from today's Republican Party), but the term stuck. The constitutional philosopher completed his transformation into an opposition party leader.[89]

Washington doubted whether he was the best choice to save the nation from its partisan vices. On October 1, 1792, he sat in Mount Vernon with Jefferson. He admitted that until recently he had no idea how much Jefferson and Hamilton despised each other. Jefferson did nothing to calm his apprehension. Hamilton was trying to turn America into Britain, he retorted, with a corrupt "squadron" in the legislature "devoted to the nod of the treasury." Washington pleaded with Jefferson to distinguish between "difference of opinion" and corruption. A call to breakfast interrupted the conversation.[90]

However much Washington questioned his own abilities, his friends believed that he alone could hold the country together in the coming years. With the rest of the country, the president knew that Americans would reelect him unless he announced his retirement. He worried, however, that announcing retirement would appear presumptuous, as if he assumed he were guaranteed reelection unless he declined it. He remained silent, knowing it meant another four years in office. If his morning conversation with Jefferson were any indication, it meant another four years of partisan brawls.[91]

George Beckwith summarized Washington's problem: The president was torn between "a difference in the political opinion of the officers at the head of the executive departments. . . . He balances amidst discordant advice, sometimes leaning to one party, and occasionally to the other. The great point of difference is on an English and a French connexion." In early 1793, that divide deepened when the French decapitated their king.[92]

4

"Kindling Parties"

Mr. Genet, the late Minister here from the French Republic, had laboured to convulse our Country, by kindling parties, and forcing us from our neutrality.

—EDMUND RANDOLPH, March 15, 1794

SORROW DRENCHED THE NATION IN late 1793. George Washington . . . dead, assassinated by a foreign agent—Edmond-Charles Genet, the official representative of France. Genet had quarreled with Washington for months, demanding the president's support in France's war against Britain. Washington refused, so Genet murdered him.

Or so thought one Concord, New Hampshire, fellow after he heard reports of Washington's assassination. At first, he bedamned "all the French to the devil." Then he learned that the story "has happily proved to be a LIE." Washington was alive and well. He assumed Federalists had fabricated the account of Washington's murder to vilify Genet. The Concord man cursed the "vile miscreants" who propagated the rumor to destroy the bonds between France and America. "May their hellish machinations be blasted forever!"[1]

Perhaps the Concordian was spreading false rumors that Genet's enemies were spreading false rumors; he might have concocted the whole thing to discredit Federalists. Either way, Americans were polishing the art of propagandizing foreign intrigues to abuse their political opponents. The process had accelerated after the actual death of Louis XVI of France earlier that year.

For eighteenth-century Europeans, regicide was the most radical political act possible. Kings personified the nation. They embodied the government. Even in England, where seventeenth-century subjects killed one king, overthrew another, and limited monarchical power thereafter, the king remained "a superior being" who could "do no wrong," according to legal convention. The awe of kingship loomed even larger in France, where the House of Bourbon reigned with few checks to their power. Assassins had murdered kings throughout Europe's medieval history only to replace them with other kings. Monarchs came and went; monarchy survived. On January 21, 1793, when the French people guillotined their king in favor of a republic, they beheaded an entire cosmology of divine right, natural hierarchy, and social order.[2]

Americans had maimed that cosmology during their revolution, but they hadn't finished it off like France had. The Continental Congress had attacked the king personally in the Declaration of Independence, an aggressive shift from earlier tirades against Parliament and the king's cabinet. Yet even John Adams, the co-author of that radical charter and Congress's fiercest advocate of independence, reverenced social hierarchy and wanted to make the presidency a quasi-royal office. Adams's fellow Federalists abhorred Louis XVI's execution and the violence against the French aristocracy. Hamilton considered the killing a "melancholy catastrophe." Like other Federalists, he refused to see parallels between the French and American rebellions. Federalists created convenient myths about an orderly American Revolution contrasted with violent frenzies in France.[3]

Madison dismissed Federalists' "spurious" claims of "the bloodthirstyness" of French revolutionaries. He could sympathize with Louis Capet, the man, but not Louis XVI, the king. The monarch had met his just end. "If he was a Traytor," Madison reasoned, recalling the specific charge against Louis, "he ought to be punished as well as another man."[4]

Lumping the king into the mass of French citizens, Madison embraced a new order premised on democratic equality for white men. Overlooking his own values of racial hierarchy, the Virginian lambasted Federalists' fondness for class elitism. He interpreted their denunciations of France as "symptoms of disaffection" from republicanism.[5]

As far as Madison could see, monarchists in Europe and crypto-monarchists in America conspired to overthrow republicanism in France and the United States. If French revolutionaries failed, he feared, Americans would face "the most serious dangers to our present forms & principles of our Governments." The two republics shared a destiny of either triumph or tragedy.[6]

If Louis's death highlighted political differences between early Republicans and Federalists, war in Europe churned those differences into policy battles. In early 1793, Britain prepared to crush its ancient enemy. The French assembly didn't wait for Britain to strike first. Less than two weeks after they executed Louis, they declared war on Britain, forcing Republicans and Federalists to debate whether their alliance obligated them to support France.[7]

Into that tinderbox stepped Edmond-Charles Genet, French minister with more "vanity than talents," as one of his friends admitted. Dependent on the palace, Genet made a more natural royalist than revolutionary. He had climbed the ranks of French civil service until he headed the Bureau of Interpreters at age eighteen and landed as Louis XVI's minister at the Russian court at twenty-six. As news of revolution sprinkled into St. Petersburg, Genet managed to accommodate whichever faction held power in France, growing more radical with the revolution. By the end of 1792, he struck the Russian empress Catherine as "an insane demagogue," and she booted him from the country.[8]

With a bourgeois upbringing, impressive civil service record, and diplomatic experience, Genet snagged the attention of the ruling Girondin Party—moderates on domestic policy but zealots for evangelizing the revolution abroad. With his fluent English, he made a natural pick to lead the French legation at Philadelphia. Genet's superiors entrusted him to ensure that Americans honored their alliance in the coming war.[9]

The Mission

Genet knew how to make an entrance. In the afternoon of April 8, 1793, onlookers in Charleston, South Carolina, spotted Genet's ship in the distance as it glided toward the harbor. The vessel was a rally cry on water. It sported one liberty cap for a figurehead and another carved into the stern. Its foremast resembled a liberty pole, an unmistakable symbol of revolution in the United States. On one mast, a banner proclaimed, "FREEMEN, WE ARE YOUR BROTHERS AND FRIENDS," while a second banner on a taller mast warned, "Enemies of Equality, relinquish your principles or tremble!" By the time Genet disembarked, a throng had assembled at the docks to welcome him.[10]

Winds had diverted Genet's ship away from Philadelphia and toward Charleston, but the minister intended to capitalize on the mishap. Once ashore, he met the French consul at Charleston, Michel Ange Mangourit.

The pair dashed to meet South Carolina luminaries, including Governor William Moultrie. In Moultrie, they found an enthusiastic supporter of the French cause.[11]

During the next ten days, the three agreed to organize a combined force of Americans, Cherokees, and Creeks to wrench the Floridas from Spain, France's latest enemy in Europe. Genet, Mangourit, and Moultrie hoped to rekindle the ancient alliance between France and the Creeks and Cherokees. France could cripple Spain, US frontier people could expand westward, and wealthy land speculators such as Moultrie could profit.[12]

Genet left Mangourit and Moultrie to sort the details and departed for Philadelphia. He sent his ship ahead with instructions to capture British vessels on the way. He preferred to travel overland to rally Americans for France as he went. At each stop, hordes of pro-French Americans fêted him, praised France, and toasted "the republic of France—May her success induce mankind to be free," "Liberty, and no king," and "the national convention of France." Genet glittered with gaiety as he traveled, ready "to laugh us into the war if he can," one Federalist chuckled.[13]

Surrounded by adulation, Genet was stunned in Richmond, Virginia, with news that Washington had declared neutrality in the conflict. Genet and his superiors had never expected the United States to declare war on Britain, but they did expect some advantages from their alliance. They especially wanted to use American ports as bases for French privateers— more or less state-sponsored pirates commissioned by the government to plunder enemy commerce. (One participant called it "Highway Robbery under the protection of law.") Dubiously splicing a couple of articles from the 1778 treaty with the United States, Genet claimed France's right to prepare, man, and launch privateers in the United States. Washington's neutrality proclamation imperiled that plan.[14]

The proclamation also deepened the chasm between Jefferson and Hamilton, with the Virginian pleading for soft language and the New Yorker for terminating the alliance. As he often did, Washington split the difference between his polarized secretaries. It took some fancy legalistic footwork, but his policy preserved the alliance while refusing France some of the privileges Genet thought his nation deserved.[15]

Startled by the first major obstacle to his mission, Genet declined an invitation to feast with Richmond's citizens and blitzed toward the capital. He took a month to travel from Charleston to Richmond, six days to travel from Richmond to Philadelphia. Crowds "flocked from every avenue," marveled one report, to greet him on the outskirts of the capital. He slipped into the city by an unexpected route, but they swarmed to his hotel the next day. His entrance marked a "triumph for liberty," he reveled.[16]

Like politicians, diplomats can believe too much in their own press. By the time he arrived in Philadelphia, Genet boasted that he had "destroyed the prejudices" that threatened his mission. Adoring crowds ill prepared him for a "cold" reception from the standoffish Washington. Genet had Jefferson's sympathy, but the secretary of state knew that he risked his influence with Washington if he defied the president. He backed Washington's message—no French privateers or their spoils in US ports.[17]

Washington frustrated Genet, but the Frenchman considered the executive office a single cog in a system of interlocking gears that composed the machinery of the US government. If he could manipulate the right gears, the others would follow, including the presidency. To that end, his superiors expected him to recruit "zealous cooperators" in Washington's cabinet and the House of Representatives. No doubt they thought of Jefferson and Madison. Together, they might outwit America's "English partisans."[18]

Genet penetrated the gray area where the people's sovereignty ends and the government's begins. In Europe, monarchs were the sovereign, whatever the limits of their power. Americans acknowledged multiple, overlapping sovereigns including the president, Congress, state legislatures, state governors, and, ultimately, the people. Foreign ministers struggled to divine what that meant for diplomacy. Would they negotiate with congressmen and senators? With the president? Or could they even bypass elected officials and appeal to the people through newspapers and political canvassing? If a foreign minister incited the people of a European nation against their monarch, the minister would be subverting the government. But what about a government in which the people reign sovereign? Could foreign ministers try to influence public opinion and feed outrage against elected officials? By teaming with Governor Moultrie and rousing popular support, Genet intended to make the most of America's multiple sovereignties. "The voice of the people," he assured his superiors with a wry pun, "continues to neutralize the declaration of neutrality."[19]

Genet knew his antics would never fly in Europe, but America was not Europe. He believed that France and the United States had unveiled a new diplomatic age, when the people directed foreign affairs through legislatures rather than executives. "Vox populi vox dei," he reminded Paris—the voice of the people is the voice of God.[20]

Vox Populi

By the time Genet sauntered into Philadelphia, Jefferson had been wrangling with Hamilton for weeks about how to receive him. Because Hamilton believed that the US-French alliance had died with Louis XVI, he pressured Washington to receive Genet in a limited capacity. Jefferson insisted that the minister receive full recognition. Washington agreed with Jefferson. The president also concurred that the alliance remained intact and that by its terms the United States could offer no special aid to Britain.[21]

The more battles Jefferson won, the more he despaired that Hamilton was winning the war. Jefferson wanted to tip neutrality in France's favor, but the president refused. The secretary of state mistook Washington's compromises as Hamilton's victories. By antagonizing Genet, he vented to Madison, Hamilton and his allies favored "the confederacy of princes against human liberty."[22]

Human liberty. Jefferson was no longer combating an unsound funding system or a misguided foreign policy. He believed himself at the center of a contest over something far greater. Madison saw the same stakes. He resented Washington's neutrality proclamation less because of its content than because Washington had issued it unilaterally, as if the president could decide between war and peace without Congress. Hamilton had duped Washington into copying Europe's "Monarchical model." For his part, Hamilton perceived Jefferson, Madison, and France as the threats to American liberty, which would erode before the chaos of the French Revolution. In the semantics of diplomacy, Madison, Jefferson, and Hamilton thought they saw epic shifts in human destinies. With so much at stake, they could grant compromise no refuge.[23]

Both sides rushed to summon supporters to their camps. They marshaled the people to their cause in the most American way possible—with newspapers. In the 1780s and 1790s, presses flowered across the United States, bold in their political opinions and formidable in their power. As one historian puts it, "the partisan press and American political parties began life as one."[24]

Republican presses cascaded praise onto Genet while they blistered the neutrality proclamation and Washington (usually couched as attacks on Hamilton and other Federalist advisers). One caustic writer implied that Washington had yielded to "the opiate of sycophancy" and "servile adulation." Others arraigned the president as "infamously niggardly," "the most horrid swearer and blasphemer," and prone to "gambling, reveling, horseracing, and horsewhipping."[25]

By mid-June 1793, Jefferson and Madison wondered whether the newspapers had gone too far. As the attacks swirled, Washington fell feverish, and Jefferson noticed that the aspersions worsened his condition. "I am sincerely sorry to see them," he wrote Madison. "Every Gazette I see," Madison frowned in agreement, criticized the "anglified complexion" of the administration. They blamed Hamilton for the president's embarrassment. Federalists had smothered Washington in the "rags of royalty" until he could only fall short of expectations. However much they wanted to indict Hamilton, Jefferson and Madison had fueled the popular outcry and, in the process, exposed their own party to accusations of foreign collusion against the administration.[26]

While Jefferson and Madison worried that the Republican press barrage was backfiring, Genet infuriated Washington with smug dismissiveness of the president's policies. He portrayed Washington as a stooge of Britain. In the United States, he reasoned, the people were the sovereigns, not the president, and the people voiced their will through Congress. He replicated Madison's logic that Washington had intruded on congressional authority. Genet would do as he pleased—including outfitting privateers—until Congress "confirmed or rejected" Washington's policies.[27]

On July 6, Alexander Dallas, secretary to the Pennsylvania governor, zipped through Philadelphia's nighttime streets toward the outskirts of the city, where Genet and his subordinates resided. Dallas had learned that Genet was preparing to launch a new privateer the next morning. The governor had dispatched Dallas to warn the minister to restrain the ship until the president could determine its legality. Otherwise, the governor would marshal the militia to stop it.[28]

An admirer of Genet, Dallas trod lightly. After apologizing for the late visit, he softly delivered the governor's ultimatum. Genet exploded with defiance ("many angry epithets," Dallas recalled). Washington is "not the sovereign of the country," the minister barked. Americans backed him and his mission, he insisted, but Washington was controlled by a few officials who hated France and liberty. If the governor sent the militia against the privateer, he would "repel force by force." Dallas retreated and sent a report to the governor.[29]

When Jefferson learned about the meeting the next morning, it seemed to confirm what he had begun to suspect: Genet wanted to turn Americans against the government, and he was becoming a liability to Republicans. Two days earlier, Genet had revealed to Jefferson secret instructions for a French agent named André Michaux. To complement Mangourit's expedition, Genet had deputed Michaux to recruit an American and Indian force to attack Spanish and British territory in the West and liberate the Mississippi. Michaux enlisted the help of prominent westerners such as George Rogers Clark and John Brown, Madison's old friend who once flirted with Gardoqui's western schemes (he again got cold feet and withdrew his support from Genet). Prior to Genet's visit, Jefferson had a vague notion of the operation. Now Genet made him a party to it, compromising his official capacity. Jefferson warned Genet that the scheme would land its participants in a noose. He didn't care what France did to Spain as long as it didn't involve Americans, he told Genet. Genet took Jefferson's weak warning as a wink.[30]

In the space of two days, Genet had threatened violence against American militia, promoted insurrection in the West, and blustered about turning the people against Washington—delicious material for Jefferson and Madison's political enemies. Hamilton had already launched a newspaper offensive to defend Washington, vindicate the neutrality proclamation, and demoralize French sympathizers. Producing some of his best rhetoric since the *Federalist* under the pseudonym Pacificus, he blended sharp arguments with piercing attacks in essays that he hurtled into the *Gazette of the United States*. His opponents did not just misjudge the issues, he warned his readers. They were hostile to the Constitution, Washington, and the government. The new revelations would seem to confirm his charges.[31]

Jefferson panicked. "Never in my opinion, was so calamitous an appointment made, as that of the present minister of F[rance] here," he agonized to Madison. "Hotheaded, all imagination, no judgment, passionate, disrespectful & even indecent toward the P[resident] . . . talking of appeals from him to Congress, from them to the people, urging the most unreasonable & groundless propositions, & in the most dictatorial style." Hamilton's essays aggravated the situation, and somebody needed to strike back, Jefferson stressed, before Americans thought Republicans couldn't counter his arguments. "Take up your pen," he begged Madison, "select the most striking heresies, and cut him to pieces in the face of the public. There is nobody else who can & will enter the lists with him."[32]

When Hamilton learned about Genet's threat to appeal to the people, he saw more than a campaign to pressure the government. He saw "evidence" that Genet wanted "*to controul the Government itself, by creating, if possible, a scism between it and the people* and enlisting them on the side of France, in opposition to their own constitutional authorities." He warned, "It would be a fatal blindness" to ignore the minister's threat.[33]

Before Madison had even received Jefferson's plea to muzzle Hamilton, the latter released a new essay. The Genet-Dallas meeting remained confidential cabinet information, so he didn't leak its details—yet. He warned, however, about "insidious efforts" to detach the people from the government. In Europe, foreign agents bribed their way into court councils; in America, Hamilton warned, they would entice "the patronage of our passions" and exploit partisanship, precisely what Genet was trying to do. "Caresses, condescentions, [and] flattery" from foreign agents, "in unison with our prepossessions, are infinitely more to be feared" than routine corruption, Hamilton admonished.[34]

Hamilton saw the problem as unique to republics. "Foreign influence is truly the GRECIAN HORSE to a republic," he declared. "We cannot be too careful to exclude its entrance." In European monarchies, foreign bribes might buy a few courtiers. In a republic that allowed free political discourse, foreign interference could turn a nation against itself. What Genet considered popular mobilization Hamilton deemed subversion.[35]

Madison received Jefferson's bitter assessment of Genet and Hamilton on July 18, in the middle of a sweltering harvest season. Judging by his correspondence, he fought a sour mood most of the summer, and Jefferson's call to a newspaper battle with Hamilton didn't help. He knew he couldn't vanquish Hamilton "by a single fire," and he hesitated to launch a prolonged newspaper contest. With little enthusiasm, time, or resources to enlist in the fight, Madison grudgingly arrayed his pen against Hamilton, a task he found even more "grating" than he expected.[36]

While Madison scraped away at his new burden, Hamilton spit another slew of essays into the press, accusing Genet of waging a disinformation campaign in Republican newspapers. Genet likely had printed pro-French essays, as Hamilton claimed. Since Genet's arrival in Charleston, the treasury secretary charged, the Frenchman had incited "popular intrigue" and allied with Republicans to undermine Washington. One artist etched Hamilton's accusations into a cartoon that depicted Genet requesting Republicans to endorse his "plan for the entire subversion of the government."[37]

With Hamilton's indictments dominating the press, Madison wrote on the defensive under the pseudonym of Helvidius. He lumbered into a

FIGURE 4.1   A Peep into the Antifederal Club, 1793, depicts the devil overseeing a group of unseemly-looking Republicans, who surround Genet as he holds a "Plan of the Entire Subversion of the Government." Courtesy Library Company of Philadelphia.

flurry of mixed messages. He needed to back France, American neutrality, and Washington while distancing Republicans from Genet and attacking Hamilton. He was embarrassed by the muddled result the rest of his life. His case whimpered into an abstruse argument about the constitutional constraints on presidential power. He tried to cast Hamilton and his ilk as imitations of British royalists, but his stilted style drowned his invective. Madison had brought political theory to a propaganda fight.[38]

Hamilton beat Jefferson and Madison at their own game, rallying Americans in the newspapers to his (and Washington's) side. He exploited Genet's meddling to gain the advantage. Genet had given Americans a crash course in how to wield foreign intrusion as a partisan weapon. Hamilton remembered the period as a critical juncture, a moment when the people turned against Genet and gave the president power to combat the "machinations" of future agents. At the same time, he remembered Genet's blunders as more "useful than pernicious to our affairs." If foreign agents could exploit partisanship, partisans could exploit foreign tampering to taint their rivals and advance their vision for the national future.[39]

Vox Dei

Most Americans remained enraptured with Washington. By challenging the president, Genet rendered himself the villain of the contest. At the beginning of August, Washington's cabinet—Jefferson, Hamilton, Henry Knox, and Edmund Randolph—convened at his house, likely in his packed study on the second floor. Each man knew they needed to request that France recall the minister. Even Jefferson agreed ("He will sink the republican interest if they do not abandon him"). The question was, how much should they publicly humiliate Genet in the process? Hamilton wanted to air Genet's transgressions to the public. Jefferson advocated a quiet ouster, aware that Hamilton intended to make Republicans collateral casualties of the minister's disgrace.[40]

Jefferson may have feared that he lost the fight after Secretary of War Knox showed Washington a printed cartoon that depicted the president as a king at the guillotine. Washington erupted, as Jefferson put it, "into one of those passions when he cannot command himself." He would rather be dead than president, he shouted, and would "rather be on his farm than to be made *emperor of the world*," but still the Republican press accused him of "wanting to be a king." Stunned silence followed, and Washington concluded the meeting and dismissed his secretaries.[41]

The press attacks might have tipped Washington to Hamilton's side had Jefferson not announced three days earlier he would resign that September. Washington needed Jefferson and wanted him to stay at least another six months. The president cooled, and within a week he decided to keep Genet's recall private. Jefferson agreed to stay in the cabinet until the end of the year. He vouched that Republicans would never side with Genet against Washington or their own government. They would abandon the minister the moment they learned of his misconduct.[42]

Washington may have spared Genet public humiliation, but Hamilton intensified his public crusade against the minister and Republicans. He leaked the details of Genet's disastrous meeting with Dallas to Federalist allies. Federalists organized public meetings to defend Washington and condemn Genet. They lauded Washington, "who is still beloved, honored and esteemed by all good men," as one supporter expressed. Federalists gathered in Richmond in mid-August to denounce all "intriguing of a foreign minister with the political parties of this country." They warned that foreign influence would beget the "dismemberment and partition" of the United States.[43]

Madison learned about the meeting at the end of August, while spending a couple of weeks at the home of his friend and political ally Senator James Monroe. He itched to return to Montpelier, but he knew that an acquaintance named David Randolph would soon arrive at Monroe's home with news from Jefferson, and Madison was keen to get it. Randolph arrived on August 30 with Jefferson's confidential letter. Genet "was absolutely incorrigible," Madison read. The cabinet would request his recall— something Madison would have learned weeks earlier in a ciphered letter from Jefferson had he not misplaced his key to the private code they regularly used to discuss sensitive information. Jefferson agreed to the recall, Madison learned, to escape "the wreck which could not but sink all who should cling to it."[44]

Madison and Monroe began organizing a campaign to counter the Federalist onslaught. They drafted resolutions that celebrated the French Revolution and endorsed America's alliance with France. They urged Virginia's Republican counties to adopt them and send them to the president.[45]

The pair suffered the same handicaps that had plagued Madison's Helvidius essays: Praise for France resembled a cheer for Genet, and a cheer for Genet sounded like censure of Washington. By the time the resolutions affirmed fidelity to the Constitution, applauded Washington, ignored Genet, and tiptoed around neutrality, they lost their bite. Madison and Monroe cast their opponents as British monarchists who despised the American Revolution, but they clearly wrote from the defensive. In two county meetings, Republicans further diluted the resolutions with denunciations of Genet's "imprudence and indiscretion" and "highly improper" conduct. Republicans struggled to trumpet a cohesive message amid Genet's spats.[46]

Genet's "conduct has been that of a madman," Madison griped. He could only hope that Federalists would overplay their hand and reveal themselves as monarchists and British pawns.[47]

In France, Jacobins had seized power, and the paranoid faction suspected Genet's failures resulted more from disloyalty than incompetence. By the time they deliberated Washington's request to recall Genet, they had condemned and executed his former Girondin superiors for conspiracy.

Even before they harbored those suspicions, they knew it made bad diplomacy for their minister to parade as if at "the head of an American party." They happily recalled the besieged minister.[48]

In early March 1794, Madison learned of the guillotining of the eminent Girondin diplomat, Jacques-Pierre Brissot, in Paris. Genet would be a fool to return to France, he thought. Brash but no fool, Genet accepted Washington's conciliatory offer to remain in the United States after his discharge. Genet's plans to invade Spanish and British territory faded with his dismissal.[49]

Much had changed by then. Jefferson had resigned and retired to Monticello. Madison had returned to Congress with a tentative Republican majority in the House. Politicians and residents crept back into Philadelphia after fleeing a yellow fever epidemic in late summer 1793.[50]

Federalists made the most of Genet as he exited the capital and Madison entered it. The British Royal Navy had begun to seize US vessels that carried goods between the French West Indies and France. Madison grasped his chance to capitalize on the insults to US neutrality and sovereignty, renewing pleas to slap punitive taxes on British products. Federalists had lost their patience with Madison, and Genet made an excellent bogeyman. One Federalist claimed that Genet formulated Madison's legislation. Madison and his friends "are in close league with the Ex-Minister Genet," agreed another. Still another condemned Madison as France's "most confidential and efficient agent," working with Genet to drive the United States to war against Britain. He had supported all "Genet's violent outrages against our government" and "his insults to our President." Once Genet became synonymous with opposition to Washington, Madison and his Republicans had lost the fight.[51]

Vox populi vox dei? Genet got it wrong. In 1790s America, the voice of Washington was the voice of God.

Terrorism

In 1813, John Adams, who had served as Washington's vice president recalled "the terrorism, excited by Genet, in 1793, when ten thousand People in the Streets of Philadelphia, day after day, threatened to drag Washington out of his House, and effect a Revolution in the Government." Time had hardly cooled Adams's disgust with Genet. Though exaggerated almost to the point of fantasy, his memory captured the panic kindled by foreign influence two decades earlier.[52]

Adams repeated a Federalist canard born of a 1794 rebellion of frontier insurgents, who despised the federal government's tax on whiskey production, one of their few viable industries. The government had failed to win the Mississippi, failed to suppress Indians, and failed to wrest its rightful western forts from the British. Westerners feared the excise tax would destroy their last strand of livelihood. Since Hamilton had ushered the tax into law in 1791, they had ignored it, circumvented it, and resisted it with sporadic violence. Hamilton antagonized western discontents with tougher enforcement until rebels fired on federal troops and torched a tax inspector's home in July 1794.[53]

The insurrection rekindled Spanish and British hopes that western dissenters might back their empires in a war with the United States. Since mid-1793, Canada's Lieutenant Governor Simcoe had advocated a joint British, Spanish, and Indian force to conquer the West and detach disgruntled Kentuckians from the union. In January 1794, Baron de Carondelet, Louisiana's governor, revived the idea of a military alliance with Simcoe to combat Genet's aggressive plans. After the July violence, one Spanish official wrote his superiors in code, "If Great Britain has a war with these states, and we join her, you know well that nothing is more important than winning over the Kentuckians and Indians before declaring it." Fortunately for Spain, he wrote, "it is easy to make them separate from the confederation and unite with us, granting them navigation of the Mississippi." A few Kentuckians threatened that if the government refused to repeal the whiskey tax, they would "renounce the allegiance to the United States and annex themselves to the British."[54]

Such grand plans never materialized, but Washington had no guarantee of that in the spring and summer of 1794. To the president's advisers, Genet had flung the United States to the precipice of war against disloyal Americans and voracious empires. The minister "had laboured to convulse our Country, by kindling parties, and forcing us from our neutrality," charged Washington's new secretary of state, Edmund Randolph. Washington confidant John Jay suspected that Simcoe plotted war due in part to Americans' "indiscreet Reception" of Genet and their affinity for France.[55]

Actually, Simcoe hardly mentioned Genet; he worried more about US general Anthony Wayne's forces fighting his Native allies in the Ohio Valley. By August 20, Wayne had driven Native families from their villages, burned their crops, occupied their hunting grounds, and overwhelmed their warriors at the Battle of Fallen Timbers. The Native fighters and refugees retreated to the British-controlled Fort Miamis. They found shut doors. Wanting no quarrel with US forces, the British commander refused the Indians shelter and reinforcement, an act the asylum-seekers considered treachery from their allies. The powerful foreign combination showed at least tepid signs of a splinter.[56]

Late in the evening on September 30, a War Department clerk named John Stagg called at Washington's quarters in a small community twenty-five miles west of Philadelphia. No doubt exhausted from a hard day's ride from the capital, he handed the president dispatches from Wayne. Washington rejoiced at the "pleasing accounts" of the triumph. After years of bloodshed and bitter defeats, the commander-in-chief had his victory over the Northwestern Confederacy.[57]

When he heard the news, Washington was headed for western Pennsylvania, by then deemed "a center of terrorism" for insurrectionists resisting the whiskey tax. In August, 6,000 rogue militiamen had paraded in Braddock's Field near Pittsburgh, promising bloodshed over the law. Warnings floated over the mountains that the insurgents would march on Philadelphia. Both seasoned war leaders, the president and Hamilton traveled west to marshal 13,000 militia troops against the revolt now called the Whiskey Rebellion.[58]

Wayne's triumph would mean nothing if rebels crippled their own government, and Washington intended to punctuate the army's success with victory in western Pennsylvania. The feats would secure the northwestern frontier and showcase the power of the young, untried federal government.

He succeeded. The rebels fled. Washington returned to Philadelphia in October, leaving Hamilton with the troops to imprison ringleaders. Though courts convicted only two men, Washington had done what he intended—demonstrate the federal government's authority to tax its citizens and enforce its laws.[59]

Washington blamed the insurrection on a mythical alliance between Genet and Republican political organizations. Republicans had sprinkled the nation with "democratic societies"—local civic leagues that cheered the French Revolution and the French alliance. The societies had no central institution and no direct connection to Genet or France. Even so, Federalists condemned the clubs as the "impure off-spring of Genêt." Washington considered them the source of westerners' sedition, with Genet as their "father" and "diabolical leader." The French minister organized them,

Washington thought, "for the express purpose of dissention, and to draw a line between the people & the government."[60]

In reality, Washington faced little threat of an alliance between the insurrectionists and any foreign government—least of all France. Hamilton charged that the new French minister, Jean Antoine Joseph Fauchet, "knew and approved of a conspiracy which was destined to overthrow the administration of our Government." Actually, Fauchet had just abandoned Genet's western schemes, and France had little appetite for more controversy. The Frenchman suspected that the British were behind the insurrection, prodded to that belief by Republican-leaning secretary of state Edmund Randolph.[61]

The French minister may have twiddled the idea of giving the rebels monetary support, but he took less interest in the Whiskey Rebellion than even British and Spanish officials did. In August, a rebel delegation had met with British minister George Hammond and requested protection for western Pennsylvania. When Hammond dismissed their pleas, one leader threatened to embrace Spain. Spanish officials had kept their finger on the pulse of the rebellion in Pennsylvania, knowing that Pennsylvanians and Kentuckians shared grievances. Spain did purchase an American agent for 200 pesos to coax westerners into Spain's fold. Still, no foreign nation actively supported the rebellion.[62]

Games

On November 19, Madison and other congressmen piled into the House chamber on the main level of Congress's red brick hall to listen to Washington's annual message. The president would no doubt address the insurrection. Senators filed down the stairs from their second-floor location to join their colleagues. Behind the House Speaker's raised podium, two fires would have blazed during the cold late fall. The audience sat in leather chairs behind long, mahogany desks that formed a semicircle around the front of the room. After all had gathered, Washington entered and paced to the head of the assembly.[63]

The president uttered more than 2,000 words about the insurrection, but Madison fixated on one phrase: "self-created societies," Washington's oblique reference to democratic societies. The president accused the associations of encouraging the rebellion. Madison boiled at the implication. Did Americans not possess the right to assemble, speak, and print freely? In a republic, the people censor the government, not the other way around. He viewed Washington's accusation as an "attack on the most sacred principle of our Constitution." Washington spared Madison apoplexy by not mentioning his suspicions of Genet and France.[64]

Believing that Federalist advisers had constructed the speech, Madison considered the president's use of "self-created societies" "the greatest error of his political life." The congressman assumed that Federalists were trying to dupe the president into subtly denouncing Republicans and make him look like the leader of their party.[65]

"The game was," Madison explained to his allies, "to connect the democratic Societies with the odium of the insurrection—to connect the Republicans in Cong[ress] with those Societies," and depict Republicans in "opposition to the President." A game, perhaps. But "a most dangerous game" that might cost Americans their liberty, he fumed.[66]

5

"A Vile Underhand Game"

There is a vile underhand game playing, with a View of injuring unspotted Characters. In this an Attempt is making to implicate You.
— Pierce Butler to James Madison, August 21, 1795

JEAN ANTOINE JOSEPH FAUCHET DETECTED a vile plan in the spring of
1794. The newly arrived French diplomat had no idea what it was, but he
knew it spelled disaster for his republic.[1]

Charles-Maurice de Talleyrand had just arrived in Philadelphia. The
French aristocrat had embraced his country's revolution before it turned
too radical for him. As a member of France's constituent assembly (the national legislature in the early years of the Revolution), he had helped craft
a constitutional monarchy. After the fall of the monarchy in 1792, though,
Talleyrand sheltered in Britain. By 1794, he seemed a stranger to the revolution he had helped spark.[2]

Fauchet despised Talleyrand, whom many suspected as being too cozy
with the British since his days as a diplomat in London. As a young Parisian
law student when the revolution began, Fauchet embraced the Jacobins'
extremism. He detested the more conservative constitutional monarchy
Talleyrand had advocated. Now Talleyrand had landed in America—no
doubt with insidious plans, Fauchet assumed. Talleyrand joined a growing
cohort of moderate French refugees in the US capital. He wielded letters of
introduction from the former British prime minister, the Earl of Shelburne
(by then the Marquess of Lansdowne), inflaming Fauchet's suspicion that
he operated as a British spy.[3]

Talleyrand failed to make much of an impression on Madison when they
met that spring. The Frenchman handed Madison a letter of introduction

from a mutual contact in Britain, but they rarely interacted thereafter. Madison had little to say about the thirty-nine-year-old (a few years his junior), who had a reputation for conversation and revelry, and whose short stature and blue eyes matched his own. Politically, they had little in common. At the same time that Talleyrand was bemoaning Louis XVI's execution with fellow French exiles in Britain, Madison was accepting honorary French citizenship and praising France's "triumphs of liberty."[4]

To Fauchet's alarm, Talleyrand struck an almost instant friendship with Hamilton. He had carried a letter of introduction from a London socialite to the Hamilton household. The émigré was fêted and presented to Hamilton's friends and political allies. To Fauchet, any Frenchman so chummy with the treasury secretary had to be a traitor and British agent.[5]

Like most other French refugees, Talleyrand arrived not with a secret commission from the British government but with a desire to return to a calmer France. In fact, the British had expelled him from London, threatening to deport him to certain death in France if he stayed. Talleyrand admired Hamilton more than any man in America—or the world, for that matter—but the pair didn't collaborate in clandestine schemes to topple the US or French republics.[6]

Nevertheless, innuendo soared in 1794 Philadelphia, and few outdid Fauchet in his suspicions. Just over thirty years old when he arrived in the city, the minister possessed more revolutionary zeal than diplomatic experience. He planned to ease the tension Genet had sparked, but he shared Genet's suspicions that monarchists in Britain, France, and the United States plotted to suffocate liberty.[7]

Fauchet even suspected that a couple of his fellow commissioners divulged sensitive information to Federalists. He may have been right, for a couple of them had served the French monarchy in the United States for years before the French Revolution. The new secretary of state Edmund Randolph refused to confer with Fauchet in their presence for fear that they would blather sensitive information to Federalist cabinet members Hamilton and Henry Knox. So the US secretary of state and the French minister trusted each other more than they trusted their compatriots in their respective institutions. The trust chasm proved plenty wide for a clever diplomat to exploit. A diplomat like the Briton George Hammond.[8]

Hammond shared Fauchet's age but far eclipsed him in diplomatic experience and skill. By the time he arrived in the United States in 1791, Hammond had held lower-level diplomatic posts at Paris and Madrid. Anxious to burnish his reputation, he accepted the US position after several others had declined the unattractive offer to sail to America's inconsequential capital.[9]

Philadelphia exceeded his low expectations, but observers still noticed a coldness, even smugness, in his demeanor. He hardly needed charm, though. He represented the most powerful empire in the world.[10]

Throughout 1793, Hammond pondered how to exploit inter-cabinet quarrels and party distrust. He watched Genet implode, learning that "wanton disrespect" for government officials accomplished little. In 1794, he refused to aid western Pennsylvanians in their rebellion. Hammond pinpointed a more subtle but effective strategy to benefit Britain. Americans may have eschewed a foreign minister who brazenly tried to turn the people against the government, but perhaps he could turn partisans against each other. The moment came in early 1795, as Americans sparred over a new treaty with Britain.[11]

Marriages

On April 1, 1795, at about three o'clock in the afternoon, Madison strode Philadelphia's busy High Street toward George Washington's red-brick, gable-roofed mansion to dine with the chief magistrate. Most congressmen had dispersed at the end of the congressional session weeks prior, but Madison had lingered. In the past, when his colleagues hurried to their home states and families, Madison, then a bachelor, enjoyed frank political conversations with the president.[12]

Washington seemed to expect more of a social than business visit this time. The executive wanted to dine "*in a family way,*" a phrase his secretary underlined on the invitation. Married only six months and suddenly the stepfather of a toddler, Madison wouldn't have yet acclimated to such social calls with a family.[13]

As family tradition told the story, Madison had spied Dolley Payne Todd while he strolled the Philadelphia streets with a friend. Taken by the dark-haired, blue-eyed, twenty-six-year-old widow, he asked her close friend, Aaron Burr, to introduce them. A bit taller than her suitor, Dolley found James's small frame endearing, calling him "the great, little Madison" before they married and "my darling little Husband" after. Madison rarely surrendered to passion, but while they courted he permitted a mutual acquaintance, Cyrano-de-Bergerac-style, to tell her that "at Night he Dreames of you & Starts in his Sleep a Calling on you to relieve his Flame for he Burns to such an excess that he will be shortly consumed."[14]

FIGURE 5.1 Detail of Residence of Washington in High Street, Philadelphia, depicts George Washington's executive mansion. Courtesy New York Public Library.

For all the romantic zeal, Dolley and James appealed to each other's senses as much as their emotions. Cheerful but no coquette, Dolley had borne two children and had experienced the heartache of losing an infant a year earlier to the same yellow fever epidemic that stole her first husband. She came from respectable but simple Quaker roots, yet she longed for a more colorful world, enough that she accepted excommunication for marrying outside the faith. James Madison came with the right combination of simplicity and elite gentility.[15]

The Virginian lawmaker and his new family moved into a residence on Philadelphia's Eighth Street, where he once boarded with James and Elizabeth Monroe. The Monroes had since left for Paris after James Monroe's appointment as minister to France, a position Washington had offered Madison but which Madison had declined—his courtship likely among the reasons. Now in his forties, the congressman suddenly found himself a family man, and Dolley suddenly found herself at the heart of national politics, receiving invitations to dine with the president.[16]

By the time the Madisons met the Washingtons for dinner that April, the congressman cringed that the president's Federalist envoy to Britain, John Jay, fixated on a marriage of a different sort. The diplomat was "betrayed,"

Madison bristled, "by his anxiety to couple us with England." He resented Jay's appointment, remembering him as the man who had tried to sell the Mississippi to Spain for New England trade benefits. Also, Jay's mission had halted his push for penalties on British trade, for Congress had needed to show good faith while Jay negotiated.[17]

At dinner, Madison doubtless hoped for a few private moments with the chief executive to talk politics. Hamilton had resigned as secretary of the treasury several months earlier, ridding Washington, in Madison's view, of the most dangerous man in government. His departure left a vacuum of influence with Washington, and Madison had plenty to discuss. He knew that Jay had signed a treaty with British negotiators in November and that Washington had received a copy several weeks prior to their dinner. The next step would be to submit it to the Senate, where a two-thirds majority would have to approve it to make it binding. Constitutionally, Madison's House of Representatives had no role in the treaty-making process.[18]

Jay had traveled to London with a long list of issues to resolve: disputes over the western forts, violations of US neutrality, compensation for American slaveholders who had lost slaves to the British army during the Revolutionary War, debts owed by Americans to British creditors, shared access to the northern Mississippi River, Genet's privateers who had outfitted in US ports and captured British ships, and Native American relations in the Great Lakes region.[19]

More than anything, Washington wanted peace. Contemplating America's conflicts with British-backed Indians and Britain's insults on the seas, Washington saw war on the horizon—a war the United States could not win. He needed Jay to cool the temperature.[20]

With other Americans, Madison itched to know the details of the treaty Jay had signed, but Washington had kept them "an inpenetrable secret," wrote a disappointed Madison. Since the president had first laid eyes on the treaty in early March, he had criticized it privately to Secretary of State Randolph. Jay scored a couple of critical victories—most important, British evacuation of the western posts—but the treaty came back predictably lopsided. It surrendered hefty trade favors to Britain and prohibited the punitive taxes Madison wanted to lay on British goods. By eliminating key commercial advantages for the French, it brushed violently close to terminating America's alliance with France. Still, it seemed the best chance to secure the peace with Britain that Washington coveted. The chief magistrate wanted to keep the treaty confidential and let the Senate decide its fate when the body met in June.[21]

Madison was floundering "as much out of the secret as others," an unusual place for the president's former confidant. For months, though, he collected unofficial intelligence about the treaty from newspapers and private correspondence. From what he could piece together, he despised Jay's work. Prone to overestimate America's leverage against the mighty British, Madison believed that Jay had stopped far short of what he could have demanded.[22]

Washington divulged nothing. As the Madisons bid adieu to the Washingtons, the congressman couldn't have known that he would never again share such intimate moments with the president. That summer, the treaty controversy would permanently rend their political partnership, thrusting them to opposing sides of an increasingly vitriolic two-party system. And it would gift Hammond a chance to turn political enmity to Britain's advantage. All that lay in the future. For the time, Madison left the mansion no more a party to the president's secret than when he entered. In politics, though, as in bad marriages, secrets rarely last.[23]

Fires

On July 25, an angry horde of several hundred Philadelphians trampled the streets toward Hammond's residence, spurred by a cry to "kick this damned treaty to hell!" Despite the long trek through the city, their passions still boiled by the time they stood outside Hammond's door. Hammond and his family gaped from the windows as the crowd hoisted the treaty on a pole and set it aflame. The fire and curses left the family untouched but shaken.[24]

The protest resembled hundreds of others throughout the states once the treaty came to light. Someone quipped that a person could travel the length of the United States by the firelight of burning Jay effigies. Other demonstrators practiced their pyrotechny on the Union Jack. Washington had feared that knowledge of the treaty would derail tranquil deliberation. The protestors justified his apprehension.[25]

In early June, the Senate had voted to keep the treaty confidential while they debated. Madison enjoyed well-placed friends, however, and South Carolina Senator Pierce Butler leaked it to him in installments throughout the month. The Virginian honored Butler's plea to show them to nobody except Jefferson, concealing them even from his friend at Monticello.[26]

Madison's silence likely stemmed more from respect for Washington than for Butler. When a friend pressed him to denounce the treaty publicly and petition Washington personally, Madison refused. The congressman sensed that the treaty put the president in a bind. He pitied Washington, no matter how much he also reviled Jay's attempt to "prostrate us to a foreign & unfriendly Nation." The president's "situation must be a most delicate one," he commiserated. Washington deserved the "solicitude" of his friends. Besides, Madison suspected that Washington could already guess his feelings about the treaty. Madison also endured a busy summer with his new family, and he hardly took time to correspond with friends, let alone write anti-treaty diatribes. Whatever the reasons, he sat uncharacteristically silent at Montpelier while America convulsed.[27]

By the time protestors lit their fires outside Hammond's house, the treaty had slipped into public by another route. On June 24, the Senate had consented to the treaty (except for one article) with the minimum two-thirds majority required by the Constitution. The body ordered that it remain secret until Washington could ratify it with his signature, but Butler and Stevens Thomson Mason of Virginia refused to honor the vote. With rogue senators likely to expose the treaty, Washington decided to release it in a handpicked venue. Mason beat him to it, leaking it to printer Benjamin Bache, one of the administration's harshest critics.[28]

And the fires began.

The treaty "flew with an electric velocity to every part of the union," Madison marveled. For twenty-five cents, Americans could snatch a copy of the soon-to-be-most-hated text in the country. In Philadelphia, July 4 celebrations turned into an anti-treaty riot, complete with a torched effigy of Jay and a skirmish with troops. "The best celebration of the Fourth of July was to burn Jay's effigy and his treaty," commented one observer.[29]

After the Senate approved ratification, Americans knew that Washington would make the final decision, and treaty opponents targeted him with their protests. He battled a sharper dilemma than ever between his own judgment and public pressure. However much a Virginian at heart, the old general shared many of the values of New England Federalists, especially deference to authority and public order. Famously jealous of his personal honor, Washington took the criticism personally. Undeterred by dissent, Washington resolved to make the decision he thought would best serve the nation. He solicited advisers, especially Secretary of State Randolph and his former secretary Hamilton, for even-handed opinions of the treaty.[30]

Randolph had risen in politics with Madison since their days as young Virginian revolutionaries. Together, they had coaxed Washington out of retirement to chair the Constitutional Convention. Randolph had served as Washington's faithful lieutenant since his appointment as attorney general in the first cabinet. The president rewarded his loyalty with the office of secretary of state after Jefferson resigned.[31]

Randolph rarely went all-in on anything. He helped Madison shape debate at the Constitutional Convention but refused to sign the final product. While Madison and Hamilton charged ahead with the *Federalist* essays, he charted a more moderate course of conditional ratification. He spent most of Washington's first term helping the president steer a center course between Jefferson and Hamilton.[32]

Randolph's moderation earned him a reputation as a political coward. "He is the poorest Cameleon I ever saw," Jefferson huffed to Madison, "having no colour of his own, & reflecting that nearest him." Madison remained his friend, but even his friends could see that Randolph had exposed himself to political assassination when he inherited Jefferson's mantle. "I fear he has placed himself on a bed of thorns," a mutual friend wrote Madison. Randolph would become the target for partisans unhappy with the government. He could expect only blame when unpopular policies, foreign threats, or party strife imperiled the country. The Jay Treaty combined all three.[33]

Eager again to pave a middle road and help his boss out of a jam, Randolph gave Washington sound treaty advice on July 12. British officials had recently renewed their directive for navy commanders to seize US ships that carried grain to France—informally called the "provisions order." The secretary of state insisted that Washington should refuse to ratify the treaty until Britain repealed it. Washington liked the idea. He could have it both ways: reject the treaty without foreclosing the possibility of signing it in the future. Anti-treaty uproars might abate if he used it as a bargaining chip and proved that he would not let Britain browbeat America.[34]

The next day, at their regular morning meeting in the president's upstairs study, Washington instructed Randolph to tell Hammond that he was considering the ultimatum. The secretary of state retreated a couple blocks north to his state department office and sent an invitation for Hammond to meet him there. Hammond sped across town, arriving within half an hour.[35]

When Randolph told Hammond about the president's condition to the treaty, the news may have disturbed but probably didn't shock the minister. Since April, Randolph had wearied him with threats that the president wouldn't approve the treaty if the captures of US vessels continued. When Hammond pressed the secretary of state with a couple of cursory questions, Randolph realized he was himself unsure how far Washington would pursue his demand. Regardless, the British minister agreed to communicate the ultimatum to his government and departed. Randolph returned to the president's house to report and learn how committed his boss was to this course. Washington confirmed that Randolph could deliver an official written notice to Hammond that he wouldn't ratify the treaty unless the British revoked the provisions order.[36]

With the president fully committed, Randolph had seized a hefty diplomatic victory, or so it seemed. Two weeks later, on July 27, Hammond sat again in Randolph's office at midday, this time at Hammond's own request. A mob had accosted his home and incinerated the treaty in front of it two days prior, he told the secretary of state in a measured tone ("very calm" is how Randolph read him). He made no demands and expected no punishments for the insult to his character and the government he represented. He would let US authorities take the steps they deemed proper.[37]

Randolph sympathized with Hammond but doubted the government could do much. The crowd harmed nobody, and laws protected protest. If Hammond would make a written statement of the facts, he would "take them into consideration." Not much of a promise. Hammond didn't fuss. He just wanted his protest on record.[38]

Behind his poker face, Hammond contemplated a more subtle strategy to discredit the anti-treaty crowd, a plan that dwarfed petty complaints about a few hundred protestors. If executed well, he wrote his superiors that same day, his scheme would tarnish "the character and principles of certain individuals" and expose "the real motives of their political conduct." He meant Randolph and other key Republicans, including Jefferson and Madison.[39]

Number 10

Hammond initiated his ploy on Sunday, July 26—the day between the treaty fire outside his home and his meeting with Randolph. He invited the new treasury secretary, Oliver Wolcott Jr. of Connecticut, to dinner. No Hamilton, Wolcott failed to command Washington's confidence. The president even concealed the treaty from him and the new secretary of war, Timothy Pickering, until the Senate convened to debate it. Ardent New England Federalists, Wolcott and Pickering despised the Republican-leaning Randolph and pressed Washington to ratify the treaty. Washington refused their pleas and confirmed to Randolph that he would not ratify it while Britain's provisions order stood.[40]

Despite his tepid relationship with Washington, Wolcott seemed the best candidate to dislodge the president's trust in Randolph. A few days before he hosted Wolcott for dinner, Hammond received delayed instructions from British foreign secretary Lord Grenville to bypass Randolph and work with Hamilton, who was still treasury secretary at the time Grenville wrote. Grenville also directed Hammond to work covertly with Federalists if necessary to sideline Randolph from treaty talks. The instructions seemed even more urgent at the time Hammond received them. He knew by then that the secretary of state had convinced Washington not to ratify the treaty unless the British repealed their provisions order.[41]

As Hamilton's replacement, Wolcott seemed like the proper contact for Hammond to fulfill Grenville's directive. The new secretary may not have shared Hamilton's drive, intellect, or intimacy with Washington, but he at least shared his politics.

As Wolcott entered Hammond's residence on South Second Street on July 26, he found a small dinner party of British subjects and sympathizers: Hammond, his family, his former secretary, an English gentleman friend, and his loyalist father-in-law. Before dinner, Hammond pulled Wolcott aside. The minister had received a packet from Grenville, he informed his guest. The stash included an intercepted dispatch from Fauchet to his superiors in France. His curiosity kindled, Wolcott sat down to dinner with the rest of the guests.[42]

On March 28, months before the dinner party, Guillaume François Need captained the *Jean Bart* as it sailed through France's Bay of Biscay toward Brest. His ship carried a packet of letters from New York to France, including some of Fauchet's communications. The high seas breathed hostility during the 1790s, with warships prowling the waters. About twenty leagues off the coast, Need spotted a British frigate in the distance. As the British vessel rushed to seize his ship, Need commanded an officer to hurl the packet of sensitive letters overboard. The officer obeyed, but the packet bobbed stubbornly on the ocean surface. After apprehending the *Jean Bart*, the British crew dropped a boat into the water and recovered the correspondence.[43]

By May, the purloined communications landed in front of Grenville. He examined them and forwarded them to Hammond, with instructions to show them to "well disposed Persons in America." He meant Federalists in high office.[44]

As he thumbed through the dispatches, Hammond discovered why Grenville thought well-positioned Federalists might like to see them. In a dispatch labeled "Number 10," written in the throes of the Whiskey Rebellion on October 31, 1794, Fauchet mentioned Randolph's "precieuses confessions" during the disorder. Likely translating the French literally, Hammond would have read "precious confessions" rather than the more appropriate "valuable declarations." The imperfect translation conjured sinister questions about what sensitive information Randolph may have leaked to the French government amid the crisis.[45]

Fauchet failed to elaborate on the "precieuses confessions," for he had listed them in an earlier dispatch, called Number 3. They amounted to little more than unflattering remarks about the influence pro-British advisers wielded over Washington. Randolph may have embarrassed the president in a clumsy effort to convince Fauchet that Washington had not abandoned France, but he had hardly divulged state secrets.[46]

Without the context of Number 3, Number 10 hinted at darker revelations. Even more incriminating, it referenced a potentially explosive conversation between Fauchet and Randolph:

> Mr. Randolph came to see me with an air of great eagerness, and made to me the overtures which I related in my [dispatch] No. 6. Thus with a few thousand dollars the [French] Republic might have decided on civil war or peace here! Thus the consciences of the pretended patriots in America already have a price!

Divorced from context, which Number 6 would have provided, Number 10 implied that Randolph had implored the French government to fund the insurrection in western Pennsylvania. Or perhaps he was selling his influence to the French government. Number 6 left a lot murky, but at least it showed that Randolph sought neither a personal bribe nor French funding for the insurrection. Without that dispatch, though, Number 10 appeared damning.[47]

Hammond received Fauchet's intercepted letters the same day he received Grenville's tardy directive to marginalize Randolph with Federalist support. Grenville had prepared the two sets of communications months apart, but they paired perfectly. Had Hammond shared Genet's impetuousness, he may have splashed Number 10 into newspapers. As Genet discovered, however, Americans reviled foreign ministers who seemed to meddle in their internal politics. Hammond devised a slower but more effective strategy: Slip the document to Federalists and let partisans destroy each other. So he arranged dinner with Wolcott.[48]

After the meal, Hammond sequestered Wolcott in a private room and retrieved Number 10. Hammond almost certainly possessed Number 6 in the intercepted packet. However, he had no interest in revealing that potentially exculpatory letter. Besides, Number 6 also introduced unsavory, albeit unfounded, suspicions about Britain's own role in the Pennsylvania insurrection. Better to keep that one concealed.[49]

As Hammond read Number 10, translating it from French to English on the spot, Wolcott listened, intrigued. Certainly, he said after Hammond finished, "something highly improper had been proposed by Mr. Randolph." Eventually, Wolcott decided that Randolph intended to subvert the government and invite "the French to aid the insurrection with money." If he were to allege wrongdoing, however, he would need the original to support his claims. Hammond hesitated, reluctant to surrender the document. Negotiations ensued, and Hammond finally agreed to relinquish it after making a copy.[50]

Early on July 28, Wolcott grasped the original of Number 10. That same day, he brought it to his Federalist partner Pickering, who was just as peevish as his thin, furrow-browed face made him look. Pickering combined high ideals with inveterate self-righteousness, making him easy to respect and impossible to admire. The next day, he and Wolcott delivered the paper and explanation to Attorney General William Bradford. It is hard to imagine three bureaucrats less qualified to judge the contents of the letter, as none, by Pickering's admission, were strong in French. Pickering used his rudimentary ability to make a clumsy translation that cast Randolph in the worst light. The three cabinet members decided that it merited calling Washington back to Philadelphia from Mount Vernon.[51]

Accusations

Washington traveled back to the capital not entirely sure why, only that Pickering wanted him to return "for a *special reason*, which can be communicated to you only in person." On the evening of August 11, Pickering hurried to Washington's High Street mansion. As Pickering remembered it, he found the president seated at the dinner table discussing state business with Randolph, who had no idea why Pickering had appeared. Washington didn't know why the secretary of war had come either, except that he had something sensitive and urgent to communicate. The president took some wine, rose from the table, winked at Pickering, and invited him into a private room.[52]

"What is the cause of your writing me such a letter?" Washington asked Pickering, correctly guessing what the secretary of war had come to discuss.[53]

"That man," Pickering said, gesturing toward the room where they had just left Randolph, "is a traitor." In three minutes, Pickering summarized his information about Randolph, and he handed his boss a translated copy of Fauchet's intercepted dispatch.[54]

Washington kept the conversation short and returned to the table, where Randolph sat in good spirits with no idea of Washington's sudden distrust. At least that's how Pickering recounted the occasion decades later, though time likely dimmed and confused some of the details in his mind, further colored, no doubt, by his own biases.[55]

However Washington learned about the dispatch that evening, it afflicted him. Fixated on the evidence against Randolph, Washington overlooked what he knew for sure: that Wolcott had cooperated with the British minister to obtain the dispatch. Wolcott had committed no crime, but Washington never paused to consider the dubious source of the evidence. He had endured treachery before, most famously by his comrade Benedict Arnold. Experience taught him that even the closest subordinates could betray him and the nation. The old soldier cherished military-inflected, eighteenth-century traditions of virtue, grounded in fidelity and hierarchy. If guilty, Randolph had wounded his sense of honor. He had to take the accusations seriously and consider the possibility that Randolph had given bad advice based on corrupt contact with the French government.[56]

The next day, Washington convened the entire cabinet to discuss Randolph's written notice to Hammond that the president would reject the treaty until the British repealed the provisions order. Washington had already approved Randolph's preliminary draft and assured the secretary that he had resolved on that course. Maybe Pickering and Wolcott would try to dilute the language a bit, but the meeting should have been mostly perfunctory.[57]

The president blind-sided his secretary of state when he asked the cabinet members if they thought he should immediately ratify the treaty. The cabinet Federalists eagerly assented. Ignorant of the accusations that had turned the president against him, Randolph recoiled with what he later called "unutterable astonishment" as Washington's resolve crumbled.[58]

"I will ratify the treaty," the president concluded.[59]

Washington ordered the incredulous Randolph to notify Hammond that he would immediately ratify the treaty, except for the one article the Senate had refused to approve. Still unaware of Washington's suspicions, the secretary announced the decision to the British minister two days later. He didn't even try to hide his disgust. If he had his way, he admitted, the president would not ratify. Hammond saw in the downcast Randolph "clear indications of the declining influence of that gentleman in the councils of his country." He must have suspected his direct role in the feat. On August 18, Washington approved the treaty.[60]

The next day, with the treaty out of the way, the president turned his attention to his secretary. At Washington's summons, Randolph entered the president's office at 10:30 A.M. and found Pickering and Wolcott already there. An awkward formality washed through the room. Washington greeted Randolph curtly and hurried to the point.[61]

"Mr. Randolph! here is a letter, which I desire you to read, and make such explanations, as you choose," Randolph remembered the president say as he handed the secretary of state a thick packet of about fifteen pages. Number 10.[62]

Randolph had never seen the letter in his life, never even known it existed. It concerned matters that had occurred nearly a year prior. He saw the potentially damning references but could hardly make sense of them without the additional dispatches that would have clarified them. He stammered a few ambiguous explanations as far as he could remember.[63]

Washington asked him to enter an adjacent room while he conversed with Wolcott and Pickering. Alone, Randolph boiled at the humiliation of the interrogation. Three men, who spoke hardly a word of French among them, were deciding his fate based on a French letter devoid of context and written by a foreign minister almost a year prior. Washington invited him back in and granted him time to prepare a written explanation of his conduct. Had Randolph just accepted the offer, he might have saved his position and relationship with Washington. He lived in an age when his sense of honor prohibited such a conciliatory course. He retorted that he would write the defense but "would not continue in the office one second" longer after such disrespect. He immediately resigned.[64]

Hammond's ploy silenced the final, most powerful voice of opposition to the treaty in the cabinet. Hammond would have accomplished little without the serrated distrust among cabinet officers. He couldn't have known exactly how events would unfold, but Randolph's assessment seems accurate: "Mr. Hammond understood the goodness of the soil, in which he was sowing the seed; and duly appreciated the fruit, which was to spring from it."[65]

Whispers

Within two days of Randolph's resignation, whispers connected Madison to the secretary's disgrace. "There is a vile underhand game playing," Pierce Butler wrote Madison, still tucked away at Montpelier, "with a View of injuring unspotted Characters. In this an Attempt is making to implicate You." Butler wrote little else about the scandal, and he didn't name his source. He apprised Madison of Randolph's resignation but wrote nothing more about it. He didn't hint that the rumors and the resignation were connected. The senator preferred to converse in person when they got the chance.[66]

In his intercepted letter, Fauchet mentioned that Republicans, among whom he listed Madison, wanted to replace Washington with Jefferson. If we believe Randolph's account, Hammond had hissed those rumors around Philadelphia to sully Republicans. Today, most Americans would hardly consider it nefarious for the opposition party to attack an incumbent. However, many early Americans considered the presidency a quasi-royal office, especially with Washington at the helm. They blended personal honor and politics in ways scarcely imaginable now. Many feared that the opposition might destabilize the entire political system by antagonizing the president.[67]

Fauchet also referenced other unknown Republicans who cooperated with Randolph. The vague allusions left critics plenty of room to speculate about who supported the secretary of state's alleged schemes. Madison and Jefferson seemed like prime suspects.[68]

Merciless summer rains abused Virginia travelers that summer, isolating Madison at Montpelier, and he struggled to learn more about Butler's cryptic report. Not until late September did additional news creep in about Randolph's resignation. No routine departure, it had resulted from some sort of "collision" with the president, Madison learned. Then a friend brought the details from Philadelphia about the scandal with word that Madison and others "stand particularly involved and named" in it. The primary accusation was bribery. Federalists twisted Fauchet's letter to say "any thing they think proper," another friend scoffed, "& the name of every man they wish to hunt down is inserted with the specific sum given to purchase him," including Madison's and Jefferson's.[69]

In the meantime, Randolph lathered his disgust with Washington, and he promised the public a written vindication of his actions. To keep Madison out of the morass, he refused to write him while he prepared it. "Every nerve has been strained to combine your name in a business, to which you were the most absolute stranger," Randolph informed him, once his response went to press. Madison sympathized with Randolph, but he didn't hide from Jefferson his irritation "that malice is busy in attempts to complicate others with his affair." With personal stake in the content, Madison awaited Randolph's defense.[70]

Madison had traveled back to his congressional seat in Philadelphia by the time he held the final product. Randolph had obtained statements from Fauchet, along with relevant portions of Number 3 and Number 6, to clear his name of bribery and treachery. But the long (nearly 100 pages), convoluted, detailed-to-a-fault rejoinder raised other curious questions about his conduct that Randolph failed to address, and it revealed poor judgment in some of his actions. Worse, Randolph exposed his new distaste for Washington, an unpardonable sin in early America. The former secretary may have exonerated himself of the worst charges, but "his best friend can't save him from the self condemnation of his political career," Madison concluded.[71]

If nothing else, Randolph's publication invited the focus back to himself and away from Madison. Rumors about the congressman faded with his return to the capital. His name never appeared in the longest, most biting criticism of Randolph, written by arch-Federalist William Cobbett, a recent immigrant from Britain who edited the pro-British *Porcupine's Gazette*. Madison could consider himself lucky to have escaped the writer's "satirical scurrility." Cobbett rarely missed opportunities to expose and exaggerate Republican sins. Even Madison admitted that Cobbett deployed "sufficient ingenuity and plausibility" to finish off Randolph. A year and a half later, Federalists still reminded each other of Number 10: "May no more 'precious confessions' stain the annals of our country," chorused one toast.[72]

By late 1795, Randolph believed, as he wrote Madison, that "the President and his party" (having abandoned the illusion that Washington stood above party) conspired "to destroy the republican force in the U.S." Federalists saw in Randolph's defense "proof of a deep-laid plot against the Federal government." With his revelations, Hammond thought he might discredit a few Republican heavyweights. In the end, he deposed Randolph, helped save the treaty, and aggravated the exact partisan differences that allowed his plan to work in the first place.[73]

Opponents

Madison may have escaped Randolph's ignominious fate, but he and Jefferson had lost their last ally, however feeble they considered him, in Washington's cabinet. Federalist shadows would immerse executive corridors, Madison feared. "Through what official interstice can a ray of republican truths now penetrate to the P[resident]?" he despaired. He missed his chance to avert the disaster two years earlier. Washington had preferred him over Randolph as Jefferson's replacement for secretary of state, but Madison had no interest in the appointment. He betrayed no hint of regret that he had declined the position, but he now had to pitch a final battle against the ratified treaty from the relatively powerless position of his House seat.[74]

Madison had made a weak foray on the political battlefield in late summer 1795, while still at Montpelier, after he learned that Washington had approved the treaty. He broke his summer-long silence, determined to prevent the final step in the treaty process—the exchange of ratifications in London. Jefferson begged him to pummel Hamilton's pro-treaty arguments, which the New Yorker had been flinging into newspapers since July. That fall, Madison produced a systematic, intensive, vehement, but utterly forgettable anti-treaty essay.[75]

The moment had passed, snatched by Hamilton, who started earlier and outpaced Madison in his volume and tenacity. Madison turned his single essay into a petition to the Virginia Assembly, requesting the body to pressure Washington not to exchange ratifications. Hamilton shot over thirty essays into public presses, praising the treaty and condemning its opponents. Madison dissertated on the treaty's "ostensible & fallacious reciprocity." Hamilton blistered the "perverse dispositions" and "hostile and malignant zeal" of the treaty's "embittered" opponents—partisans of France led by "fawning or turbulent demagogues."[76]

Even had Madison matched Hamilton's copious, venomous style, he had nothing to gain by it. He knew by then that attacks on the treaty were attacks on Washington, who approved it. As one of his allies cautioned, other anti-treaty writers "are too violent in their attacks on the P[resident]. Such licencious charges will injure rather than promote the Republican interest."[77]

Back in Congress in February 1796, Madison found some consolation in a treaty that Thomas Pinckney negotiated with Spain and sent to Philadelphia. The United States won access to the Mississippi and a right to deposit goods for export at New Orleans. It also secured a favorable boundary for the nation in the disputed regions of the Mississippi Valley. Madison couldn't help but contrast its "very satisfactory" provisions with the catastrophic Jay Treaty.[78]

That same month, Madison learned that US and British diplomats had exchanged ratifications of the Jay Treaty in London. Refusing to abandon hope, Madison conjured a sophisticated but dubious argument that the House must approve treaties that affect commerce, a realm constitutionally reserved for that chamber. Behind Madison's leadership, the House passed a non-binding resolution avowing its right to authorize treaty articles that impinged on its domain. Madison then insisted that the House apply its new self-assigned power to kill the treaty by refusing to fund it.[79]

Madison succeeded only in killing his rapport with Washington. The more he spoke, the more the contest appeared to be a personal battle of wills between America's most prominent Republican and the president. Federalists rallied behind the president, and Republicans buckled. In May, the Republican-controlled House approved funding. The treaty survived; Madison and Washington's friendship did not.[80]

The two Virginians remained cordial but not close. A year earlier, neither could have known that their joint family dinner would be perhaps the final intimate moment they shared. Madison attended a couple of state dinners at the executive mansion, but those were formal affairs with other political elites. He felt less animosity than Washington, and he chastised a bellicose South Carolinian who wanted him to impeach the president over the treaty. Besides the fact that the move would amount to political suicide, he still believed Washington merited the gratitude of his compatriots. For his part, Washington seethed that Madison and Jefferson "are now stronger, & foremost in the opposition to the Government." Like other Americans, the president began to brand political opponents as seditious usurpers.[81]

Defeated, Madison decided to retire. Weary, Washington did the same.[82]

Farewells

"Against the insidious wiles of foreign influence . . . the jealousy of a free people ought to be *constantly* awake," Washington implored his fellow Americans in his Farewell Address. History proved "that foreign influence is one of the most baneful foes of Republican Government." Most Americans today remember the exhortation as a timeless piece of non-partisan wisdom. Madison considered it a poorly masked attack on Republicans.[83]

Washington relied on Hamilton to prepare the final text of his address. To Madison, the message proved that Washington languished "in the snares of the British faction." Madison still preferred to believe that Federalist advisers misguided the honorable but hoodwinked president. In truth, Hamilton had tempered Washington's language. In his initial draft, the president condemned the House's effort to scuttle the treaty and subtly rebuked Madison for his accusations of presidential overreach. When Washington warned against foreign encroachments, he meant France. When he warned against party spirit, he meant Republicans. Hamilton helped him dress the Federalist message in non-partisan prose.[84]

Washington never considered himself a partisan. He insisted that "peace has been . . . the order of the day, with me." He longed for his compatriots to "advocate their own cause instead of that of any other Nation under the Sun; that is, instead of being Frenchmen, or Englishmen in Politics—they would be Americans—indignant at every attempt of either of these—or any other Power to establish an influence in our Councils, or that should presume to sow the Seeds of distrust, or disunion among ourselves." He had tried to steer the nation between France and Britain.[85]

In return, "factious papers"—meaning Republican newspapers—heaped "a torrent of abuse" on him, he complained. The French and "the opposition party" spread the falsehood that anybody who sought peace did so because they possessed an unhealthy attachment to Britain. However non-partisan Washington considered himself, Republicans received the brunt of his ire by the end of his public career.[86]

For years, Washington had split the difference between the competing factions as well as any president could have done. By the end of his presidency, though, even he couldn't avoid party conflict in a country where the parties increasingly demanded loyalty and eschewed compromise. In the polarized political climate, his anti-Republicanism made him a default Federalist.

Washington's conversion to Federalism highlighted a growing anti-French, pro-British sentiment in the United States. French émigrés felt the shift. One Federalist woman suspected erstwhile French aristocrats as spies for their former government. The political climate threatened to make "the sojourn of French people in the United States very disagreeable," one émigré confided to his diary.[87]

Charles-Maurice de Talleyrand, the refugee whom Fauchet had suspected of espionage, grew "bitter" against the United States and longed for France. He had outlasted Fauchet in America. By 1795, politics had moderated in France, and the new governing faction, the Thermidorians, sent Pierre-Auguste Adet to America. Fauchet departed the United States that summer, days after Randolph had resigned. Talleyrand remained in Philadelphia another year, when he received permission to return to France and keep his head.[88]

Befriended by Hamilton and other political elites, Talleyrand had enjoyed an intimate study of US politics during his stay. He conversed with Hamilton on the Jay Treaty. In fact, on an unguarded night of drinking, Hamilton divulged negative opinions about the treaty that he never would have admitted in public. Talleyrand authored an essay on the Fauchet-Randolph fiasco. He learned the strategic importance of Louisiana to North American geopolitics. And he concluded that France could treat America as a weak dependency.[89]

On June 13, Talleyrand departed Philadelphia, about a month after Madison fixed his decision to retire. The men had interacted little during their time in the city. They couldn't have guessed that over the next decade their lives would intersect more from a distance of 4,000 miles than they ever had when they lived blocks apart in the US capital. For the time, Talleyrand returned to his native country convinced that France needed to reestablish a North American empire to counter the British, a sentiment shared by French leaders.[90]

6

"Jefferson's Election as President"

Try by every possible means to bring about Jef[ferson]'s election as President.

—GEORGES-HENRI-VICTOR COLLOT

ON A FALL MORNING, PROBABLY in early October 1796, Georges-Henri-Victor Collot sighted a large dugout canoe gliding toward his wilderness camp along the Arkansas River in Spanish-held Louisiana. On a secret reconnaissance mission for the French government, the tall and rugged Collot had been expecting this arrival. But something was wrong. In the distance, he could see only two men in the boat. There should have been three.[1]

A couple of days earlier, Collot had sent his second in command, Joseph Warin, and two guides to reconnoiter the White River. Collot would lead his remaining few men up the Arkansas, and the two parties would reunite at a channel that connected the two waterways. Even taller than Collot but ten years his junior, Warin loaded his dugout canoe with supplies, and the groups separated before dawn.[2]

Twelve hours later, Warin and his two men reached the channel that would lead them back to the Arkansas River. The trio pitched camp for the night. One guide went hunting while the other collected wood. They would float the channel and rejoin Collot on the Arkansas the next day.[3]

Alone by the canoe, Warin spotted two Chickasaw men approaching. One carried a *casse-tête*—a deadly war club, usually made of sharpened stone, steel, or bone to resemble a tomahawk. The visitors asked to trade food for rum. After some haggling, Warin offered them each a cup. They demanded a second, but he refused. Tempers flared, and one Chickasaw man jumped into the dugout to seize a barrel of rum. Warin sprang for his

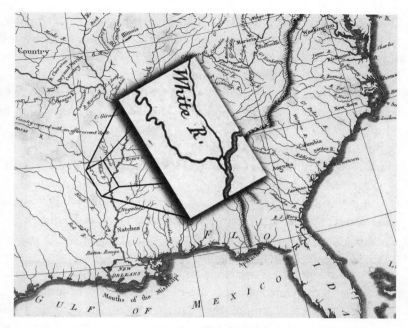

FIGURE 6.1 Detail of General Map of North America (Collot, *Voyage dans L'Amérique Septentrionale*, 1826). Drawn by Georges-Henri-Victor Collot, this map shows the area where the White and Arkansas Rivers flowed into the Mississippi. Collot represented the small channel that connected them, not far from their mouths. Courtesy David Rumsey Map Collection.

musket. The Chickasaw careened his casse-tête toward Warin's head. The Frenchman jerked back and caught a vicious blow to the chest. He slumped to the canoe floor.[4]

One guide saw the violence from a distance, snatched his musket, and fired. The ball tore through the Chickasaw assailant's arm, a fortunate first shot for the notoriously inaccurate firearm. His slow-loading weapon fired, the guide sat vulnerable to a counterattack by the second Chickasaw, who wielded his own gun. Instead, the Chickasaws fled, leaving Warin near death in the canoe.[5]

Two days later, Collot saw the two guides paddling toward his camp. Only as they came to shore did he discover Warin sprawled at the bottom of the vessel, fighting for breath and barely able to talk. One of the guides recounted the attack for Collot. He swore that the Chickasaws were the same two men whom Collot had seen periodically along his Mississippi journey, beginning 500 miles back in Illinois country.[6]

Questions disturbed Collot. Had the attackers tracked the Frenchmen hundreds of miles down the Mississippi? Did the Chickasaw pair mistake Warin for him? He and Warin shared a similar build and dress, after all. Collot considered the Chickasaws "the true tyrants of the river," a nod to the power they still wielded in the region. Did they want him dead? Or had somebody enlisted them to kill him—somebody who knew about his secret mission?[7]

Collot had traveled to the Mississippi Valley to gauge what kind of empire France could build in the West once it pried territory away from Spain and the United States. By then, Spain had reconsidered its alliance with Britain and was easing back to France's side. The previous year, to weaken Britain's attractiveness to westerners, Spanish diplomats finally granted Americans access to the Mississippi and agreed to evacuate US-claimed territory. With their ancient Spanish alliance rekindled, French rulers hoped to strong-arm their weaker partner into ceding Louisiana. They might then strip the United States of southwestern territory and resurrect the vast North American empire they had possessed just over thirty years earlier. Louisiana might not profit the French Empire much, but French rulers could better protect their lucrative dominions in the Caribbean if they possessed North American land. Since spring, Collot had traveled the Ohio and Mississippi rivers, mapping waterways and reconnoitering British, Spanish, and US strength in the western valleys.[8]

The French minister in Philadelphia, Pierre-Auguste Adet, had recruited Collot. Adet cast the mission as a harmless geographic exploration, a ruse he hoped would allow Collot to travel openly and without suspicion. Spanish and US officials early on suspected Collot's true purpose, and they planned to keep eyes on him. Whether or not a foreign government had recruited the Chickasaws to spy on the spy, Collot was right to suspect that anything was possible. He was just one operative in a land fraught with intrigue.[9]

Adet interpreted Washington's neutrality as a cover for an informal alliance with Britain, and to his mind, the Jay Treaty proved it. He applauded raucous crowds that torched Jay's effigy and pelted Hamilton with stones for defending the agreement. To him and his superiors, the treaty terminated France's alliance with the United States.[10]

Americans may have abandoned their partnership with France, but Adet would never let them "deprive us of the price of the sacrifices that we have made for them." As Adet saw it, France had freed the United States during the Revolutionary War, and in return he expected Americans to keep the British at bay in North America. Instead, the US government had sided with the enemy, and France would have to intervene. With Collot, Adet developed a two-pronged strategy. First, prepare the West to fall into French hands. Second, as Collot put it: "Try by every possible means to bring about Jef[ferson]'s election as President."[11]

Candidates

At Montpelier, Madison succumbed to defeatism about Jefferson's chances in the coming presidential election. "His enemies are as indefatigable as they are malignant," he glowered. The election would be close; everybody knew that. Jefferson could count on the South and West, but the Federalist frontrunner, Vice President John Adams, would almost certainly carry the entire North. Eighteenth-century voters expected candidates to deny presidential ambition and wait for their allies to advocate their candidacy. Federalists and Republicans had separated into two broad coalitions, but they had no formal party apparatus or nominating system. They made informal, non-binding agreements about whom they would advance. If a potential candidate truly wished to stay out of office, they asked their friends not to promote them. Madison didn't want to give Jefferson the chance to do that and so scrupulously avoided him. Republican leaders had settled on Jefferson as the man who could win them the presidency, but Madison knew that he preferred retirement. If word spread that Jefferson disavowed his own candidacy to his friends, it might torpedo Republican chances. The two Virginians didn't visit or write all summer and fall.[12]

The arrangement suited Jefferson, who didn't want the presidency but also didn't want to turn it down if elected. He would have preferred that Madison receive the party mantle, but strategists knew that Madison had operated in the trenches for too long. Federalists couldn't settle on John Jay or Alexander Hamilton for the same reason. Jefferson and Adams made good choices as respected men who hadn't been bloodied in the recent Jay Treaty feud.[13]

With their champions selected, both sides prepared to win the Electoral College—an even more haphazard system in the 1790s than its current form. Each state voted for its electors in its own way, and each elector voted for two men. The top choice won the office if he garnered over 50 percent of the Electoral College votes, and the runner-up received the vice presidency. If multiple candidates split the vote and nobody won more than 50 percent, the House of Representatives would decide among the top five vote getters. Rather than each representative casting a vote as they did in normal procedures, each state delegation cast a single vote for their state.

Madison and his fellow Framers had expected the House to settle far more presidential elections than it has. They had anticipated such a multitude of candidates that nobody could win a majority outright. With more electors, large states would enjoy more influence in the Electoral College and determine the top five choices. In the House, where each state had just one vote when it came to selecting the president, small states would wield more power in the final selection among those five. A nice compromise, the Framers thought.[14]

They failed to calculate a two-party system into their theory—two political behemoths contending for the majority vote. If party leaders wanted to avoid the volatility of a House election, they needed to cement their coalitions and compete for the Electoral College vote. Americans thought their constitution would repel a two-party system. It reinforced it.

Nobody knew quite how to maneuver their candidate to victory, for nobody had contested Washington's two elections. In 1796, Americans clashed over the office for the first time. That fall, political operatives around the country finagled the Electoral College like a chess match to ensure that their side won both the presidency and vice presidency. Madison had disliked the idea of allowing the House to decide elections—that is, until he feared Jefferson could not win a majority of electoral votes. He felt confident the House would vote for Jefferson if the Electoral College failed him. First, though, Republicans needed to keep Adams from winning a majority in the Electoral College.[15]

Everything hinged on Pennsylvania, Madison gauged. If Adams and Jefferson split the North and South, Pennsylvania would cast the deciding votes—a "swing state" in modern parlance. Republicans might take the presidency if they won Pennsylvania. And they might win Pennsylvania if Adet didn't ruin it for them first.[16]

The Election

Adet loved chemistry more than politics, but diplomacy paid better. Like other ministers sent to the unenviable American post, he possessed limited diplomatic credentials. Under the monarchy, he had traveled to Saint-Domingue—present-day Haiti—to help suppress a slave rebellion on the Caribbean island. The rebellion turned into a full-blown revolution that forced the French government to abolish slavery in the empire in 1794.

Adet resented the measure. He held some minor government positions and served in Geneva at the time of his appointment to Philadelphia.[17]

Adet came to the United States with even less diplomatic experience than Genet, but he seemed to have learned two important lessons from the former minister. First, Americans wouldn't tolerate a foreign agent who publicly flouted the president. Second, partisans could stomach foreign meddling if it remained clandestine and promoted their politics. Adet had arrived while Washington and the Senate were still keeping the Jay Treaty confidential. Rather than accost Washington, he purchased a copy of the treaty from a friendly senator, jotted a summary of its main points, and anonymously slipped the synopsis to a Republican printer. The contraband information gave the public its closest glimpse of the treaty to that point. It prompted Senator Mason to share the complete version with the press, which triggered the nationwide protests of 1795.[18]

By hiding his more egregious tactics, Adet bought some goodwill with Federalists. Hamilton considered him less objectionable than either Genet or Fauchet. Even as Adet opposed the treaty, he stayed out of trouble, co-ordinating with Republicans behind the scenes rather than in open enmity with Washington. "Adet seems to [have] conducted himself with great cir-cumspection throughout the crisis," Madison approved.[19]

Adet's stealth failed to sink the treaty. So long as Federalists controlled the presidency and Senate, France's influence would evaporate in America, he concluded. The answer? Get Republicans into office, especially Jefferson.[20]

Adet calculated that "men who are devoted to us" would vault Jefferson into office if France encouraged them. In September 1796, he traveled to Boston to take the pulse of Republicans there in the heart of Federalist ter-ritory. He found a dispirited lot, ready to "abandon the upcoming election to their adversaries." In his own (likely exaggerated) words, he "raised their downtrodden courage," "revived their hopes," and extracted promises that they would "act with energy to appoint Jefferson president and to discard John Adams." He concealed how he really felt, that in fact "they will have great difficulty countering" Federalists.[21]

If they hoped to succeed, some influential Republicans implored Adet, France would need to pressure New England merchants, who tended to support the Jay Treaty. If France squeezed them financially by capturing their ships bound for Britain, they might realize the need for pro-French policies and a France-friendly president. Somehow, Adet thought it wise to court Americans by informing them that France intended to attack their trade. In fairness, the strategy had worked for the British, who menaced Americans on land and sea until they secured the Jay Treaty. However, France lacked Britain's presence in North America, its might at sea, and its influence over US commerce. Undeterred, Adet forged ahead.[22]

One week before Pennsylvanians selected their vital presidential electors, Adet published a letter in a Republican newspaper in Philadelphia. Like everybody, he knew that Pennsylvania would decide the outcome. In modern media, the publication would be called an open letter, for he addressed it to recently named secretary of state Timothy Pickering, but he intended it for the public. He published it before Pickering even had a chance to show it to the president. He warned that France would seize US vessels that carried prohibited wartime goods to their enemy, nothing less than Britain already did. If the US government pressured Britain to cease the practice, France would reciprocate. Only fear spoke to Federalist merchants, Adet had noted elsewhere. Perhaps he could threaten them into Jefferson's column with lost trade.[23]

While presidential electors were still pondering and deliberating their final choices, Adet threw two more open letters into print. Americans had abrogated their treaty with France and allied with Great Britain, he declared. "Let your Government return to itself, and you will find in Frenchmen faithful friends and generous allies." The implication: Elect Thomas Jefferson and institute pro-French policies or risk war with France.[24]

When Pennsylvania's popular vote tipped slightly toward Jefferson, some disgruntled Federalists credited Adet's "strokes of diplomatic finesse." In such a close contest, Adet wouldn't have needed to sway many voters to swing the outcome. Whatever Adet's influence, Republicans carried the state. Pennsylvania's complex rules created a wide gap between the popular and electoral counts. Jefferson collected fourteen of the state's fifteen electoral votes.[25]

It wasn't enough. Federalists rallied against the tawdry "Arts," as Abigail Adams called them, practiced against her husband by a combination of "Jacobins," Virginians, and "foreign influence." Adet may have "thrown Some Electioneering Nutts among the Apes," but his gimmick will backfire, John Adams assured his family. One Federalist considered secession a better alternative "than to be under the government of a French agent." New England electors would "sooner be shot" than vote for Jefferson after Adet's intrusion, cried an Adams supporter. Another affirmed that even the opposition feared a national backlash. He was right.[26]

"Adêt's note ... is working all the evil with which it is pregnant," Madison desponded while election returns were still creeping in. Predictably, Federalists cast it as "an electioneering manoeuvre" (which it was) and accused Republicans of masterminding the scheme. If French authorities didn't stop gifting political ammunition to Federalists, gnarled Madison, they would reap a permanent rupture with the United States.[27]

"Mr. Adams will be President," a resigned Madison informed his father in late December. Adams had plucked two electoral votes from the South and one from Pennsylvania. He snatched the Electoral College majority by three votes. Republicans had squeezed Jefferson into second-place, making him vice president.[28]

In his inaugural address, Adams railed against "the spirit of sophistry, the spirit of party, the spirit of intrigue, the profligacy of corruption, and the pestilence of foreign influence, which is the angel of destruction to elective governments." The litany was a partisan accusation masquerading as a nonpartisan conviction. To Adams, each element interconnected with the others. And as far as he could see, Republicans had used all of them to try to nab the election.[29]

Adet had learned a lot from Genet, but not enough. He thought he had precisely timed and executed his intervention. Despite his precautions, he failed to mask his electioneering as diplomacy. Some partisans may have appreciated covert foreign scheming on their behalf, but Americans still repudiated open intervention. Enemies denounced it; friends disclaimed it.

The Conspiracy

While Adet promoted Jefferson's election in Philadelphia, Collot and Warin languished in New Orleans, oppressed by the syrupy air and "surrounded by bayonets." Suspicious of the French expedition, Spanish officials had arrested the pair on October 27, 1796, and stuck them in a fort guardhouse. Warin had been slowly dying since his assault weeks earlier. Confined at New Orleans, he finally succumbed, and Collot buried his companion. The Spanish governor, Baron de Carondelet, found in Warin's effects a detailed diary with drawings of Spanish forts and instructions that exposed Collot as a spy.[30]

Collot lied that his mission was a coordinated effort between France and Spain "to demolish the United States" now that the nations had renewed their alliance. He had scribbled copious records about how to defend the region against Britain. He and the governor even discussed the possible dangers of Spain's recent decision to allow Americans access to the Mississippi. As "sworn enemies" of France, Federalists spread alarming rumors about him to foil his mission, he told his captor.[31]

He also possessed valuable intelligence about a vast conspiracy of British agents, their Native allies, and American crypto-loyalists, who planned to attack Spanish forts. Secret sources had divulged the plot to him weeks earlier. On paper, the adversaries were formidable: A thousand Tennesseans; the Creek and Cherokee nations; 1,500 British royalists from Louisiana's Natchez district matched by the same number of British regulars; 700 Canadians; 2,000 Natives of the Northwestern Confederacy, led by the tenacious Joseph Brant.[32]

The conspiracy hadn't actually advanced that far, but a few ringleaders relished its potential, especially Tennessee Senator William Blount. A Republican, Blount acted for money, not ideology. Desperately indebted, he eyed Britain as the savior of his tottering private empire in the West. Rumors swirled that France might reacquire Louisiana from Spain, something the British could not tolerate. Westerners such as Blount feared that France would reclose the Mississippi to them, gutting their commerce. Also, the French Republic had abolished slavery in 1794. If slavery disappeared in Louisiana, Americans who owned real estate there might see their investments plummet. Even worse, those enslaved in America might be inspired to start slaughtering their masters—to use slaveholders' imagery—as they had in Saint-Domingue. Blount and Britain shared an interest in keeping France off the continent.[33]

Blount started to discuss the details with the new British minister in Philadelphia, Robert Liston. Captivated but cautious, Liston dabbled at the edges of the conspiracy. He vouched for the feasibility of the plan and sent one American to London to make the case to his superiors.[34]

Collot knew few of the specifics of the conspiracy, and he got others wrong, but he shared at least some of his intelligence with the Spanish governor. Impressed with Collot's information, the governor paroled the Frenchman, coerced a promise that he would not survey New Orleans, and shipped him back to Philadelphia.[35]

In Philadelphia by early 1797, Collot briefed Adet and Spain's minister to the United States, Marquis de Casa Yrujo. Collot informed them of the Blount conspiracy and other possible British aggressions, and he recommended strategies to prevail. The spy preened that he had done nothing less than save France and Spain from British conquest in Louisiana.[36]

Collot's information arrived at a perfect time for Yrujo. Realigned with the powerful French, Spanish rulers had begun to second-guess their decision to open the lower Mississippi. They expected Yrujo to stall the conferral. Spain couldn't yield the Mississippi because Britain was planning an invasion, Yrujo explained to Secretary of State Pickering. Pickering demanded evidence. Yrujo had none other than the word of a French spy in charge of a supposedly purely scientific expedition. Then he caught a break.[37]

That spring, one of Blount's co-conspirators got drunk and began to prattle about secret correspondence he carried—a letter that outed Blount and Liston. The conspirator ignored Blount's instructions to burn the incriminating correspondence after reading it. Authorities seized the letter, which had landed in Pickering's hands by early summer. The man who ousted Edmund Randolph now stared at evidence that the British minister was conspiring with Americans to attack Spanish dominions.[38]

The letter damned Blount, but it left room for Liston to claim that Americans had tried to involve him in the plot but that he disapproved. Liston asked Pickering to keep the matter secret, but Adams wouldn't squander the chance to trounce the Republican Blount. At least that's how Liston interpreted events. Besides, the president couldn't risk the appearance of covering up the evidence. He informed the Senate of the plot, and the body promptly expelled Blount. Anxious to exonerate Britain, Pickering accepted Liston's explanations.[39]

Enraged by Pickering's selective naiveté, Republicans lumped the secretary into the plot. Pickering "has been behaving in a very devilish manner," Yrujo's American wife, Sally McKean, wrote Dolley Madison. Republican printer Benjamin Bache decried Pickering's "collusive practices with the British minister" and the double standard that Federalists applied to Liston and Genet. After a string of problematic French agents, Republicans relished a British target.[40]

Yrujo helped. He waged a newspaper war with Pickering, a fight more audacious than even Genet had dared launch. In fact, Yrujo's wife told Dolley Madison, "Some of the Timothy [Pickering] gang says he is worse than Gennett, Fauchett, or Adett." Yrujo charged British wrongdoing and cast the secretary as a British partisan. The ploy coaxed Federalists to accuse Yrujo of exploiting America's free press to appeal to the people over the government. "The government is the creature of the people," retorted Yrujo—in the press, no less. America was no European monarchy. Foreign ministers had every right to bypass government officials and address the true sovereigns of the nation.[41]

Like Genet, Yrujo demanded that Americans probe the most fundamental question about their democracy: Who held sovereignty, the people, or the rulers? Most would have agreed it belonged to the people, but no one was quite sure what that meant. Unable to distinguish the government from the people, Americans turned foreign policy disagreements into accusations of subversion and corruption—a war between liberty and tyranny, order and anarchy.

The Bribe

In early March 1797, while Yrujo pondered Collot's recent intelligence, President Adams entered Madison's Philadelphia house several blocks south on Fifth Street. He found Jefferson alone in a room the Virginian occupied at the Madisons'. Happy to find Jefferson unaccompanied, Adams stepped into the room and closed the door. He needed to speak with the new vice president in private.[42]

Adams worried about France, he confided to Jefferson. However much he distrusted the French, he wanted to preserve peace. Although a Federalist, Adams considered himself above party squabbles. Like many presidents since, he commenced his administration with grand visions of national unity. He wanted to send a bipartisan (as it would be called today) delegation to France to smooth recent differences. Adams knew Madison was retiring from Congress at the end of the session, and he wanted to include the Virginian in the mission. Madison would accompany Federalist Charles Cotesworth Pinckney and moderate Elbridge Gerry in Paris. Adams wondered whether Jefferson could ask his friend to join. Jefferson agreed but knew Madison would never accept.[43]

Madison had made a habit of declining diplomatic positions in the 1790s. Washington had wanted him to succeed Jefferson as secretary of state, but Madison wouldn't take the position. In May 1794, the president asked him to serve as minister to France. Madison refused. He had rebuffed Washington's offers, and he had, if possible, even less desire to accept them from Adams. Madison rejected the position and slipped into retirement just as the Blount conspiracy broke.[44]

Cozied with his family at Montpelier, Madison absorbed the rhetoric about the conspiracy. He wrote little about politics that summer, but talk of the scandal whirled around him. His congressman friend John Dawson rejoiced to him that Republicans could expose "the criminality of the British minister, & the partiality of our polite secretary," Pickering. House Republicans planned to drag Liston and Pickering down with Blount. Even as the chamber impeached the disgraced senator and the Senate held impeachment hearings, Madison preferred the term "Liston's Plot," refocusing attention on the British.[45]

By early 1798, Madison feared that Federalists careened the United States toward war with France and Spain, which would bury "the misdemeanours of Liston and his partizans." Just as they had threatened, the French had begun to seize US ships that carried British goods, mostly to prevent Americans from aiding France's rebellious colony of Saint-Domingue. However, Madison preferred to blame the Jay Treaty, and the accord did give France cover to plunder its former allies. Spanish and US troops assembled in the Mississippi Valley. The Jay Treaty avoided war with Britain but might start one with France, brooded Madison.[46]

Adams hoped that the mission to France would cool temperatures. In September 1797, three Americans had traveled there to negotiate with the new French minister of foreign relations, Charles-Maurice de Talleyrand, the former exile who had lived among them in Philadelphia. To accompany Gerry and Pinckney in place of Madison, the president tapped John Marshall, a Virginian like Madison but no Republican. Marshall gave the three-man commission an odd dynamic of two southern Federalists and an uncommitted New Englander who leaned Republican. By spring 1798, Madison could congratulate himself for dodging a spot on one of the most inglorious diplomatic errands in US history.[47]

It all started one evening the previous October at a shabby hôtel particulier on the Rue de Grenelle in Paris. Bare floors, stained furniture, cracked mirrors, and decrepit chimneys greeted Jean Conrad Hottinguer, a Swiss banker and Talleyrand's fixer. The hôtel's residents—Pinckney, Marshall, and Gerry—had finished dinner, and Marshall and Gerry still lingered on the main floor, which Pinckney occupied with his family, when Hottinguer arrived. The Swiss man and Pinckney retreated into a private room.[48]

If the Americans were serious about a new treaty, Hottinguer told Pinckney, Talleyrand had conditions. The three men needed to give a good explanation or apology for a speech by President Adams that French rulers thought insulted France's honor. Also, the United States must pay French debts to private Americans, cover the cost of American losses to French privateers, and give France a large loan. Finally, Talleyrand required a 50,000 pound *douceur*—a sweetener, a bribe—before he would even talk to the Americans. Talleyrand wanted to avoid war, but he felt little pressure to negotiate. If he could just buy enough time, France might turn the tide of war against Britain and strengthen his hand. In the meantime, he could continue to blame French aggression on the Jay Treaty.[49]

The ultimatum kept the envoys up all night. Would they submit to a personal bribe and outrageous terms just to commence negotiations? The entire demand smacked of the corruption Americans equated with Europe and Federalists associated especially with France. They decided to buy time and acquire more information from Hottinguer.[50]

Over the next couple weeks, the three Americans quibbled with Hottinguer and other informal representatives of Talleyrand while the two Federalists argued with Gerry about their options. If the envoys didn't comply, the Frenchmen warned, French agents could convince Republicans that Federalists had scuttled negotiations to invite war. Time ticked away with no progress. By December, Talleyrand sensed that his weakest prey was Gerry, the one commissioner still willing to consider his demands. He had isolated Gerry by early spring 1798, threatening to send home the Federalists and allow the New Englander to remain and negotiate. Heated arguments rebounded off the stale walls of the Rue de Grenelle residence as the envoys barked accusations of duplicity and incompetence at each other. The mission unraveled, and they returned with nothing.[51]

That spring, an infuriated Adams learned about the failed enterprise and revealed Talleyrand's antics to Congress. To protect the envoys, he redacted the names of Talleyrand's contacts, replacing them with W, X, Y, and Z, giving the episode its famous moniker, the XYZ Affair. The day he laid the dispatches before Congress, he hinted at possible war. Within a week, Congress voted to publicize the relevant documents.[52]

Madison's fellow Republicans mounted a feeble campaign to blame Federalists for the failure. The rogue Talleyrand had befriended Hamilton during his Philadelphia days, some of them reminded Americans. They insisted that Federalists Marshall and Pinckney had crippled negotiations and that Adams preferred war with France. Madison seethed that the president released the documents "more to inflame than to inform the public mind." By publishing them, Adams committed "libel" against the French government with insufficient evidence. The attack ignored the fact that the president had been even quicker to release the Blount papers, which implicated the British. Madison berated Adams for the curious sin of transparency.[53]

First Lady Abigail Adams delighted to hear "the Common people" say that "we should all have been sold to the French" were Jefferson president and had Madison and Aaron Burr accompanied the mission. The proof was that the publicized dispatches quoted an exasperated Hottinguer, who grumbled that France and the United States would have come to terms had Madison and Burr been there. The French wanted nothing more, Adams claimed, than to foster division and unseat her husband. The French orchestrated the entire fiasco to make him look bad, she bristled.[54]

Actually, Talleyrand cared little about Republicans or Federalists. He hardly mentioned parties in a report on US relations to his superiors. He needed time and wanted money, things he would have extorted from negotiators of either party. Even so, Talleyrand's indiscriminate graft benefited Federalists, and Madison knew it. Then as now in US politics, perception was more important than reality.[55]

Madison might have expected Talleyrand's "depravity," as he wrote Jefferson, but not his "unparalleled stupidity." He had not known the Frenchman well during his stay in America, but Talleyrand had enjoyed a reputation for intelligence. How then, wondered Madison, could he have thought it sensible to solicit a bribe from the American diplomats? The man had lived in America, where he knew nothing remained secret in politics. He should have known that his move would play right into the hands of Federalists anxious to discredit France and embarrass its Republican sympathizers.[56]

With Republicans on their heels, Federalists led the nation to an undeclared, limited war in the summer of 1798, now called the Quasi-War. Adams dispatched US Navy vessels to protect American ships, and private vessels armed to repel French attacks. He appointed Washington as commander-in-chief and Hamilton as inspector general—fueling fears that he prosecuted a partisan war. Congress voted to abrogate the treaty with France. The alliance was dead.[57]

The Pole

On March 18, 1798—the day before Adams revealed the XYZ dispatches to Congress—Collot visited a Polish soldier and a hero of the American Revolution, Tadeusz Kościuszko, in a tiny Philadelphia boarding room. Six or seven others joined him. The room barely fit Kościuszko's bed and armchair, so the guests took turns entering two or three at a time.[58]

The group included France's consul general, Philippe Joseph Létombe. Federalists despised him ("a rash sour uninformed man," scorned one). Adams would strip him of his exequatur within months. Letombe's friend Jacques Flamand came along. Also in attendance was the French émigré Médéric-Louis-Élie Moreau de Saint-Méry. By then, Moreau was "the only person in Philadelphia" who still dared wear a French cockade, a symbol of the French Revolution. The remainder included others in Philadelphia's French circles, such as, very likely, Constantin-François de Chasseboeuf, Count de Volney, the French government's unofficial eyes and ears.[59]

It is possible that these Frenchmen gathered merely to salute the famed revolutionary. Maybe they had other motives. In any case, Kościuszko's company attracted the suspicion of Federalists. Federalist printer John Fenno noted that the Pole's most frequent visitors were Republicans who defamed the US government and applauded France, including Vice President Jefferson. By the time Kościuszko met with Collot and his French associates that March, he had acquired a reputation as an ally of Republicans and France.[60]

Born among the minor nobility, Kościuszko started his military career during the American Revolution, joining Washington's forces as a volunteer after his lover's father harried him out of Poland in 1775. American officers respected his engineering abilities, and he played critical roles at the crucial Battle of Saratoga and in southern campaigns. A decade after the war, he returned to Poland and incited an ill-fated uprising against Russian dominance of his homeland. At the final battle, in October 1794, Russian troops destroyed the rebels. They sliced Kościuszko's head with a sword and stabbed him in the back and hip with pikes. Some reports had it that cannon shot blew off part of his thigh. As his men scattered and his enemies surrounded him, he stuck the barrel of his pistol in his mouth and pulled the trigger. The gun misfired, and he slipped into merciful unconsciousness for two days. When he awoke, he was a Russian prisoner. His beloved Poland disappeared, partitioned among Russia and Eastern European powers. The Russian emperor exiled him in 1797.[61]

Kościuszko arrived to applause in Philadelphia that August, his head and leg still bandaged. He spent almost all his time in his little room, traveling only with difficulty. Though at fifty-two he still looked young, he struggled for every movement and needed to be carried even short distances. US dignitaries streamed to his cramped quarters to pay him homage. Mild-mannered and amiable, he spoke with his guests in decent English. They greeted him as he lay in the bed or sat in his chair, unable to move due to the pain of his wounds.[62]

When the guests were gone, however, he would spring up and walk un-aided around the small room. Not even his closest friends knew. While Kościuszko had suffered in prison and traveled to America, his scattered rebel comrades had allied with France against their common enemy, Russia. Kościuszko preferred his adversaries mistake him for a cripple convalescing in America while he someday stole back into Eastern Europe to reignite his rebellion. He dared not lower his guard even on the other side of the Atlantic. Americans spoke and wrote too much—"unwitting spies," he called them.[63]

At least one of his French visitors of March 18, Létombe, knew that the Polish soldier had come to America "only to mislead his enemies." Kościuszko had tracked down the French diplomat the day after he arrived in Philadelphia. He wanted Létombe's help to get to France as soon as pos-sible. His pleas apparently paid off. Around March, he received an invita-tion from French executive officers—the Directory—to travel to France and consult about the Polish rebel alliance.[64]

The timing was flawless for Jefferson, Kośiuszko's friend and a fre-quent visitor. The vice president saw the disastrous XYZ dispatches the day after Kościuszko's March meeting with Létombe and the others. He needed somebody in Paris to convince France to negotiate before war rav-aged his nation and ruined his party. With his affinity for Republicans and connections at the Directory, Kościuszko was ideal.[65]

Kościuszko knew that Adams had not authorized the mission, but he needed Jefferson as much as Jefferson needed him. He would be journeying in secret across the ocean, vulnerable to warships and imprisonment if captured. He needed passports, which at the time functioned more like certificates of safe transport against potential captors at sea. He required a cover, and Jefferson could help.[66]

Jefferson submitted requests to the British, Spanish, Portuguese, and French ministers, asking them for passports for "Thomas Kanberg," the alias he assigned Kościuszko. The fictional Kanberg was supposedly a personal friend of Jefferson's from German regions, going to Europe on private business and completely uninterested in politics, Jefferson lied. The ministers granted their passports without questions.[67]

Jefferson created a secret code to communicate with Kościuszko, arranged the Pole's finances, and devised his covert departure. Until the last minute, Kościuszko refused even to reveal his plan to Julian Ursyn Niemcewicz, a fellow Polish exile who had stuck with him since his time in Russia. After agonizing delays, Kościuszko prepared to leave on May 4, 1798. That night, he instructed Niemcewicz to tell others that he had gone to Virginia's mineral baths for his health. Niemcewicz would journey that direction three days later under the pretext of joining him. At 4 A. M. on May 5, Jefferson fetched Kościuszko in a coach, and the pair clattered through the darkness to a small port at Newcastle, where a ship waited to carry the Pole to France.[68]

Jefferson was a bad liar, so he was relieved a month later when nobody had interrogated him about Kościuszko. "Your departure is not yet known or even suspected," he wrote his friend, using their code. He assured Niemcewicz, "As far as I have heard there is not the smallest suspicion here" that Kuściuszko had sailed for France. Niemcewicz, though, was "overwhelmed with questions" and hated playing "the role of liar." Gossip flooded his ears about his friend: Some bought the story about the Virginia mineral springs while others thought the two Poles had quarreled and separated. A wild rumor floated that Jefferson had kidnapped Kościuszko and was hiding him at Monticello.[69]

Then the ruse began to crumble. Somebody had seen the general at Newcastle—walking. Chatter spread that the general's lameness was all a show. Still unaware that Kościuszko had faked his disability, Niemcewicz denounced the blasphemous attack on the poor invalid. As word crept out, some Republicans rejoiced that "the *Polish hero*" would soon fight the British alongside the French.[70]

By September, the press confirmed that Kościuszko was in France. Safely arrived, he dropped his alias and false disability and embraced the adoration of French republicans. One reported (based on an interview with Kościuszko) that while in America the Polish soldier had refused to see Washington because the former president had championed the Jay Treaty. He mostly ignored Adams. Instead, the interviewer claimed, "he has lived constantly with Jefferson, that worthy American, who has not forgotten that the English were the tyrants of his country, and that the French were its liberators."[71]

Federalists suspected "the foulest duplicity" and "blackest ingratitude," as Federalist John Fenno wrote, once they learned that Jefferson facilitated Kościuszko's departure. "Jefferson's connection with [Kościuszko] was as singular, as I fear, it will prove disgraceful," Fenno chided. While Americans praised Kościuszko, he collaborated with their French enemies, assisted "incendiaries," and encouraged treason.[72]

Jefferson's ally, George Logan, fueled Federalist suspicions with his clumsy exit to France a month after Kościuszko's. Logan harbored irascible hatred for Britain, a "madness," Niemcewicz called it. He and Kościuszko had visited Logan at the American's Germantown home that April—a rare venture beyond the confines of the room for Kościuszko. Logan could hardly get through a conversation without blasting "a volley of invectives against England" and its aristocratic supporters in the United States.[73]

"We must have revolution," Logan told his guests (as Niemcewicz remembered it). "That alone can save us." He yearned to travel to France.[74]

"Your brain is sick," Niemcewicz wanted to tell him. The "madman" Logan would trade the "tranquility" and "abundance" of America for the gore of revolution. "But go to France," Niemcewicz thought, "go to Europe, see what goes on there and you will return cured of your madness."[75]

Logan sailed to France on June 12. Like Kościuszko, he intended to negotiate unofficially in Paris with Jefferson's tacit backing. He tried but failed to leave secretly from Newcastle. Federalists lambasted his mission within a week of his departure, suspecting that he planned to lead a French invasion of the United States and introduce "the bayonet and guillotine." American blood would flow in the gutters. Federalists' "extravagance produced a real panic among the citizens," Jefferson lamented to Madison.[76]

After they learned about Kościuszko's secret exodus, Federalists coupled it with Logan's journey. They spread false reports that the two men departed on the same vessel as Volney—next to Collot the most suspected Frenchman in the country—who left for France about the same time as Logan. Logan and Kościuszko had visited often in Philadelphia, they noted. There existed "an evident connection" between the American and the Polish "mutilated rebel," *the hired agent of France.*" Fenno exposed those who he believed "secretly meditate, if not the overthrow, the disgrace of the American government," including Jefferson, Kościuszko, Volney, and Logan.[77]

Working on parallel tracks rather than as a team, Kościuszko and Logan joined an informal cohort of Americans and French who advocated peace. With thousands of Polish rebel disciples, Kościuszko had the most to offer France—men willing to fight in Europe. As early as August, the Directory appeared amenable to formal treaty negotiations, mostly because by then France couldn't afford another enemy. Still, observers in Paris credited Kościuszko and his allies for the positive turn.[78]

Logan returned in September 1798 to the wrath of congressional and cabinet Federalists who wanted war, not renewed talks. For months, they had pressured Adams for action. The president hesitated, unconvinced that France would actually invade and distrustful of his fellow Federalist Hamilton, who had effective command of the new army. Congressional Federalists accused Logan of treason and introduced evidence that they said proved he had colluded with Talleyrand to help Republicans seal the next presidential election. Republicans dismantled the evidence, proving that it had nothing to do with Logan. "Why . . . do the French think they have a party in the United States?" asked Swiss-born Republican Albert Gallatin. "Because the Federalists are constantly saying so on the floor of the House and in the press." Federalist conspiracies fed foreign intrusions, not Republican disloyalty, argued Gallatin.[79]

Federalists introduced legislation that prohibited private individuals from intervening in disputes between the US government and foreign powers. Republicans decried the bill as a political weapon. Despite their protests, the act, still known as the Logan Act, passed in early 1799. Jefferson's shadow channels aggravated Republicans' greatest vulnerability—accusations of secret collusion with France.[80]

As Madison observed events over the summer and fall of 1798 from retirement, he frowned that the entire US government had spiraled into a "tragicomedy." He watched resignedly as Federalists trampled his vision for the republic. Adams knew better than to suppose that Madison would stay silent for long, though. He would emerge stronger than ever, the president predicted, for "political Plants grow in the shade."[81]

Shade

As congressional Federalists armed the nation against France, they trained their legislative arsenal on Collot. Rumors had sprinkled the nation about Collot's mission from its beginning, due, in part, to Collot's inability to stay quiet about it. He had discussed his plans, including the confidential portions, with Americans who he believed sympathetic to his cause. After his return to Philadelphia, Collot mingled with prominent Republicans, including Jefferson, toasting France and death to British rulers.[82]

Federalists glimpsed an alliance between Republicans and French agents at least as sinister as the one from the days of Genet. Wolcott insisted that the Swiss-born Gallatin had fed Collot intelligence about the West. Under the banner of "FRENCH INFLUENCE, STILL TRIUMPHANT," one Federalist publication insisted that Blount worked with the French rather than the British—"a match for the defection of Randolph." Nobody could deny it, he claimed, knowing that Collot had tried to convince Blount's fellow Tennesseans to secede from the union and vote for Jefferson.[83]

Few outperformed New York assemblyman William Wilcocks, who pelted Republicans with charges of corruption in marvelous array. Even if most Republicans had "come to their senses" after the XYZ Affair, a few "unnatural monsters" and "dark assassins" remained devoted to France. Like a "silent, concealed worm," the traitors advanced "under the privilege and concealment of the press." Cheered by Republican printers such as Thomas Greenleaf and Benjamin Bache, they would destroy "the tree of liberty" and support France "in plundering and murdering (for in this it must terminate) their own fellow citizens!" Wilcocks yearned for the day when "treason and sedition must hide their heads, no longer supported by the vehicle of newspapers."[84]

In April 1798, Jefferson informed Madison that Federalists had introduced legislation to expel Collot and one other suspected spy, "But it will not stop there," he warned. That summer, true to his prediction, Congress passed the Alien Act—"a monster that must for ever disgrace its parents," Madison fumed. The act empowered the president to expel foreigners he deemed dangerous. It followed an onerous new naturalization law targeted at Irish and French immigrants, strong voting blocs for Republicans. Weeks later, Congress approved the Sedition Act, a law to punish those who published "scandalous and malicious writing . . . against the government of the United States" or the president. However egregious the violation of the First Amendment may appear today, Federalists conjured creative legal justifications for the act.[85]

With varying degrees of sincerity, Federalists insisted that the laws repelled foreign interference and corrupt collusion. The republic would perish unless Americans "reject foreign Influence and resist foreign Hostility," Adams warned. In a world where men safeguarded fragile senses of personal honor, attacks on statesmen might doom the nation, portended his Federalist companions. They panicked that without the Sedition Act, the Republican press would lure Americans away from their own leaders and into French and Spanish ranks.[86]

Madison saw nothing but a Federalist power grab. Of all the powers the federal government enjoyed, "the management of foreign relations appears to be the most susceptible of abuse." Leaders can conceal or disclose information at a whim. "Perhaps it is a universal truth that the loss of liberty at home is to be charged to provisions against danger real or pretended from abroad." He echoed his own speech before the Constitutional Convention over a decade earlier: "The means of defence against foreign danger, have been always the instruments of tyranny at home."[87]

Friends pleaded with Madison to return to politics. "He should not be permitted to remain at home under any circumstances," Virginia Senator Henry Tazewell exhorted Jefferson. Federalists and the British angled for the coming elections, and "no Stone will be left unturned" to win, Tazewell cautioned.[88]

Not ready to return to Philadelphia but unwilling to remain silent, Madison sprang to prove that Federalists were the real culprits of foreign collusion and that their recent legislation jeopardized the republic. Had he shared Hamilton's impetuous intensity, he may have started churning out anti-Federalist material that summer. Even had he wanted to move quicker, house renovations and other personal business sucked time away from politics. Instead, he and Jefferson crafted a careful offensive over the fall.[89]

The two Virginians each anonymously prepared a set of resolutions— Jefferson's to be adopted by Kentucky's legislature and Madison's by Virginia's. Fearful that Federalists would spy on their mail, they conferred sporadically in person. However conjoint their strategy, they each produced their own series, independent from one another.[90]

Jefferson's came first. He declared that if the federal government overstepped its bounds, as it did with the Alien and Sedition Acts, state governments could deem the laws "void and of no force." Jefferson considered the proposal moderate, but Madison saw that taken to its logical extreme, the idea would return the United States to a loose assembly of states rather than a nation. At the Constitutional Convention, Madison had advocated a federal veto of state laws. Jefferson was proposing the exact inverse. Madison never believed his constitutional philosophy had changed during the 1790s. Until his death, he maintained that Hamilton had abandoned the true vision of the Constitution. He may have altered some of his

PLATE 1 James Madison, 1783, by Charles Willson Peale. During the Confederation Congress, Madison labored to devise a government that could protect liberty and repel foreign intrusion. Courtesy Library of Congress.

PLATE 2 Thayendanegea (Joseph Brant), 1776, by George Romney. An Iroquois leader, Brant tried to maintain a shaky confederacy of Native nations and the British Empire while Madison tried to ensure the survival of the union of states. Courtesy National Gallery of Canada.

PLATE 3 Diego de Gardoqui, ca. 1785. As a Spanish diplomat in the United States, Gardoqui encouraged Westerners to form a client state of Spain. Courtesy Cano de Gardoqui Family.

PLATE 4 John Brown, 1792, by John Trumbull. Brown conversed with Gardoqui about the possiblity of western independence from the United States. Courtesy Yale University Art Gallery.

PLATE 5 Alexander Hamilton, 1792, by John Trumbull. Hamilton and Madison cooperated to publish the *Federalist* essays before becoming bitter political opponents early in George Washington's first term. Courtesy Crystal Brides Museum and Metropolitan Museum of Art.

PLATE 6 Thomas Jefferson, 1791, by Charles Willson Peale or Sarah Miriam Peale. During the 1790s, Jefferson and Madison established an enduring political partnership in opposition to the Federalists. Courtesy US Department of State.

PLATE 7 George Washington, 1795, by Gilbert Stuart. Washington consulted Madison as a close adviser before the Jay Treaty controversy damaged their partnership. Courtesy Metropolitan Museum of Art.

PLATE 8 George Beckwith, 1808/16. Described as a "petty spy," Beckwith cooperated clandestinely with Alexander Hamilton to strengthen ties between the United States and Britain. Courtesy Trustees of the British Museum.

PLATE 9 Edmond-Charles Genet, 1793, by Gilles Louis Chrétien. The French diplomat aggravated US relations with France by meddling in US politics to win support for France's war against Britain. Courtesy Metropolitan Museum of Art.

PLATE 10 George Hammond, 1793, by John Trumbull. As a British diplomat in the United States, Hammond exposed Secretary of State Edmund Randolph to allegations of corruption, which helped ensure ratification of the controversial Jay Treaty. Courtesy Yale University Art Gallery.

PLATE 11 Edmund Randolph, by Casimir Gregory Stapko. Randolph's career as secretary of state was ruined due to allegations that he colluded with France to promote insurrection. Courtesy Department of State.

PLATE 12 Oliver Wolcott Jr., ca. 1790, by John Trumbull. Wolcott replaced Alexander Hamilton as Washington's treasury secretary and was instrumental in promoting allegations of corruption against Edmund Randolph. Courtesy Yale University Art Gallery.

PLATE 13 Timothy Pickering, 1792/93, by Charles Willson Peale. A virulent Federalist, Pickering helped end the career of Edmund Randolph and was involved in discussions about New England secession. Courtesy National Park Service.

PLATE 14 Pierre-Auguste Adet. During his time as a French diplomat in the United States, Adet tried to encourage support for Jefferson's candidacy for president and supported the reconnaissance mission of George-Henri-Victor Collot. Courtesy New York Public Library.

PLATE 15 John Adams, 1793, by John Trumbull. John Adams presided over the controversial XYZ Affair and Quasi-War with France but was also instrumental in a rapprochement with the European power. Courtesy National Portrait Gallery.

PLATE 16 Charles-Maurice de Talleyrand, 1808, by Baron François Gérard. Madison first met the Frenchman Talleyrand in the United States, but they interacted more frequently from across the Atlantic after they both became the top diplomats for their respective nations. Courtesy Metropolitan Museum of Art.

PLATE 17 Tadeusz Kościuszko, 1797, by Benjamin West. The Polish revolutionary Kościuszko feigned a disability, posing as a convalescing cripple during his travels through Britain (where West painted this) and his stay in the United States before Jefferson helped him sneak back into Europe to help restore harmony between France and the United States. Courtesy Allen Memorial Art Museum.

PLATE 18 Aaron Burr, 1802, by John Vanderlyn. After his term as vice president and (in)famous duel with Hamilton, Burr's movements in the West invited suspicion from Federalists and Republicans as many feared that he might be an agent of foreign powers. Courtesy New York Historical Society.

PLATE 19 The Emperor Napoleon in His Study at the Tuileries, 1812, by Jacques-Louis David. Madison and Jefferson faced frequent accusations of acting as puppets for the French emperor. Courtesy National Portrait Gallery.

PLATE 20 Secretary of State James Madison, 1804, by Gilbert Stuart. As secretary of state, Madison tried to steer US foreign policy through the treacherous waters of European warfare. Courtesy Colonial Williamsburg Foundation.

PLATE 21 Marquis de Casa Yrujo, 1804, by Gilbert Stuart. The Spanish diplomat Yrujo mounted a press campaign to challenge the Jefferson administration's policies in the West, exposing unanswered questions of the nature of sovereignty in the United States. Wikimedia Commons.

PLATE 22 Louis-Marie Turreau, 1806, from detail of Tableaux historiques des Campagnes des Français sous la Revolution et l'Empire. As the French envoy in the United States, Turreau tried to mediate between Madison and the Marquis de Casa Yrujo after Yrujo's controversial diplomatic tactics infuriated Madison. Courtesy Trustees of the British Museum.

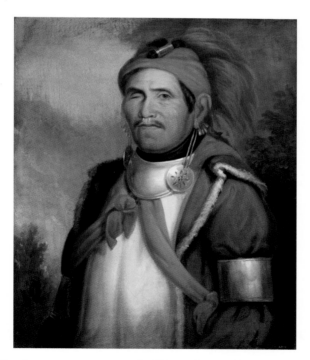

PLATE 23 Tenskwatawa, 1830–1833, by Henry Inman. To resist US expansion, the Shawnee prophet tried to revive the British-Native confederacy that had dwindled since the 1790s. Courtesy National Portrait Gallery.

PLATE 24 Tecumseh, ca. 1808. The brother of Tenskwatawa, Tecumseh was a pivotal diplomat for the confederation Tenskwatawa was trying to build. Courtesy Toronto Public Library.

PLATE 25 Paul-Émile Soubiran from Puech, "Un Aventurier Gascon," 116–117. Soubiran teamed with former British spy John Henry to con the Madison administration into purchasing documents President Madison supposed would prove a conspiracy between Federalists and Britain.

beliefs in response to what he considered Hamilton's overreach, but not enough to condone Jefferson's resolutions. He had fought for a stronger national government to protect against foreign incursion and secure individual rights. Now, he believed that Federalists exaggerated the first point to trounce the second, but he couldn't agree with Jefferson's language.[91]

Used to restraining some of Jefferson's overzealousness, Madison moderated his constitutional arguments in his Virginia version. He pledged "a warm attachment to the Union of the States." He insisted that states retained the vague right to "interpose" if the federal government exceeded its authority, but he mentioned no right to nullify or ignore federal laws.[92]

However accommodating to the union, Madison lambasted the acts as "palpable and alarming infractions of the constitution." The Alien Act made the chief executive judge and jury and granted him powers not defined in the Constitution. Even worse, the Sedition Act flagrantly violated the Constitution. Virginia would sink to "criminal degeneracy" by standing silent while the federal government annihilated one of the most essential rights guaranteed by the charter. If the government could deny Americans freedom of the press, they could strip them of their freedom of conscience—the most sacrosanct of all rights to Madison's mind.[93]

Icy air clawed at Montpelier in January 1799, but the slow winter months finally freed Madison to prepare an assault on Federalists and produce his most effective writing since the 1780s. As before, when the stakes seemed immense, he retreated into books and writing. Not content to excoriate the laws that made Federalists politically vulnerable, Madison wanted to reverse the narrative, to prove that Federalists prostrated the nation before foreign power.[94]

Madison beat Hamilton to the newspapers as his opponent was overseeing military preparations. He unleashed his tirade with an essay unsubtly titled "Foreign Influence" in the Republican *Aurora*. Federalists had charged that the French were turning the people against the government, but they got it backward, Madison argued. British influence had turned the government against the people, a far more dangerous prospect.[95]

Madison finally found the right balance between logic and rhetoric. "Great Britain, above all other nations, ought to be dreaded and watched," he warned. The empire had stronger motives and greater means than France to subdue US sovereignty. Since the 1780s, Britain had desired the decay of America until anarchy reigned over "misery and horror," disgracing republicanism and bolstering monarchy. Britain hated the French and American republics, but especially the American because of its success. It tried to counter that success by turning Americans against France, pitting the people against each other, provoking America's government against its people, and making puppets of British sympathizers. The ultimate goal: shape America into a monarchy. British intrusion was more insidious than French, he warned, because Britons shared language and manners with Americans. British diplomats could meddle in US newspapers without detection. British subjects posed as American citizens to canvass during elections. They advocated the Jay Treaty and war with France.[96]

Madison condemned Federalists for subjecting the free press "to a foreign taint." The Sedition Act might give the impression that Republican newspapers were flooding the nation with criticism of Adams. Actually, that was a result of the Sedition Act more than a cause, a self-inflicted wound the president and Federalists invited with their censorship. Before 1798, Federalist presses drowned out their Republican counterparts. Madison saw a poisonous link between Britain and Federalist newspapers. Printers needed merchants and traders to purchase advertisements in their newspapers, and merchants and traders depended on British commerce. As a result, Federalist editors prostrated before advertisers and their foreign commercial overlords.[97]

Even more egregious to Madison, the British government enjoyed an unofficial mouthpiece in William Cobbett's *Porcupine's Gazette*. Madison fulminated against the "foreign newspaper, conducted by a British subject, avowing his allegiance to his King, glorying in his foreign attachments and monarchical principles, and vilifying with the most unparalleled audacity, the revolution which obtained our Independence, and the republican principles which are the basis of our constitution." He lamented that the free press had become "tainted with partiality," unfazed by the irony that he was publishing his essay in a Republican newspaper. Partisans excel in accusing others of partisanship.[98]

A month later, he shot another essay into the *Aurora*. By then, Federalists and Republicans debated a non-intercourse bill with France. Federalists warned Americans that the French executive Directory was growing increasingly despotic. Rather than dispute the charges, Madison reminded readers that Federalists were trying the same things in the United States. He repeated for the public what he had told Jefferson nearly a year earlier: Governments might forge chains for citizens out of weapons meant to repel foreign danger. The people must guard their liberty by retaining their sovereignty over the government. Their political duty didn't end after they elected their representatives. "In no case ought the eyes of the people to be shut on the conduct of those entrusted with power." By electing representatives, the people did not abandon their authority over their representatives or their right to censure them, as the Sedition Act implied.[99]

Federalists countered that Jefferson wanted to sacrifice the US Constitution and independence on the French altar. Anti-Jefferson newspapers reprinted copies of a 1796 letter he wrote to an Italian friend after the Jay Treaty fight. Jefferson had condemned the "harlot England," who sheared the hair of once-mighty "Samsons" (such as Washington, Jefferson hinted) and lured them to the "Anglican, monarchical, and aristocratical party." The letter revealed Jefferson's "subserviency" to France, insisted one Federalist. Another called the letter proof that Jefferson's election would be "more ruinous and destructive to the liberties and happiness of America, than almost any other event that could occur."[100]

Strategy

"Collot is a pernicious and malicious intriguer," spat John Adams in August 1799. By all rights, he should expel the Frenchman under the Alien Act, he thought. He couldn't, though; the spy might know too much. If Collot stayed in the United States, he would sow "corrupt divisions" among the people. If deported to France, he might return with a French army and valuable knowledge of western military preparations. Timothy Pickering asked the British diplomat Liston to detain him in Philadelphia, since he had first arrived there as a paroled prisoner of war following his surrender at Guadeloupe, the Caribbean island he once commanded. Collot stayed in the city for the next year, under British custody and US surveillance.[101]

Adams never expelled Collot or anybody else, but the Alien and Sedition Acts were no idle threats. The Alien Act intimidated enough of its targets to leave the United States before the president had to enforce it. The administration persecuted some of its leading critics under the Sedition Act. Over a dozen Republican printers landed in jail. Others that walked free still faced trials and harassment. Fears of foreign meddling and foreign collusion gripped Federalists until they struck at the heart of civil liberty and political opposition.[102]

Between 1796 and 1800, Americans developed minority and majority strategies to implicate their rivals in foreign collusion. Minority partisans accused the majority of wielding corrupt, foreign-supported power, while

THE PROVIDENTIAL DETECTION

FIGURE 6.2 The Providential Detection, ca. 1797. This image depicts the American Union, overseen by Providence, preventing Jefferson from sacrificing the Constitution and independence of the United States to the altar of "Gallic [French] Despotism." The altar is surrounded by bundles of money depicting France's corrupt means of acquiring wealth and power. Jefferson's other hand frames his controversial letter to his Italian friend, Philip Mazzei. The devil leers from the corner. Courtesy Thomas Jefferson's Monticello.

the majority alleged that their opponents cooperated with foreign agents to seize illegitimate power. Not all partisans defaulted to such extremes, but those poles defined the political divide.

By 1800, Americans muddled ideological disagreements, partisan posturing, and foreign intrusion until they became indistinguishable. They believed they competed for the nation's soul—a soul that would reflect the image of either France or Britain. Those stakes made electoral victory vital, exacerbating partisanship. Foreign manipulation became simultaneously a real national security threat and a political cudgel. It stoked Americans' most legitimate fears and fueled their most outlandish accusations, perpetuating a cycle of partisan distrust.

Collot had failed to secure Jefferson's election as president, at least in the way he expected. He did contribute, though, to the political paranoia that prompted Federalists to adopt the Alien and Sedition Acts, which exposed them to Republican outrage. To Republicans, the acts confirmed their narrative that Federalists wanted to surrender the country to a client monarchy of Great Britain. Madison fine-tuned that narrative and prepared to launch Jefferson into a rematch with Adams.

7

"Embryo of a Tornado"

This little event, of France possessing herself of Louisiana . . . is the embryo of a tornado.
                    —THOMAS JEFFERSON, April 25, 1802

MADISON BORE A "PASSION FOR CHESS," as one of his friends described it. He and Jefferson could play for hours at a time. Sometimes they enjoyed the challenge of wits with Madison's sister-in-law, Anna Payne. Jefferson hated to lose. During his time in France, he refused to play at a Parisian chess club after he endured a swift defeat his first time playing there. He considered Anna Payne an equal or superior talent (a "Chess heroine," he called her), but even Payne could scrape just two wins and a draw from twenty-one games against chess master Lucy Knox. Jefferson was a fine player, but he was out of his depth against true chess genius.[1]

If Jefferson's chess game suffered the same flaws as his political savvy, the opposition could sometimes goad him into impulsive moves. Federalists had criticized the disloyal tone of the Virginia and Kentucky Resolutions, especially Jefferson's hint that states should nullify laws they deemed un-constitutional. Some states lent the resolutions tepid support; others ignored or denounced them. Hamilton thought they evinced a "conspiracy to overturn the government" and to encourage French hostilities against the United States. Hamilton didn't explain why the resolutions would in-vite French aggression, and it would have required impressive logical gym-nastics to blame a Federalist-supported war on Republicans. Unrepentant, Jefferson insisted that Virginia and Kentucky should threaten to secede if the Federal government usurped their rights.[2]

Madison disagreed. However their chess skills matched, Madison usually kept a more level head when it came to politics. At Monticello in early September 1799, he convinced Jefferson to drop the inflammatory ultimatum. The threat would only reenergize Federalists and syphon focus from their violations of civil liberties. Republicans needed to win power and reform the federal government, not disband it. With James Monroe, they decided to vindicate the Virginia and Kentucky Resolutions through pen. The agreement spawned Madison's most penetrating political theory in a decade.[3]

Desperate to win elections, Republicans coaxed Madison out of the "sin" of retirement, as Jefferson called it. Madison allowed his allies to advance him as a candidate for the Virginia House of Delegates. In early December 1799, he rented a dingy room at a tavern in Richmond, ready to begin the upcoming assembly session as the delegate from Orange County. He waited for Dolley to arrive later during the session, apprehensive about how she would feel about the living quarters.[4]

Alone in Virginia's capital, Madison prepared an assault on Federalists and their Alien and Sedition Acts. Crippled for a week by dysentery, he picked up his pen again even before he recovered, literally writing feverishly. He was composing a vindication of the Virginia Resolutions, and he wanted the assembly to adopt it.[5]

In his *Report of 1800*, endorsed by the assembly that January, Madison addressed each of the Virginia Resolutions, defending their logic and shepherding them into a coherent philosophy on limited government. Madison maintained his devotion to civil liberty, but he reversed his theory about how to safeguard it. In the late 1780s, he had believed a strong federal government would protect individual rights from domineering state governments. By 1800, he saw the federal government as more prone to trample liberty. States retained the right to judge the constitutionality of laws, he insisted. Otherwise, the government would consolidate into a single national sovereign and "pave the way to monarchy." To prevent that travesty, the federal government needed to prove that it exercised constitutional power—something it could not do with the Alien and Sedition Acts.[6]

Madison weaved through technical legal theories while condemning the British system of government and every pretension to it in the United States. The British government had failed to protect liberty because it trusted in a supposedly infallible king and omnipotent legislature. Yet Federalists wanted to replicate that system, as proven by the Alien and Sedition Acts.[7] Madison reminded his readers that in the United States, "the people, not the government, possess the absolute sovereignty." As sovereigns, the people retained the right to criticize and scrutinize their representatives. Madison noted that the Sedition Act would expire in March 1801, on the books just long enough to shield current power holders—Federalists—from criticism through the upcoming presidential election.[8]

To restore sovereignty to the people, Republicans needed the presidency. Madison imagined that once in power, his party would serve as stewards of the government, not sovereigns of the nation. From his Richmond tavern room, he began to arrange the chess pieces to secure victory.

Chess

Three votes. As if Madison needed a reminder, South Carolinian Charles Pinckney stressed that Jefferson had lost the 1796 election by three electoral votes. Even worse, to Pinckney, two southern electors had voted for Adams and denied Jefferson the presidency, including one in Virginia. Southern states needed to alter their election laws to favor Republicans, Pinckney implored Madison.[9]

Madison obliged. As a member of the Virginia Assembly in 1799 and 1800, he helped draft state legislation to benefit Republicans in the coming election. Virginians would choose electors on a state-wide basis, replacing the district-by-district process that had led to the election of an Adams supporter in an anti-Jefferson part of the state in 1796. With the change, the state's Republican majority could swing all twenty-one electors to Jefferson. Madison contended that the law would enhance Virginia's influence in the coming presidential contest by forcing the state to speak with one voice in the Electoral College. Northern Federalists decried it as partisan manipulation. The Assembly squeezed the law through by five votes.[10]

Virginia Republicans listed Madison on their slate of electors certain to vote for Jefferson. Pro-Jefferson luminaries organized a central committee to coordinate with subcommittees to promote their man—an early version of a get out the vote drive. Madison chaired the Orange County subcommittee. Convinced that only party organization could salvage the America he envisioned, he shelved his earlier discomfort with the idea of a governing majority faction. Americans had begun to edge past amorphous partisan coalitions and into the early stages of party organization. With others, Madison manipulated the gears of government to operate for his side.[11]

Southerners had a now-defunct clause of the Constitution in their corner. The notorious Three-Fifths Clause counted three-fifths of the enslaved people in a state toward that state's representation in Congress. (Madison had inspired the compromise with a similar, though defeated, proposal under the Articles of Confederation.) The provision increased the South's representatives, which meant additional electoral votes, since those votes equaled a state's total number of senators and representatives.[12]

Many southerners believed that even with the clause, the North's free voting population would overpower the South and monopolize federal power. The opposite occurred as southerners spread slavery west and populated Kentucky and Tennessee, giving the South a decided advantage in the Electoral College. Despite some popular notions, the Framers did not create the Electoral College to protect southern slavery, and Madison never endorsed it for that reason. Combined with the Three-Fifths Clause, though, the system did benefit slave states.[13]

Southern Republicans needed the middle states, and nothing united the two sections more than the Alien and Sedition Acts, as well as high taxes born of Adams's Quasi-War with France. Americans flooded Congress with written protests, which cascaded from Kentucky and Virginia to Pennsylvania, New York, and New Jersey. However prominent Madison and Jefferson's Virginia and Kentucky Resolutions, they formed just a part of a barrage of remonstrances against the government's overreach. Madison's *Report of 1800* disappointed in its circulation outside of Virginia, but paradoxically that boded well for Republicans. His voice was one of many attacking the administration.[14]

As Republicans chorused against the Adams administration, Federalists split between Adams's moderate wing and the more virulent disciples of Hamilton. Most of the cabinet agreed with Hamilton—still the effective head of US forces—that the United States should escalate hostilities with France. Despite sharing some political opinions, Adams and Hamilton hated each other. The president suspected that Hamilton might manipulate the army to install himself at the head of "a regal government." Instead, Hamilton planned to finesse electoral politics to topple Adams, thwart Jefferson, and promote a Federalist candidate more to his liking.[15]

Adams and his supporters conceded that indeed there existed an "English Party" in the United States—Hamilton's faction. Hamilton supplied his opponents ammunition in 1798 when he tried to coordinate with the British to attack New Orleans if the Quasi-War accelerated. Hamilton denied Britain an alliance, but he did want its navy to support the planned, though ultimately aborted, US invasion. The distinction didn't shield him from criticism even from Federalists. "That there is a party in this country who wish to strive to bring about an alliance with Great Britain, I presume you will not deny," an Adams backer wrote a Hamilton ally in 1800. "If this is a 'British Party,' there certainly is one." The Adams bloc replicated Republican attacks to down their interparty rivals.[16]

Madison and Jefferson knew that New York was vital to translate Federalist fractures into Republican victory, which meant cooperating with Aaron Burr. By the mid-1790s, the New Yorker Burr had amassed a reputation as an effective political operative or unscrupulous opportunist, depending on one's relationship to him.[17]

The party had backed Burr for vice president in 1796. Before 1804, electors cast two votes each, and the second-place candidate won the vice presidency. Technically, then, Burr ran for president but with the under-standing that he would finish second to Jefferson. Burr schemed to use the peculiar system to leap past Jefferson into the presidential slot. Some Virginian electors refused to cast their second vote for him and relegated him to fourth place in the contest, a slight he didn't forgive. Since then, New York Republicans distrusted their Virginian allies.[18]

Republicans splintered even further in New York, torn among factions loyal to a few elite power players, including Burr. After Federalists made impressive gains in 1799 state elections, Burr began to retool political ma-chinery to unite New York Republicans in 1800. Behind his efforts, they snatched control of the state legislature that year.[19]

Since New York's assembly chose the state's presidential electors, Burr essentially guaranteed the presidency to Jefferson. "The republic is safe," an ally wrote Madison after New York swung Republican. The party owed Burr, and Republicans invited him back to run for vice president. Burr wouldn't accept unless Virginians guaranteed him their votes. He refused to finish an embarrassing fourth place again. Madison assured him he could count on Virginians' loyalty this time.[20]

They proved a little too loyal. Republican electors planned to cast one vote for Jefferson and another for Burr. Only one or two electors would cast their second vote for somebody other than Burr, ensuring that Jefferson finished first and Burr a close second. Madison had considered withholding his vote from Burr but didn't want to violate his word. He should have run with his first instinct. If he had, Jefferson would have won, Burr would have finished second, and all would have worked according to plan for Republicans. Instead, he turned his political chess match into one of the stormiest elections in US history.[21]

Storms

A snowstorm drubbed Washington, the new federal district, on February 11, 1801. Still under construction, the town struck visitors as a swampy backwater or idyllic landscape, but hardly a national capital. The snow would have made the few roads—precarious in the best conditions—almost unmanageable.[22]

Despite the weather, the Senate and House gathered in the north wing of the capitol, the only portion of the building near completion. House members filed down staircases from their temporary, nondescript meeting room on the principal floor to the Senate's ground floor chamber. They entered a spacious hall nearly forty feet high. A tall arcade hugged the politicians' desks and red leather chairs into a semicircle on the lower portion. Atop the arcade was a second story gallery, where stately ionic columns stretched to the ceiling.[23]

Jefferson stood at the front of the chamber, ready to execute one of his few official duties as vice president: count the certified electoral votes. He opened New Hampshire's certificate, counted the votes, and announced the tally to the assembly. He repeated the process fifteen more times for each state. A few men seated at a table in front of him recorded the votes, double-checked the certificates, and handed the totals to Jefferson.[24]

He announced the result. Seventy-three electoral votes for Jefferson. Seventy-three for Burr. Not a single Republican elector had deviated from the New Yorker. The two Republicans tied ahead of Adams and Thomas Pinckney, who was Hamilton's man. Jefferson reminded the body that according to the Constitution, the tie swung the decision to the House of Representatives. Each state delegation would cast a single vote for Jefferson or Burr, giving the victory to the man who won a majority (nine) of the states.[25]

The tie surprised nobody but vexed everybody. Since December, political insiders had forecast a likely draw between Jefferson and Burr. Even so, once Jefferson announced the outcome, they were wading into uncharted waters. What if the states split evenly in their votes for Jefferson and Burr? What if they failed to decide by March 4, when the new president was to be inaugurated? Would Adams remain president? Would the Federalist president pro tempore of the Senate become president? Would there be a president? Would there be a government?[26]

The storm outside the capitol reflected the moment inside. For months Americans had compared the anticipated chaos to tempests. Republican political organizer John Beckley called it a "tempestuous moment of party violence and collision." Adams mourned, "Clouds black and gloomy hang over this country threatening a fierce tempest, arising merely from party conflicts." Winds tossed the United States "in the tempestuous sea of liberty," he lamented, with only ports of "political convulsion" in sight. Jefferson predicted that "storms of a new character" would maul the country that winter.[27]

Republicans suspected that Federalists would use the maelstrom to steal the election, and some supposed that they would recruit foreign governments to do it. "Unfriendly foreign ministers should be observed," Tench Coxe warned Jefferson, for Federalists would hazard everything for the election. For over a year, Coxe and his fellow Republican strategists had warned the public that Adams led "an English Monarchical Party," devoted to Britain and aristocracy. "A secret connexion or league subsists between the British government and ours," and British ministers controlled US officials "as if . . . we were colonies once more!"[28]

Federalists warned of Republican insurrection if the House failed to vote for Jefferson. One predicted that Republicans would "Septemberize the nation," evoking bloody images of the French Revolution's September 1792 massacres.[29]

Republicans hardly calmed such fears. Jefferson thought armed resistance a "certainty" if House Federalists denied the clear intent of the electors to make him president. One Republican armed a handful of men and kept a night watch outside the capitol so Federalists could not sneak in and vote without his party. Virginia congressman John Dawson apparently participated: "*We* are resolv'd never to yield. . . . I have not closed my eyes for 36 hours," he updated Madison. One observer prayed, "Heaven grant that we may not become a Prey to foreign Enemies, nor given up to intestine Broils, & that ever dreaded scourge a civil War."[30]

Most Federalists conceded that either Jefferson or Burr would be president, and they debated which one would most likely betray the United States to France. One contended that "Burr is not enthusiastically devoted . . . to the French nation," unlike Jefferson. If the House elected Burr, the United States could repel "the *foreign incendiaries*, who . . . have called

Hell to their assistance, in order to make this government the devoted victim to their malignant passions."[31]

Hamilton disagreed. Jefferson may have a dangerous infatuation with France, he reasoned, but Burr would "listen to no monitor but his ambition." A bankrupt charlatan, Burr would sell his allegiance to foreign governments. "Let the Fœderalists vote for Jefferson," Hamilton implored. An amused Jefferson informed Madison that Hamilton and his league "have been zealous partisans for us."[32]

Jefferson's allies expected Burr to announce that he would decline the presidency and clear the way for Jefferson. Burr refused, claiming that a withdrawal would insult his honor. He would neither pursue nor forswear the presidency. Historians have debated Burr's motives, but the most recent evidence suggests that he did angle to take the top spot. Burr denied the charges, but Madison always suspected they were true.[33]

Another blizzard pummeled the region while the House deadlocked. Gouverneur Morris captured the symbolism in a one-line diary entry for February 13: "Still cold and another Snow Storm—No President yet chosen." By then the House had balloted twenty-nine times without a victor. The representatives played their political chess "Game" for days, Abigail Adams scoffed, but "the Castles can not be stormed nor the Kings taken, tho they have met with *check & mates*."[34]

After thirty-five ballots over five days, a few Federalists who had backed Burr abstained and threw Jefferson the states he needed to win. Jefferson prepared to govern in a new era of Republican control. "The storm through which we have passed has been tremendous indeed," he wrote a friend, but the American ship had weathered it. His administration would "put her on her republican tack, & she will now shew by the beauty of her motion the skill of her builders."[35]

Madison shifted from minority opposition leader to executive official when Jefferson nominated him as secretary of state. Finally in the majority, Republicans suspected that Federalists would consort with foreign powers to retake illegitimate power. On the eve of the inauguration, Monroe warned Jefferson that Federalists were "desperate" and "will intrigue with foreign powers & therefore ought to be watched."[36]

The Inauguration

Just before noon on March 4, 1801, Jefferson left his Washington boardinghouse where he had lived since November. The house sat just south of the capitol, perched atop a shrub-covered hill, called Capitol Hill. It overlooked a broad plain laced with a creek and dotted by trees and buildings as it stretched to the Potomac River. Jefferson strolled about 200 paces to the capitol with an entourage of House members. A rifle company saluted him at the capitol door, and he stepped into the Senate chamber, where, weeks earlier, he had announced the indecisive election results.[37]

A crowd of over a thousand people crammed into the Senate hall as Jefferson moved to the front. The president-elect disliked public speaking, preferring more intimate climates of political persuasion. Now he faced undoubtedly the largest throng he had addressed in his life, swarming the chamber around him and amassed in the gallery above. He spoke so low that only a fraction of the audience could hear.[38]

Near the end of the short speech, Jefferson promised to pursue "honest friendship with all nations, entangling alliances with none." Without rehashing past accusations, he subtly assured his audience that he would neither play the dupe of France nor needlessly provoke Britain.[39]

The time seemed ripe to dispense with the French–British debate. A young, incorrigibly ambitious French usurper named Napoleon Bonaparte had leaped to the head of French civic councils in 1799. Born to impoverished nobility on France's recently acquired island of Corsica, he had risen through the revolutionary military ranks with a mix of impressive and disastrous military campaigns. Decisive, bordering on brazen, Napoleon advanced his reputation for leadership even as his success in battle seesawed. In 1799, he laid a coup against the French revolutionary government and emerged as First Consul of France, a dictator in all but name. He melded his autocratic style with revolutionary ideals to become the latest version of the enlightened despot, a ruler who uses dictatorial power to ensure an orderly society with equality before the law.[40]

With Napoleon's rise to power, France no longer made an obvious proxy for Federalist and Republican disagreements. As one Federalist put it, his party "rejoiced" at the coup that they believed restored some order to France. At the very least, it seemed to prove them right all along about the ungovernable chaos of the French Revolution. Jefferson described Napoleon as "a cold-blooded, calculating unprincipled Usurper, without a virtue, no statesman, knowing nothing of commerce, political economy or civil government, and supplying ignorance by bold presumption."[41]

Napoleon intended to amass as much goodwill with neutral nations as possible and in 1799 had agreed to receive US envoys in good faith to negotiate peace. In a judicious evaluation underappreciated in history, Adams saw that his limited war with France had neither a clear objective nor any obvious end point. Bucking his party hardliners (and ultimately dooming his reelection), he had sent three Federalist negotiators to France over the summer of 1800 to conclude hostilities.[42]

Atoning for the XYZ fiasco, Napoleon welcomed Adams's new team in grand style. He even sponsored a solemn ceremony in memory of George Washington, who had died in December 1799. The negotiators worked into the fall of 1800 and signed an agreement on October 3, ending the Quasi-War. The ratification debate stirred some partisan accusations of foreign partialities, but the treaty (called the Convention of 1800) garnered bipartisan support. The Senate ratified it, aside from one article, a month before Jefferson's inauguration.[43]

With the change in presidency that March, it fell to Jefferson to complete the exchange of ratifications. For all the divisiveness of the recent campaign, Adams and Jefferson would share a legacy of peace with France in a way few could have predicted a year earlier. Perhaps Americans could move past the foreign discord that had divided them for more than a decade.[44]

Jefferson avoided any suggestion of foreign collusion in his inaugural address, any hint of Federalist or British corruption. "We are all republicans: we are all federalists," he exhorted. Both parties shared a blessed land and noble principles, sheltered from "the exterminating havoc" of Europe's wars.[45]

Weeks later, a different treaty threatened to bring that "exterminating havoc" to America's borders and to reignite phobias of foreign conniving and partisan corruption.

The Territory

Located about thirty miles south of Madrid, the royal palace of Aranjuez reposed on the banks of the Tagus River, the main pavilion flanked by two others, each with a large dome and cupola, framing a courtyard. It overlooked a magnificent parterre. Just beyond the garden lounged the stately palace of Spain's most important minister, Manuel Godoy, titled none-too-modestly Prince of Peace.[46]

On March 21, 1801, Lucien Bonaparte, Napoleon's younger brother, headed to the palace to negotiate a settlement between the governments of Spain and France. Bonaparte and Godoy had squabbled for hours the day before and exchanged testy notes that morning. At four o'clock that afternoon, they finalized a secret arrangement devised months earlier: Spain would transfer possession of its Louisiana Territory to France. The massive region stretched from New Orleans north to Canada and west to the Rocky Mountains.[47]

Spain had controlled the territory since France had relinquished it in 1763, at the end of the Seven Years' War, and now Napoleon wanted it back. Alone, Louisiana promised little to Napoleon, but coupled with Saint-Domingue it could resurrect France's once-sprawling North American empire. Napoleon's plan depended on subduing revolutionaries on the Caribbean island and restoring France's control over it. Until 1791, Saint-Domingue had hosted one of the harshest slave regimes in the world, which had produced fabulous wealth for the enslavers and for the empire. That year, a slave rebellion had turned into revolution that by 1794 had compelled France to abolish slavery and introduce a new social order on the island. Under the leadership of a slave-turned-general named Toussaint Louverture, they had repelled a British invasion.[48]

By 1800, Louverture claimed to govern Saint-Domingue on behalf of France, but he tended to disregard Napoleon's authority. Adams and his Federalists had cultivated economic ties with Louverture and tried to entice him to declare independence. Napoleon prepared to reconquer Saint-Domingue, arrest Louverture, re-enslave the island's black population, reinvigorate its production, and cut Americans from the French-Caribbean economy.[49]

Napoleon wanted Louisiana to extend France's renewed strength from the Caribbean to Canada. Since the American Revolution, French leaders had hoped the United States would check British power on the continent. Instead, they had signed a treaty with Britain, strong-armed France's Spanish allies into ceding western land, gained access to the Mississippi, abrogated their agreements with France, nabbed part of rebellious Saint-Domingue's trade, nudged it toward independence, and battled French warships. Americans made very poor pawns. With Louisiana, Napoleon devised a play for direct power in North America.

Spanish rulers agreed that their French allies could better fortify Louisiana and create a stronger buffer between the United States and Spain's dominions in Mexico. French and Spanish negotiators had reached a preliminary agreement on October 1, 1800, hours after French and American diplomats signed an end to the Quasi-War. Napoleon kept the deal a secret for fear that Britain or the United States would invade Louisiana before France could acquire it. Adams might have rethought

the peace had he known. Spain made a troublesome but hardly formi-
dable neighbor. France could inflict real damage on US sovereignty.
One former French official had recently admitted that France coveted
Louisiana, "which would have given us so great an influence over the
United States."[50]

By the time Lucien Bonaparte and Godoy met at Aranjuez, rumors
about the transfer echoed around Europe. David Humphreys, the US minister in Spain, noted a lot of official bustle between Madrid and Aranjuez
in mid-March. On March 23, he met with Lucien, who told Humphreys
that France had just granted the kingdom of Etruria to a member of Spain's
royal family. The information was true, and Humphreys sensed its real
significance: Spain must have given something in exchange. The intelligence "affords an additional reason for believing the cession of Louisiana
to France," he wrote in a coded message to Madison, the new secretary of
state.[51]

The Secretary

Madison missed Jefferson's inauguration. While Congress wrestled over
the election in February, he had tended to his sick father at Montpelier.
Just as James Madison Sr. seemed about to revive, his health plunged, and
"very gently the flame of life went out" on February 27, Madison wrote
Jefferson. As executor of his father's complicated will, Madison remained
at Montpelier through April. He arrived at Washington on May 1 and
swore the oath of his office the next day.[52]

As chief diplomat, Madison wielded national executive power for the
first time in his career. No longer in the minority, he oversaw US foreign
policy, and he soon learned the difficulty of juggling America's interests
amid the miasma of European politics. He had little practical experience
to prepare him as secretary of state, but he had pondered foreign affairs for
nearly two decades.

The new position would require more than diplomatic theory, though.
Madison would need to cultivate personal connections quickly with
people he knew little. The skill was his weakness but Dolley's strength, and
he relied on her combination of political savvy and social grace to nurture those relationships. Not that James was socially illiterate. Margaret
Bayard Smith reported on a dinner party with him and Jefferson that
May, describing both men as possessing "easy and familiar" manners. But

Madison was surrounded by those closest to him on that occasion. Dolley excelled at mixing the social and political.[53]

The Madisons lived and worked in unsettled conditions that month. They resided with Jefferson in the executive mansion (not yet called the White House), where Dolley acted as a sort of surrogate First Lady for the widower president. Just west stood a new executive office building that housed the State Department, cluttered with records and furniture as laborers relocated it from a temporary home down the street. Madison's department shared the building's thirty-six rooms with the War Department, Navy Department, General Post Office, and city post office—a measure of the still-infant state of US bureaucracy. A small cadre of State Department clerks occupied the rooms allotted to Madison's personnel. Madison inhabited an unimpressive office, about seventeen by twenty feet, with plastered and whitewashed walls lined with bookcases.[54]

The unremarkable building suited the image of the Jefferson administration, which prepared to govern with republican simplicity. Jefferson broke precedent when he wore no ceremonial sword to his inauguration. Madison had already acquired a reputation for wearing suits of all black. Washington and Adams had each tried to temper expectations of executive grandeur with republican modesty, but never to Jefferson and Madison's satisfaction. "Never were there a plainer set of men," Margaret Bayard Smith observed of the president and secretary after her May dinner with them. However exaggerated her description of two elite Virginians, it captured the tone Jefferson wanted to set for his new administration.[55]

Jefferson and Madison planned to infuse their foreign policy with those same ideals of republican simplicity. Unlike European monarchies, the United States needed no large army or heavy-handed state apparatus to achieve its international goals, they theorized. A republic could depend on the public spirit of a free (white) citizenry to defend it. It would invite freer commerce with foreign nations to nourish prosperity. That prosperity would afford it leverage in diplomacy. The government's smallness was its strength. During his inaugural address, Jefferson had trumpeted, "I believe this . . . the strongest government on earth." It would endure because the people held a personal stake in its success, he and Madison believed.[56]

Louisiana tested their optimism. As news crept in about the transfer to France, Jefferson saw "the embryo of a tornado" on the horizon.[57]

Neighbors

In late May 1801, Madison received a letter from Hamilton. By then a private New York lawyer again, Hamilton forwarded intelligence from a correspondent in Paris: Spain had ceded Louisiana to France. The New Yorker must have scribbled with haughty vindication. Two years earlier, he had proposed an invasion of New Orleans to prevent just such a scenario. During the recent presidential campaign, his own party had denounced him as a British partisan for his plan. Now France would master the region, exactly as he warned. Madison already knew about the transfer, of course. And he blamed Hamilton for it, at least in part.[58]

Madison assumed that Napoleon wanted to counter Americans who might scheme with Britain to conquer the region, Hamilton among them. Spanish rulers likely heard rumors of Hamilton's plan to take New Orleans with British help, Madison supposed. French officials definitely knew of Blount's conspiracy. With some Americans so dangerously devoted to Britain, France would of course seek a stronger position on the continent. Madison instinctively viewed the issue through his anti-British, anti-Federalist lens.[59]

Madison ranked the three major European empires according to their desirability as neighbors. He preferred the status quo, with weak Spain in control of Louisiana, sharing the Mississippi with the United States. The more powerful French might cause trouble, but they could prove friendly and improve commerce in the region. Predisposed to think the best of France, Madison hoped that it would adopt a policy "conciliatory to the minds of the Western people" if it possessed the territory. Any nation would be better than Britain.[60]

With Jefferson, Madison feared that Louisiana would cause quarrels between France and the United States, propelling Americans into an unwanted alliance with Britain. He could imagine few worse geopolitical nightmares. As Jefferson put it to a Frenchman whom he used as a sort of shadow diplomat, "It is in truth our friendship for France which renders us so uneasy at seeing her take a position which must bring us into collision." The administration needed to dissuade Napoleon from acquiring the land or persuade him to implement friendly policies once he obtained it.[61]

On July 11, 1801, Madison received Napoleon's new minister, Louis-André Pichon in his State Department office. Most of the conversation focused on Saint-Domingue. Madison wore an inscrutable face in his diplomatic talks—an "austere impartiality," Pichon called it. Pichon was stepping toward the door as the meeting concluded, when Madison startled his guest with the subject that really weighed on his mind: Louisiana. If the rumors about the transfer were true, Madison predicted "daily collisions" between France and the United States. Americans wouldn't flinch, he warned Pichon.[62]

Pichon feebly denied knowledge of the acquisition, but he countered that if the French did control Louisiana, they would make excellent neighbors. The empire could grant Americans "all they can reasonably desire as to commerce and safety."[63]

Madison repeated that he could see the transfer end only in "some collision." Pichon departed, worried he had said too much and that France and the United States were heading toward a new rupture.[64]

However dismissive in their meeting, Madison found comfort in Pichon's assurances. After the Frenchman left the office, Madison wrote Robert Livingston, a New York Republican about to embark as US minister to France, that the empire would likely adopt a "conciliating policy" in Louisiana. Madison saw his plan working; he just might bluff France into friendship in the West.[65]

His optimism withered once Livingston started sending reports back from France. "The fact is that Talleyrand is decidedly unfriendly to the United States," Livingston grizzled in a coded message to Madison. Talleyrand had endured a brief spell of disfavor under France's revolutionary government, but Napoleon restored him to power, making him the minister of foreign relations after the coup. Well-practiced at spurning US envoys since the XYZ Affair, Talleyrand ignored Livingston's pleas to discuss Louisiana. Livingston had arrived with instructions to prevent or undo the transfer, or to convince France to guarantee Americans access to the Gulf of Mexico. Talleyrand ignored him. "The first quality of a diplomatic agent is to know how to keep quiet," Napoleon told Talleyrand—a summary of France's approach for much of the year.[66]

A once-devout Francophile, Livingston could hardly believe the France he found: "It has nothing that can be called republican in its form." Napoleon would have preferred Federalists to "Jacobins" such as Jefferson—a message Livingston wrote in code so Federalists wouldn't learn that Jefferson was too French even for the French. Republican solidarity between the nations had died—slaughtered by Napoleon.[67]

France in Louisiana spelled disaster for the United States, Livingston cautioned. Napoleon would infiltrate western politics and commerce. The

French would renew alliances with southeastern Native American nations. They might garrison Louisiana with black troops—a dangerous example to the South's enslaved population. Most ominously, Napoleon was preparing a massive force to impose his will in the Western Hemisphere.[68]

Fragile peace draped Europe in the summer of 1802 after France and Britain agreed to the Treaty of Amiens, freeing Napoleon to pursue his American empire. He recruited his brother-in-law General Charles Victoire Emmanuel Leclerc to lead 40,000 soldiers (though not all reinforcements arrived) to subdue Saint-Domingue. More than a passing fancy, the expedition demanded fifty-six war vessels—two-thirds of Napoleon's navy.[69]

With other Americans, Madison feared that the invasion was the French military's first step toward Louisiana. Headed by slaveholders fearful of the contagion of rebellion, the Jefferson administration helped supply Leclerc's expedition against the formerly enslaved Saint-Dominguans. At the same time, they allowed US merchants to keep trading with the rebels. Leclerc lost Madison's goodwill when he began to seize US goods and pay for them with devalued currency. The practice boded ill for the type of neighbor France would make. By the end of the summer, Madison considered Napoleon no better than France's former monarchs.[70]

The crisis worsened in October 1802, when a Spanish official at New Orleans, Juan Ventura Morales, expelled US trade from the port, violating America's 1795 agreement with Spain. The incident reminded Madison of his nation's fragile hold on the Mississippi. If France controlled the river, it could inflict even more devastating harm. The administration sent seasoned diplomat James Monroe to join Livingston in Paris. Together, they were to negotiate the United States' continued access to the Mississippi once France took control of Louisiana.[71]

Meanwhile, Madison was pelted with warnings that France would imperil western loyalty. Livingston reported that Napoleon might close the Mississippi to Americans in an "attempt to corrupt our western people." Monroe guessed that France sought "the opportunity of interfering in our affairs." The American consul at New Orleans advised that most westerners would secede from the union with barely a nudge, "a measure which will be the foremost in the Mind of every Frenchman in Office in this Country."[72]

Madison learned that one Kentucky man, Francis Flournoy, was advocating western secession and an alliance with France and Spain. A US attorney indicted Flournoy for violating the Logan Act, the dubious Federalist-backed legislation passed during the Adams administration after Logan's controversial mission to France. According to the indictment, Flournoy met the standard of entering into indirect communication with a foreign power. Maybe, as Kentuckian Harry Toulmin told Madison, Flournoy was no more than a "crack'd brained individual" unworthy of attention. The US attorney never even prosecuted the case. Nevertheless, Flournoy seemed like a small reflection of a more ominous threat.[73]

By early 1803, Madison believed that French rulers intended to control the United States by infiltrating western loyalties. Or they might seduce westerners "into a separate Government, and a close alliance," as he warned Monroe and Livingston. Reports from the West confirmed that many Native Americans anticipated a reunion with their old French allies. Madison worried also that enslaved laborers would flee to French territory, believing that they considered "the French as patrons of their cause." Not since the 1780s had Madison found the combination of foreign menaces and potential subversives so potent. France might steal his nation's sovereignty without sending a single soldier into US territory.[74]

With other Republicans, Madison subscribed to a comforting but fanciful hope that Napoleon might abort the acquisition of Louisiana once he realized that Americans disavowed Britain. One rumor claimed that Napoleon had discarded his plans when he discovered that the "hostilities" of the Adams administration were "acts of an abandoned and desperate monarchical faction corrupted by" British agents, unsupported by the American people. According to Madison's calculation, Napoleon thought he needed westerners because he believed that Britain controlled easterners. The secretary of state pleaded with Monroe and Livingston to cure the French ruler of that delusion. Had Madison followed his logic to its natural conclusion, he could have blamed himself for Napoleon's interest in Louisiana. He and his party had spent years trying to convince anyone who would listen that the British manipulated US councils.[75]

Federalists hesitated to blame Jefferson and Madison for France's imminent presence, knowing that Spain and France had negotiated the transfer during the Adams administration. Instead, they accused Jefferson of responding weakly to the new threat. Many advocated an attack on New Orleans.[76]

Federalists merged their anti-French ideology with the opportunity to entice westerners to their party. Some charged that Spain had shut the port to Americans at the secret behest of France. They derided Monroe's mission to Paris as "timid and yielding." If Jefferson failed to attack, one feared, westerners "must become vassals of France." They would "be made

EMBRYO OF A TORNADO" 157

the sport of all the arts and intrigues of their new visitors, and perhaps renounce their allegiance to us," another Federalist agreed. The same writer
feared that Napoleon would manipulate Monroe into surrendering the
sovereignty of the entire nation. He might summon deputies from each
state to decide the nation's future under his direction at Paris, a fate he had
inflicted on Switzerland just months before.[77]

Jefferson critic Charles Brockden Brown concocted a letter to Napoleon
supposedly from a French counselor of state. France controlled Republicans'
loyalties, the letter insisted. "Their hearts are ours. . . . They conceal or
palliate our crimes; they pity our calamities; they connive at injuries and
insults from us. . . . What obvious and convenient tools will these prove in
any critical affairs? . . . They will eagerly swallow the opiates that we shall
provide for them." Commenting on the fictitious letter, Brown declared
that the French were "spreading among us, with fatal diligence, the seeds of
faction and rebellion." He chided the Jefferson administration for sending
envoys to France instead of armies to New Orleans.[78]

Some Federalists renewed calls for a partnership with Britain to take
New Orleans, a proposal that Madison couldn't dismiss. By April 1803, he
prepared to embrace the unholy alliance if necessary to keep France off
the continent, but he doubted he could trust the British. Besides, such a
partnership might just confirm Napoleon's suspicions that Americans
sympathized with Britain, accelerating his takeover rather than averting
it. Even worse, Britain might claim the land for itself after it helped the
United States boot France out, an outcome Madison considered more dangerous for America than French occupation.[79]

Monroe warned Madison that if the administration appeared too moderate, Federalists—"enemies of free government," as he called them—might
regain power, the greatest of all calamities. Reminded of their tenuous
grasp on the Mississippi, westerners demanded outright possession of New
Orleans by peace or force. If Madison wanted to avoid a war and a perilous
alliance with Britain, Monroe needed to return with nothing less.[80]

The Purchase

After Easter services on Sunday, April 10, 1803, Napoleon returned to
his palace at Saint Cloud, just outside Paris. He invited two advisers,
Denis Decrès and François de Barbé-Marbois, to discuss Louisiana. "I
am thinking of ceding it to the United States," Napoleon told them, as
Barbé-Marbois remembered it. "They ask no more of me than a city in

Louisiana; but I already consider the entire colony as lost, and it appears to me that in the hands of that nascent power it will be more useful to the policy and even to the commerce of France, than if I tried to keep it. Each of you tell me your thoughts?" It was a stunning proposal. Americans wanted New Orleans; he wanted to hand them the entire colony of Louisiana.[81]

Things had gone poorly for Napoleon in 1802, despite a promising summer. He had declared himself Consul for life in August, and he was gathering control around Europe. He had reacquired several Caribbean islands through the Treaty of Amiens. Leclerc's army prevailed in the early months of the invasion of Saint-Domingue, subduing influential resistance armies. The general captured Louverture and transported him to France, where he died in prison.[82]

Then Napoleon overstepped. He instructed his generals to reinstate slavery in the French Caribbean when possible, a directive issued "three months too soon," Leclerc snapped. Saint-Dominguans stiffened their resistance when French designs became clear. They "laugh at death" and would never surrender, Leclerc despaired. Ice and then storms cornered French reinforcements in European ports. At the same time, yellow fever ravaged French camps and killed Leclerc in November. By the end of the year, Saint-Dominguans had forced the French to evacuate. Napoleon would not regain France's prize colony in the Americas, rendering Louisiana useless to him.[83]

While French forces staggered off the island, Europe stumbled toward war. Few had expected the Peace of Amiens to last, for few on either side liked much about the agreement. It stunted British commerce in Europe and restricted Napoleon's ambitions in the Mediterranean. By spring of 1803, Napoleon expected renewed warfare with Britain. That war might strip him of Louisiana and award it to the British. It would also require money.[84]

Hence why Napoleon had summoned Decrès and Barbé-Marbois to Saint Cloud to ask their opinion about selling Louisiana to the United States. Barbé-Marbois suspected that Napoleon, a man rarely plagued by indecision, cared less about their advice than their assent. Napoleon had probably made up his mind to sell a month earlier. France might as well sacrifice "that which will slip away from us" anyway, Barbé-Marbois advised. Better to profit from Louisiana's sale to the Americans than lose it to the British. The three men talked into the night, and the counselors retired to quarters in the palace.[85]

Famous for needing little sleep, Napoleon summoned Barbé-Marbois the next morning at dawn. "The time has passed for waffling and deliberation. I renounce Louisiana. It is not just New Orleans that I will cede, it is the entire colony without any reservation."[86]

Later that day, Talleyrand hosted Livingston at his office on Rue de Bac in Paris. Did the United States want all of Louisiana, he asked? Livingston responded vaguely, as he had no instructions to discuss such a purchase and could hardly tell if the offer was serious. It was, Barbé-Marbois assured him at a near-midnight meeting two days later. Livingston agreed to consider the offer, but he wanted to cut Talleyrand from negotiations, and he needed a lower price than the $22.5 million Barbé-Marbois was asking. Barbé-Marbois agreed, and the two concluded what one historian has called "the most portentous exchange in the chronicle of American diplomacy."[87]

Barbé-Marbois, Monroe, and Livingston negotiated the details over the next two weeks. On Sunday May 1, the American team, including their two secretaries, met Napoleon at the Louvre Palace, a sprawling complex in the heart of Paris. After some pleasantries, the French ruler told them they had a deal. For $15 million, Monroe and Livingston had doubled the area of the United States.[88]

The Americans dined with Napoleon that afternoon, and then the party retired to the Louvre's salon. Fine artwork enshrouded the massive room, which by then had already become a center of art and culture. Napoleon envisioned the palace, which he renamed Musée Napoléon, as the artistic center of Europe, adorning it with treasures acquired by purchase and plunder.[89]

As the company mingled, Napoleon approached Monroe. He asked if the federal city—Washington, DC—had grown much.

Monroe replied that it had.

"How many inhabitants has it?"

"It is just commencing," Monroe prefaced his answer. If he included the two adjacent cities, Georgetown and Alexandria, "the federal city would make a respectable town," though "in itself it contains only two or three thousand inhabitants."

Insecurity saturated Monroe's defensive response. He and Napoleon talked in the middle of a vast metropolis of about 550,000 residents. Napoleon obsessed over his capital as a mark of his power and imperial

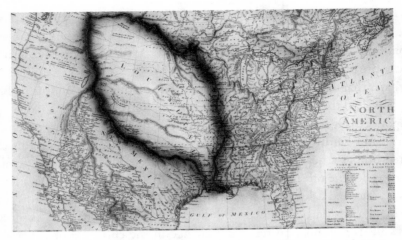

FIGURE 7.1 Detail of North America by Robert Wilkinson, 1804. This map shows the vast Louisiana Territory after the United States purchased it from France. Courtesy Stanford University.

triumphs. He dreamed of making Paris, as he put it, "not only the most beautiful city to exist and the most beautiful city to have existed, but also the most beautiful city that could exist." Its opulence overwhelmed Monroe. He complained to Madison about "the great splendor of the government, and the obligation it imposes on every one, especially foreign ministers, to imitate" its lavishness. Napoleon believed capitals reflected national prestige. If Washington's size represented US grandeur, the nation boasted almost nothing.[90]

Napoleon asked a few questions about Jefferson. How old was he? About sixty. Was he married? Widowed. Did he have children? Yes, two daughters (it was actually three daughters and a son, but Monroe didn't count—probably didn't know about—the boy and girl born to Jefferson and Sally Hemings).[91]

Did Jefferson always reside in the federal city? Generally.

The subject again on the city of Washington, Napoleon asked, "Are the publick buildings there commodious, those for Congress & President especially?"

Monroe was standing in the grandest hall of one of the greatest palaces in Paris. Just across the way stood Napoleon's residence at Tuileries. To the west, Saint Cloud overlooked the Seine River. Not far south, beautiful gardens graced the palace of Luxembourg. The surroundings made a pathetic image of Washington's half-built US Capitol and modest executive mansion, surrounded by muddy roads, wooden houses, cattle, pigs, and geese.[92]

"They are," came Monroe's flat response.

Napoleon complimented Monroe on America's spunk during the Revolution. "Americans did brilliant things in your war with England," he said. "You will do the same again."

Americans would always perform well if war were forced upon them, Monroe assured him, sidestepping the insinuation that the United States might join France's fight against Britain.

"You may probably be in war with them again," Napoleon pressed.

Maybe, maybe not, evaded Monroe.

As recorded by Monroe, the conversation underlined Napoleon's logic behind his decision to sell Louisiana. Americans made useful partners— too weak to worry France but strong enough to help defeat the British. The United States was growing, and the Louisiana region would strengthen it, though that mattered little for the moment. In the immediate future, the sale would avert a potential alliance between the United States and Britain, keep Louisiana out of Britain's grasp, and maybe even rekindle a shared war against the British.[93]

Napoleon had made the same point to Barbé-Marbois when he explained the Louisiana sale during their sunrise meeting weeks earlier: "Perhaps it will also be objected to me that the Americans could become too powerful for Europe in two or three centuries; but my foresight does not embrace those distant fears." Napoleon couldn't see the United States surviving, much less thriving. He reminded Barbé-Marbois, "Confederations which are called perpetual last only as long as one party does not find it profitable to disband them." The United States was too fractured to endure. All that mattered to him were "the present dangers to which the colossal power of England exposes us." Like French rulers before him, Napoleon saw the United States as doomed collateral in the preeminent geopolitical contest between France and Britain.[94]

Madison wrote Monroe a letter with a very different opinion of US prospects. He exulted that the United States could soon replace Britain as the "admiration & envy of the world." Unaware that Monroe and Livingston had just secured a deal that exceeded anything he imagined possible, he cautioned that one thing might impede that happy future: the Louisiana crisis.[95]

Madison worried more about national security than national expansion. During his July 1801 meeting with Pichon, Madison laughed off the prospect of expanding US borders beyond the Mississippi. It was no ruse. Throughout the crisis, Madison betrayed no hint that he wanted land west of the river. Even after he secured the purchase, Monroe thought the United States might grant Louisiana independence and make it an ally, an idea shared by Jefferson. Madison's main goal was to keep the French off the continent. If that failed, he wanted just enough land, meaning New Orleans and the Floridas, to give westerners their vital outlets to the Gulf of Mexico. That access was essential to "the very existence of the United States," he stressed. With it, the nation could secure western loyalty, avoid collisions with France, dodge an alliance with Britain, and save the union.[96]

Jefferson agreed. The president had coveted Spanish territory across the Mississippi since the 1780s, but he saw that as only a distant possibility. In the immediacy of the crisis, his main concern was New Orleans. Whichever power possessed the city "is our natural & habitual enemy," he declared. In the months before he knew of the treaty, Jefferson hoped to defuse tension between Federalists and Republicans, fearful that disunity would expose the nation to "foreign force & intrigue."[97]

When Madison and Jefferson learned about the purchase on July 3, 1803, they believed they had rid the nation of an existential threat. Jefferson wavered over the treaty, concerned that it violated Republicans' strict reading of the Constitution, which left unaddressed the government's power to purchase foreign territory. Madison harbored no such doubts, and soon Jefferson agreed that the moment was too important to lose. He would submit the treaty for ratification. The purchase "removes from us the greatest source of danger to our peace," Jefferson exulted.[98]

The Minority

Madison and Jefferson believed that the Louisiana Purchase vindicated their vision of republican government. They had doubled the size of the nation and dispatched the powerful French from their borders without a massive army or onerous taxes. Federalists wanted to win a city with a war; Jefferson won a continent with diplomacy. The triumphant president predicted that he had delivered Federalists their "coup de grace."[99]

Federalists had banked on the failure of Monroe and Livingston, which would have handed them western votes and a war with France. When the envoys succeeded beyond expectation, Federalists faced the unenviable choice of praising their opponents or criticizing the nation's triumph. The tension divided the party. Some, such as Fisher Ames of Massachusetts, tried to split the difference, hinting that the United States should have vindicated its rights by war, not a "mean and despicable" purchase. Others, such as John Adams, his son John Quincy, Gouverneur Morris, and Rufus King acknowledged the importance of the purchase to US security. "I am content to pay my share of fifteen millions, to deprive foreigners of all pretext for entering our interior country," Morris assented. Even Hamilton had to admit that the acquisition deserved the "exultation which the friends of the administration display."[100]

A few influential party leaders forwent bipartisan congratulations and led a charge against the purchase. They feared that the vast territory would dilute their power, which remained concentrated in New England. They worried, too, that if slavery spread west, their power would collapse under the weight of the Constitution's Three-Fifths clause. Suddenly, those Federalists agreed with Jefferson about the strict constraints of the Constitution. They charged that Jefferson was ramming an unconstitutional treaty through the Senate to deprive Federalists of political power and fund Napoleon's war against Britain. One writer warned that the purchase was a clever ploy of Napoleon to give "France the right of interfering in [the United States'] domestic concerns." Behind the incensed leadership and Federalist newspapers, most congressional Federalists opposed ratification. Nonetheless, the Republican supermajority ratified the treaty that October.[101]

Federalists slipped into the minority rhetoric Republicans had innovated during the 1790s, accusing their opponents of monarchical designs undergirded by a foreign enemy. Napoleon "conferred the kingly honor of Louisiana" on Jefferson and made him president for life, jeered a satirist. One griped that Republicans "seemed disposed to make Mr. Jefferson Lord Paramount over Louisiana." Comparing Jefferson to Napoleon, Timothy Pickering warned that "in four years it [will] be proposed (Frenchman like) to elect him President for life." The minority couldn't make up its mind whether Jefferson loved the French because of their radical democracy or their dictatorship.[102]

Even after Jefferson ousted France from North America, some partisans still insisted that "this administration has partialities against England," the bewildered president complained. The transatlantic radical Thomas Paine sneered that Federalists "who last Winter were for going to war to obtain possession of that country [Louisiana] and who attached so much importance to it that no expense or risk ought to be spared to obtain it, have now altered their tone and say it is not worth having." Jefferson concluded that with "bloody teeth & fangs the federalists will attack any sentiment or principle known to come from me."[103]

By the end of 1803, Timothy Pickering and a tight circle of New England Federalists conspired to secede from the United States. Never reconciled with Jefferson, even Vice President Burr gave the plan an uncomfortable nod. The conspirators tried to recruit Federalist heavyweights but received a muted response. Hamilton and others campaigned against the scheme: "Cease these conversations and threatenings about a separation of the Union," pleaded the party's founding luminary. The conspiracy fizzled after Republicans leaped into power in key state elections throughout New England. Hamilton's death at the hands of Burr in 1804 also blunted Federalist resolve and dampened the conspirators' hopes.[104]

Despite its failure, the plot unveiled the precarious union of the young republic. Even when both sides agreed on a common foreign threat, they failed to bridge the chasm of their mutual suspicion. Americans may have repelled foreign dangers from their western border, but they still cultivated plenty of differences that outside powers could exploit. Those vulnerabilities surfaced in force as Madison tried to strengthen the US grip on its new territory.

8

"Corrupting the Citizens"

> How often has it been found that . . . all their [foreign ministers'] address is employed in the evil task of corrupting the Citizens?
> —JAMES MADISON, January 30, 1807

"THE MARQUIS DE CASA YRUJO presents his compliments to Major Jackson, and would be very happy to know from him when and where he could have the pleasure to see him in the course of this day."[1]

William Jackson read the note on September 6, 1804, in his Philadelphia printing office, where he published news along with his Federalist opinions. Jackson had never "exchanged one word" with Yrujo. He could scarcely fathom why the Spanish diplomat desired a meeting. Yrujo wanted to keep the encounter discreet. He contacted Jackson through a Philadelphia merchant named Francis Breuil. A member of Breuil's household delivered the message around noon that day. Jackson was out when it arrived; his clerk delivered it to him upon his return.[2]

Perplexed, Jackson jotted a reply: "Major Jackson presents his compliments to the Marquis de Casa Yrujo—in reply to his note of this morning, just now received, Major Jackson will be at his office, until 2 o'clock—and at his house in Chesnut street, next to Genl. Dickinsons until four o'clock, at either of which places he will see the Marquis de Casa Yrujo—or, if more convenient, he will wait on him." Jackson's clerk delivered the message to Yrujo.[3]

Soon after, Breuil arrived at Jackson's office in person. Yrujo would like to meet him at 5 o'clock at the diplomat's house, the visitor informed him. Jackson asked him why Yrujo wanted to meet. Breuil didn't know.[4]

That afternoon, Jackson met Yrujo in a large house near the busy Second Street market on the south side of Philadelphia. The Portuguese minister in Washington described Yrujo as "very perceptive and able." Yrujo spoke Italian, Portuguese, French, and English as well as he spoke his native Spanish. He charmed people with a melodious singing voice and talents on the Spanish guitar and fortepiano.[5]

With nearly a decade of experience in the United States and six years as the son-in-law of Pennsylvania governor Thomas McKean, Yrujo had an excellent grasp of US politics. He understood that foreign powers needed the esteem of public opinion more than they needed the good graces of the president. As he put it to his superior in Madrid, Spain's minister of foreign relations Pedro Cevallos, "By the nature of the Government it is necessary to speak to many, and listen to all." He faulted his subordinates for failing to grasp "the state . . . of the parties" and "public opinion" in the United States. More important, Yrujo knew that foreign interests could benefit from the quarrelsome parties. He insisted that his deputies understand "the intrigues, passions, and interests of the parties that divide this country." And he knew that the press shaped public opinion.[6]

FIGURE 8.1 Detail of New Market, in South Second Street Philadelphia, by W. Birch & Son. This image shows a distant view of Marquis de Casa Yrujo's house (*far right*) at the corner of Second and Pine in Philadelphia across from the Philadelphia New Market. Courtesy Library Company of Philadelphia.

Yrujo "accosted" Jackson with a candid greeting: "You will be surprized Major Jackson at the liberty I have taken in sending for you," Yrujo began, using Jackson's title since his Revolutionary War days, "but I trust an explanation of the motive will excuse me." Yrujo didn't know it, but he was beginning a conversation that would ensnare him in controversy for nearly four years—a controversy that would expose the republic's inherent vulnerabilities to foreign manipulation.[7]

The Gulf

One year earlier, Yrujo had whisked a letter to Madison when he learned that France had sold Louisiana to the United States. Following the lead of his superiors in Madrid, he charged that the transfer violated the French government's agreement not to alienate Louisiana except to return the colony to Spain. The Spanish king would never have ceded the colony to France had he known France would sell it to the United States. Spain's rulers feared that the transfer left the Spanish Floridas isolated against encroaching Americans. Yrujo urged Madison to withdraw the United States from the agreement.[8]

Far from withdrawing, Madison countered that the Louisiana boundary included a large portion of West Florida as well, based on a specious interpretation of decades-old treaties. Spain assailed the dodgy reading and refused to surrender the colony. With the Louisiana Purchase, the United States had hemmed in Spain's Gulf region, and Madison assumed it would soon fall into US hands. He especially wanted West Florida, with its outlets to the sea.[9]

Madison still considered Spanish West Florida a security threat, for the Jefferson administration expected trouble in Louisiana. Before the Louisiana Purchase, the government had never acquired foreign land. Now it needed to organize a vast territory of people who had little stake in its survival—Louisiana creoles, Acadians, Haitian refugees, Spanish natives, and descendants of Rhineland Germans, to say nothing of the Native American nations that inhabited the land. When US troops raised their flag in New Orleans on December 20, 1803, longtime residents met the whoops and hollers of the US minority with, in the words of one observer, "silence and quietness," and even "sighs and tears."[10]

As secretary of state, Madison oversaw the new territory and shouldered the responsibility of incorporating it into the United States. The Louisiana Purchase had taken the Jefferson administration by surprise, so it had no other apparatus ready to manage the monumental process. The administration appointed William C. C. Claiborne territorial governor of the newly created Orleans Territory, which encompassed the southern portion of Louisiana. The young governor—he was still in his twenties—complained to Madison that when he assumed control, "the People were split into Parties, divided in their affections, and the sport of Foreign and Domestic Intriguers."[11]

The region hosted people with dubious loyalty or outright hostility to the United States. General James Wilkinson remained on the Spanish payroll even while he served as commanding general of the US Army and governor of the Louisiana Territory. The US consul at New Orleans, Daniel Clark, also lent his loyalty to Spain from time to time for the right price, as did the surveyor William Dunbar. The Spanish governor of the Natchez region, Manuel Gayoso de Lemos, had toured the West in the late 1790s, gauging the desire of westerners to separate from the United States. Gayoso had reported to Madrid that some western elites remained enamored with France and regretted the failure of Genet's invasion of the region. Given the right circumstances, they might still secede from the union, he believed. A lot had changed since Gayoso's 1797 reports, but figures like Wilkinson, Gayoso, Clark, and Dunbar remained formidable actors in the region.[12]

The United States and Spain competed for alliances with Choctaw, Caddo, and other Native nations in the area. Native Americans leveraged the conflict to demand guarantees of their autonomy. One Choctaw leader reported that Spanish authorities wanted his people to purchase US supplies and use them to construct Spanish forts. Spanish officials assumed that Meriwether Lewis and William Clark, who had embarked on their expedition in May 1804, intended to secure Native alliances against Spanish dominions in the West. At the suggestion of the spy Wilkinson, the Spanish recruited Native Americans to reconnoiter the party and imprison its members if possible. Mutual suspicion reigned.[13]

Even if the United States had secured the loyalty of most of those living around Orleans, many maintained a "great partiality for France as their Mother Country," Governor Claiborne warned Madison. Besides, Claiborne reported, Spanish troops and high-ranking officials remained in the region, endangering fidelity to the United States. Madison responded, "In every view it is desireable that these foreigners should be no longer in a situation to affront the authority of the US or to mingle by their intrigues in the affairs of your territory." Rumors spread that Louisiana would soon return to Spanish hands. Madison feared that the slightest foreign manipulation would dissolve shaky allegiances.[14]

To hasten the acquisition of West Florida, Jefferson signed the Mobile Act in February 1804. The act permitted the president to establish a customhouse on West Florida's Mobile River, implying US ownership. Yet it acknowledged the disputed status of the region, delaying implementation until an unspecified future date, ostensibly after Spain recognized US possession of the colony.[15]

On March 5, Yrujo marched into Madison's State Department office and unleashed his fury at what he considered "one of the greatest Insults" the United States could heap on Spain. Tempers flared in a fiery exchange. Yrujo knew he had crossed a line, but he blamed Madison as much as himself for the "altercation." The secretary succumbed to one of his intermittent "streaks of excessive irritability," Yrujo insisted. Madison accepted no blame: Yrujo had "remonstrated . . . in a stile so insolent as to produce a painful dilemma."[16]

The relationship eroded as the two men exchanged letters over the following weeks. Yrujo implied that the Mobile Act was an act of war. Madison resented Yrujo's "insulting language," "ill humour and indecorum," and "intemperance and disrespect." He warned him that the United States might break communications with him if he forgot his civility again. Yrujo relocated to Philadelphia for the summer, in part to avoid Madison. He refused to meet with the secretary before he left. He asked his wife to give his regards to Dolley, her good friend.[17]

By mid-summer 1804, "the passions of Yrujo," to use Madison's phrase, reached Cevallos in Madrid. Cevallos threatened to torpedo an unrelated agreement if the United States refused to rescind the Mobile Act. A US diplomat in Spain began to make hints of war. Jefferson wanted to avoid bloodshed, but he did order additional troops to the Gulf area as a precaution.[18]

Yrujo desponded that Republican presses inflamed the tension by calling for annexation of West Florida and prodding Americans toward hostilities. "The newspapers opened their batteries and began to wage a war of the pen against us," he complained to Cevallos. If not checked, the press would incite "public opinion, which possesses so much influence in a popular government, to intrigues, and hostile designs" against Spain.[19]

Yrujo needed to counter the Republican narrative, so that September he contacted Jackson, the Federalist printer.

The Proposal

Jefferson and Madison wanted war, Yrujo told Jackson. "*You* have it in your power to do much good by espousing the part of peace."[20]

Jackson had survived as a Federalist customhouse surveyor in a Republican administration since 1801, but Jefferson had finally purged him from office months before Yrujo called on him. Yrujo assumed he had picked the right target—someone booted from his post by "political intolerance" and forced to adopt the "useful" profession of a Federalist printer.[21]

Yrujo complained that the presses encouraged the administration's worst impulses toward war. He wanted to feed anonymous essays to Jackson's paper, advocating Spanish interests and countering the administration's designs on West Florida. For Jackson's cooperation, Yrujo promised compensation.[22]

Jackson suspected Yrujo meant a bribe. The printer mostly listened. He seemed indecisive to Yrujo. Internally, Jackson "stifled the emotions" and "restrained my indignation" to learn more of Yrujo's corrupt plan. At least that's how he told it later. Yrujo accompanied him to the front door and pressed him for an answer. In Yrujo's account, Jackson promised to think about it. In Jackson's account, he "suppressed the indignation of my feelings, and left the house." Both versions may have been true.[23]

Whether Jackson played Yrujo or really did consider the proposal, he found city alderman Jonathan Inskeep the next day and swore an affidavit about the conversation. He sent it to Jefferson. Whatever his disagreements with the president, he had no interest in running pro-Spanish essays at the behest of a Spanish agent.[24]

Unaware that Jackson had apprised Jefferson of his proposal, Yrujo requested a meeting with the president, asking to bypass Madison due to their strained relationship. Though uncomfortable about sidestepping his secretary of state, Jefferson acquiesced. Yrujo wrote the pro-Spanish essays he wanted to publish, handed them to the secretary at the Spanish consulate with instructions to find a printer, and left Philadelphia with his wife, Sally.[25]

The secretary, longtime Philadelphia resident Charles Mulvey, carried the essays to William M'Corkle of the *Freeman's Journal*. He refused to reveal their author until M'Corkle agreed to publish them. Mulvey offered compensation to M'Corkle, which the printer, like Jackson, considered a bribe. M'Corkle rejected the anonymous overtures, especially due to the apparent bribe and because, he maintained, "the contents appeared to be very exceptionable, coming from a foreign government." Although

M'Corkle didn't know Yrujo's identity, he suspected "the bearer to be in personal and familiar connection with a Spanish public officer."[26]

Mulvey either exercised more caution or found a less scrupulous editor in Samuel Relf of the *Philadelphia Gazette*. Relf printed Yrujo's three essays in mid-September, under the pseudonym "Graviora Manent." Yrujo posed as an American who was defending Spanish claims to West Florida and denouncing the Mobile Act. The king of Spain must have viewed the Mobile Act "as an aggravated offence," Yrujo's fictitious American explained. He denounced the "peevish levity" of the US minister in Madrid who was threatening war.[27]

Republicans saw through the charade, reprinting the essays with caveats that they came "from a *Spanish official* source" and assuring their readers that the author played fast and loose with facts. William Duane's *Aurora* mocked the apparent coincidence that the essays ceased as soon as Yrujo departed Philadelphia. With his usual officious paranoia, Tench Coxe wrote a confidential, unsigned letter to Madison to inform him that "a foreign interested agent" had produced the essays. Two days later, Jacob Wagner, Madison's chief clerk in the State Department, confirmed Yrujo's identity when he found in the essays an identical phrase in a letter Yrujo had sent Madison earlier in the year.[28]

Meanwhile, Jackson had published the affidavit he sent to Jefferson, exposing the supposed bribe Yrujo had offered. M'Corkle compounded Jackson's accusations when he published his own account of Mulvey's approach and alleged bribe. He could scarcely imagine why Relf would publish essays "calculated to give fuel to the dangerous fire which foreign agents appeared to be lighting up among us."[29]

Republicans decried, as Yrujo later reported to Madrid, "what they called my attempt against the purity of the American press." One Republican editor condemned Yrujo's "shocking imposition" that "must blast his character in the eyes of the world." Another targeted the Federalist presses that published his content. The editors insisted that "to every blow" leveled by Yrujo, Federalist printers "added two."[30]

Hesitant to defend Yrujo, Federalist printers charged Jefferson with hypocrisy because he had once consorted with the French minister Genet. If Jefferson requested Yrujo's recall over the matter, chortled one critic, Yrujo could move in with "another disgraced minister who married another Governor's daughter, the unfortunate Genet." Another labeled the affair "Spanish Intrigue—a la mode de François."[31]

Isolated on his journey to Monticello, and lodging at "miserable little places" without a newspaper, Yrujo traveled "peacefully" with no idea that the "world burned behind my back," as he'd later report. He arrived at Monticello, where Jefferson received him cordially and never mentioned the affidavit Jackson had sent him, even as they discussed the West Florida dispute.[32]

When Yrujo returned to Washington and learned that Jackson had divulged his maneuvers, he dashed a letter to Madison to defend his conduct. He argued that he had the duty to protect his king by repelling "the attack with the same weapons which are made use of for his Injury"—the press. The US government could not deprive foreign agents of that right "enjoyed by every individual who breathes the air of the United States." Otherwise, the newspapers could reduce foreign ministers to "*distinguished Slaves* in the very centre of the Land of Liberty." Yrujo insisted that he had not committed "diplomatic intrigue," claiming that he merely hoped to sway public opinion in favor of peace by revealing facts otherwise "concealed" from Americans.[33]

To Jackson's claim that Yrujo had bribed him, the minister countered that he innocuously offered to pay him for print space. The explanation made little sense. Yrujo had planned to submit the essays as opinion pieces written under a pseudonym. He had lived in the United States long enough to know that newspapers didn't charge for such material.[34]

Yrujo's defense failed to move Madison, especially because he sent it to the newspapers before he delivered it to the secretary. Yrujo told Madison that a sudden illness seized him and caused the breach in etiquette. To his government, however, he explained that he "printed, and circulated it immediately" so that it did not fall "among the dusty files of the Secretary of State, in which it would have stayed buried." By publishing the letter, he hoped to stem the tide of "infamous attacks" that printers "vomited" against him. He cared little if he convinced the administration of his innocence. "Public opinion," he declared, "is the true sovereign of a democracy." The press had damaged his reputation, and "only the press could wash the stain." Yrujo understood the paradoxes of US politics.[35]

Madison fumed that for the second time in a month Yrujo had bypassed diplomatic channels with "an appeal to the people." Even worse, Yrujo practically admitted in his defense that he had attempted "to debauch a citizen of the UStates . . . into a combination with a foreign functionary in favor of a foreign Government."[36]

Yrujo caught Madison in a war with his own ideology. Before his party took power, Madison had chastised Federalists for restricting the free press and trying to deny constitutional rights to foreigners. Now Yrujo lectured him that any attempt to restrict his access to the press amounted to an attack on the Constitution. Yrujo explained the Jefferson administration's hypocrisy to his superiors. When administration members had floundered in the minority, they "greatly applauded" his press attack on the Adams administration during the Blount conspiracy. When Jefferson claimed the presidency, he even rescinded Adams's demand for Yrujo's recall.[37]

Yrujo recognized the inconsistencies, and he knew how to account for Jefferson's and Madison's changed opinion of him by 1805. "In this country, they never look on the right, or wrong of a subject, but on how the two parties that divide them principally look on it." Yrujo knew the parties used him as a pawn. The parties seemed oblivious that he reciprocated.[38]

The Recall

Despite Yrujo's pleas of innocence, Madison instructed US diplomats in Madrid, Charles Pinckney and James Monroe (who had gone there from Paris), to demand his recall for bribing a US citizen into violating the Logan Act. His appeal to the Logan Act dripped with irony. The act was born of partisanship, passed by Federalists fearful that Republicans would cooperate with foreign powers to undermine the executive's foreign policy. Now Madison resorted to it for the same reasons. Not a single person had been prosecuted under the act (nor has one ever been). It remained so obscure that Pinckney barely remembered if such an act existed. For convicting criminals, it did little; for bludgeoning political foes, it proved useful.[39]

When Pinckney and Monroe requested Yrujo's recall in April 1805, they repeated Madison's complaints against the minister: his attempt to bribe Jackson to violate the Logan Act, the publication of his defense to Madison, and "the whole tenor of his conduct." Cevallos alerted them that Yrujo had already requested to return to Spain. The two governments agreed to allow Yrujo to remain in the United States until he could travel to Europe in safety. The agreement would spare Yrujo the personal embarrassment of an official recall. Monroe and Pinckney thought "safety" meant better weather, and they transmitted that understanding to Madison. But Cevallos had hedged his language. Nearly a year passed before Madison realized that the court intended to leave Yrujo in the United States until the Napoleonic Wars ceased and British privateers no longer preyed on Spanish ships.[40]

Meanwhile, Cevallos pressured Yrujo to reconcile with the US government. In his draft letter, he instructed Yrujo to make peace with Madison, before scratching out the word "minister" (meaning Madison) and changing it to "government." The first iteration revealed that Cevallos understood that personal animosity between Yrujo and Madison was aggravating official affairs. Even with the change in the text, Yrujo knew that mending his relationship with the government meant repairing the breach with Madison, whom he blamed for the rupture. "There have been certain personal piques between the Secretary of State and me of little importance in themselves, but of significant influence in their animus due to his excessive irritability." Still, in early August 1805, he promised to return to Washington from Philadelphia and restore calm.[41]

Yrujo got his chance almost immediately, for the Madisons had arrived in Philadelphia at the end of July 1805. Dolley had suffered in bed since May with an ulcerated knee. On July 26, she and James rode into the city to consult a renowned doctor. They lodged in a fashionable boarding house on Sansom Street, near the statehouse and Congress Hall, where James had spent so much of his career. The doctor splinted Dolley's leg, confining her to bed to recover. "Not a step can I take," she complained, though grateful for the remedy.[42]

Within a week after the Madisons arrived, the Yrujos visited them and brought Dolley well wishes. Madison reciprocated, visiting Yrujo and even dining at his country house "with all appearances of harmony, and I might say friendship," Yrujo wrote Madrid. After James returned to Washington and left Dolley for another month to continue her recovery, she ate with the Yrujos several more times. Yrujo was confident he had regained Madison's good graces.[43]

Yrujo misinterpreted Madison's gestures. The secretary of state bore no ill will because he assumed that Yrujo was preparing to exit his post, as arranged earlier in the year. His demeanor changed when he learned that Yrujo intended to return to Washington in his official capacity.[44]

Madison told Alexander Dallas, by then a US attorney in Philadelphia, that the government would not "continue the diplomatic intercourse" with Yrujo, given the request for his recall. Madison wanted to avoid the fiasco that might occur if he publicly refused to receive Yrujo in Washington. On November 20, he requested that Dallas persuade Yrujo to remain in Philadelphia.[45]

Dallas may have thought back to the last time an executive asked him to intervene with a meddlesome minister. His attempt to tame Genet's antics could hardly have inspired confidence in his new assignment. Besides, Yrujo possessed two advantages Genet had never enjoyed: a less popular president and a full-fledged two-party system. Federalists dared attack Jefferson in ways that Republicans of the early 1790s could never have attacked Washington. With the hardening of party lines, an assault on Jefferson was an assault on Republicans, not on the government. Dallas had little prospect for success with Yrujo. Dallas had two or three conferences with the minister, entreating him to stay in Philadelphia. Despite Dallas's "tone of friendship," Yrujo knew the attorney worked for the administration. He ignored the pleas.[46]

Yrujo strutted into Washington on January 15, 1806, and headed to the residence of the French minister, Louis-Marie Turreau. The Frenchman lived in a fine house in the "Seven Buildings" district on the corner of Nineteenth Street and Pennsylvania Avenue, just northwest of the president's mansion. It was large enough for a later resident to host a ball with 400 invitees.[47]

Nearly fifty years old, Turreau had arrived in Washington in 1804. Unlike Yrujo, he spoke only broken English. Abrasive and fastidious in dress, "his countenance indicates a ferocious disposition," one senator recorded, "unfeeling as a brute" and "a heart devoid of morals." Others agreed. Turreau had earned a reputation of cruelty in war and cruelty to his wife (beating her even when she was well advanced in pregnancy) but friendly enough to the United States.[48]

Talleyrand had charged Turreau to keep peace between Spain and the United States, an impossible task given the discord between Madison and Yrujo. Turreau had once convened a dinner between the adversaries, but Madison "does not know how to forgive," he brooded. While Yrujo was in Philadelphia, Turreau had pestered him about returning to Washington. With Yrujo's return that January, Turreau tried again to reconcile the two men. Turreau told Yrujo that he could hardly believe that the administration would condemn his presence in Washington. They agreed to arrange a conference with Madison the next day and "reconnoiter the terrain." Yrujo spent the evening at dinner with Turreau and then returned to his boarding house, Stelle's Hotel, just east of the capitol.[49]

Though known for its Federalist clientele, Stelle's accommodated a diverse array of lawmakers and diplomats. At the time, it was hosting members of a legation from Tunis, on special assignment to resolve issues stemming from US hostilities with the North African state. One persnickety observer marveled at the "perfect harmony" with which "Turks" and "Christians" mingled in the boarding house's barroom, testing strength with good-natured wrestling matches. The hotel converged a menagerie of political, cultural, and diplomatic interests. The cosmopolite Yrujo would have felt at ease there.[50]

It was late at night when Yrujo traveled through town in the frigid air. Most of that January was uncharacteristically warm in Washington, with temperatures sometimes reaching the mid-60s. But mid-month experienced a cold spell with the "usual severity of the Winter," John Quincy Adams wrote his mother.[51]

When Yrujo stepped into the boarding house, he was handed a letter, a message from Madison as icy as the night air he had just escaped. The secretary of state had heard that Yrujo arrived that day, and he wondered how the Spaniard dared show his face in the capital months after Madison assumed he would have left the country. "Under these Circumstances, the President has charged me to signify to you," Madison wrote, "that your remaining at this Place is dissatisfactory to him." They wanted him out of the city. The message wasn't a termination of diplomacy—no declaration of war—Madison emphasized. The administration's quarrel was with Yrujo, not Spain. Once a new minister arrived, they could resume normal relations. As one senator put it after he heard of Madison's letter, Yrujo "is now considered more as a spy than a minister."[52]

Yrujo could hardly believe the conduct of the administration, so "insulting and ridiculous at the same time." The next day, he penned a defiant letter, asserting his right and his intention to remain in Washington. To Cevallos, he stated his case even more coarsely: neither the president nor Congress possessed the authority to expel "even . . . a negro, or the least of the citizens of this country," let alone a foreign ambassador.[53]

Yrujo's arguments carried an ironic echo of Madison's *Report of 1800*. In his *Report*, Madison had decried Federalists' arguments that the Alien Law was preventative rather than punitive. He declared that the law unconstitutionally punished exiled foreigners by exposing them to the hazards of the ocean, especially when war made the seas even more dangerous.[54]

Yrujo used the same logic. The administration could not, in good conscience, "insist that I depart in the middle of a maritime war" and risk life and property to flee the country at the "caprice" of the government. The Spaniard insisted that the administration had violated its own constitution. The charter protected foreigners as well as citizens.[55]

If a minister could be "persecuted, insulted, and reviled by the liberty, or license that the Constitution gives to printers," Yrujo demanded the right to defend himself by the same means. He argued that "in a country like this," where the press shaped public opinion, he could vindicate his honor only in the press. Congressmen used newspapers to shoot "all kinds of insults" at nations that oppose their agendas, he explained. Even if he had insulted Madison or Jefferson—as the US government had complained to Madrid— he did nothing different from citizens and politicians across the country.[56]

Jefferson and Madison had assumed executive office ready to restore the rights they believed Federalists had tried to deny Americans. Now Yrujo exposed the worrisome possibility that foreign powers could turn those rights from agents of liberty into tools of subversion. He struck a persistent fear: the US government must either suppress freedom or succumb to foreign incursion.

The Press

Weeks later, almost taunting Madison, Yrujo published accusations that Jefferson had misled Congress in his recent annual message. Yrujo had penned the rejoinder to Madison as a diplomatic letter on December 6, 1805. He addressed the letter to Madison, but he intended it for the press, to "open the eyes of the public" to the "machinations" of Jefferson and Madison.[57]

Mindful of his instructions to calm the situation rather than to stir it, Yrujo nudged the letter toward printers without compromising his position. He passed copies to members of the foreign diplomatic corps and permitted them to distribute them "to whomever they judged appropriate." Yrujo knew he could count on his fellow foreign diplomats, for Madison had outraged the community with his attempt to expel Yrujo from Washington. As Yrujo told it, the clamor had embarrassed Madison to the point that in private conversations the secretary blamed Jefferson for the misstep, claiming that he merely followed orders. As Yrujo expected, his colleagues in the foreign diplomatic corps circulated his letter until it landed in the hands of a printer and multiplied in newspapers throughout the country.[58]

Jefferson's allies in the Republican press launched a counterassault, hurling "an infinity of personal invectives" at Yrujo, as the Spaniard complained. "In no other country under heaven would the ambassador D'Yrujo, be suffered to remain one hour, but in this," fumed one

Republican newspaper, "thanks to the liberality of our institutions, which can tolerate the most insidious and daring intriguer, with equanimity, and suffer the artifices of a corrupt and abandoned diplomacy to pass without the controul of any other ordeal than that of public opinion." The editor saved some ire for Yrujo's Federalist sympathizers. "Whenever a foreign nation or a foreign agent is guilty of any outrage or any indecorum towards our government—the cry of these muddy headed beings is not against the *aggressors*, but *against our government*."[59]

Yrujo retaliated by again posing as a US citizen to berate the Jefferson administration and defend the publication of his correspondence with Madison. He published the piece in the Federalist *United States' Gazette*. "We are as attached to our own government as any of our fellow citizens," the writer declared, "but let us not forget, that this attachment is directed to its principles and not to persons." Americans owed their loyalty to the United States, not to Jefferson. They should admit when the president stood in the wrong, and he was wrong about West Florida.[60]

Days after Yrujo's attack appeared, Federalist presses published the correspondence he and Madison had exchanged when he arrived in Washington in mid-January. Yrujo had delivered the correspondence to the diplomatic corps along with his rebuttal to Jefferson's message. He waited for its certain appearance in newspapers. The *United States' Gazette* again obliged. The editor's commentary echoed Yrujo's logic so exactly that it must have come from the minister. As the arguments went, the administration had no just cause to expel Yrujo or demand his recall. Instead, it grasped the "miserable pretence" of the William Jackson episode to justify the ouster. The US government could not treat "the meanest of our citizens" as it did Yrujo. The editorial repeated one of Yrujo's favorite talking points: the administration wanted the minister out of Washington because he threatened Jefferson's "golden dream" of taking West Florida by conquest.[61]

Argent

While Yrujo and Madison exchanged angry letters in mid-January, Congress convened in a secret session to deliberate the West Florida issue. On February 7, they voted to grant the Jefferson administration $2 million as an advance to purchase the Floridas from Spain, though the terms were cushioned in vague language. Yrujo interpreted the move as a recognition that Spain controlled the disputed territory, and he declared victory in his "guerrilla" (little war) against the administration. He gloated that Congress had spurned Jefferson's appetite to appropriate the land by war, unaware that the president had requested the funds for the purchase.[62]

Publicly, Jefferson advocated force against Spain, but he and his cabinet devised a secret plan to buy the Floridas, with France as a mediator. At the time of the Louisiana Purchase, Napoleon had promised to support US claims to the disputed part of West Florida. By 1805, though, he wanted more money for his war and depended on Spain as an anti-British ally. If he coerced Jefferson to pay Spain for the Floridas, then Spain could forward the money to France as part of a war subsidy it owed. One US envoy described France's interest in brokering the West Florida deal: "l'argent— beaucoup d'argent." Money—a lot of money.[63]

For several months in 1805, Jefferson had toyed with the idea of a British alliance to take West Florida by force. Ever skeptical of Britain, Madison advised against the idea. Treasury Secretary Albert Gallatin seconded his concerns. By November 1805, Jefferson agreed to pursue the purchase through France. He asked Congress for the $2 million. Jefferson and Madison knew that the money would end up in French coffers, but what Spain did with the money was its own business. The administration preferred to spend millions on peace rather than millions on war. Conquest without war, as one French official framed Jefferson's policy.[64]

Congress granted the money but did so over howls from Federalists and some disaffected Republicans claiming French intrigue. Rumors flooded Congress that, as the moderate Federalist Senator William Plumer recorded it, "the President was immediately, to send the whole of the $2,000,000 . . . to France—That the real object & design was to expend it in *bribes*." The day after the Senate started to deliberate the legislation, Plumer suspected that "France has several ministers in disguise—spies— in this country." Federalist Timothy Pitkin of Connecticut suspected that the money "is going into the pockets of Bonaparte and Talleyrand." The administration had duped Congress, he soured, "by a species of duplicity disgraceful in a Chief Magistrate." Another suggested, "The *haste* to pass this bill looks more like a design to purchase *men in Europe* than a province in America." Senator James Hillhouse, also of Connecticut, doubted that Jefferson cared about the Floridas, assuming the president intended the money to aid France in its war with Britain.[65]

During the same session, at Jefferson's behest, Congress voted to prohibit US trade with the new nation of Haiti, intensifying accusations that he was groveling to France. "The national sovereignty, which had been achieved by the best blood of our country, has been surrendered" to France, accused one Federalist editor. "If there is an individual who doubts the truth of this assertion, let him consult the law, which annulled our commerce with St. Domingo [Haiti] . . . let him refer to the still more disgraceful tribute of 2,000,000 of dollars, which . . . has been granted to the Great Nation [France]." John Quincy Adams told his father that the trade prohibition against Haiti "is nothing comparatively speaking." He couldn't divulge the Senate's confidential discussions about the $2 million payment, but he summarized Jefferson's foreign policy as "unqualified submission to France."[66]

John Adams couldn't decide whether Jefferson was leading the nation to war with Spain or prostrating it at the feet of France. "If We get into War," Adams feared in late 1805, "in my opinion our Country at Home, and especially our Elections will become the Sport of foreign Nations." War would welcome dangerous foreign alliances. Like Rome, America was "for sale, and soon to perish should it find a buyer," he wrote, using the original Latin, quoting Jugurtha, a man famous for bribing Roman officials. Adams hardly changed his tune when he learned Republicans opted for a peaceful alternative. "We are . . . become the Shoelickers of Bonaparte," he grumbled. Whether Republicans chose war or peace, Federalists accused them of inviting foreign corruption.[67]

The Federalist press joined the fray once the payment request became public. A Federalist newspaper declared that "the money was demanded by France, and goes to France." One creative opponent wrote a parody script depicting French and Spaniards pillaging a house built by George Washington. The scene changes to Napoleon's Saint Cloud palace where two treasure caskets lie side by side labeled "Louisiana, 15,000,000" and "AMERICAN TRIBUTE, 2,000,000."[68]

Federalists followed the lead of Virginia Republican, John Randolph. Youthful in looks and, by his own description, effeminate in nature, Randolph fit uncomfortably in a political arena that prized masculinity. Still, his fiery wit and stalwart principles carried him up the ranks of congressional leadership. For more than a year, he had nurtured personal and policy disagreements with the administration. Jefferson was acting like a Federalist, he charged, conducting covert diplomacy and harvesting inordinate power.[69]

Randolph had initiated the rumors that Jefferson intended the money for French bribes. He saw an ugly reflection of the XYZ affair, but this time the administration was caving to foreign demands. He claimed that in a meeting with Madison, the secretary of state had told him that France wanted money "and that we must give it to her." Jefferson opened the "public purse to the first cutthroat that demanded it."[70]

Randolph reserved special ire for Madison, whom he viewed as a proponent of an overreaching national government, starting with the Constitutional Convention. Randolph believed that Jefferson wanted to boost Madison's image for the 1808 election by publicly taking a hard line against Spain even though privately he cowered to foreign pressure. Randolph's suspicion grew when he learned that Madison might have withheld from the House Monroe's recommendations of tougher measures against Spain.[71]

Randolph fancied himself the leader of a new faction. "If we belong to a third party, be it so," he announced. Jefferson and Madison had abandoned Republican principles. The administration reduced Congress to a subordinate body meant to legitimize Jefferson's whims. It had corroded statesmanship into surreptitious "cunning."[72]

According to Randolph, Yrujo was working under Napoleon's orders. Randolph theorized that Napoleon instructed Yrujo to antagonize Jefferson into buying the Floridas, which would land money in France. "Are the people of the United States, the real sovereigns of the country, unworthy of knowing what . . . has been communicated to the priviledged spies of foreign governments?" By "priviledged spies," he meant Yrujo. The Spaniard was France's "diplomatic puppet," he insisted. "He has orders for all he does. Take his instructions from his pocket to-morrow, they are signed 'Charles Maurice Talleyrand.'" Jefferson's secrecy, the requested money, Yrujo's offenses—they all stemmed from France.[73]

For all Randolph's invective against Yrujo, the pair shared the same grievance against the administration: Jefferson and Madison were acting as though sovereignty resided with the executive branch, a reversal from their days in the minority. Reminding Americans that the people are "the real sovereigns of the country," Randolph foreshadowed Yrujo's main defense against Madison's demand for his recall.

Sovereignty

On February 13, 1806, less than a week after Congress voted Jefferson the $2 million for the possible purchase of West Florida, John Quincy Adams introduced a bill to empower the president to expel offensive foreign diplomats. Adams's bill unapologetically targeted Yrujo. Like his father, Adams aligned with Federalists but considered himself above party.

The PRAIRIE DOG sickened at the sting of the HORNET——or a Diplomatic Puppet exhibiting his Deceptions!

FIGURE 8.2 This political cartoon depicted Randolph's accusations against Jefferson, Yrujo, and France. Jefferson is shown as a prairie dog vomiting cash to Yrujo, who holds maps of the Floridas and instructions from Talleyrand in his pocket. Napoleon is portrayed as a hornet stinging Jefferson into ejecting the cash. Yrujo dances and shouts "A gull for the people." Napoleon as a hornet was a play on rumors that Jefferson shipped France $2 million in specie aboard the US warship USS *Hornet* (*Repertory*, April 15, 1806). Jefferson as a prairie dog suggests dissatisfaction with the Louisiana Purchase, seen by some as a waste of funds on the vast plains—a reminder that, as some elected officials argued, Congress had once allocated funds for the purchase or conquest of the Floridas, and Jefferson squandered them on Louisiana (Plumer, *Plumer's Memorandum*, 395–396). The caption repeats Randolph's claim that Yrujo was a "Diplomatic Puppet," and Yrujo's posture is reminiscent of a marionette. Courtesy Library of Congress.

However skeptical of Jefferson's foreign policy, he was a nationalist offended by Yrujo's behavior. Like some in Congress, he may have suspected Yrujo as a source of French mischief. He also likely remembered Yrujo's misconduct toward his father during the Blount conspiracy.[74]

Two days after Adams introduced the bill, a large party of Washington elites convened at the Georgetown house of his brother-in-law, Walter Hellen, where he and his family lodged. Adams spent part of the evening at a game of whist, but such gatherings were never purely social. Turreau was there, and he wanted the Massachusetts senator's ear. If the bill passed, Turreau joked, he would "be afraid of being ship'd off" also, sentenced to certain capture by the British. His lighthearted banter carried an element of real concern. Members of the foreign diplomatic corps worried that Jefferson "might abuse his power," as one put it, and remove them at a whim. Adams was confident that Turreau would never misbehave in a way that would trigger his expulsion. Turreau iterated that he was only joking, but the quip segued into the topic he really wanted to discuss: Yrujo. Yrujo shouldn't have published his letter to Madison, Turreau conceded, but his actions hardly warranted his removal.[75]

Adams responded with a list of Yrujo's sins. Besides publishing his correspondence with Madison, Yrujo had shared it with the foreign diplomatic corps; he had also offended the president beyond all decorum for a foreign minister. Adams told Turreau that he had read a misguided justification of Yrujo's conduct in the newspapers (unaware that Yrujo had authored it). As Adams explained, the piece claimed that in 1786 British, French, and Prussian ministers had set a precedent by circulating their correspondence with Dutch officials and printing it in newspapers. That precedent aggravated Yrujo's assault rather than legitimized it, Adams protested. Holland had teetered on civil war in the 1780s due to "civil dissensions and internal party struggles." In that atmosphere, the three foreign powers sought to decide the country's fate and manipulate its laws to their benefit. "Did the Marquis pretend," Adams asked, "that he and the French and English Ministers ... were by concert to give us the Law?" For Adams, Holland's case found an unsettling parallel in the United States, a nation riven by party strife whose free press made it vulnerable to foreign intrigues.[76]

Adams conceded, "The President of the United States did not in most respects stand on the footing of an European Sovereign." When he sends his annual message to Congress, though, he is fulfilling a similar capacity, Adams argued. Yrujo had disrespected the president by publicly attacking that message. Adams challenged Turreau: How long would France allow a minister to remain in the country if he openly criticized Napoleon and his policies? The Frenchman smiled. "Probably not long," he admitted.[77]

The conversation illustrated Americans' struggle to determine who held sovereignty in their republic. They usually insisted that the people possessed it; the president was a representative, not a sovereign. When foreign agents followed that logic and provoked the people against the administration, however, Americans treated the president as a sovereign, especially those of his own party.

Yrujo rejected the double standard. "The American people cannot be considered as separate from their government," he insisted to Turreau. He echoed Madison's own argument that "the people, not the government, possess the absolute sovereignty" in the United States. As Yrujo saw it, by addressing Americans in the press, he had appealed to the "true sovereign" of the nation.[78]

Yrujo distinguished between the Jefferson administration and the government, for the president and his cabinet comprised only one branch of the government. Americans tried to overthrow administrations every election cycle. In Madrid, Cevallos argued that even if Yrujo used insulting language against the president, opposition presses did the same thing every day. Americans had blurred traditional lines between dissent and disloyalty, so they could hardly claim that Yrujo had conspired against the government. The Spanish court rejected Madison's attempt to apply European diplomatic tradition to a non-traditional nation. Americans couldn't have it both ways.[79]

Adams's bill crumbled to bipartisan defeat in the Senate. Federalists voted against it to deny Jefferson additional power; Republicans voted against it because they assumed Jefferson already possessed such authority. Jefferson and Madison both delighted in the bill when they first heard about it. They rethought their position when they realized the bill might look like it was censuring them for trying to expel Yrujo months earlier without congressional authorization. Better to assume they had always possessed the power, they reasoned. Also, Jefferson had not decided what he wanted to do about Yrujo. He worried he would appear weak if he failed to use the new authority to expel the Spaniard. Unaware that Jefferson had withheld his support for the measure, Yrujo exulted that by scuttling the "ridiculous bill," the Senate had rebuked the administration.[80]

Given that he had never tried to overthrow the US sovereign or government, Yrujo labeled Madison's attempt to oust him a "notorious and scandalous infraction of the laws of nations." Until the spring of 1806, he had assumed that Madison wanted him out of Washington for fear that he would unmask the administration's flawed West Florida policy. In March, he landed on a new explanation, one that knocked Jefferson and Madison on the defensive: They wanted him gone so he couldn't detect their clandestine attack on Spanish sovereignty.[81]

The Venezuelan

Months earlier, on the evening of December 6, 1805, Venezuelan Francisco de Miranda had arrived by stage in Washington. He proceeded to Capitol Hill and lodged at Stelle's. The following day around noon, he found Madison, who received him with "pleasure and friendship." The secretary had heard of the South American's arrival in the United States. Miranda told Madison that he wanted to arrange a meeting "under . . . the most inviolable secret" with the president. Madison replied that he would talk to Jefferson and contact Miranda as soon as possible. Three days later, just as Miranda was finishing dinner in Stelle's tavern, a State Department messenger (probably John Maul) delivered a note. Madison wanted a meeting the next day.[82]

On December 11, the two men met without Jefferson. Madison told Miranda that he had the president's authority to hear Miranda's message. The administration moved cautiously, aware of Miranda's notoriety as an anti-Spanish revolutionary.[83]

Miranda had first tasted revolution in 1781 at Pensacola during the Revolutionary War, helping Spain win West Florida. He fled to the United States two years later, wanted by Spanish authorities for illegal trading. He befriended some of the most influential leaders of the future Federalists, including Hamilton, John Adams, and Rufus King. He then traveled to Europe, where he spent years indulging fantasies of South American independence and courting potential allies in France and Britain. Eventually he gave up and sailed for New York, arriving in November 1805. A month later, he sat across from Madison, explaining his objectives.[84]

Miranda recounted to Madison his decades-long campaign for South American independence. To achieve it, he claimed, he needed nothing more than tacit consent—only a wink from the US government, as he put it. Yet he withheld his plan to break US law by recruiting US citizens as fighters, implying he wanted only to purchase supplies and materiel.[85]

Madison told Miranda that the government would supply no clandestine finances or munitions. He affirmed, however, that US citizens could assist if they chose, something he probably wouldn't have said had he known the kind of help Miranda wanted. Two days later, the pair met again. The government wouldn't help, Madison reiterated. Still, private citizens could do whatever they wished so long as they didn't violate US law. According to Madison's account, he told Miranda that "it would be incumbent on the United States to punish any transactions within their jurisdiction which might . . . involve an hostility against Spain." Even had Madison left the language as vague as Miranda's account suggested ("private individuals could do whatever the laws did not absolutely prohibit"), he had given a clear signal that the United States refused its support.[86]

That afternoon, Jefferson hosted Miranda at a dinner party with Jefferson's daughter and some congressmen. Sitting next to the president, Miranda opined that Spain should cede the Floridas to the United States. In turn, Jefferson predicted the future "glory and splendor of America, which marched quickly in its universal independence." The two men made no formal anti-Spanish agreement, but each understood what the other wanted. Even if it wasn't winking, the administration was smiling.[87]

Beginning with a Brazilian conspiracy in 1786, Jefferson had received periodic visits from South American revolutionaries who desired US support for their causes. He treated Miranda as he did the others—with distant warmth. Despite his personal sympathy for Miranda's cause, he could not commit the US government to support potential or ephemeral insurrections. US officials may have applauded republican revolution but not at the expense of their reputation among European powers.[88]

Despite the guarded response, Miranda insinuated to others that he enjoyed the support of the administration. "Their tacit approbation, and good wishes is evidently with us," he wrote a fellow conspirator. Good wishes, perhaps, but not tacit approbation, especially since he apparently never admitted that he wanted US citizens to sail south to fight with him. He returned to New York and began to recruit (or more often dupe) Americans into an insurrectionary force to liberate Venezuela. He secured a ship and, on February 2, 1806, sailed for the Caribbean on a doomed mission that landed ten US nationals in a hangman's noose in Venezuela.[89]

When Yrujo learned about Madison's meetings with Miranda in late December, he initially thought little of the matter. He was suspicious of Miranda but not distressed. He noted that the Venezuelan had left the capital without the support he had sought from the Jefferson administration. While Yrujo made his trip to Washington, he missed three letters from the Spanish consul in New York, who detailed Miranda's preparations. Yrujo did not receive them until he returned to Philadelphia two days after the Venezuelan had sailed.[90]

Having learned more about Miranda's activities, Yrujo spread word of Madison's conferences with Miranda. According to his version, Madison promised that the government would "shut its eyes" if private citizens volunteered to help, so long as he did not compromise the administration.

As Yrujo told it, Madison fed Miranda's hopes that they could collaborate in the future if Congress declared war on Spain.[91]

The minister alleged that Madison had tried to keep him out of Washington so he couldn't expose the intrigue, but the allegation carried little substance. Madison and Jefferson had considered expelling Yrujo from the country before they even knew that Miranda was sailing for the United States. They agreed to ask Dallas to keep Yrujo out of Washington weeks before they knew Miranda intended to visit the city, and probably before they even knew he had arrived in New York. His accusations were meant to distract from his own failure to detect and impede Miranda.[92]

But Yrujo would not give up. He anonymously authored a series of "questions"—mainly insinuations—for Madison and delivered them to Samuel Relf, the Federalist who had published his Graviora Manent essays. "Did Miranda go to Washington about the middle of December last? Had he two long interviews with you? Did he not present you a plan of an expedition against the province of Caracas [Venezuela]?" From there, the subtle accusations escalated: Miranda had told the administration specifics about his plan, and they agreed to "*shut their eyes*" to his maneuvers. Due to this "criminal connivance," some Americans converted to Miranda's mission, filled US ships with ammunition, and sailed on a "depredatory expedition." They would invite a retaliatory embargo on all American property in Spanish dominions, leading to "ruinous and disastrous consequences."[93]

Republican printers discredited Yrujo's account—his anonymity hardly fooled them—as foreign disinformation. "Every man will know how to distrust the truth of an assert[i]on made by the Spanish *Ex*-minister," chided one. Given Yrujo's recent disgrace, another scoffed, he would "take any measures for revenge." The *National Intelligencer*, the mouthpiece for the Jefferson administration, snapped that Yrujo was "aiming a deadly blow at the character of the whole government." Another newspaper suggested that Yrujo had again bribed his way into a US newspaper to accomplish "his intriguing purposes."[94]

One French official wondered if Yrujo was secretly working for the British, intent on provoking the United States to ally with Britain in a war with Spain. If one traced his conduct from the Louisiana Purchase until the Miranda affair, "one will see, perhaps, that the Marquis has not lost for one instant the intention of enflaming his court against the government of the United States." Even if Yrujo weren't a spy, the official complained, his erratic behavior was throwing America into the arms of Britain.[95]

188 SERPENT IN EDEN

The administration answered Federalist accusations of complicity by prosecuting Samuel Ogden and William Steuben Smith, who had helped Miranda outfit the ship and recruit the ill-fated crew. The trial spiraled into a political fiasco. Federalists accused Jefferson and Madison of sacrificing Smith and Ogden to cover their own sins. Smith and Ogden's Federalist lawyers subpoenaed Jefferson, Madison, and the rest of the cabinet, intent on making the trial a referendum on Jefferson with a heavily Federalist jury. The executive officials ignored the subpoenas. The jury acquitted the defendants.[96]

In Europe, the scandal shook the already tenuous talks over West Florida. Talleyrand was trying to broker a purchase with the $2 million Congress had authorized. Spanish negotiators complained that the United States operated in bad faith, something they had suspected even before the Miranda disaster. Negotiations fizzled, and France advised Spain to fortify West Florida rather than sell it. The region remained Spanish.[97]

The People

Yrujo exploited the early American myth that newspapers were the voice of the people. More often, they were the voice of partisan elites. Yrujo understood that political culture and made them the voice of a foreign government by appealing to the people—the sovereigns of the United States. To his mind, he did nothing more than work within the democratic institutions Americans had created.[98]

Madison disagreed. In January 1807, he composed a thirty-four-page indictment against Yrujo and sent it to the US chargé d'affaires in Spain, George Erving, as a basis to demand Yrujo's departure. In addition to presenting a diplomatic case against Yrujo, Madison wrestled with his own beliefs about constitutional protections for the press and foreigners. Madison fumed that Yrujo would dare assert the right, "in common with the Citizens, and under the Constitution of the Country, to employ the press in vindicating and advancing the objects of his Government, and in turning the opinion of the people against their own." In denying Yrujo constitutional protections, Madison saw no contradiction with his *Report of 1800*. Yrujo wanted to "claim, in the same breath, all the rights of a citizen, and all the immunities of a public minister." He could not enjoy both. The minister pledged no allegiance to the United States, and claimed accountability only to Spain for his "abuses" of the freedom of the press.[99]

Madison wondered what would become of US democracy if the government allowed the free press to propagate "the intrigues of a foreign Minister, in poisoning the public opinion, in biassing the elections, and in turning both against the interests and government of the Country." Madison revealed his quandary. The free press constituted the most important guardian of citizens' rights, but it also served as "the most operative of all modes" for foreign powers to meddle in US politics. Madison recognized that foreign powers need not topple the US government with armies. If they could use the press to sway public opinion and meddle in elections, party politics would do the rest.[100]

The secretary of state refused to concede that diplomatic immunity allowed an ambassador to "tamper with the virtue and fidelity of the citizens," "corrupt the presses," or "arraign [the president] before the community" by publishing insults against him. Madison believed that the United States was particularly vulnerable to such intrusions due to the "peculiarities in their political principles and institutions." The country allowed broad rights to its citizens that foreign powers could exploit if not checked by international law. Too often foreign ministers were "employed in the evil task of corrupting the citizens." Madison invoked a host of diplomatic philosophers who declared that ministers who conspired against the government, disturbed public order, or offended the sovereign could face recall or expulsion.[101]

With his diatribe, Madison revealed the blurry line between political partisanship and foreign collusion—a problem unique to republics. By claiming that Yrujo sought to "corrupt the presses" and "tamper with the virtue and fidelity of the citizens," he implicitly equated loyalty with assent and corruption with dissent. Yrujo thought he was addressing the national sovereigns; Madison thought the Spaniard was "corrupting the citizens." With that mindset, Madison exposed the contradictions of Jefferson's Republicans, who believed their party to be the people's servants in opposition to Federalist overlords. While in the minority, he had proclaimed that sovereignty rested with the people. Once in the governing party, he found the question more complicated, especially when the interests of domestic political opponents seemed to align with the interests of a geopolitical foe. For all his intellectual firepower, he failed to address Yrujo's underlying assumption—that the government and the people were the same.

As a vehicle of public discontent, the free press provided foreign governments a tool to exacerbate partisan tension and influence policy.

By corroding political disagreement into criminality, partisans ironically facilitated rather than suppressed Yrujo's designs. Yrujo had waged press wars with Adams's Federalists and Jefferson's Republicans. He didn't depend on a single party; he depended on political enmity. And he knew he could aggravate it in the free press. So long as an opposition party existed, he could pressure policymakers. He and Madison both recognized the country's quandary: A republic faced a perpetual conflict between protecting its citizens' rights and protecting its own survival.

By the time he wrote his directive to Erving, Madison suspected that Yrujo was engaging in even more sinister enterprises. From the West, Madison heard muddled but alarming rumors that the Spaniard and other foreign agents were sponsoring alleged subterfuge perpetrated by Aaron Burr. The former vice president seemed the spark that might detonate disaster in the West.[102]

9

"The Burr Fever"

A fever is raging among them [Republicans] denominated by Federalists *the Burr fever*.

— MORRIS B. BELKNAP, 1806

YRUJO RELISHED THE IRONY: A declaration of independence targeted at President Thomas Jefferson, the author of the original Declaration of Independence. Former vice president Aaron Burr had written it, so Yrujo's sources told him. Burr had left office in March 1805, scrapped from Jefferson's second term due to his suspected antics during the election of 1800. Now, a year and a half later, as Yrujo understood the plan, Burr would gather a small army under the pretext of leading an expedition to settle new land in the West. The troops would raid a federal arsenal at Cincinnati and descend the Mississippi toward New Orleans. The Assembly of New Orleans would declare western independence from the United States and invite Burr to head the new government.[1]

The Spaniard recounted perhaps the most enduring image of Burr, that of a traitor bent on revolutionizing the West and governing a new nation. It is tempting to accept Yrujo's version as accurate, assuming that as an outside observer he enjoyed objectivity in the matter. Yet Yrujo knew only what Burr and his allies told him. Also, he had Spain's interests to consider, and those interests connected with the destiny of the western United States. He had good reason to want his interpretation to be true.[2]

Burr's actual objective still eludes historians, though many have advanced conclusions with unwarranted certainty. From the quagmire of conflicting, confusing, and missing evidence, scholars have advanced a range of theories to explain Burr's movements between 1805 and 1807. Some believe the Jefferson administration's official line that Burr contemplated treason and disunion. Others have judged that Burr intended to invade Spanish dominions and even hoped to win the sanction of the US government for the offensive. When that plan failed, the argument goes, he gathered recruits to settle legally and peacefully in Spanish territory, just as he claimed he was doing. Or maybe Burr intended to invade Spanish America and assumed western states might unite with his new republic. Since the Louisiana Purchase, many in the East and West, including Jefferson, thought that westerners might eventually form a new nation. Burr may have considered his plot potentially separationist, but not treasonous.[3]

As the conclusions shift, so do the villains. Burr has varied between a treasonous reprobate and a persecuted citizen. Jefferson has been cast either as a perceptive leader or vengeful oppressor, with Madison's reputation tracking close to his. In all versions, the commanding general of the US Army, James Wilkinson, fares poorly, ranging from opportunistic traitor to paranoid traitor. His precise role in the Burr episode remains unclear, but archives outside the United States have long exposed his other acts of treachery.[4]

Burr's project may have remained undefined even in his own mind. He almost certainly contemplated an invasion of Spanish Mexico (a broad term for Spain's remaining dominion west of the Mississippi) and may have considered disunion if necessary—whatever it took to rebuild his reputation as the man who double-crossed Jefferson and killed Hamilton. In 1805, he traveled from Pennsylvania to New Orleans, gauging the political climate and seeing how far he could push his luck.

Many believed Burr's alleged conspiracy the most immediate threat the United States faced, and they saw foreign governments behind it. Mingling their fears with party politics, partisans accused each other of aiding or emboldening Burr and his foreign allies. As the rumors intensified, so did partisan invective. Burr's project—whatever it was— touched every nerve in US political culture: foreign meddling, internal dissent, and party strife.

Republicans and Federalists disavowed Burr, each side with their own reasons to despise him. Since 1800, Republicans had suspected him as a toady of Federalists, while Federalists reminded Americans of his Republican loyalties. Amid the political theatrics, it became and remains impossible to ascertain Burr's motives and objectives. Partisan politics muddied foreign meddling and foreign collusion to the point that Americans could hardly tell—sometimes didn't care to tell—legitimate from exaggerated threats.

Merry

On August 6, 1804, Charles Williamson visited British diplomat Anthony Merry. Merry had arrived in Philadelphia from Washington the week before and lodged at the Franklin Inn in Germantown, just northwest of the city. Distinguished visitors had slipped in and out of his quarters to greet him since his arrival, including Yrujo. Williamson's visit was different; he brought a secret message from Burr.[5]

Scottish by birth, Williamson first came to the United States as a British soldier during the Revolutionary War. Captured, imprisoned, paroled, and finally released in a prisoner exchange, he married a Connecticut woman and returned to Scotland. He moved back to the United States on business in the 1790s and became a US citizen.[6]

Still sympathetic to the British, Williamson wanted to recruit Americans to attack the French Caribbean and possibly Spanish Florida. He befriended Vice President Burr, whose ambition matched his own. Burr had killed Hamilton in July 1804 and fled vengeful Hamilton allies in New York, sheltering in Philadelphia. There, he and Williamson made a plan to secure British aid for their hazy scheme.[7]

Williamson approached Merry with details. After Williamson departed, Merry wrote a coded message to his superior in London. Burr would "lend his assistance to His Majesty's Government in any manner in which they may think fit to employ him, particularly in endeavouring to effect a separation of the Western Part of the United States from that which lies between the Atlantick and the Mountains, in its whole Extent." Williamson headed to London and would provide more information, Merry wrote.[8]

Merry entertained fantasies of western secession with British help. He detested Jefferson, who spurned social etiquette that Merry thought essential to diplomacy. Jefferson had broken what Merry considered correct protocol by improperly seating Merry's wife at dinner (a small but significant slight in honor-obsessed circles of the elite). He hoped to see the union crumble under Jefferson's care. He argued that if his government gave commercial advantages to westerners, they would secede and become a British economic dependency. When Williamson explained Burr's plans, Merry saw his vision materializing.[9]

Either Merry misunderstood Williamson, or Williamson tailored his account to fit Merry's predispositions. When Williamson arrived in London, he gave a tamer version of the plan than Merry had described. He advocated a coordinated US-British attack on Spanish lands and cast

Burr as the leader of an army, not as a traitor requesting help to dissolve the union or pledging his services to Britain. Burr gave different versions of his plan to different people, depending on where he thought their loyalties lay. Williamson likely told Merry whatever he thought might win the diplomat's support.[10]

While Burr waited for the British cabinet's response, he finished the final months of his vice presidency. He spent most of the time presiding over the impeachment trial of Supreme Court justice Samuel Chase, who was eventually acquitted by the Senate. On March 2, 1805, Burr delivered a farewell speech to the Senate that moved many to tears. Friends and enemies described it as a masterpiece. He pleaded for reason and impartial dialogue in the Senate, averring that he had "known no party."[11]

More than most politicians of the time, Burr defied strict party identity, and that contributed to many of his problems. He had organized for Republicans, and he had depended on Federalists to support his move for the presidency in 1800. He had created an open rift with Jefferson, the nation's most eminent Republican, and he shot and killed Hamilton, the nation's most eminent Federalist. He had recently presided over the partisan-tinged impeachment trial of Chase with impartial poise. Then as now, many partisans interpreted non-partisanship as weak-kneed inconstancy or crass opportunism. Burr's enemies usually accused him of the latter.[12]

With no natural political home, Burr invited suspicion from all sides when he began to pursue his cryptic plans weeks after he left office, beginning with secret conversations with Merry. That March, he told Merry that Louisianans craved independence from the United States. They waited only for "protection & assistance from some foreign Power" and cooperation with other western regions. Burr kept the details vague, but he wanted to facilitate those connections, Merry reported in code to London. Westerners preferred to ally with Britain, Burr assured Merry, but he threatened that they would contact France if the British refused.[13]

Some historians have questioned Burr's truthfulness with Merry, but their reasoning has limited appeal. As one theory goes, Burr planned an invasion of Mexico and the Floridas, not disunion. He knew that Britain would not fund a scheme to overthrow Spanish dominions, so he lied and told Merry that he planned western secession. The theory fails to explain why Burr believed Britain would sooner aid a treasonous plot against the United States than an attack against the Spanish Empire. The first option would only turn the neutral United States into an adversary. The second would potentially maim an enemy. Besides, Burr eventually told Merry about his plans to invade Spanish lands, something he wouldn't have done if he wanted to fool Merry about his true purpose. Most likely, Burr was following his pattern of telling others what he thought they wanted to hear while keeping all options open.[14]

While he waited for a response from London that would never arrive, Burr plunged westward to kick-start his operation. Between April and October 1805, he traveled into the Ohio Valley, down to Tennessee, onto New Orleans, and back up toward Indiana Territory. Along the route, he socialized with some of the region's most prominent figures and consorted with potential collaborators. Many westerners considered Burr a man who had fought for their interests in the Senate, where, for example, he supported Tennessee statehood. Away from the polarizing politics of New York and Washington, he still enjoyed connections in high places.[15]

As he toured the West, gossip began to trail his heels until one Federalist newspaper turned the whispers into howls. In July, the *United States' Gazette* insinuated that Burr might "form a separate government" in the West, ally with Britain, and invade Mexico. Yrujo probably authored it.[16]

Yrujo

Yrujo heard about Burr's alleged conspiracy in the spring of 1805. At first, he thought Burr was a British agent who intended to revolutionize the West and maybe invade Spanish dominions. He knew Burr had met secretly with Merry while in Washington. Burr had also requested passports to travel to Mexico, which Yrujo denied. The diplomat began to warn other Spanish officers of Burr's possibly nefarious designs.[17]

On December 5, 1805, former New Jersey Federalist Senator Jonathan Dayton appeared at Yrujo's Philadelphia house. Dayton possessed impeccable political credentials. At twenty-six, he had been the youngest signer of the US Constitution. He rose to the House Speaker's chair in the 1790s and then served as a US senator. By the time he stepped into Yrujo's residence that winter, Dayton had become an important ally of Burr, a friend since youth.[18]

Dayton played the double agent with Yrujo, hinting that he held secrets that Spain might want to purchase. He told Yrujo that Burr had proposed a joint military expedition with Britain to take the Floridas from Spain and win western independence. The Floridas would become part of an independent West, which would grant Britain special economic privileges for its help. The army would then invade Spanish Mexico and make republics of it.[19]

Dayton was working for Burr, not betraying him. Burr knew that Yrujo was suspicious of his plans, and he guessed that the Spaniard had published the piece in the *United States' Gazette*. Some historians have doubted Yrujo's authorship, but it conformed perfectly to his modus operandi—pressuring his enemies by posing as an American in US periodicals. The Federalist gazette had become one of his favorite outlets. The writing also followed the style he used against Madison during the Miranda affair, building unsubtle accusations through a series of rhetorical queries. According to one of Burr's allies, Yrujo once spied on Burr's lodging for two hours to catch him with Merry. Burr knew he needed to divert Yrujo, paradoxically by confirming his suspicions. By first admitting that Burr contemplated an attack on Mexico, Dayton was priming Yrujo to believe him when he told him Burr had changed his mind.[20]

Burr had abandoned hope of British support, Dayton told Yrujo later in December. He lied; London officials had little interest in Burr's project, but Burr didn't know that at the time. Dayton knew Yrujo wouldn't cooperate if he thought Burr still counted on Spain's British enemies, so he proposed a different scheme to the Spaniard. No longer interested in Spanish territory, Burr wanted to seize Washington, depose Jefferson, dissolve the government, then dismember the West. If Spain wanted to redirect Burr from Mexico and aid his attack on the American capital, he just needed between $500,000 and $1 million from Yrujo's government.[21]

Over the next several months, Burr hopped between Philadelphia and Washington, and whispers flitted about secret encounters with Yrujo. Some reported late-night meetings between the two at Stelle's hotel when Yrujo made his controversial trip to Washington in January 1806. One senator's sources told him that Burr and Yrujo made frequent private contact in Philadelphia. Erick Bollmann, one of Burr's lieutenants, confirmed the meetings and even remarked that Yrujo began to pester Burr with his visits.[22]

Burr and his associates may have mistaken Yrujo's interest for enthusiasm, a misstep some historians have followed. Yrujo wanted to believe Dayton. "Spain would view with extreme satisfaction the dismemberment of the colossal power which was growing up at the very gates of her most precious and important colonies," he gushed to Spain's minister of foreign relations Cevallos. Nevertheless, the Spaniard remained suspicious that Burr aimed for Mexico and the Floridas. Besides, his superiors in Madrid warned him not to commit Spain to Burr's cause, though they had some in-terest in where his plans might lead. Yrujo asked Madrid for an agent to spy on Burr. Yrujo likely badgered Burr to extract information from him rather than to back his plan, feigning excitement to get close to him.[23]

Many believed that the encounters indicated Spanish support for Burr's plot. Rumors already floated from the West that Spain conspired against the United States. "Spanish intrigues have been carried on among our people:—we have traitors among us," a Federalist Kentucky prosecutor named Joseph Hamilton Daveiss warned Jefferson in January 1806. "A seperation of the union in favour of Spain is the object," he continued. "This plot is laid wider than you imagine. Mention the subject to no man from the western country however high an office he may be:—some of them are deeply tainted with this Treason." Among others, Daveiss suspected "a very exalted magistrate of this country," a man known to Spanish rulers as Number 13: James Wilkinson.[24]

Number 13

After rising in US military rank, Wilkinson had cooled his espionage for Spain for a short time in the 1790s. The United States had emerged as the clear power in the Mississippi Valley, making it the more attractive op-tion for the incurably self-interested general. By 1798, however, he worried that Spanish officials would expose his earlier activities, so he crept back into their confidence to keep them quiet. Within two months after the United States received Louisiana from France, Wilkinson had met with West Florida's Spanish governor, Vicente Folch. He promised inside infor-mation in return for $20,000 in back pay and a renewal of his pension as a Spanish agent.[25]

While he divulged US secrets to Spain, Wilkinson secured governorship of the upper region of the Louisiana Territory, which stretched from the Arkansas River to Canada. Jefferson knew his choice of Wilkinson as ter-ritorial governor ran risks. He had heard rumors that Wilkinson spied for Spain. He considered it more important, however, to entice Wilkinson to the United States with a carrot than beat him into the arms of the Spanish with a stick. Besides, one of Wilkinson's main accusers was a Federalist in whom Jefferson deposited little trust.[26]

Wilkinson wanted Spain's money, but he also wanted its North American land. He fantasized about seizing Mexico and promoted the idea of inva-sion to his superiors in Washington. He was not averse to abandoning his commitments to Spain with the promise of greater glory and wealth. His ambition, duplicity, position, and contacts made him a peerless ally. Like most two-timers, Wilkinson kept all paths clear while he assessed likely victors—the United States, Spain, or Burr.[27]

Burr and Wilkinson met at Fort Massac in June 1805 while Burr toured the West. They had shared private conversations dating back at least to May 1804, probably earlier. Wilkinson claimed that at Fort Massac they had a harmless discussion about Burr possibly representing some western region in Congress. Those who knew Wilkinson's double-dealings and who suspected Burr of treasonous intentions believed not a word of it. Wilkinson became a prime suspect with Burr, especially after Burr left the fort with a letter from Wilkinson to Daniel Clark, a prominent New Orleans resident, that sounded like an invitation to a secret plan. "You are spoken of as [Burr's] right hand man," Clark wrote Wilkinson after the rumors started to grow. Whatever he and Wilkinson discussed, Burr believed Wilkinson his ally. Yet among his three options—the United States, Spain, and Burr— the general rejected Burr first.[28]

In late 1805, Wilkinson ceased contact with Burr after Spanish forces crossed the Sabine River into what Americans considered their territory. The occupation tested Wilkinson's conflicting loyalties. After diplomacy failed, the Jefferson administration expected him to lead a force to repel the Spanish troops. The general depended on his US appointment, because without it, he was a useless spy to Spain. In late summer of 1806, he led troops to confront the Spanish.[29]

War seemed imminent until a leader of the Kadohadacho—a major tribe among the Caddo in the Red River region—named Dehahuit intervened in late August 1806. Spain and the United States competed for land occupied by Dehahuit's Native nation. A "remarkably shrewd and sensible fellow," according to one American observer, Dehahuit could recruit hundreds of warriors if needed—enough to turn the tide in the small-scale conflict. He also possessed a gift for diplomacy, growing up with his father, Tinhiouen, a man known as the "Great Peacemaker." Dehahuit gave a loose pledge to the United States in return for greater autonomy, prompting Spanish forces to return west of the Sabine. Over the following two months, Wilkinson, the Spanish commander, and Dehahuit negotiated the Neutral Ground, a small strip between Louisiana and Texas that both armies agreed to vacate.[30]

Peace stunted Burr's plans. He had counted on violence with Spain, which would have given him a pretext to launch his incursion. He had continued his preparations during the spring and summer of 1806, recruiting a handful of lieutenants back East and hundreds of other followers with varying loyalties. He told most of them that he targeted Mexico, and many joined assuming they would aid the United States in war against Spain, not mount an illegal invasion or commit treason. Even if Burr decided to forge ahead, he doomed his plan when he sent Wilkinson what came to be called the "cipher letter"—one of the most controversial documents in American history.[31]

In early October, a young Burr ally named Samuel Swartwout found Wilkinson at his headquarters along the Sabine. Swartwout had first met Thomas H. Cushing, Wilkinson's second-in-command, and Cushing introduced him to Wilkinson. Swartwout said he had come to fight Spain, though by then Wilkinson knew no fight would occur. Cushing excused himself.[32]

That's when Swartwout dropped the pretense. He retrieved a packet from his coat and handed it to Wilkinson. A message from Burr, he told the general. Wilkinson asked Burr's location. Swartwout replied that he was still in Philadelphia, so far as he knew. Burr had actually left for the Ohio Valley to launch his mission months earlier. Swartwout stepped out of the headquarters, and Wilkinson carried the packet to his private chambers. Burr had authored the letter on July 22 at Philadelphia. He wrote in a mish-mash of plain text and codes that Burr and Wilkinson had used for earlier secretive correspondence. Wilkinson deciphered the code by candlelight that night. It made tedious work, matching each numbered code to a page and line in a dictionary and translating symbols into words with a key.[33]

After Wilkinson deciphered the code, he stared at a letter as perplexing as the rest of the Burr Conspiracy. The letter deepens the mystery of Burr's objective rather than clarifies it. Some scholars have even disputed Burr's authorship, though he seems the probable choice, and Wilkinson forever claimed that it came from Burr.[34]

For all its ambiguity, the letter was potentially damning for Wilkinson. "I have at length obtained funds," Burr exulted, "and have actually commenced." "Naval protection of England is secured," he lied. "A navy of the United States ready to join," he misled again, suggesting that Commander Thomas Truxton planned to deliver US naval support. Then the most incriminating (and humiliating) lines for Wilkinson, written, as Burr's notes often were, in third person: "Wilkinson shall be second to Burr only. . . . Our project my dear friend is brought to the point so long desired." Burr would move between 500 and 1,000 men down the Mississippi River in November, meet Wilkinson (and by implication team up with his army), and continue to their unspecified final destination. "The people of the country to which we are going are prepared to receive us," Burr assured Wilkinson. "The gods invite us to glory and fortune."[35]

Less conniving minds would have seen a potentially incriminating letter that threatened to implicate Wilkinson in an illegal plot, but Wilkinson saw opportunity. Peace had ruined whatever plans he and Burr may have conjured, making Burr expendable. For years, Wilkinson had served two masters, and he nearly brought them to war against each other at the Sabine. He couldn't please one without antagonizing the other. Now, he could win the thanks of both if he turned on Burr, and Burr had given him the evidence to do it.[36]

Wilkinson faced the problem that the letter mentioned him as a Burr associate—second only to Burr, in fact. No problem. Only he and Burr knew the code. Wilkinson could make it say whatever he wanted, and Burr couldn't challenge him without exposing himself. Wilkinson began to tweak the letter, erasing his own role. He turned "our project" into "the project," for example. With the altered letter, Wilkinson joined the chorus crying treason against Burr.[37]

Wilkinson dispatched an emissary to Mexico City to warn Spanish authorities of Burr's plot and collect payment for the intelligence. He told officials nothing they hadn't already learned from their own network of spies and informants. They refused to pay.[38]

On November 6, the day after Wilkinson made a final peace with the Spanish commander at the Sabine, Wilkinson received a duplicate of the cipher letter from a second Burr agent named Erick Bollmann. Wilkinson learned that Bollmann had spent over a month in New Orleans. Bollman may not have known the content of the letter, but he could have told any number of people about Wilkinson's involvement in the plan.[39]

With peace secured on the Sabine, Wilkinson wheeled his army toward New Orleans to act as the savior of the city and to silence those who could connect him to Burr. He warned officials in New Orleans and Washington of "a deep, dark and wicked conspiracy" that threatened the city. In fact, rather than the thousands Wilkinson claimed, Burr's forces had dwindled to an anemic couple dozen or so. Even so, the general arrived in New Orleans on November 25, casting himself as the city's protector and flashing the doctored cipher letter to support his case. He needed to arrest anybody involved in the plot, including Swartwout and Bollman.[40]

The same day that Wilkinson entered New Orleans, Madison entered the executive mansion in Washington, probably greeted by Jefferson's courteous French maître d'hôtel, Étienne Lemaire. Lemaire would have shown Madison through the grand Entrance Hall, into Jefferson's antechamber, and through another door into the president's large private study. With its high ceiling, the room featured Jefferson's favorite things: tall bookshelves, plant-lined windowsills, walls draped with large maps, fine mahogany furniture, and probably natural specimens from the West, which the president loved to collect. The study may have exhibited some of the samples sent by Wilkinson a year earlier, such as a Native chart drawn on a buffalo hide, plant samples, and horned frogs. Whether or not the treasures were in the room, Wilkinson made his presence felt.[41]

Madison sat with Jefferson and other cabinet members—Albert Gallatin of the Treasury Department and War Secretary Henry Dearborn—to discuss recent news from Wilkinson. Jefferson had just received a dispatch from the general about an army of 8,000 to 10,000 men. Wilkinson hadn't included specifics; he even denied knowing the "prime mover." He believed, however, that the forces planned an insurrection in Orleans Territory followed by an attack on Mexico. If so, he assured Jefferson that he would "throw myself with my little Band into New orleans, to be ready to defend that Capital against usurpation & violence."[42]

Wilkinson's dispatch arrived just in time to salvage his standing with Jefferson. Before November, the president had started to doubt Wilkinson's loyalty. The month before, he had received a credible report that Burr and Wilkinson were working together. In a series of October cabinet meetings, the administration wrestled with the alleged conspiracy. Madison sent a secret agent west to investigate Burr. But Wilkinson? "What is proper to be done as to him?" the cabinet agonized. He enjoyed the loyalty of the army, making it possibly more dangerous to cut him loose than retain him in command, especially if he did connive with Burr. With peace on the Sabine and his campaign against Burr that November, Wilkinson had reassured Jefferson maybe not of his integrity but at least of his reliability.[43]

Wilkinson cemented that confidence when he sent Jefferson a deciphered version of the cipher letter, which reached the president on January 18, 1807. Jefferson pleaded with Wilkinson for the original ciphered version and the key. Wilkinson never sent it, knowing that the key would expose his falsifications. In fact, the administration asked mystifyingly few questions of Wilkinson—questions that other Americans did ask—including why he and Burr shared a cipher in the first place. The question probably occurred to Jefferson. He may have assumed that Swartwout delivered the key with the letter (an improbable scenario since a cardinal rule of cryptology is to keep the lock and key separate). More likely, Jefferson knew he needed Wilkinson and, therefore, ignored some of the troubling questions. The general had provided the firmest proof yet of a conspiracy that had existed only as a rumor. And he commanded the army that might smother it. "Scoundrels have their uses," as one historian has put it, "and Wilkinson was the president's scoundrel."[44]

The administration wielded the cipher letter to condemn Burr before the public. On January 22, 1807, Jefferson submitted it to Congress as part of a general proclamation accusing Burr of planning an attack on Mexico and disunion in the West. Jefferson weaponized the office of the presidency—the proverbial "bully pulpit"—against Burr. Americans had heard conflicting rumors about Burr's plans for nearly two years; Jefferson cemented the suspicions of treason. He assured Congress, Burr's "guilt is placed beyond question."[45]

Arrests

Two days later, Jefferson and Madison interrogated Erick Bollmann, now held prisoner at the Washington marine barracks. Had Burr received financial backing from foreign governments? Had he cooperated with the ministers of Great Britain or Spain? Had he sent agents to those nations to win their support?[46]

Wilkinson had apprehended Bollmann, along with Swartwout, two months earlier, when he began his heavy-handed military reign in New Orleans. The two men had delivered Burr's ciphered message and could connect Wilkinson to the plan. Wilkinson swore an affidavit that accused them of trying to recruit him, using his distorted version of the cipher letter as evidence. He sent them under guard to Washington, where they had arrived on January 22.[47]

In the message he sent to Congress that day, Jefferson had discounted the possibility that foreign governments aided Burr. He declared that the United States pursued "paths of peace and justice" with Spain and Britain, making it unlikely that they would support treason. In fact, Jefferson did suspect Yrujo and Merry, but he had barely avoided bloodshed with Spain along the Sabine, and he now had envoys in London trying to rework the Jay Treaty. It wasn't the moment to fling about charges of foreign subversion. Even so, the president and Madison wanted to learn more, so they met with Bollmann.[48]

Convinced that Burr's plans were more patriotic than treasonous, Bollmann had asked for a private conference with Jefferson to explain the mission. The president agreed and invited Madison, the pair promising not to use the information against Bollmann at trial. The meeting marked a singular moment in US history: the president and secretary of state personally interrogating an accused traitor to investigate a former vice president.[49]

As Bollmann narrated it, Burr masked his plan to invade Mexico by telling Yrujo that he planned to detach the West from the Union. "Yrujo . . . entered eagerly & zealously into the plan," Bollmann told Madison and Jefferson. The Spanish minister met frequently with Burr and "*pestered* him with his advice & exhortations, offered him the use of 10,000 stand of Arms & money to any necessary amount." Yrujo "was in fact so full of zeal, that he would have gone to Spain, in order to put his Government into the course of effectual Cooperation."[50]

Burr knew that France wanted Louisiana back, Bollmann told them. Unless Burr stripped Spain of Mexico, Napoleon would establish a puppet government in the West and revive the threat to the United States. Burr wanted to coordinate with US authorities to counter the "deadly hatred" and "dangerous designs of Spain & France." Burr was a hero, not a traitor.[51]

Madison and Jefferson asked the obvious question: Why did Burr try to hide his actions from the US government, then?

Events would fly too quickly for Congress, Bollmann explained. Had Burr divulged his scheme, he would have ruined the surprise strike against Mexico. He couldn't tell Jefferson the plan because the president had no authority to approve it on his own. Burr needed to assume that the government would favor his designs.[52]

What about Britain? Jefferson and Madison wondered.

Burr "communicated freely with Merry," admitted Bollmann. The diplomat "entered warmly into his views," promising that the British government would support the expedition. Bollmann clarified that Britain wanted to hurt France and Spain, not the United States. (That statement would have surprised Merry, who had actually tried to advance the treasonous part of Burr's supposed plot.)[53]

From Bollmann's report, it seemed more critical than ever that Yrujo leave the country. Just days prior, Madison had sent his lengthy report against Yrujo to the American chargé d'affaires in Madrid. He could add Bollmann's revelations to "the perfidious conduct which Spain has long been pursuing towards the United States through her diplomatic and other Agents on this side of the Atlantic." His thoughts drifted to the 1780s, when Gardoqui had tried to manipulate his friend John Brown and trigger disunion. Yrujo "entered eagerly" into Burr's plan, Madison seethed a week later in a coded letter to Monroe, by then an envoy in London. As far as Madison could see, Spain had spent decades trying to dismantle the nation through conspiracies with disaffected Americans.[54]

"Burr intrigued with Merry," Madison added to Monroe. The British diplomat may have convinced his government to support the scheme had the prime minister not died, he explained, relating information from Bollmann. Madison instructed his friend to investigate further in London.[55]

Despite the danger, Burr's enterprise was "pretty effectually crushed," Madison reassured Monroe. Burr's army numbered "a handful of men only" by then, and Wilkinson had arrested central conspirators such as Bollmann and Swartwout. Then in February, 1807, US troops arrested Burr and sent him to Richmond for trial. Jefferson flaunted the wilted conspiracy as a vindication of his governing philosophy: "THE GREAT SECRET OF GOVERNMENT IS TO LET EVERY THING TAKE ITS OWN COURSE." The president exulted that, unlike the tyrants of Europe, he hadn't needed an army to cripple the conspiracy. A few proclamations had starved it of support.[56]

Blame

Tench Coxe warned Madison that the president may have prematurely declared victory. Like most Americans, Coxe possessed only secondhand knowledge of the alleged plot, but (again, like most Americans) that sufficed for him to form tenacious opinions about it. He briefed Madison that Burr had coveted an independent state *"confederated with a great power."* Spain may be the dupe, or the submissive partner in the plan. It matters not which. [Yrujo] seems ready for such things." Burr counted on "direct or indirect foreign aid" and "deeper internal treason than we know." Jefferson may have saved the country from Burr in the short-term, he cautioned, but a deeper conspiracy with foreign powers still simmered.[57]

For Republicans like Coxe, Federalists made prime suspects for such a scheme. "I am satisfied that extreme party men ... would have been willing to see Burr dissever us to alter the local position of the public authority, to obtain army and navy, to change the principles of our government, to accomplish foreign connexions, and for all this kind of purposes. Party was never more extreme than now," he lamented. By "extreme party men" he meant Federalists. Burr threatened to combine "those wicked men" with foreign powers to subvert the nation.[58]

Coxe illustrated for Madison why Federalists supported Burr: If the West seceded, they would regain the power they enjoyed before the Louisiana Purchase. According to Coxe, Federalists hoped that Burr would convert the West into an "antirepublican Neighbor" and invite European domination. Europe's *"hostile," "secret cabinets"* could then pressure the United States to abandon democracy.[59]

Coxe feared that the French lurked behind the entire scheme. Burr and Yrujo likely plotted to make the West "a subconfederate state" for France "with Burr at the head." A French official stirred Coxe's suspicions when he reportedly declared in Philadelphia, "Your government cannot go on— you must or will have an Emperor." Paradoxically, though, France's supposed subterfuge condemned Federalists in Coxe's eyes. Federalists hated Burr, he explained to Madison, but "they sigh for the objects they think he might have accomplished, even in concert with a power whom they hate still more." Federalists would promote their "illegitimate and monstrous objects ... by any means and any men however odious and despised." They may hate Burr and France, Coxe reasoned, but they would use them to overpower democracy and bury freedom's defenders *"under the ruins of the constitution.* ... Tis a wild ambition and a revengeful spirit with which the party is possessed."[60]

As Coxe's somewhat tortured explanation shows, partisans struggled to fit Burr's untidy political and diplomatic loyalties into their partisan framework. Burr had tried to secure British aid; he also tried to recruit Britain's Spanish enemy, which introduced suspicions of French influence. Burr had enjoyed support among some Federalists and anti-Jefferson Republicans, but some Jefferson allies had also backed him early on. When anti-Burr Republicans raised cries of insurrection, some Federalists dismissed their warnings as *"Burr fever."* Burr's Republican allies claimed that Federalists were persecuting him. Those claims escalated when Federalist US attorney Joseph Hamilton Daveiss tried and failed to indict Burr in November 1806.

By January, 1807, however, most Americans seem to have accepted the Jefferson administration's official version that Burr contemplated something illegal at best, treasonous at worst. Though he defied party lines, Burr became a useful means to taint political opponents.[61]

Some Federalists believed the French backed Burr. American newspapers had recently published purloined dispatches from a French commander to Louis-Marie Turreau about a "*secret expedition*" about to sail from Cuba. The commander instructed Turreau to help coordinate with French ships in the Chesapeake. For Federalist editor Thomas Fessendon, the dispatches exposed a joint attack on New Orleans among the French, Spanish, and Burr. Fessendon promised to "leave the deductions to the public," but he helpfully hinted that Republicans aimed to "trust our national Independence to the keeping of Turreau, Burr, and Yrujo."[62]

Other Federalists impugned Jefferson for his weak response to Burr. As one Federalist poet put it:

> How chanc'd our chief to make no stir,
> Full nine months to stop that Burr?[63]

Federalist editor Stephen Cullen Carpenter derided the president's "proclamation force and pop-gun armaments." Republicans had convinced Americans that they needed no army, and now Republicans had orchestrated the very insurrection that made an army necessary, he bristled. Carpenter marveled that Republicans had not tried to implicate Federalists in the plot.[64]

The Republican *Public Advertiser* obliged. "Open and avowed federalists" had flocked to Burr's ranks, the newspaper declared, reviving their antics from the 1790s when they cooperated with British diplomat Liston during the Blount conspiracy. The editors assured readers that "*Liston* was as notorious for his intrigues then, as *Yrujo* or *Burr* are now." Merry now intrigued with Federalists to continue the "plan of dismemberment," they argued. Carpenter was "a *hired emissary*"—a British tool to spread its propaganda in the United States. According to Republican James Sullivan, Burr seemed the last "miserable hope" of Federalists who wanted to remake the United States into a British-style monarchy. Another Republican believed it only a matter of time before Americans learned that "leading federalists" supported Burr. Most already knew of the Federalist Senator Dayton's involvement. In the meantime, the writer fumed, British sympathizers accused the French of aiding his scheme. "But who is so foolish as really to believe France would join these buccaneers in dismembering the Spanish dominions!"[65]

Yrujo made a conspicuous target due to his infamy, and Federalists and Republicans scrambled to tarnish the opposing side with him. "*Yrujo* was the intimate friend of *Merry*," the *Public Advertiser* contended, "and it is well known that he did excite *Merry* to improper acts against our government." With Yrujo's prodding, the editors claimed, Merry informed his superiors about Burr's treason and happily allied with him. British rulers hoped for the ruin of American institutions and the subversion of its government. Federalists and British agents backed Burr's conspiracy, but "adulators and *emissaries* of the government of England" wanted to fault Jefferson for it, they complained.[66]

For Federalists, Yrujo was a French lackey, who, with Turreau, was "intriguing and bullying at the seat of Government," as one writer accused. Burr's conspiracy, the Spanish invasion along the Sabine, Yrujo and Turreau's intrigues—they were all part of Napoleon's plan to use his agents ("pioneers of hell") to prepare the United States for his conquest. Just as the president failed to move swiftly against Burr, he failed to extinguish the French threat. The "hirelings of Napoleon" used "the most diabolical industry to divide the people [and] sow the seeds of distruction among them." Like most Americans, the author diagnosed the problem as "political controversy and party heats" that "lay bare the bosom of the country to every hostile sword." And like most partisans, he blamed his opponents for the division.[67]

According to one Federalist rhyme-smith, Burr conspired with Talleyrand and Yrujo to invite Napoleon back to the continent:

> You'll find [Burr's] schemes, I fancy, plann'd
> In union with one Talleyrand:
> A certain Marquis [Yrujo], like as not,
> Has had a finger in the plot.

The Burr/Yrujo/Talleyrand conspiracy formed part of a wider effort by French sympathizers to "open our gates" to Napoleon:

> Have not the tyrant's friends, so steady,
> Invited foreign troops already?

> Yes, sent the French an invitation,
> To set their feet upon the nation!!![68]

A Federalist satire summarized the fight to smear political opponents with Burr's name. The author imagines a conversation between Republican stalwarts William Duane and Michael Leib. "I think," Duane tells Leib, "we have gained something on the general scale by charging *Burr's* defection to the account of the federalists." Though fictional, the comment represented the political strategy of both parties. Voltaire once quipped, "If God did not exist, it would be necessary to invent him." If the Burr Conspiracy didn't exist, partisans would have been obliged to invent it.[69]

Prisoners

In late January 1807, while Swartwout lingered with Bollmann in the marine barracks, his lawyers begged Madison for the chance to talk to their client. Swartwout and Bollmann had languished in prison for days, under military guard and without a civil arrest warrant. The marine commandant had refused them access to counsel. The lawyers had appealed to Secretary of War Dearborn, who declined to help. Finally, they contacted Madison, asking him to petition the president if he could do nothing for them.[70]

The petitions went nowhere because Jefferson had ordered that the men have no access to an attorney. Jefferson had declared Burr guilty before the nation. To stop Burr (or perhaps to punish him for his behavior during the 1800 election), Jefferson had accepted Wilkinson's version of events and praised the general's "honor" and "fidelity," though he knew that the general might have cooperated with Burr before turning on him. He defended Wilkinson's power grab in New Orleans, when the general declared martial law, imprisoned Burr supporters on his own falsified evidence, and arrested Burr even after a grand jury refused to indict him. Whether in good or bad faith, Jefferson had committed himself to the treason charges and wanted guilty verdicts.[71]

On January 30, a federal prosecutor asked the DC circuit court for arrest warrants against Bollmann and Swartwout for treason. He acted with "instructions received from the president of the United States." The court featured two Jefferson appointees and one Federalist. Despite flaws in the prosecution's case, the two Republicans outvoted their Federalist colleague and issued the warrants—the first party-line vote in a federal court in US history.[72]

The political friction worsened when Swartwout and Bollmann's lawyers—"a solid phalanx of seasoned Jefferson critics," as one legal historian has called them—appealed to the Supreme Court in February. The appeal brought the case before Chief Justice John Marshall, Jefferson's second cousin and a Federalist. The two despised each other. Jefferson still seethed about Marshall's opinion several years prior in *Marbury v. Madison*, a suit against Madison to require him to deliver a justice of the peace commission to an Adams appointee. Though the court didn't direct Madison to deliver the commission—a technical victory for the administration— Marshall expanded the court's power at Jefferson's expense. He declared that a lower court could order Madison to convey the commission (and seemed to suggest that it should), arguing that the courts had some power over executive actions. Madison said almost nothing about the case, but Jefferson complained about Marshall's "gratuitous interference" and "the perversion of the law" for the rest of his life. In 1807, the cousins prepared for a rematch.[73]

The defense lawyers commended the *Marbury* decision, arguing that the court again needed to curb executive overreach, and Marshall agreed. The chief justice held that the prosecution presented no evidence that Swartwout and Bollmann had levied war against the United States, a criterion for treason under the Constitution. He freed the prisoners and gave the administration a high bar for prosecuting Burr.[74]

Nevertheless, prosecute they did.

The Trial

That summer, Madison received an unexpected visitor at his F Street house in Washington: Jonathan Dayton. A grand jury had indicted Dayton along with Burr and a few others for treason in late June. The charges stemmed from events in mid-December 1806, when some of Burr's men had allegedly mustered on Blennerhassett Island on the Ohio River, waited for boats to ship them to New Orleans, threatened a militia officer, then fled. The Jefferson administration hoped the gathering would meet Marshall's standard of "levying war." Like Burr, Dayton was far from the island when the events occurred, but he was a suspected ringleader.[75]

Uncertain why one of the indicted conspirators would call on him, Madison didn't hide his distaste for the visit. Attorney General Caesar Rodney happened to be in the house, which may have increased the discomfort. Dayton sensed tension, uttered some excuse for his call, and left.[76]

In early August, Dayton wrote Madison to explain: He had appeared at his house that day to plead his innocence and to ask the secretary's permission to post bail, which he believed he needed. In "wretched" health, he feared authorities would throw him in a jail cell, where he would die and leave behind his wife and two daughters. Desperate, he wrote to Jefferson asking the same favor. Madison and Jefferson discussed the request and decided the question belonged to the courts rather than the executive—an obvious conclusion today, less so at the time. Both on extended breaks to their Virginia plantations by mid-August, the president and secretary exchanged five letters to ensure they agreed on their response to Dayton. The exchange illustrated how closely Jefferson and Madison superintended the case and how closely they worked together. By no coincidence, Dayton believed he needed Jefferson's and Madison's personal help. They may have left the question of bail to the courts, but, like others all around the country, Dayton knew that this was Jefferson's case.[77]

With Madison's help, Jefferson managed nearly every facet of the trial and steered it toward a partisan battle. Jefferson and Madison decided to try Burr in Richmond—a cynical political maneuver. At the time, Supreme Court justices headed trial cases at circuit courts, and Marshall would be the trial judge in Richmond that summer. As Jefferson explained it, even if they lost the case, the defeat "will heap coals of fire on the head of the judge." They could lose legally and still win politically. Jefferson hoped the people might even amend the Constitution to give voters more control over federal judges, whom he viewed as the last Federalist holdouts in the government. Jefferson predicted that Burr would walk free only if "his federal patrons give him an opportunity of running away."[78]

Jefferson tried Federalists in the court of public opinion while his administration tried Burr in the courtroom. "The federalists appear to make Burr's cause their own"; "the fact is that the Federalists make Burr's cause their own"; "the federalists too give all their aid, making Burr's cause their own," he repeated ad nauseam. Federalists only regretted that Burr failed to "overturn the government," introduce a monarchy, and "rid them of this hateful republic."[79]

Other Republicans chorused with him. The "main springs, at least, of the federal party were English in their feelings, monarchical and disposed to support Burr as far as they could venture," Tench Coxe assured Madison. Burr's indictment pleased everybody but Federalists, chimed in another. Joshua Hatheway saw a dangerous plot forming ever since Federalists supported Burr for president. Now, he elaborated, "we hear the tongue of every federalist excusing him, and calumniating our executive for his energetic measures against Burr—taking all these things into view, they irresistibly force a conviction on the mind, that a PLOT has long since been laid by the *Federalists* and *Burr*."[80]

Some Federalists switched from associating Burr with Republicans to arguing that the Jefferson administration was persecuting him. They walked a tightrope between withholding support for Burr and condemning Jefferson. "For Burr we care not," one Federalist wrote. "But against such horrible acts of tyranny and persecution, we will continue to raise our voice." Another agreed that they had little respect for the man who killed Hamilton, "yet we would be disposed to do him ample justice, to afford him those rights and privileges, which the constitution of our country secures."[81]

On September 1, 1807, the jury acquitted Burr, likely not for partisan reasons, but because the prosecution failed to meet Marshall's standard for proving treason. Just over two weeks later, the jury acquitted Burr on the lesser charge of violating US neutrality by invading Mexico. The verdicts stoked Republican fury. One complained to Madison that they "furnished the federalist with repeated triumphs" over Republicans' attempts to execute justice against traitors. Jefferson warned that Burr would "become the rallying point of all the disaffected, & the worthless of the US. and to be the pivot on which all the intrigues & the conspiracies which foreign governments may wish to disturb us with are to turn." Three years later, Jefferson was still complaining to Madison about Chief Justice Marshall's "twistifications" in the cases of Marbury and Burr.[82]

Madison could have predicted the spectacle had he read his own writing. In *Federalist* no. 43, which he wrote in 1788, he argued that "new-fangled and artificial treasons have been the great engines by which violent factions, the natural offspring of free government, have usually wreaked their alternate malignity on each other." Madison may have disputed that the administration had conjured "artificial" treason against Burr, but he could have hardly denied that his party used the trial to heap hatred on Federalists.[83]

10

"The Election of Mr. Madison"

If Mr. Jefferson continues this experiment [of the embargo] a few Months longer it will to a certainty prevent the Election of Mr. Madison.

— JOHN HOWE, June 1808

IN THE LATE AFTERNOON OF June 22, 1807, nine miles off Virginia's Cape Henry, cannon shot ripped through the American warship USS *Chesapeake*. Frantic sailors scrambled to their quarters, stumbling around the cables, canvas, and lumber that littered the decks. From fifty yards away, the British HMS *Leopard* poured a barrage of fire from twenty-six cannons into the *Chesapeake*, discharging several broadsides. The Americans responded with one or two shots that struck nothing but water. After fifteen minutes, the *Chesapeake*'s commander, Commodore James Barron, ordered his crew to lower the flag. Three men lay dead. Eighteen sustained wounds, including Barron and one who later died from injury.[1]

Before the bloodshed, the *Leopard*'s captain, Salusbury Pryce Humphreys, had hailed the *Chesapeake* and sent Lieutenant John Meade aboard. Meade handed Barron a note from Humphreys, demanding access to search the ship for British deserters.[2]

"I know of no such men as you describe," Barron replied. He enjoyed plausible deniability. The British and US governments struggled to distinguish between subjects of the empire and citizens of the republic. In a world where crew lists—with names and brief physical descriptors—were the primary tool of identification, British deserters could discard their former identities and evaporate into American crews. British Rear-Admiral Philip Patton once complained, "The Thirteen Provinces of America [actually fifteen at the time he wrote] have opened an Asylum for the discontented as they may remain with safety on their shores or be employed in their Ships without danger of discovery. The language, the customs, the manners, being similar to ours."[3]

Even had Barron suspected that he had British subjects onboard, he held a legal duty to retain the men who had joined his service. He vouched for the citizenship of all his men and denied Humphreys's demand to search his ship. Meade's men rowed him back to the *Leopard* with Barron's message, Humphreys shouted a warning, and the firing started.[4]

Fifteen minutes after the US flag disappeared and shooting ceased, a British boarding party arrived on the *Chesapeake*. They examined the ship's lists and searched the crew. About two hours later, Jenkin Ratford, William Ware, Daniel Martin, and John Strachan stood on the quarterdeck, prisoners of the Royal Navy. The party rowed the accused deserters to the *Leopard*. Three would land in prison and one at the end of a rope in front of his former British comrades. The tattered *Chesapeake* crawled back to Hampton Roads, Virginia.[5]

Years of quarrels collided in the Atlantic on that June afternoon. Americans interpreted the problem as one of impressment—the Royal Navy's practice of stopping US vessels, searching for British subjects, and pressing them into service to fight France. Sometimes British boarding parties hauled off US citizens, and those numbers reached the thousands. Madison complained that they impressed more Americans than they did British. The unfortunate victims entered a life of toil and danger in the service of an empire to which they pledged no allegiance. Americans lamented the plight of their compatriots and vilified the attacks on their national sovereignty.[6]

British rulers considered desertion the trouble. They subscribed to a doctrine of perpetual allegiance, denying subjects the right ever to renounce their loyalty to the Crown. That notion clashed with the US idea of naturalization, which assumed that people could exchange one national loyalty for another. An almost unfathomably large administrative system for the time, the Royal Navy needed every available recruit to operate its more than 900 ships. It demanded the right to retrieve British subjects for service, including those who had naturalized as US citizens. Press gangs often dragged away native US citizens as well, relinquishing them only if they could prove their birthplace. If Americans stopped harboring deserters, British leaders reasoned, naval officers wouldn't have to extract them from US ships. British commanders usually confined their searches to private merchant vessels. The *Chesapeake* marked the first attempt to pry sailors out of the US Navy.[7]

The incident threatened to spark simmering conflict into open war. Americans of all political persuasions decried the violation of US sovereignty. Underneath the apparent unanimity, however, political enmity still festered. The coming months tested whether Americans could speak with one voice against foreign outrages.

Conflict

A week after the attack on the *Chesapeake*, Madison gave Jefferson a multi-page manuscript, containing his suggested changes to a proclamation Jefferson had drafted that would ban British warships from US ports. Madison often tamed Jefferson's passion, but when it came to Britain, he stoked it. The secretary wanted a fiercer response. He turned Jefferson's judicious complaint into a tirade against "insults as gross as language could offer," "an act transcending all former outrages," and "lawless and bloody" intentions. Jefferson denounced other instances of "maltreatment" of US citizens. Madison wanted him to condemn the "violence" against them.[8]

Madison had spent the prior year trying to get a British officer convicted for a similar incident against a private US ship. In April 1806, Captain John Whitby of the British warship *Leander* had fired a stray shot, trying to halt the *Richard* near New York. The shot tore into the vessel and killed John Pierce. Americans exhibited Pierce's body in public, burned a British flag, and cried for vengeance. Several of the most ardent Republican newspapers mentioned war. Madison monitored Whitby's trial in London and learned of his acquittal about a month before the *Leopard* crippled the *Chesapeake*. He considered the attack on the *Chesapeake* part of a pattern of "uncontrouled abuses." "Even the murder of a Citizen peaceably pursuing his occupation within the limits of our jurisdiction has been stamped with impunity," he suggested Jefferson write in the *Chesapeake* proclamation. Concluding his revisions, Madison hinted at war if Britain failed to control its officers.[9]

Jefferson incorporated some of Madison's changes, moderated others, and omitted a few of the most incendiary. Other cabinet members probably modulated more of the language at a meeting on July 2, the day Jefferson issued the proclamation. For example, the final version struck the specific reference to the killing of Pierce, something both Jefferson and Madison had included in their drafts. It also expelled Madison's subtle threat of war.[10]

Two days after Jefferson issued the proclamation, James Jay could hardly concentrate while writing a letter to Madison from New York: "Guns firing, Drums beating, Men women & children roaring . . ." It was July 4. The same sounds would have echoed through America's cities any other Independence Day, but the din rang more portentous of war less than two weeks after the *Chesapeake* disaster.[11]

"I must just hint . . . that we have sufficient means, properly employed, to take or destroy the British Ships in the Chesapeak [Bay] or other parts of our Coast," Jay wrote Madison. War probably was unwise, he conceded, but perhaps it was unavoidable. If it erupted, it would leave the British "a poor, degraded & ruined people."[12]

However delusional, Jay captured the feverish spirit of many Americans, especially Republicans. "The Indignation of the People of the United States, has been excited to the most violent Extent," British diplomat David Erskine wrote his superior in London. On July 2, Philadelphia rioters stormed and immobilized a small, armed British vessel docked in the port. They cut its rigging, broke its gun carriages, confiscated its arms, and dismantled the rudder, which they dumped in front of the British consul's house. When the mayor tried to intervene, the crowd beat him away. "The probability of war is very strong," one Republican summarized.[13]

Madison had tried to steer the nation between Britain and France much as ancient Greek heroes navigated between Scylla and Charybdis, to use a metaphor popular at the time. The task had grown more difficult after 1805, when British magistrates made it harder for US vessels to furnish France with Caribbean goods, a practice France used to avoid capture of its own ships. The British insisted that any trade prohibited during peace was also off-limits during war, meaning it would seize US vessels trading French goods that France would have proscribed in peacetime. In a 204-page pamphlet, Madison attacked British logic, to no avail. British rulers had no interest in allowing France to slip its provisions past British warships under the protection of a neutral nation.[14]

Also in 1805, the Battles of Trafalgar and Austerlitz had left Britain supreme on the seas and France in control of the continent. At a tactical military impasse, the empires tried to maim each other's commerce, harming nations like the United States that wanted to remain neutral and trade with both. In May 1806, the British ministry blockaded Europe's northern coast. Napoleon tried to choke the British economy by confiscating any British goods entering the continent. Britain retaliated by prohibiting ships from sailing port to port along France's coast, a common practice of

US vessels. Both governments tried to convince the United States that the other disrespected its neutrality. The *Chesapeake* affair threatened to tip the balance toward war with Britain.[15]

The president wanted to avoid war, but the war cry vindicated his party's anti-British stance. Tench Coxe assured Madison that the "criminal and offensive" act had convinced some Federalists to back the administration. Even the most inveterate exhibited more "discretion" than they had before. The affront reunited Republicans, which had started to fracture under the anti-Madison leadership of congressman John Randolph. Coxe pressured Madison to publicize as much damning evidence as possible against the British "to decrease the British and monarchic party." As Jay put it to Madison, the time seemed ripe to prove that "the Clamors of federalists against the imbecillity & timidity of [the] Administration, are destitute of foundation."[16]

The outrage "is abolishing the distinctions of Party," Madison exulted to Monroe, who was in London trying to resolve the disagreements with Britain. When Jefferson and Madison first deputized Monroe and William Pinkney to make a treaty in 1806, they insisted that the agreement terminate impressment. The two commissioners negotiated into the summer of 1807, but Britain refused their demands to end the practice. Suspicious of large militaries, the Jefferson administration possessed two frigates and fewer than seventy smaller gunboats to answer Britain's nearly 1,000-ship navy. British negotiators had no interest in surrendering a point the United States was powerless to challenge.[17]

Madison hoped that the more unified, aggressive spirit in the United States would pressure the British finally to abolish impressment. He directed Monroe to require it as amends for the *Chesapeake* "outrage." If the British refused to atone for the misdeed, Madison instructed Monroe to send home quietly all US vessels in British ports—a hint that hostilities might ensue.[18]

Even on the off-chance that British leaders would have blinked in the face of united fury, Americans never shared the unanimity Madison imagined. Party strife had increased with British aggression in the months before the *Chesapeake* affair. Earlier that year, Republicans exposed a letter that seemed to show the British consul-general advocating the release of a US ship from British custody because its owners were "warm Federalists." The Republican *Aurora* made the phrase "warmly federal" a snickering epithet for British–Federalist collusion. Months later, the newspaper derided "warmly federal" merchants, who used recommendations from

British officials to obtain thousands of dollars of credit. The miscreant "swears allegiance to the United States to cover his ships, and toasts king George to cover his credits. . . . [H]e goes to the election, damns democracy, and votes as [British consul] Phineas Bond directs him!" Partisan distrust proved difficult to surmount, even after the strike against the *Chesapeake*.[19]

On July 1, 1807, a Philadelphia meeting revealed the perceived American unity more as a delicate détente. The participants condemned Britain's "hostility, injustice, and oppression" and resolved to support the administration in avenging "the wrongs our country has suffered." No spontaneous anti-British or pro-Jefferson voice, the resolutions emerged from a carefully crafted negotiation to sound a bipartisan tone. The night before, a Federalist committee told Republican organizers that they would agree to no resolutions that expressed friendship for the administration or approved its past conduct. Announcing the meeting, Republican newspapers called for the "enemies of British OUTRAGE and MURDER, and the Friends of this country and its administration" to gather. Federalist newspapers dropped language about the "friends" of the administration.[20]

Perpetually suspicious of Federalists, Tench Coxe noticed the nuances. He griped to Madison that Federalist newspapers refused to "carry any idea of attachment to the administration." Further, "federalists would not meet to support the Country & to bear testimony against these British outrages, unless our democrats would agree to omit or obliterate expressions of friendship to the administration." He warned against trusting people who made "a negative censure of the administration a condition of their patriotism." Writing Madison almost daily at that point, Coxe exhorted the secretary to receive all aid offered by Federalists but never to trust them. The violence against the *Chesapeake* shoved partisans into a short-lived, distrustful cooperation.[21]

By August, Federalists began to unite "again in favour of great britian, and against their country," Massachusetts Republican James Sullivan warned Jefferson. Less prone than Coxe to conspiracy theories, even the moderate Sullivan feared that a small wing of Federalists would collude with Britain "to change our government."[22]

With such accusations, Republicans revealed more about their own partisanship than that of Federalists, though some Federalists did grasp the chance to chide Jefferson as weak. As Coxe hinted, some started with moderation, denouncing the attack but calling for more facts. Others launched more direct partisan insults at the president, claiming that the administration invited attacks with its weak military. "We hope," bristled one Federalist newspaper, "that the American people, as they are now feeling the sad consequences of the pusillanimous conduct of [the] administration, will awake from their slumber, and withdraw their confidence from the men who have proved themselves so unworthy of it." By slashing the navy, the administration was "virtually guilty of the plunder, devastation, and murders which have ensued." More sympathetic to British arguments for impressment, Federalists also blamed Jefferson and Madison's unwise policy of, as Federalists saw it, protecting British deserters.[23]

As time passed, some Federalists questioned the character of the sailors taken from the *Chesapeake*, a less controversial tactic than it would seem today, given the already poor reputation of sailors at the time. Reports described Daniel Martin as a "colored man" and William Ware as a "mulatto boy," making them even less sympathetic to many whites. Their names first crossed Madison's desk in January 1807, when he was informed that they were Americans escaped from British service and vulnerable to recapture. Jefferson critic John Lowell Jr. seized the information about their identities (along with some misinformation) to challenge the citizenship of three of the men snatched from the *Chesapeake*. Lowell argued that those born in slavery (which probably only included Ware), were natives, but not citizens.[24]

Madison ignored the argument and spent months gathering evidence of their nationality. The State Department contacted Ware's former enslaver for proof of US birth, making Ware's freedom from the British morbidly dependent on his former enslavement in the United States. He died in a British prison.[25]

Republicans held the political advantage, with any defense of Federalist principles sounding like a defense of the *Leopard*'s recent attack. One Federalist outlined their party's ordeal. If a Federalist failed to assail the British, "he is at once stigmatised as a British emissary or hireling—as an idolizer of monarchy and every thing that is connected with it—as a sworn foe to his own friends and the freedom of his own nation, a tory or a traitor." If they complained of British atrocities and suggested the government respond with strong action, "then are federalists denounced as the friends of war, as restless spirits who aim at embroiling our government in a dispute for the sake of embarrassing it and making way for their favourite objects, armies, navies and oppressive taxes."[26]

Republican John Page demonstrated his party's rhetorical strength, warning Jefferson that King George III "is bent on a War with the *U.S.*"

The monarch would rely on "the support of federal partizans, avowd Tories, his own Subjects here, & *Burr's Choice Spirits*"—a wise crack about Aaron Burr's followers—"& I suppose Insurrections of Slaves in the Southern States." The accusation lumped Republicans' favorite domestic villains onto Britain's side. Like many others, Page saw all his disparate fears as a coherent unit mobilized by a foreign threat.[27]

Embargo

The Royal Navy court-martialed the four men taken from the *Chesapeake*. Though enlisted in the British service, Ware, Martin, and Strachan claimed US citizenship. British officers threw them in prison. As a British subject, Jenkin Ratford received no mercy. On US shores before he sailed with the *Chesapeake*, he had paraded his defiance with a "contemptuous gesture" to his former British officer. On August 31, 1807, he was hanged in front of his former comrades aboard the British warship *Halifax*.[28]

On September 19, news of Ratford's fate stunned and disgusted Madison, who was on his late summer retreat to Montpelier. If the cold, torrential weather that plagued central Virginia and swept away Montpelier's milldam hadn't dampened Madison's spirits, the news from British minister David Erskine did. "Upon a solemn Investigation," Erskine wrote, "it was clearly proved . . . that [Ratford] was a British born subject, that he had enter'd His Majestys Service voluntarily, that he had deserted from His Majesty's Ship Halifax, for which Offence, clearly established, he had been convicted and had received the Sentence of Death." According to Erskine, the court-martial also revealed that American officers knew of Ratford's identity when they signed him into the US Navy, along with several other known deserters.[29]

Madison couldn't have cared less what the trial revealed. The attack violated US sovereignty, and the British should have returned all four men, he shot back after returning to his Washington office in early October. The execution "aggravated" the offense against the United States, he charged, and it ruined Britain's ability to right the wrong.[30]

Madison admitted to Jefferson that Ratford "was probably a British subject" and that the Royal Navy could not have suffered the poor example of releasing a known deserter. If any good could come of the execution, Madison hoped that it would give his negotiators in London more leverage to demand an end to impressment as a "radical cure." Erskine suspected correctly that Madison and Jefferson hoped the incident would keep

Americans riled against Britain while the administration grasped for the illusory goal of ending impressment.[31]

The British cabinet disavowed the violence against the *Chesapeake*, but Ratford's execution revealed their disinterest in any real atonement. On October 16, George III issued a royal decree reemphasizing Britain's right to search foreign ships for its sailors, though forbidding violence against foreign naval vessels. Weeks later, the cabinet released an "order in council" that punished neutral trade by declaring that all vessels destined for Europe stop at British ports and pay a duty. If they failed to entice neutrals to their side, British magistrates planned at least to bludgeon them away from France.[32]

Napoleon posed an equal menace to Americans. In September, he declared that France would seize US vessels sailing for Britain and all British merchandise, even if carried by neutral vessels. The emperor had instituted the policy nearly a year prior but had wavered on whether to enforce it against the United States. Meeting Britain blow for blow, he no longer tolerated US neutrality.[33]

Madison believed that the government could constrain European empires to respect US neutrality—and avoid a war for which it was unprepared—if it withheld vital commodities. He had favored economic coercion for decades. The policy had been a key factor in his support for the Constitutional Convention. In 1785, he longed for "Retaliating regulations of trade" effected "by harmony in the measures of the States," something unattainable under the Articles of Confederation. In the First Congress of the new government, he had pleaded to no avail for discriminatory taxes on British imports to punish Britain's perceived thuggery. The Framers had constructed the Constitution for just such a purpose, he had insisted. His thinking had remained constant: Britain could not survive without provisions from the United States. By 1807, he had the governing system and the political power to make his vision a reality. The government had passed a limited Non-Importation Act about a year and a half earlier but left it dormant while Monroe tried to negotiate in London.[34]

In December 1807, Madison urged Jefferson to level US economic might against Europe and prohibit all US ships from sailing to foreign ports—a blanket embargo on US exports. Madison drafted a message for Jefferson calling for the legislation, and the president submitted it to Congress. On December 22, Congress passed the Embargo Act, which would demolish any goodwill that remained between Federalists and Republicans after the *Chesapeake* calamity.[35]

Madison knew the embargo would hurt the economy in the short term and dispirit some Americans. To control the political damage and rally support for the act, he threw several anonymous editorials into the *National Intelligencer.* He celebrated that Congress overcame the "habitual opposition of party spirit" to pass the bill with overwhelming majorities. The boast carried little weight since Republicans held overwhelming majorities in both houses, anyway.[36]

In fact, bipartisanship skewed against the bill, with Federalists holding firm against it and some Republicans joining them. Jefferson dismissed the bill's opponents as partisan dogmatists or misinformed, a defense offered by many politicians since to justify bad legislation. Madison saw warning signs, otherwise he wouldn't have been writing to defend the law the day after it passed.[37]

Documents

"Mr. Jefferson has imposed an embargo to please France, and to beggar us!" raged one New Englander to the Federalist opposition leader and former secretary of state, Timothy Pickering. By then a Massachusetts senator, Pickering agreed and identified the embargo "*as only another mode of shutting our ports against British commerce in compliance with the requisition of Napoleon.*" The criticisms echoed over the coming year: Republicans intended the embargo to please Napoleon and punish Federalists.[38]

New Englanders rejected Madison's description of an "impartial" embargo. Britain commanded a stronger share of US trade than did France, and the Federalist stronghold of New England depended on that commerce. Federalists suspected that Republicans concocted the embargo to ruin them and Britain with one swipe.[39]

Federalists indicted the Embargo Act as Napoleon's scheme since its earliest days. The day Jefferson signed it into law, Federalist Samuel Taggart mourned, "My country is no longer independent; we have been legislating under an imperial decree of the Emperor of France and sanctioning a plan matured in Paris." He repeated rumors that Napoleon had threatened war unless the administration passed the embargo. According to Napoleon's supposed plan, Britain would respond with war on the United States, and he could then rope the republic into an alliance with France.[40]

Jefferson fueled the conspiracy theories by withholding from Congress dispatches received from the US diplomat in Paris, John Armstrong. Jefferson had political and practical reasons for concealing the documents. In a letter to Madison, Armstrong had admitted that Napoleon devised his blockade to invite retaliation from Britain and disrupt peace between Americans and the British. Armstrong's assessment could have caused problems for the administration among those who saw France as the worse aggressor. Armstrong also vented his unflattering opinions about the progress of negotiations in London, which Jefferson would not have wanted to air in Congress. More practically, though, Madison had no time for his State Department clerks to make copies of the recent mass and tangle of correspondence from Britain and France. He knew that a British envoy would arrive in Washington any day to try to settle the *Chesapeake* issue, and the administration wanted the embargo as leverage. Jefferson withheld less controversial letters from the diplomats in Britain as well. There were no hints that those letters existed, though, so they never became a political lightning rod like the omitted Armstrong correspondence. For several reasons, then, the president submitted a minimal number of documents that summarized the unfolding dilemma in Europe.[41]

The president did send Congress some correspondence between Armstrong and the new French minister of foreign relations, Jean-Baptiste Nompère de Champagny, but prohibited its publication. In fact, the Senate's official printing of Jefferson's message scrapped any mention of the documents. The suppressed documents looked like a cover-up after US newspapers learned about them. Pickering assumed Jefferson wanted to keep Champagny's letter private because it "contained a sentiment or two" that would embarrass the administration. He probably meant the closing lines, in which Champagny hinted at the "common interests" and "support of the same cause" that the United States and France shared against Britain. Jefferson could have argued that publication of the material might disrupt ongoing negotiations, but the lines undoubtedly would have ignited critics who thought him too friendly to France.[42]

The secrecy invited its own trouble. During the congressional debates, opponents of the embargo had demanded to see Armstrong's correspondence to Madison. When the Republican majority refused to request it, some congressmen concluded that it outlined an ultimatum from Napoleon to shut US ports against Britain or face war with France.[43]

By asking for the embargo, the theory went, Jefferson played Napoleon's patsy, and the missing correspondence would prove it. One congressman wrote to a friend about the House's secret debates: "Of course I am not permitted to inform you either what the President has communicated to us, or what we have done in consequence of it. But I may be permitted to tell you we are doing *no good*. I fear we are about to plunge the nation into the most dreadful calamities—unnecessarily and wantonly—I am now more than ever persuaded that there is but too much FRENCH INFLU-ENCE." Another wondered "Is it not probable that an intimation has been received through Armstrong, or in some other way, that our ports must be shut against the British?" The congressman continued, "Or is it not the plan for us to make common cause with the august emperour, whose sympathies and ours are the same." The line paraphrased the Champagny letter that the president had submitted in secret—an apparent attempt to leak the information without violating confidentiality.[44]

John Randolph's anti-Madison Republicans outrancored even Federalists. With the 1808 presidential election approaching, Randolph allies hoped to prevent Madison's nomination. Josiah Masters made the most strenuous accusations of foreign collusion. "My life upon it," he re-portedly declared, "this measure is from the mandate of Napoleon." Randolph closed the final debate in the House with a tear-filled lament that a Bonaparte would likely rule the United States in the near future. Randolph's faction promoted charges that the embargo "is a Sacrifice of the national Dignity and Independence to the Views and Mandates of France," one Madison confidant groused.[45]

The charges tumbled out of Congress and into the public. "The letters of Messrs. Champagny and Armstrong are said to contain a menace of war from Bonaparte, unless we shut our ports against England," Federalist newspapers cried. The *United States' Gazette* wanted answers: "What was the tenour of Mr. Armstrong's last letter to the government of the United States? Did it mention any declaration of menace of the French govern-ment with respect to any power desirous of remaining neutral? What was the purport of what was received from Mr Champagny? . . . Did he, or did he not, intimate or require an alliance of the United States with France?" One Federalist sardonically suggested, "Perhaps Mr. Armstrong has been consulting the magnanimous emperor on the subject of our quarrel with England." Another writer suspected that the omitted correspondence would prove "that we are at this moment under the secret controul and direction of Napoleon."[46]

A Republican editorial paradoxically multiplied the accusations when it tried to vindicate Jefferson and the embargo. The editor, James Cheetham, argued that the legislation was born of "DISGRACEFUL PROPOSITIONS made by Napoleon to our executive through the medium of Messrs. Champagny and Armstrong, *whose letters have not been published*." The embargo targeted France to retaliate Napoleon's abusive demand, "throwing defiance in the face of the tyrant." Those who suspected Republicans as Napoleon's puppets had their facts wrong, Cheetham implied. Gleeful Federalist newspapers overlooked Cheetham's Republican-friendly twist and reprinted the editorial, fixated on the "disgraceful propositions" it mentioned. They dropped the portions that justified the embargo and reproduced those that fortified their own message about corrupt French influence in the administration. After stripping the editorial of its unsavory conclusion, Federalists trumpeted the support of "the leading democratic print" in New York.[47]

On March 9, 1808, Pickering amplified the Federalist charges with what was essentially an open letter to the governor of Massachusetts. New Englanders could pick up a Federalist newspaper or splash nine pence at a bookstore, receive a copy, and wonder, with Pickering, "Why, in this dangerous crisis, are Mr. Armstrong's letters to the secretary of state absolutely withheld, so that a line of them cannot be seen? Did they contain no information of the demands and intentions of the French Emperor? . . . Are we still to be kept profoundly ignorant of the declarations and avowed designs of the French Emperor, although these may strike at our liberty and independence?" They might then conclude, again with Pickering, "In this concealment must be wrapt up the real cause of the Embargo." Thousands of copies flowed throughout New England, into the South, and across the Atlantic.[48]

The Junto

Within a week after Pickering published his letter, Senator John Quincy Adams trekked the evening streets of Washington to the Executive Mansion. After the Louisiana Purchase, the senator had drifted away from his father's Federalists and into Jefferson's camp. He had completed the transition with his vote for the Embargo Act. Like his father, he considered himself non-partisan, a Cicero caught between Caesar and Pompey, as the elder Adams styled it. On March 15, 1808, the younger Adams brought information to the president and wanted answers in return.[49]

Inside with Jefferson, Adams described a letter from Lieutenant Governor John Wentworth of British Nova Scotia that had circulated in

New England the previous summer. As Adams related it, the British magistrate had warned that France planned to establish a monarchy on the ashes of British North America under Jean Victor Moreau. Napoleon had exiled the famed French general to the United States three years earlier, but rumors spread that the two had reconciled. According to Adams's account, Wentworth claimed that with Moreau in power, Napoleon would introduce monarchy into the United States.[50]

Adams was probably referring to a letter that Federalist newspapers had reprinted the previous summer and fall, though the author was concealed as "a very respectable source." If not the same letter, it sketched the same anti-British plot and apparently came from an official in Halifax. Moreau would convince Americans to declare war on Britain, receive 10,000 French troops, join with American forces, and "drive the English from the continent." France would retake Canada with Moreau as monarch, while the United States would get the Floridas and a few Caribbean islands. Napoleon would then help Jefferson consolidate power and become a sort of monarch for life. The writer concluded that "the Americans who are now loudly crying out for a war with England, may know how completely they have been made the tools of France and its pensioners."[51]

The letter echoed fears among British-Canadian commanders that Napoleon schemed with Moreau and Americans to conquer the rest of British America. One reported that Moreau was cooperating with Irish dissidents to provoke Americans to war against Britain. Admiral George Berkeley suspected that US leaders had agreed to transfer any British colonies that fell into US hands to France or to a French puppet government. One British Canadian official sent an outline of the dreaded plan to the under-secretary of the colonies.[52]

In a secret dispatch to London, Wentworth heartened his superiors with news that New Englanders were "offended at the interference of France in the affairs of the Union." They worried that Moreau's supposed invasion would "bring the power of France so near to New England as to entail war and corrupt means for their subjugation." They might refuse to fight even if war erupted, he reassured London.[53]

In the months before Adams met Jefferson, Moreau had attracted suspicion in the United States with a trip to New Orleans. Some suspected that he met other French officers there and planned to finish what Burr had started, taking New Orleans for Napoleon. "I am told indeed," John Adams wrote his son John Quincy, "there are great Numbers of French officers and Soldiers Scattered all over the United States. . . . Moreau is gone to New orleans, and Napoleon is about to buy or beg the Floridas. And Apprehensions are entertained that Napoleon could Stamp his foot and raise an Army in a moment in the midst of Us." Probably spurred by those recent fears, John Quincy Adams wanted answers about Wentworth's alleged letter.[54]

Jefferson assured Adams that he had no plans to ally with France and that France had never requested it. Had Jefferson been candid with the senator, he might have admitted that someone had suggested to Madison that the government ought to recruit Moreau against Britain. The administration never pursued the idea, however. In fact, Moreau hungered for a fight with Napoleon more than he did one with Britain (he died fighting the emperor in 1813), though Jefferson probably knew nothing of that.[55]

Other Republicans seized the supposed Wentworth letter as evidence of British disinformation. Eleven days before he met with Jefferson, Adams had revealed the content to Congressman Wilson Nicholas during an hours-long conversation in the capitol. Nicholas called the letter "merely a British device to divide and distract us." Next, Adams discussed the letter with Virginia Senator William Giles, who reveled in the irony that British authorities had planted accusations of French meddling in Federalist circles. He growled on the Senate floor, "This idle and ridiculous tale of French influence, I have strong reasons to believe, was originally suggested by British influence. . . . I have heard it said, and believe it to be true, that the Governor of Nova Scotia made the suggestion, in a letter addressed to certain British partisans in Boston."[56]

Pickering made an easy target as a former proponent of New England secession and leader of what Republicans called the Essex Junto, a loose conglomerate of radical New England Federalists. More a bogeyman of Republican imagination than an actual political bloc, the junto often bore blame for any ills that plagued Republicans. Moderate Republican James Sullivan summarized Republican opinion: "From the Time General Washington retired, the federal faction, called the Essex Junto here, were determined to reconnect us with, and place us under the guidance and protection of the English Crown." Sullivan glowered to Jefferson, "The deep laid plot of Pickering's letter, added to the embargo, gave [radical Federalists] fresh confidence, and uncommon impudence; and they have done the most wonderful things with them." But they overreached, he added. They wanted to dissolve the national government and separate the

North from the South, expecting the support of London. Pickering's extremist wing had not shed its British-supported secessionist fantasies.[57]

Republicans exchanged whispers that Pickering was collaborating with Britain's special envoy, George Rose, who had come to the United States to settle the *Chesapeake* affair. As the rumor went, Pickering and Rose had spent a long evening in secret talks not long before Pickering published his letter. At the very least, the two men did enjoy friendship and shared common opinions about Rose's mission.[58]

Madison and Rose had talked in circles since mid-January. Rose refused even to discuss reparations for the *Chesapeake* unless the United States swallowed preliminary demands it could never stomach. Madison terminated the talks on March 5.[59]

Cynical Republicans noticed a string of suspicious coincidences: Rose and Pickering met for one of their private conferences; soon after, Rose announced the failure of the negotiations; Pickering published his letter, which blamed Madison for the failed talks; congressional Federalists moved to repeal the embargo. Federalists intended all those events "to operate in concert," grumbled Jefferson's secretary of war. A more caustic Republican seethed that Pickering would sell the United States "for fewer pieces of silver than Judas did his Master."[60]

If anything good came from the end of the Rose mission, it was that it allowed Jefferson and Madison to release many of the documents for which Federalists had clamored for months. The administration had withheld them while the sensitive situation unfolded. Free to display them after the failed negotiation, Jefferson believed that they would "effectually put down mr Pickering." On March 22, Jefferson and Madison flooded Congress with papers: hundreds of pages of diplomatic dispatches to Madison, correspondence with foreign authorities, and documents related to the Rose mission. Despite the deluge, Jefferson and Madison never released the letters from Armstrong. Federalist Jacob Wagner had recently resigned from the State Department after years as Madison's chief clerk, and he knew the department's workings better than anybody. He guessed right when he doubted that "those wretched shreds of dispatches [that Jefferson showed Congress] are all that Mr. Armstrong or others have furnished." Jefferson and Madison did suppress several Armstrong letters, but they had revealed enough to prove that Napoleon hadn't masterminded the embargo.[61]

The release kept Republicans on the offensive, despite the influence of Pickering's letter. "Pickering's seditious sentiment & Copies of his letter were sowed, much thicker, among us by the enemies to our Government, than were the tares by the enemy of goodness among the wheat," carped New England Republican Levi Lincoln. He was confident that the trove of documents Jefferson sent to Congress would help "eradicate these noxious weeds" of "british agents, british emissaries British advocates & the old tories."[62]

Just over a week after Jefferson dropped the documents in Congress, Adams launched an anti-Pickering barrage into the press, denouncing his fellow Massachusetts senator's letter and defending the embargo. Adams had received a copy of Pickering's letter on March 16, the day after his meeting with Jefferson. For the next two weeks, he spent every spare moment penning a response as an open letter to Federalist leader Harrison Gray Otis.[63]

Despite Pickering's "pretences," Adams scolded, "The French emperor . . . had *not* required that our ports should be shut against British commerce." Pickering may have thought he served the nation by dissuading the people from a French-induced war, but he was subjecting the country to "the servitude of British protection." Adams grew more acerbic as he concluded that Pickering exploited fear of France "to lash us into the refuge of obedience to Britain." Pickering wanted to trade the mirage of French influence for the reality of British domination.[64]

"The countenances of the Junto are fallen," James Sullivan exulted to Madison in April. "The Letter of Mr. Adams . . . is a fatal overthrow to them."[65]

A British spy saw things differently.

The Spy

On April 22, 1808, a British secret agent named John Howe glided past two decrepit redoubts and a frail fort as he drifted through Massachusetts Bay on the ship *Emulous*. The pitiful sight boded well for his mission, he thought, a mission commissioned by the new governor of Nova Scotia, George Prevost. Pretending to visit friends, he arrived to report on US military preparations and the state of the political parties.[66]

Howe had grown up in Boston but fled the city with other loyalists when the British evacuated. Like many of the others, he moved to Halifax. Americans had done nothing to endear him to their nation over the decades. "When I observe the licentiousness of this country," he griped, "their continual recurrence to Elections, the manner in which all the Officers of the Government are obliged to cringe for popular favor . . . I cannot help experiencing the most pleasing sensations on reflecting that I am a subject of Great Britain." Despite his hatred of the United States, he retained a fondness for New England and especially Boston, which he now approached in the *Emulous*.[67]

With British warships restricted from the harbor, Howe perched in a smaller boat and drifted toward the docks. As the boat crept by Fort Independence, he studied the structure, sensing it had degenerated since its pre-Revolutionary War days, when it had belonged to the British Empire. Rickety redoubts offered the fort minimal protection.[68]

Howe likely disembarked at Long Wharf, where outsiders usually docked. The wharf connected to State Street, leading to the city center. A couple of blocks down the busy street stood the customhouse. Howe strode toward the building to apply for an exemption for the *Emulous* to enter US waters, claiming that the captain carried official dispatches but sticking to his story that he came to visit friends.[69]

Howe was astonished by the "great number of new and elegant buildings." Boston had just invested heavily to revitalize the waterfront near State Street, constructing over a hundred four- and five-story brick buildings, stores, waterproof cellars, and the new India Wharf. The harbor dazzled as "the most elegant and commodious seat for mercantile business in the United States," boasted the Boston Directory.[70]

The renovated commercial zone drew a stark contrast with the infirm military establishments. New Englanders wanted business, not war.

Months into the embargo, the policy had failed to budge Britain. The same month that Congress had passed the Embargo Act, the Portuguese court was sailing for Rio de Janeiro under British protection. Driven from Lisbon by a French invasion, the Portuguese prince regent re-centered the imperial seat in Brazil and opened the country's ports to foreign commerce. Britain turned there and elsewhere in South America for goods it couldn't get from the United States. Tens of thousands of bags of cotton flooded into London from Brazil that year, more than compensating for the loss of US trade. The same occurred for other goods that Britain normally would have received from the United States, according to a report from a US consul in Salvador. One London firmed scoffed, "What is the Embargo for, but to throw the U States back 50 years, and divert all their trade to other channels?"[71]

Howe found Americans' political turmoil as promising to Britain as their deficient defenses. Because of the embargo, he reported to Prevost, "wealth and prosperity" met "suffering" in New England. Ships stuck in harbors. Tradesmen unemployed. Empty stores and houses. Bankruptcies. He wrote the governor, "You scarcely meet a person who is not complaining." Fortunately, he beamed, "they appear more disposed to blame their own Government than ours." The embargo produced "the very best effects" for which Britain could hope—misery in the United States that was blamed on the Jefferson administration.[72]

Howe hoped the discontent might launch Federalists back to power in the upcoming presidential election, in which Madison emerged as the most obvious successor to Jefferson. To demolish confidence in Republicans, Howe informed leading Federalists that the embargo failed to dent British commerce, much less ruin it: "I assure them very gravely that our Manufacturers have new sources open to them in the trade to the Brazils, St Domingo and other Channels." He urged his government to retain its policies and endure any ill effects of the embargo if for no other reason than to preserve the discord and keep Madison from winning the presidency.[73]

Howe sowed and nourished suspicions among Federalists that, as he put it to his government, Jefferson's "real object in the Embargo, has undoubtedly been to league with France." He reported that Republicans were planting French schoolmasters in New England under the guise of teaching French but with nefarious purposes. The plan unveiled "the readiness of the Executive of this Country to forward the most extravagant wishes of the Emperor of France."[74]

British cartoonist Isaac Cruikshank contributed to the cause. In October 1808, one month before the election, he drew Jefferson trying to justify the embargo to angry and suffering constituents. Napoleon leers from behind Jefferson's chair and promises him: "You shall be King hereafter." A bull dog—representing John Bull, the embodiment of Britain—notices the scandalous collusion and barks in vain to warn the Americans in the room.[75]

It required no genius to divine that Britain wanted the Jefferson–Madison faction out of power. Rumors had spread since the previous year that Britain backed John Randolph as a Republican presidential candidate instead of Madison. Howe ventured no opinion of other possible candidates, but he believed that anybody would be better for Britain than Madison. "It is therefore the manifest interest of Great Britain that Mr. Jefferson and his confidential friends should be removed from the Administration of this Government if possible." Even Howe admitted that Madison had bested

FIGURE 10.1 In this image, Napoleon promises Jefferson that he will make him king in return for implementing the embargo as Jefferson tries to justify the measure to discontented Americans. Jefferson characterizes the embargo as "a Grand Philosophical Idea," a play on Federalist derisions of Jefferson as the "Philosophical President," unconcerned with reality (for one example among hundreds, see "Dreams of a Philosopher," *New York Commercial Advertiser*, January 20, 1802). Petitions from suffering states lay on Jefferson's desk. A bulldog representing the British caricature John Bull (as written on the collar) notices Napoleon and tries in vain to warn the Americans in the room. Courtesy Trustees of the British Museum.

Rose in his arguments during their negotiations, but by championing the embargo, Madison had squandered whatever popularity he had earned. If the embargo persisted, Howe assured Prevost, Jefferson would "prevent the Election of Mr. Madison."[76]

One cartoon summarized a year's worth of accusations. It depicted Jefferson and his "mad son" Madison restraining a ship at Napoleon's orders. Madison exclaims, "God send the Emperor may make me a President!" A group of congressmen peer at the scene through a curtain, with Federalist Barent Gardenier lamenting, "We are forging chains to fasten us to the car of the imperial conqueror [Napoleon]." Republican George Campbell shoots Gardenier, representing a duel the men fought after a heated House debate on the embargo. The artist captures Josiah Masters's line, "My life upon it the hand of *Napoleon* is in this Embargo bill!!!"[77]

FIGURE 10.2 This brilliantly detailed political cartoon depicted many of the major events and accusations surrounding the embargo. The title, *An Old Philosopher Teaching His Mad Son Economical Projects*, played on Madison's name to depict him as little more than a crony of Jefferson, a common canard from Madison's critics. Appearing in late 1808, it depicts Napoleon holding a copy of the Embargo Act and related documents. The "United States" seems to be fading from the wording on the document held by Napoleon, suggesting evaporating sovereignty. In a secret Congress ("Galleries cleared by order of the house"), Republicans chastise Federalists for revealing the embarrassing scene, while an ineffective House Speaker calls for order. The cartoon includes an allusion to a duel fought between Barent Gardenier and George Campbell over the embargo and Masters's affirmation that Napoleon ordered it. "Spitting" Matthew Lyon is in the *bottom right* of the panel (holding a "spitting record" in his pocket [for the nickname, see Freeman, *Affairs of Honor*, 174]). The *left lower* panel shows the *Leopard* firing on the *Chesapeake*, while a harmless US gunboat returns fire with meaningless bills and acts. The *right lower* panel shows an American sailor taking his own life to free himself from Napoleon in the *background* (who mocks Madison's phrase of a "dignified retirement" to describe the embargo ["Embargo," *National Intelligencer*, December 23, 1807]) and a member of a British press gang in the *foreground*. For approximate publication date, see *Washington Federalist*, December 13, 1808. Courtesy Free Library of Philadelphia.

Napoleon hadn't demanded the embargo but accepted it as the best thing short of war between the United States and Britain. A French report praised the "great and courageous sacrifice" Americans offered against Britain's repression. As the election year of 1808 heated up, Americans learned of Napoleon's decree from Bayonne calling for the capture of US vessels that violated the Embargo Act, shutting US ports even tighter against Britain. Jefferson and Madison hardly appreciated his help, which reinforced their image as his stooges. "It is evident that Bonaparte and they are acting in concert," seared a Federalist newspaper, "from the decree he has lately issued at Bayonne, to enforce the American embargo."[78]

As Howe surveyed the political anger, he rejoiced, "It is now nearly reduced to a certainty that Mr. Madison will not be the President."[79]

The Suit

The following March, 1809, Madison stood in the House chamber to take his oath as president. To the joy of the Republican press, he wore a black suit made of American-spun wool sheared from Merino sheep raised in the United States. British traders had fretted that Merino sheep herds, which produced fine quality wool, might wean Americans off British manufactured cloth. Republicans had trumpeted US-made fabrics over British imports. Yet against Madison's wishes, several days before his inauguration Congress had voted for the demise of the embargo. They replaced it with a feebler act that prohibited trade with France and Britain but bared few teeth. Like the suit Madison wore, it did little more than symbolize defiance in the face of European might.[80]

The black suit contrasted Madison's pale face as the almost fifty-eight-year-old trembled and began a weak-voiced inaugural address before hordes of onlookers. He gained composure as he talked. His voice rose in volume, fully audible by the time he promised "to exclude foreign intrigues and foreign partialities" from US politics. Even less subtle than his suit, the line was an obvious jab at Britain and its Federalist colluders.[81]

Madison took office convinced that his opposition was conspiring with Britain. He believed in the integrity of most New England Federalists but also thought the "Junto" was "ready to sacrifice the rights interests & honor of their Country, to their ambitious or vindictive views." They plotted disunion with British help, he fretted in a coded message to his minister in Britain. Madison's charges boded ill for Abigail Adams's hopes that he could "ride in the Storm, and stem the torrent" of partisan divide that swept the nation. "If Mr. Madison can, he will perform wonders," she sighed. "The people are so divided that it is like a House which cannot stand."[82]

II

"Murdered by British Intrigue"

> The blood of our fellow-citizens murdered on the Wabash by British
> intrigue calls aloud for vengeance.
>
> —Kentucky *Reporter*, December 10, 1811

BEFORE HE RECEIVED THE VISION, the Shawnee Lalawauthika had been
a village drunk. His visage screamed mediocrity—"common size, rather
slender, & of no great appearance." Even his average physical traits glossed
his subpar life accomplishments. After meandering from village to village
with other Shawnees, he landed in a small town nestled against the White
River in Indiana Territory. Thirty years old in early 1805, he had a family he
couldn't support, a vocation he couldn't practice, and a heritage he couldn't
honor. He drank away his livelihood and most of his friends, along with
the pain of failure.[1]

The vision changed all that.

In April 1805, Lalawauthika smoked his pipe near his wigwam campfire.
Two young men approached him, sent by the Master of Life. They led him
to a fork in a path. Casting his eyes to the right, he beheld a strange but
beautiful world prepared for the righteous, a world of bounteous game and
fertile cornfields. He saw it, but he could not enter. He shifted his gaze left.
Fire engulfed the second path. Unworthy Indians traveled the blazing road
to a land of fiery torture reserved for drunks like him.[2]

Lalawauthika awoke to the gasps of his family and fellow villagers, who
were preparing his body for a funeral. Tears streamed his face as he recounted
the vision to his stunned audience, who had thought him dead minutes
before. He renounced alcohol and adopted a new name, Tenskwatawa—
Open Door. He had entered the trance a failure and emerged a prophet.[3]

It was an age of dreams, visions, and prophets throughout most societies of North America. The era spawned the latter-day restorationist Joseph Smith, the Jewish prophet Matthias, the enslaved apocalyptic Nat Turner, and (closer to Tenskwatawa's tradition) Native reformer visionaries Neolin and Handsome Lake. Tenskwatawa taught in a style of prophets who promised fiery hell for Indians who embraced white culture—an ironic warning, given its Christian basis.[4]

Over the next two years, Tenskwatawa circulated Indian villages preaching an uncompromising creed of Native revival through moral purity and sovereignty. Hardly alone, he joined other Indian prophets and leaders who called for a renewed confederacy among Native nations throughout North America. From across the Great Lakes region, Indians rallied to their side, ignoring older leaders who remembered past military tragedies and who encouraged accommodation with Americans.[5]

Rumors flew that Tenskwatawa conspired with Britain to support his movement. He denied British backing, however. One British official even believed Tenskwatawa was a French agent. Though a decade removed from the Battle of Fallen Timbers, Shawnees still remembered the closed doors of Fort Miamis, where the British had refused them shelter from US General Anthony Wayne's troops. They had hesitated to trust the British ever since. Still, Tenskwatawa entertained a possible British partnership in the future, and his denials failed to dispel American fear of a resurrected British–Indian alliance within US borders.[6]

Small wonder that one of the earliest pieces of advice President Madison received was that "an early Attention to the Indian Department will be indispensably requisite." The giver of the gratuitous counsel, James Stevens, lived in New York State and just fifty miles from Britain's powerful Fort Niagara. He felt well placed to feed the new president intelligence. Stevens lamented that the United States had promoted Native neutrality while the British had courted Native alliances. "Let us not underrate the Importance of the Indians," he admonished the new president. If the United States won their friendship, they could help invade Canada and annex it to the United States, a dream of many Americans since the Revolutionary War.[7]

Stevens cautioned that Federalists skulked in the region's post offices, "decidedly inimical and uncommonly virulent" against the administration. "Some secret Treachery is in operation," he warned, hinting that Federalist postmasters would spy for the British if war erupted. With his unsolicited opinion, Stevens summarized Republican fears of a threefold threat of external enemies and internal colluders: the British, Indians, and Federalists.[8]

Land

"I really fear that this said Prophet is an Engine set to work by the British for some bad purpose," Indiana governor William Henry Harrison had confided to Jefferson's secretary of war in July 1807, weeks after the *Chesapeake* incident.[9]

Harrison mirrored Madison's decades-old fears of Native American alliances with Britain. After Madison lost an aunt, uncle, and two cousins to such a coalition during the Revolutionary War, tales about the family's torture spread and probably grew with time. By 1822, the narrative had Cherokees cutting his uncle into pieces alive while he was forced to watch the murder of his wife and children. Whatever Madison believed about the deaths of his extended family, and however gruesome their demise, the rumors matched Americans' nightmares of Indian bloodlust. Since 1779, when Madison and the rest of Jefferson's council clapped the "scalp-buyer" Major Henry Hamilton in irons, Madison viewed British–Indian alliances as a preeminent threat to US independence. In June 1780, he wrote to Jefferson, "Savages are making the most distressing incursions under the direction of British Agents."[10]

After observing the bungled talks at Fort Stanwix in 1784, Madison advocated stronger federal power to negotiate with Indian nations. Three years later, he signed the Constitution, which reserved that function to the federal government. The text of the Constitution exposed the ambiguity with which early Americans viewed Native nations. Congress controlled the power "to regulate Commerce with foreign Nations, and among the several States, and with the Indian Tribes." The clause distinguished between foreign nations, the states, and Indian tribes. As conceived by Madison and his fellow Framers, Native nations weren't foreign nations, but they also weren't part of the domestic body politic. They fell somewhere in between. They occupied land claimed by the United States even as the government recognized them as sovereign actors. Madison had helped create a Janus-faced standard by which Americans viewed Indians simultaneously as dangerous foreign adversaries and duplicitous dependents.[11]

When Madison imagined the trans-Appalachian valleys, he saw "a mine of vast wealth to the United States," as he wrote in *Federalist* no. 38. The federal government could control the land, sell it, pay off debt, and "furnish . . . liberal tributes to the federal treasury." Along with that "vast wealth," however, he saw dangerous confederacies of Native nations allied with British and Spanish empires, blocking westward expansion and suffocating Americans in the East. Rather than rejoice when the Jay Treaty obliged Britain to surrender western forts, he bristled at the thought that it allowed British Canadians to keep their property and trade with Indians in US territory. Britain had surrendered nothing. Its subjects could retain "both their land & their allegiance at the same time, and consequently . . . keep up a foreign and hostile influence over the Indians, within the limits of the United States."[12]

Madison failed to appreciate that George Washington supported the Jay Treaty for at least one of the same reasons that Madison opposed it: the British–Indian alliance. "All the difficulties we encounter with the Indians; their hostilities—the murders of helpless women & innocent children along our frontiers, results from the conduct of the Agents of Great Britain in this Country." Washington felt that he couldn't lose the chance to push the British out of western forts and disrupt their alliance with Native Americans.[13]

It worked. When the British shut the gates of Fort Miamis against the Native fighters at Fallen Timbers, they signaled a tepid desire for peace with the United States. The Jay Treaty secured that peace with the surrender of the western forts. With their major ally evacuating the region, Ohio Valley Natives made a calamitous peace with the United States at Greenville, Ohio, in 1795. They ceded large portions of their land in return for annuities that mostly benefited a few Native oligarchs.[14]

The most virulent Federalists, such as Timothy Pickering, dreaded white frontier folk as "little less savage than the Indians." Like most Americans, they considered westward expansion inevitable, assuming Native nations and cultures would disappear as Indians were assimilated into "civilization." If unruly classes frayed into the West, however, they would sap strength from the nation, cause problems with Native nations, and invite trouble from empires on the border. Westerners needed the firm hand of the national government to impose order and keep peace with Native Americans. Federalists argued for a slower, well-regulated expansion that kept populations high in the East to support the labor necessary for an industrializing nation.[15]

With the Jay Treaty and Treaty of Greenville, Federalists had ironically laid the groundwork for Jefferson and Madison's more aggressive expansionism. Madison agreed that the federal government needed to control the unincorporated West and Indian policy, but he viewed westward movement as a benefit rather than a threat. The government should encourage it, not stymie it. Madison envisioned a future in which farmers would receive cheap land, cultivate it, export their crops, and keep the nation prosperous and free of the degraded, British-like society Federalists advocated.[16]

In Madison's mind, Americans balanced precariously between two opposite but equally dangerous fates. They might return to primitive "savagery" like Indians, whose society had not developed into what he considered a civilized state. Or they might march toward industrialized debauchery like Britain, whose society had advanced so far it withered into corruption. If Americans moved west with insufficient land to cultivate, they would adopt Indian hunting and gathering practices and devolve into the first outcome. If they stayed east, they would overpopulate, become a manufacturing society, and rot into the second. To avoid either fate, the United States needed western land free of Indian control and British threats.[17]

Madison complied with Jefferson's program of purchasing the land to diminish Native hunting grounds. The process would "abolish the savage manners of those tribes," he asserted, by encouraging them to adopt US-style agriculture and gradually assimilate into white society. The administration used treaties to acquire millions of acres from Native nations, usually purchasing them far below market value and often by coercion, bribery, or artifice. Jefferson and Madison viewed the policy less as malicious dispossession than a benevolent solution to help Native Americans survive the tide of change that would sweep over them.[18]

More pessimistic than Jefferson about human nature, Madison lacked confidence in the plan, though he never discarded it. He later observed "a disinclination in human nature to exchange the savage for the civilized life." He applied the view to whites and Native Americans alike but thought it boded ill for the project of assimilation. When Jefferson mentioned Indians' "sanctimonious reverence for" their traditions in his Second Inaugural Address, Madison urged him to change it to "a blind attachment to" them. A decade before he became secretary of state, he hinted at his preferred course when he praised white attacks on Native Americans as "the true method of dealing with the savages."[19]

However they subdued Native Americans, Jefferson and Madison considered the objective a vital geopolitical strategy to dismantle Indian friendship with European empires. Jefferson had accelerated Native American dispossession in early 1803, when he feared Napoleon would park his empire next door and renew old French alliances with Native Americans. More than a decade after the Jay Treaty was signed, Madison still complained that British traders incited "Indian partizans" against the United States. He received reports that the British army paid Native Americans to apprehend deserters on US soil and that the British government and traders had promised military aid to Indians if necessary. If Indians became farmers, they would have no need of British weapons.[20]

Lingering nuisances became imminent threats after the *Chesapeake* drubbing in 1807. With war looming, the British Indian Department scurried to revive the military alliance with Native Americans that had dissolved after the Treaty of Greenville. While they enticed Native Americans with diplomatic gifts and half promises of returned land, they encouraged discretion. They wanted their allies prepared for war should it occur but not to precipitate premature hostilities.[21]

Prophetstown

Like other leaders of revivalist movements of the period, Tenskwatawa wanted not only to spread a doctrine but to gather a people. At first, the place was Greenville, Ohio. Resonant with symbolism, the site marked the spot where Shawnees, Miamis, Wyandots, and Delawares surrendered vast lands to the United States in 1795. A decade later, Tenskwatawa intended it to represent the revival of Native resistance.[22]

The point was not lost on the governor, William Henry Harrison. "The sacred spot" where the United States and Native nations made peace "has been selected for dark and bloody councils," he complained in a message to the gathering Shawnees. Suspecting a British scheme, he tried to convince them that the "fool" Tenskwatawa spoke "not the words of the Great Spirit but those of the devil and of British Agents."[23]

In the spring of 1808, Tenskwatawa moved his people over a hundred miles west, into Indiana Territory. He selected a spot near the Wabash and Tippecanoe rivers and called it Prophetstown. Indians gathered there by the thousands, and its population soon outpaced that of every city west of the Appalachians except New Orleans. Prophetstown sat on land claimed by the US-friendly Chief Little Turtle. The region's Native inhabitants had fled the US armies that burned their homes in the 1790s. Like Greenville, Prophetstown signified the redemption of Native land from US aggression. The move west was symbolic and politically savvy, leading Tenskwatawa away from US-allied Shawnees, Wyandots, and Miamis who spurned his revival. It crept him nearer to tribes who lived near the Canadian border region and who were more receptive to his message. With them came closer ties to potential British allies.[24]

Tenskwatawa envisioned Prophetstown as a place of peace. Native Americans would gather there, discard their tribal affiliations, and share the land. Under a common Indian identity, they would resist US trickery to acquire their territory. The city brought Tenskwatawa closer to Vincennes, where Governor Harrison resided. Tenskwatawa assured the governor that he desired friendship with the United States.[25]

The Prophet sought peace but prepared for war, spurred less by aggression than by fear. He wanted ground where his people could, as one Indian agent quoted him, "watch the Boundry Line between the Indians and the white people—and if a white man put his foot over it . . . the warriors could easily put him back." Tenskwatawa's brother, Tecumseh, conjured the image of a coiled snake when he told British officials, "If the Americans encroach upon them they are resolved to strike." The rivers protected the new city to the north and east. Residents cleared trees to strip possible enemies of cover.[26]

While Tenskwatawa prepared Prophetstown for defense, he inched toward British friendship. With war talk saturating the air in 1808, Native nations needed to decide whether to pursue partnerships or neutrality. Tenskwatawa's most ardent followers flooded his gathering places from the Canadian border, where they had long traded with the British. That April, he told a British emissary that he wanted to travel north to talk with His Majesty's commanders in Canada.[27]

William Claus managed British efforts to nurture Native alliances. The son of a loyalist and grandson of famed British Indian agent William Johnson, Claus had spent his life in British–Indian alliance networks. As deputy superintendent of Indian Affairs in early 1808, he began to convene Native American leaders in the Great Lakes region to talk possible war with the United States. He struggled to find chiefs he thought he could trust with British secrets. Starting in February, he grew more aggressive, looking deeper into US territory to Britain's former Shawnee allies. Claus knew that Black Hoof, Little Turtle, and other US-friendly leaders despised Tenskwatawa, which made him an enticing potential ally. He wanted the Prophet on his side.[28]

In the summer of 1808, Tenskwatawa declined Claus's invitation to Amherstburg in the Great Lakes province of Upper Canada for diplomatic talks. With Prophetstown's newcomers in need of physical and spiritual nourishment, the Shawnee leader refused to abandon his city for negotiations 300 miles away.[29]

He sent his brother, Tecumseh, instead. An able negotiator, Tecumseh withheld a commitment without foreclosing a future alliance. The Native confederation might consider it if the British could guarantee support. Thirteen years after Fort Miamis, distrust still ran deep.[30]

While Tecumseh negotiated with the British, Tenskwatawa met Governor Harrison at Vincennes and made him rethink his initial assessment of the Prophet. Harrison had made no secret of his initial distrust. "I have heard a very bad report of you," he said to his visitor, "that you are endeavoring to alienate the minds of Indians, from the great Father, the President of the 17 fires [the 17 US states], and once more bring them under the influence of the British." Tenskwatawa defused the tension by promising neutrality. His people would "never take up the tomahawk, should it be offered by the British, or the Long Knives [Americans]." By the time Tenskwatawa left Vincennes, Harrison had no idea what to think. "I was not able to ascertain whether he is, as I at first supposed, a tool of the British or not," Harrison admitted. Tenskwatawa might even prove useful to the United States, he hoped.[31]

During his final months in office, Jefferson received several such contradictory reports about Tenskwatawa's spreading movement. Assuming the Shawnee showed no "preference between the English & us," he hoped the government could buy off the "scoundrel" (Jefferson's term) as it had other Native leaders. Tenskwatawa considered the annuities a betrayal of Native sovereignty. Indian nations must protect their land, he argued, not bargain it away for empty promises. Though hardly the first to criticize US treaty-making chicanery, Tenskwatawa and Tecumseh became the most energetic opponents of it.[32]

The Treaty

When in his First Inaugural Address Madison promised "to carry on the benevolent plans which have been so meritoriously applied to the conversion of our aboriginal neighbours from the degradation and wretchedness of savage life, to a participation of the improvements of which the human mind and manners are susceptible in a civilized state," he fanned the flames of Tenskwatawa's revival. Native Americans began to realize, as some Wyandots later wrote Madison, that "this pretence of bettering our situation, it appears, is only for a temporary purpose" until Americans took their farmland, too. A former British agent saw that the "discontent of the Indians arises principally from the unfair purchases of their lands," no matter how much "Americans ascribe it to the machinations of our government."[33]

In July 1809, months into his tenure, Madison authorized Harrison to secure more land east of the Wabash for the United States. Conscious that Indians grew restless with what they considered US deceit, he urged transparency to mute suspicions of wrongdoing "if practicable." The qualifier gave Harrison a lot of latitude.[34]

That September, Harrison negotiated land purchases with Delawares, Potawatomis, Miamis, and Eel River tribes at Fort Wayne, resorting again to coercive ploys. When the Miamis refused his offer of 2¢ per acre rather than the market value of $2 per acre, Harrison threatened to withhold annuities the United States already owed them. Supplemented with alcohol, the threats did the trick. The United States purchased almost 3 million acres. The Senate consented, and Madison ratified the treaty on January 2, 1810.[35]

A former British army officer named William McIntosh excoriated the treaty to Madison. McIntosh clamored that Harrison had done exactly what the president had instructed him not to do—negotiate a legally questionable treaty. Not only had Harrison forced an unfair and illegitimate bargain, but he had also lied to the administration about the proceedings, McIntosh claimed. He pleaded with Madison not to ratify the treaty, something Madison had done nine months before McIntosh wrote.[36]

Even had Madison received McIntosh's remonstrance earlier, McIntosh likely would have had little impact on Madison's opinion of the treaty and not just because Harrison denounced the man as "a Scotch Tory." The president wanted transparent agreements to avoid diplomatic disputes, but ultimately Native Americans were responsible for their own decisions, he reasoned. As he told Creek leader Hobohoilthle about a different treaty, "The line was drawn by us both. Your land is your own. Nobody can make it smaller without your consent. The Trees and the Game and everything which your land produces is also your own. Nobody can touch them without your leave."[37]

Madison viewed the transactions as the hard realities of diplomacy moderated by US benevolence. Some powers bargained from strength and others from weakness. As far as Madison saw things, he treated with Native nations more honorably than the British had treated with the United States. In fact, he had their best interests at heart, he believed. "Look at your Father, the President," he implored Hobohoilthle, appealing to Native diplomatic language long used to describe a senior partner in an alliance. "Turn your ear to him, and believe what he says." Madison exhorted Indians to adopt agriculture, domesticate livestock, and train women to spin. The president "knows that his red Children can live well if they will follow his advice. . . . He is your Friend. He holds out his hand to you." Madison believed he sought a workable and benign solution for both parties. That was more than the British or French could say about their diplomacy with the United States, Madison might assuage his conscience.[38]

Tenskwatawa and Tecumseh saw things differently. Enraged by the purchase, they jettisoned hopes of friendship with the United States. They fumed that the chiefs who signed the treaty possessed no right to sign away millions of acres, land that Tenskwatawa and Tecumseh believed all Native Americans held in common. Though not present at the signing, Tecumseh claimed that US-friendly Potawatomis forced the others to sign and "held the Tomhawk over their heads," something Harrison denied.[39]

The Shawnee brothers combined Tenskwatawa's religious charisma with Tecumseh's military and diplomatic intelligence to galvanize Native nations against the United States. They provided leadership to a diverse and angry array of Indians who saw the treaty as evidence that the United States intended to usurp all Native land. Together, they turned a religious revival into a political confederacy.[40]

Tecumseh traveled south to invite Creeks, with whom he shared heritage, to join the growing confederacy. Like their northern neighbors, Creek militants had tired of US intrusions on their land. Creek spokesman Hobohoilthle warned Madison that if the US government persisted, "there may be some mad crazy people who would do mischief." Those were the people Tecumseh wanted.[41]

Tenskwatawa and Tecumseh abandoned neutrality and fixed an alliance with eager British commanders. Conscious of his growing power, Tecumseh warned Harrison that his followers would enlist British support if the United States tried to acquire more Native land. He promised the Creeks that the confederacy would war against the United States once Britain gave the signal. The British heaped ammunition on the confederacy in 1810 and 1811. The brothers' influence grew so strong that one British

Indian agent feared they would push the empire into overly hasty warfare with the United States. It became difficult to gauge who was the senior partner in the resurrected alliance.[42]

Harrison spilled a barrage of charges onto Madison's desk, renewing his accusations against Tenskwatawa as a British minion. The Prophet is "inspired by the Superintendant of Indian Affairs for Upper Canada, rather than the Great Spirit"; Tenskwatawa's complaints are a "mere pretence, suggested to the Prophet by British Partizans & Emmissaries"; British Indian agent Matthew Elliott wanted to marshal "the most warlike of the Tribes, as a kind of barrier to Canada." The governor summarized his contempt in a message to the Indiana legislature: "The Prophet is a tool of British fears or British avarice, designed for the purpose of forming a combination of the Indians, which in case of war between that power and the United States may assist them in the defence of Canada, or as the means of keeping back our settlements."[43]

Harrison's allies echoed his fears. A meeting of his supporters warned the president, "We are fully convinced that the formation of the Combination headed by the Shawanoe Prophet, is a British Scheme and that the agents of that power are constantly exciting the Indians to hostility against the United States." One waggish writer alluded to Hebrew scripture, quipping that Britain controlled Tenskwatawa and wished to govern US law, thereby dictating "both the law and the prophets." Americans like Harrison believed that if not for British intrigues, docile Indians would accept US claims to Native land.[44]

The Battle

A mid-August heat wave suffocated central Virginia during Madison's annual retreat to Montpelier in 1811. The thermometer hovered around the mid- to high eighties—not torrid by current conditions but stifling enough for someone who lived during what climatologists now call the Little Ice Age. He considered it too hot to travel for social calls. Then overnight, on August 24, the weather turned mercifully cool, almost unseasonably so. That same day, Madison authorized an operation destined to surge political temperatures in Prophetstown. For almost a year he had refused Harrison's pleas to detach troops to secure the region of the Fort Wayne purchase. Such a march would have challenged Tenskwatawa's vow that Americans would never possess the land. For the time, Madison prized peace over a

show of force, despite Harrison's apocalyptic warnings of "a general combination of all Tribes against us."[45]

That August, Harrison prepared troops to ascend the Wabash and again
asked for approval. He assured William Eustis, secretary of war, that he
could disband the confederacy without fighting. They needed to move
fast, Harrison insisted, because a British agent had told the Prophet that
"the time had arrived for taking up arms"—certainly faulty intelligence.
While Tecumseh traveled south to visit the Creeks, Harrison planned to
lead a force up the river, threatening Native Americans into submission.
The Prophet's supporters would cower and the confederacy crumble, he
predicted.[46]

Harrison convinced Madison that the march would cause no bloodshed.
The president assumed that his recent cautions against "needless hostilities"
would temper the governor. And he overestimated the Prophet's desire for
peace. Madison approved the expedition in the comfort of Montpelier's
mild weather. It seemed like a poignant fulfillment of Tecumseh's scoff to
Harrison that the president was too distant and comfortable to care about
their problems. "He may sit in his town, and drink his wine, whilst you and
I will have to fight it out."[47]

While Tecumseh journeyed south in October 1811, Harrison slogged toward Prophetstown with about 2,000 men, a mix of regular troops and militia. The Prophet and the governor each assumed the other would attack,
and their scouts and sentries danced around each other as the American
force advanced toward the Indian city. On November 6, Harrison's force of
about 800 (he left the others at a hastily constructed fort down the river)
camped just outside Prophetstown. The governor posted sentries around
the site.[48]

Tenskwatawa and Harrison tottered between peace and war, agreeing
to a conference the next day while suspecting the other might attack that
night. Indian patrols reconnoitered Harrison's camp in the early hours of
November 7. Tenskwatawa may have sent them, but the evidence is not
conclusive. However it happened, somewhere in the pre-dawn darkness
Native scouts stumbled across American sentries. Shots cracked in the
nighttime silence, and Harrison and Tenskwatawa tumbled into a battle
that both expected but neither intended, at least not that morning.[49]

Around 4:30 A.M., war cries pierced the air as Native Americans
penetrated sentry lines and rained bullets into Harrison's camp. Confused
violence dominated the early fighting, with half-slumbering troops
snatching firearms, dousing fires (to obstruct the Indians' vision), and

returning fire. Sometimes they couldn't tell friend from foe. They scrambled into formation. Harrison mounted a horse and barked orders.[50]

Though surprised by the timing, Harrison had desired a nighttime attack like this. He wanted a fight with Tenskwatawa's followers but knew strategic and political catastrophe would ensue if he attacked in open warfare during the day. Despite his assurances to Madison of bloodless victory, he expected to route the confederacy and burn Prophetstown. He coveted a rationale to do it, and now he had one. "In night attacks," he reckoned, "discipline always prevails over disorder," and he believed his troops more disciplined than Native American soldiers. He would not waste this moment of potential glory.[51]

The US troops rallied and held the ground for over two hours in heavy fighting. In the gray dawn, they fixed bayonets and took the offensive. The Prophetstown fighters retreated from the woods and crossed the nearby prairie, out-ammunitioned more than out-maneuvered at what became known as the Battle of Tippecanoe. The Americans began to count their casualties and scalp the enemy dead.[52]

Tenskwatawa and his people evacuated Prophetstown, and Harrison burned the city the next day. He claimed victory but at a disastrous cost—188 US casualties compared to 120–130 of the Prophetstown soldiers, though Harrison's troops outnumbered Tenskwatawa's. The governor may have routed the Prophet for a few months, but he had come nowhere near destroying the confederacy. However indecisive the triumph, Madison and fellow Republicans tried to turn the military mishap into a cudgel to beat the British, the confederacy, and Federalists.[53]

The Triumvirate

Madison spun the bloody debacle in his favor when he disclosed Harrison's account of the battle to Congress. He praised "the dauntless spirit and fortitude victoriously displayed" by the US soldiers and Harrison's "collected firmness." The president portrayed the battle as an unqualified victory that would save the region from Native American violence. He needed a positive interpretation of Tippecanoe because his enemies charged him and Harrison with botching it.[54]

Most criticism originated with Federalists keen to discredit the administration's Indian and British policies. Early on, some Federalist editors misreported that Harrison had retreated despite a force double the size of Tenskwatawa's. So much for "the ability of our administration to conduct a war," chortled one. Even after another Federalist editor Alexander Hanson received more facts, he still exaggerated the losses. He did, however, accurately assess the cause of hostilities, blaming the Indians' aggression on "an enormous cession of their lands" rather than British intrigue. Another was more blunt: "Mr. Madison knows, that the British government has no hand in Indian hostilities."[55]

Even so, British wickedness made a fine target for Republican rage. Harrison vilified the critics as corrupt British allies who ignored the sins of Britain and the Prophetstown fighters. One newspaper described the battle as an "ANGLO–SAVAGE WAR." Tenskwatawa's fighters shot Americans with British arms and ammunition, another charged. One Republican demanded, "The blood of our fellow-citizens murdered on the Wabash by British intrigue calls aloud for vengeance." In an address sent to Madison, one group of Pennsylvanians declared that "the tomahawk of the savages is prompted to the butchery of our unconscious settlers by the infernal Stratagems of ruthless England." In a House floor debate, a Republican congressman roared that the nation needed to drive the British off the continent to save women and children from Indian tomahawks. Some erased any distinction between Native Americans and the British, one calling Indians "British savages" and another calling the British "half-Indian, scalping assassins."[56]

Reports of the attack arrived just in time for Republicans to deflect attention from riots in Savannah, Georgia, in which French and US sailors had brawled, inflicting death on both sides. One Federalist decried the violence as "*a bloody massacre of American seaman, in our own streets.*" Republican printer Duane countered that the same British government that "lets loose the savages upon our citizens" must have deployed agents to instigate the riots and inflame public opinion against France. With little sense of irony, the editor based his claim of British meddling on a report from a French commander.[57]

As the 1812 election year launched, Republicans assailed Federalists as the final member of a villainous triumvirate. One warned that during the coming election cycle, Federalists would make the British look "as angels of unsullied piety" and tell Americans that Napoleon had sent the Prophetstown Indians to murder Americans. A Massachusetts Republican told voters that Federalists had countenanced the British and Indian violence. Madison supporters deluged him with anti-British memorials that linked British contrivance, Native American violence, and the infidelity of Britain's sympathizers—one comparing Federalists to assassins in the dark.

FIGURE 11.1 A Scene on the Frontiers as Practiced by the Humane British and their Worthy Allies, 1812, by William Charles. This image depicts Native Americans scalping US troops, carrying British-supplied weapons and medals (emblazoned with "GR," meaning Georgius Rex [King George]). They receive a reward of secret service money from British officers for the scalps. Courtesy Library of Congress.

Federalists, the British, and Indians were conspiring to murder Americans and their liberty.[58]

Britain's diplomat in the United States, the young and adroit Augustus John Foster, protested that Britain had played no role in the Battle of Tippecanoe. He shared letters between British rulers, revealing their repeated admonitions to restrain Native American warfare. He failed to convince a president inundated by the roar of outraged Americans. James Monroe, Madison's new secretary of state, retorted that no matter what British superiors instructed, "subordinate agents" had provoked the western Native nations to hostility.[59]

Besides, Monroe reminded Foster, even if British magistrates hadn't approved the violence, they had authorized the mission of the by-then notorious secret agent, John Henry. Time to revisit Henry and the con artist Soubiran, beginning in the weeks before they boarded the New Galen.[60]

12

"A Serpent, in the Shape of a Spy"

We have seen a serpent, in the shape of a spy, stealing to our fire-sides
and altars, and attempting to sting us in the very heart of our Union.
—Inhabitants of Richmond, Manchester, and
Vicinity to Madison, May 30, 1812

IN OCTOBER 1811, IN AN apartment on Britain's Isle of Wight, the Count
de Crillon watched a bed-ridden Irishman named John Henry spout deliri-
ous nonsense. Crillon had previously crossed paths with Henry in British
society—dined with him at MP William Wellesley-Pole's, then at MP
Lord Yarmouth's, and seen him at fashionable London clubs. Just a month
earlier, the nearly six-feet-tall Henry had enjoyed a reputation for good
looks and polite manners. Now, he cut a very different image. While he
waited for a Boston-bound ship, Crillon had brought Henry to the apartment he rented in the island town of Ryde. There, his servants attended to
the poor man.[1]

Among his incoherent stammers, Henry peppered the name "Lord
Liverpool," Britain's colonial secretary. Crillon observed visitors floating in
and out of Henry's room over the course of several weeks. One arrived with
a packet of letters from Sir James Craig, the governor-general of Canada.
Henry refused them.[2]

By November 19, Henry had recovered from his fever. That day, a mes-
senger brought another letter, this one bearing the seal of Lord Liverpool.
"What more does he want of me?" Henry bristled, flinging the letter onto
the table and marching out of the room. Crillon discerned easily that
Henry was connected with some of the most powerful men in the British
Empire and that those connections for some reason left him spiteful and

vindictive. The next day, Crillon and Henry boarded the *New Galen*, destined for Boston.[3]

Then came that fateful night on the deck when they began to divulge their plights to one another. Crillon explained that Napoleon's imperial police had exiled him from his native country, a common enough occurrence in Napoleonic France, even for men of distinction such as Crillon. In return, Henry explained that he felt betrayed by Lord Liverpool and James Craig, who had employed him to spy on American Federalists in 1809 only to insult him with inadequate compensation.[4]

That is one telling of how John Henry met the Count de Crillon.

The problem with the account is that the *real* Count de Crillon was probably hundreds of miles away in Paris at the time, with no idea that Paule-Émile Soubiran was impersonating him. Soubiran invented much of the narrative to play a long con on the US government.[5]

Despite the difficulty of reconstructing the past out of Soubiran's lies, we can piece together a general framework. He did befriend Henry in Ryde on the Isle of Wight while they waited for the *New Galen* to bring them to Boston. It's doubtful they met earlier at dinner parties with MPs, though Henry did attend some of those and Soubiran had a knack for worming his way into elite society. It's even less likely that Soubiran nursed Henry back to health from near-death. When Soubiran later wrote Henry a letter recounting the services he had rendered him, he never mentioned that kindness.[6]

Soubiran likely lodged with or near Henry, and he may have seen letter packets from James Craig and Lord Liverpool as he claimed, alerting him that Henry might be a man worth conning. He apparently met Henry under his own name or an alias other than Crillon. Then, probably after he learned who Henry was and the information he possessed, Soubiran adopted the guise of the Count de Crillon. He told Henry that he had earlier used his mother's name because he was "in hiding from everybody." However the conversation unfolded, Soubiran convinced Henry that he was Count Edouard de Crillon, a son of the late Duke de Crillon.[7]

Once in Henry's confidence, Soubiran extracted details about Henry's 1809 mission and his sense of betrayal by Craig and Liverpool. He probably did so during a chance nighttime encounter on the ship, as he described. During the conversation, Henry also raged against Britain's repression of his native Ireland—"loaded with the chains of despotism," as Soubiran quoted him. Whether Soubiran remembered or invented the phrase on

Henry's lips, the Irishman confirmed elsewhere that he despised England for its crimes against his birthplace.[8]

Soubiran convinced Henry to show him the documents he had retained from the mission—letters detailing Henry's movements and conversations among New England Federalists. At worst, they revealed Federalist sympathy for Britain and Craig's hope that New England might secede— hardly revelations to even casual political spectators. With the right gloss, though, the papers could imply a more sinister plot between Federalists and Britain to sever the union.[9]

Soubiran saw not just manuscripts, but, as he wrote later, a "treasure"—a treasure that would "produce an immediate explosion between America and Great Britain." France would hail him a hero if he sparked the war and diverted British resources from the fight against Napoleon's troops in Europe. He began to formulate a plan that, whether he realized it or not, would culminate the toxic synergy of foreign meddling and political paranoia in the United States. He glimpsed what only a rogue of his caliber could—a chance to profit from Henry's bitterness, Craig's subterfuge, Napoleon's ambition, and Madison's suspicion.[10]

The Irishman

John Henry wore national affiliations loosely—a British subject born in Ireland and an immigrant to the United States then to British Canada. He roamed looking for financial security—editing a newspaper, selling wine, and commanding US artillery companies during the 1798–1800 Quasi-War with France. His travels took him to Philadelphia, Harper's Ferry, New York, and Vermont. Widowed with two daughters by 1806, he had moved to Montreal, Canada, where he befriended traders and magistrates.[11]

Henry felt little love for the republic he had left behind. When war between the United States and Britain lurked after the attack on the *Chesapeake* in 1807, he scrambled for a position in the king's service. To prove his usefulness, he transmitted intelligence to Canadian magistrates from his connections in the United States. "Democrats in power are in the French interest," he warned a Canadian administrator. If war erupted, though, party divisions would dissolve the union, and Canada could siphon New England into its column. "By good management a war will make half of America ours.... That wretched republic already totters under its own weight."[12]

His applications for a government appointment failed, but he scraped for attention, promising British officials more intelligence while in New England on private business in the spring of 1808. If Jefferson's embargo lasted much longer, he reported to a Canadian official, New Englanders would secede, establish their own government, and come to better terms with Britain. New Englanders would need to leap, though, before they "awake in the chains" of Napoleon. He worried only that Jefferson would capitulate before northerners jumped back into the arms of the British.[13]

Like his fellow agent John Howe, Henry believed that the longer the embargo lasted the better for Britain, but Henry had a more extreme vision. Howe hoped Federalists would take the presidency and improve relations with Britain. Henry worried that such success would appease Federalists, who would then abandon the goal of "a northern Coalition allied to England." He pressed some of his Boston acquaintances to support his more radical scheme but received no firm commitment.[14]

Impressed with Henry's information, Governor Craig commissioned him on a secret mission to Boston in 1809. Henry delighted to read that Lord Castlereagh of the British ministry had praised his letters from London. Had Henry read Craig's evasive language more carefully, he may have realized that the British government had no real plans to promote him for his service. Nevertheless, hoping for his long-awaited sinecure, he leaped at his chance even though it included no immediate compensation except for travel expenses. He left again for New England in February.[15]

Craig sent Henry to gauge how New Englanders viewed the union, the likelihood they would secede from it, and their desire "to make a connection with us" in case of war. The governor also authorized him to recruit American agents, if possible.[16]

On March 7, Henry wrote his most damning letter. If war commenced, the "federal States" would secede and form their own union, he informed Craig. Britain could send a few vessels from Halifax to defend their ports against the anemic US navy. Even that letter involved a vague hypothetical rather than a concrete plan, and the suggestion to protect New England with British vessels came from Henry, not Federalists. Madison's critics said nothing openly about secession, "finding it a very unpopular topic," Henry admitted. He could only explain the hesitancy by the "giddy, inconstant multitude," who act "inconsistently and absurdly."[17]

Less than a week later, Henry lamented that Congress had repealed the Embargo Act, for it had offered the best promise of "a revolution" that would destroy the republic. If British rulers aimed for that goal, he advised, they would need to pursue steady, long-term policies to divide northerners and southerners, Republicans and Federalists. The repeal calmed war talk, terminating Henry's hopes for the dissolution of the nation.[18]

At the same time, Madison and Secretary of State Robert Smith consented to reopen trade with Britain if Britain would lift its onerous orders in council—the executive orders that harassed neutral trade. They made a preliminary agreement to that effect with British diplomat David Erskine. Madison had scored a major diplomatic victory, but Henry believed that the president would never follow through on the overtures of peace. "It seems impossible that he should at once divest himself of his habitual animosity" to Britain, he wrote Craig. Whatever Madison's motives, Henry believed, his party wouldn't support him; they depended too much on anti-British rhetoric.[19]

Henry was wrong. It was the British foreign secretary George Canning who would eventually refuse to approve the deal. In the meantime, Federalists and Republicans praised it, inviting "a temporary suspension of conflict of parties," as Henry soon realized. For the time, there would be no war, no northern confederacy, no British alliance with New England. Henry returned to Montreal.[20]

Henry began his path to bitterness when he learned that Canning had rejected the agreement to lift the orders in council. By reneging on the deal, Britain ceded the high ground to Madison, who had lifted trade prohibitions from Britain and retained them against France. The French cabinet couldn't have concocted a better scheme to "injure the English party" in the United States, Henry derided. Madison could resurrect enmity with Britain and reinstate the trade restrictions while clearing himself of charges of French influence. British rulers should have taken his advice and fostered party strife when they had the chance, he believed. He had terminated his mission in New England due to an agreement made in vain.[21]

Meanwhile, Henry saw men appointed to positions in Canada that he coveted and believed he deserved. In early 1811, he traveled to London to plead his cause to Lord Liverpool, the new colonial secretary. He received some weak pledges that came to nothing. His government had sent him on a worthless mission, refused to compensate him, and continued to oppress his native Ireland. Frustrated and poor, he prepared to return to the United States, where his daughters resided with their aunt.[22]

Henry kept copies of his correspondence, which described his exchanges with New England Federalists. He crossed the Solent to the Isle of Wight, where he boarded in the town of Ryde while he waited for the *New Galen* to carry him to Boston. While he waited, he chanced on a flamboyant French count.[23]

The Count

Born the son of a goldsmith, Paul-Émile Soubiran hailed from Lectoure, a town of just over 6,000 surrounded by the low hills of France's south-western Gascony region. With blood "always so boiling," as one acquaintance remembered him, Soubiran was unfit for a life of daily toil or subordination. The short Frenchman deserted the National Guard in 1793 then suffered a miserable career in Napoleon's forces. In legal peril (unjust persecution, if you asked him) since his tour on the island of Malta around 1798, he was arrested a year later in Bayonne for impersonating a French general. He vanished from prison within a month. He tried to climb military ranks. According to his own dubious story, he lost a promotion to aide-de-camp for Jean Lannes, slipping through the cracks after Napoleon deposed the Spanish monarch and made his brother Joseph king of Spain in 1808. Soubiran served under the celebrated Marshal Michel Ney until he pilfered some official funds and fled.[24]

In his own version, Soubiran traveled Europe with a couple of servants through Barèges, Bordeaux, Paris, Brussels, Amsterdam, Bremen, Hamburg, Copenhagen, Stockholm, Gothenburg, and many spots in between. He lost some money gambling, charmed his way into some elite homes, and gave the slip to a creditor—a situation so common a French satirist wrote a manual about how to do it. He admitted to shameless flattery but painted himself as no criminal. He even tried to legitimize his impersonation of Crillon, insisting that he befriended an old Monsieur de Crillon Partorias in Britain, who made him heir "of his name, of all his property, and of twelve hundred quadruples."[25]

The French police told a different story. The "intriguer of the first order," as the files describe him, scammed his way across the continent, eluding police from "Spain to Hamburg" and playing "the roles of Colonel, Consul, Ambassador, and Chevalier of all the Orders." The chase apparently began after he defrauded the French Army. Soubiran admitted elsewhere that he had "been obliged to quit France and assume every sort of mask."[26]

By mid-1811, Soubiran, now forty, landed in Britain, possibly, as he claimed, after trying to sail for the United States but suffering capture by a British warship. He would later tell people that he attended lavish dinners and elite clubs. One of his tales even had him meeting Prince Regent George IV, who offered him command of a British legion in Spain if he turned against France. More likely, Soubiran spent his time in London trying to claim an old gambling debt and then fled the city after shooting the debtor in the shoulder on a dueling ground.[27]

He slunk off to the Isle of Wight, where he met, like a gift from the patron saint of frauds, a dejected Irishman with important secrets. He assumed the identity of Count Edouard de Crillon and won Henry's trust. Aboard the *New Galen*, the fake count learned about Henry's documents that just might earn him a slick profit and turn him from a disgraced scoundrel into a French hero.[28]

Trust

At the end of January 1812, French diplomat Louis-Barbé-Charles Sérurier hosted Soubiran at Kalorama, the elegant Washington, DC, estate Sérurier had leased since his arrival the previous spring. The *New Galen* had deposited Soubiran and Henry onto Boston's docks about a month earlier. From Boston, Soubiran had written Sérurier, promising intelligence that might cause war between the United States and Britain. Sérurier smelled a scam from over 400 miles away ("The letter . . . might cover a trap," he worried). Skeptical but intrigued, Sérurier arranged to meet Soubiran in Washington.[29]

At the Kalorama estate, Soubiran summoned his most shameless flattery, praising Napoleon, lamenting his own faults, and bemoaning the wrongs done to him. Sérurier recognized the "romance" in his stories and contradictions in the details. Even so, Soubiran convinced Sérurier of his contrition and desire to serve Napoleon. In exchange for information that would provoke war between the United States and Britain, Soubiran asked nothing but a return to the emperor's favor. (The swindler planned more subtle ways to profit from his long con.) Sérurier saw that the man before him could benefit France if he possessed documents that would push the United States to war with Britain and, as Soubiran put it, see the "English Party . . . entirely annihilated." Rather than make the papers an official French enterprise, he suggested Soubiran bring them to Madison's new secretary of state, James Monroe. Sérurier was still unsure he trusted Soubiran, but that mattered little so long as Madison and Monroe did.[30]

Madison hosted Soubiran as the Count de Crillon in the executive mansion. The president had received a letter from Massachusetts governor Elbridge Gerry, introducing the con artist. Soubiran walked into the lion's den, dining with the British diplomat Foster, who denounced him as a French spy. Soubiran's indignant retort elicited a sheepish response from Foster, and Soubiran solidified his place among Washington diplomats as a French count. To support Soubiran without endorsing him, Sérurier entertained him with the rest.[31]

With Soubiran legitimized in the highest circles in Washington, Henry arrived in town to sell his documents to the Madison administration. While his French partner campaigned for validity, Henry lay low in a Georgetown boarding room. On February 1, he and Soubiran met Monroe and Virginia Senator Richard Brent, who worked under Madison's orders.[32]

Ecstatic about the potential dirt on British–Federalist collusion, the secretary of state broke the first rule of negotiation and betrayed eagerness. Republican hawks in Congress were pressuring Madison to declare war against Britain, and the president scrambled for national unity. Since Congress had repealed the Embargo Act in 1809, he had clawed for other ways to assert US strength against British and French insults. He sparred with, as he saw it, an "unhinged" Congress unwilling to muster backbone. By 1810, Congress lifted trade restrictions against both European powers, leaving a feeble threat to reinstate them against one if the other started respecting US neutrality. In response, Napoleon made an empty promise to repeal his anti-neutral decrees. Madison tried to use this flimsy pledge to convince British rulers to lift their orders in council, but Napoleon failed to fool British rulers that he would follow through. They would retain their orders until the emperor's defeat. By early 1812, Madison considered Britain the greater of the two sinners, given impressment, the *Chesapeake* affair, unlawful blockades (as he saw them), Indian alliances, and the empire's harder line (at least in word) against neutral trade. By early 1812, the president wanted war, but he needed to convince a skeptical nation. He had ironically placed the decision to declare war beyond his—or any president's—reach during the Constitutional Convention, when he helped lodge the power in Congress. Most important, he needed to dissuade wary Republicans from joining with Federalists to dilute war preparations. Henry's documents might give him the ammunition against Britain and Federalists to do that.[33]

Henry's stash might also tip Republicans into power in the coming elections, especially in the critical state of Massachusetts, where Governor Gerry, a moderate Republican, stood for reelection. If US armies invaded Canada during a war, as Madison intended, they would need the unequivocal support of northern states. Madison never admitted as much, but he must have seen that the disclosures might embarrass Federalists and favor Gerry, the man who had written letters of introduction for the fake Count de Crillon and Henry. According to one cynical interpretation of the time, Madison wanted Republican legislatures in New England, as they would select Republican electors and secure his own reelection.[34]

Sensing his bargaining power, Henry started the price at the astronomical figure of £25,000 sterling, nearly $125,000. Monroe agreed to the price but the next day informed Soubiran that the treasury lacked the funds. The president could pay $50,000, and even to do that he would need to empty the secret service budget (the fund for espionage expenses). Henry roared that he would rather burn the papers than sell them at that amount.[35]

Watching the deal start to crash and likely seeing his own chance to profit, Soubiran intervened with the alarmed Monroe and promised to bring the price down. At 5 o'clock in the morning on February 5, Soubiran wrote Monroe good news: Henry was ready to sell. He wanted £18,000, still about $34,000 more than the United States could afford. To compensate the difference, Soubiran had promised Henry his Spanish estate, St. Martial, and the United States could reimburse Soubiran later for the gift. Soubiran owned no such property, though neither Henry nor Monroe knew that.[36]

As a supposed aristocrat, Soubiran couldn't appear to be angling for a portion of the upfront payment, but he had schemed a way to get his cut. Henry would later learn that Soubiran was no count and that he would receive no estate. For the time, Soubiran had secured the purchase of the documents. To others, he insisted that he made the offer to finalize the deal and serve his country. Sérurier doubted the claim, but he had no interest in arguing with the man who was about to reveal documents that might hurl the United States to war with Britain. He and Monroe witnessed the transfer of the bogus Crillon's forged deed to Henry.[37]

Madison had dealt with frauds before. While secretary of state, he tussled with Anthony Morales, who impersonated the Dutch consul general so well that, at least for a short while, he received an exequatur (official recognition) from Thomas Jefferson. Blinded by political paranoia, however, Madison ignored past lessons and abandoned caution with Henry and

Soubiran. He believed that Henry's letters would prove British–Federalist collusion without even seeing the papers. He authorized the $50,000 purchase, a sum equivalent to the cost of a warship at the time. The parties transacted the business on February 10, and Henry left Washington a rich man.[38]

If Madison had scrutinized the situation better, he might have learned what Henry hinted at in private: the documents were basically worthless. "You may be assured that I made the disclosures as palatable to the persons I had to deal with as I possibly could," Henry wrote a Canadian friend. He considered the exaggerations necessary "to make it appear to be worth the purchase." The Irishman could hardly believe how much money the US government offered him. Henry could have caused some damage had he sold copies of letters from his first mission, in which he named a couple of Federalist discontents. He never sold those documents, perhaps because he had not retained copies of them. Even had Madison seen them, he would have discovered nothing but the names of a handful of Federalists who flirted with the idea of disunion but never committed to it.[39]

With the papers in their possession, Madison and Monroe began to verify their authenticity, a step a less avid buyer would have taken before purchasing them. The pair learned that they were authentic but essentially useless. They had just spent $50,000 and promised another $34,000 for papers that revealed no sedition, no plot, no crime, and no names.[40]

Madison and Monroe needed to make the most of their blunder, and they began by trying to conceal what they had paid for Henry's cache. When Monroe prepared a bill of exchange for Amsterdam bankers to pay Soubiran his share (a payment never made), he left the order vague to conceal its purpose. He directed the US minister in France to take a receipt for the payment from somebody besides Crillon and without mentioning Crillon's name.[41]

Monroe extracted a cover letter from Henry that implied the Irishman had given rather than sold his papers to the administration. Henry wrote the letter February 20, ten days after he delivered the documents and received payment. Aware that Madison would likely publish his words, he promoted the intelligence in the same exaggerated terms he had pitched it to the administration. By exposing the intrigue of British rulers, the letters would inspire "*unanimity among all parties in America*" and "melt all division and disunion among its citizens."[42]

Despite the bloviating tone, Henry had accurately appraised the nation's dilemma: foreign powers could insult the United States at will, knowing that the people would never retaliate as one. Madison counted on Henry's earlier promise that the letters would "extinguish every thing worth the name of opposition to the Government." Even if the papers exposed no Federalist conspiracy, they offered proof that Britain wanted to instigate one. The president gambled that they betrayed enough to shame Federalists and unite Americans against Britain.[43]

Some of the information would embarrass Federalists, but that embarrassment paled against Madison's folly of blowing his secret service fund for trivial intelligence. And it withered before the irony that Madison paid foreign nationals an unconscionable amount of public money to reveal that his political opposition had not conspired with a foreign power. By 1812, Madison lived in and had helped create a nation in which it seemed rational to trust a former British spy and mysterious French gascon more than his political opponents.

Distrust

On March 9, 1812, Madison released Henry's manuscripts to Congress and colored them in their darkest hue. "They prove," the president touted, that a British secret agent had tried to foment "disaffection to the constituted authorities of the nation." British rulers pursued "intrigues with the disaffected, for the purpose of bringing about resistance to the laws, and, eventually in concert with a British force, of destroying the Union and forming the eastern part thereof into a political connexion with Great Britain."[44]

Madison studiously avoided mention of Sérurier's involvement, "as such mention might injure its effect by giving it a French color," as Sérurier reported to Paris. Presumably, Madison revealed nothing about the man whom he knew as Crillon for the same reason. Yet Monroe had consulted Sérurier about how best to word Madison's message. The French minister knew more than Congress when Madison released the documents. Political trust ran thin in Washington in early 1812.[45]

The same day, Madison tried to convince others, and maybe himself, that the trove proved more than it did. "This discovery," he wrote Jefferson, "or rather formal proof of the Co-operation between the Eastern Junto, & the B[ritish]. Cabinet will, it is to be hoped, not only prevent future evils from that source, but extract good out of the past."[46]

The manuscripts proved no such cooperation, as Federalists soon bellowed. Not a single "individual was ever intimated as being concerned with Henry," Josiah Quincy protested. "By Henry's own declaration," a Federalist crowed two days after the release of the documents, "he did not find the least prospect of success." Henry substantiated the claims. He wanted to damage Craig and Liverpool, not incriminate his New England friends. His letters implicated nobody, he declared. Madison hoped the documents would nourish unity; they bred enmity. Enraged Federalists wouldn't even cross his threshold after the disclosure, Dolley Madison reported.[47]

Federalists could think of no reason for Madison to release the documents other than to manipulate coming elections. British diplomat Foster agreed. "No event could happen more opportune for this Government to influence the approaching Elections," he sighed to London. One of the president's old friends lamented, "I think it a most pitiful electioneering Manoeuvre" unworthy of Madison. The most cynical Federalists insisted that Madison wanted Republicans in control of the Massachusetts legislature to secure its electors for his own reelection bid that fall. Josiah Quincy blistered Madison, "To such arts could a man placed at the head of the nation condescend, to give food to party malice, and to increase the chances of his re-election . . . to the Presidency of the United States!"[48]

Even worse for Madison, word leaked about the payments—including the pretend Crillon's and Sérurier's roles—after Henry cashed $48,000 worth in checks and flashed around the forged deed of his new estate. Rumors flew that Crillon was an intimate friend of Napoleon and chummy with Sérurier. One Federalist theorized that Napoleon would reward Crillon for "what he had done for Madison, his Vice-Roy." Rather than proof of a British plot, the documents became "proof positive of 'French influence!!!'" Another Federalist mixed biblical metaphors: "A Frenchman stole, like the serpent, into Eden, upon the slumberers of the garden." Federalists boiled that the president had fallen into a French scheme and misused public funds to target their party and ensure his reelection.[49]

Some of Madison's confidants almost validated Federalist suspicions about his political motives. Treasury Secretary Albert Gallatin exulted to Jefferson, "The discoveries made by Henry will have a salutary effect in annihilating the spirit of the Essex junto" and even Madison's Republican opposition. Likewise, Jefferson congratulated Madison that the "double treachery of Henry . . . prostrates" British partisans in the United States.[50]

Madison operated less from corrupt political impulses than the conviction that leading Federalists must be nothing less than criminal. The Federalist backlash forced the president to double down, convinced that he could read subversion between the lines of Henry's pages. Monroe believed a British–Federalist conspiracy "the obvious meaning" of the correspond-ence, even if not explicit.[51]

Names

Convinced that a plot existed, Madison began to search for names. After Henry sailed for France, where he intended to claim his non-existent es-tate, Monroe asked the US minister in Paris, Joel Barlow, to collect names of Federalists involved in the supposed scheme. To save face and explain why they had bought the non-incriminating letters, Monroe feigned that he and Madison initially preferred to "reclaim" rather than "punish the offenders," so they had sought no names from Henry. They had rethought their approach and now wanted names. It took months for the letter to land in Barlow's hands, too long to do the administration any good. Barlow died before he could contact Henry.[52]

In the meantime, Madison remembered an anonymous letter he had received while he was secretary of state in late 1808. "If the present crisis should eventuate in a war against England," the correspondent warned, "an immediate severance of the Union will be attempted." Madison suspected (correctly as it turned out) that Jonathan Dayton, the former Federalist senator from New Jersey implicated in the Burr Conspiracy, was the au-thor. Dayton continued, "There are men of the highest standing, & first respectability & influence in society, who are engaged in it, & some indeed who are at this time very near to you, & whom you would no more suspect than your brother." At the time, Madison ignored the warnings because, as Dayton informed him later, the repeal of the Embargo Act and shaky 1809 détente "completely confounded" the potential traitors. Even so, the cor-respondent promised names of the conspirators if occasion called for it.[53]

The occasion had arrived, Madison concluded in mid-March 1812—"a moment singularly critical." Linking Dayton's intelligence with Henry's, he implored Dayton for the names of the conspirators promised years earlier. Henry had exposed the "British designs agst our Union," but the "domestic plotters" evaded detection, the president fretted. With war imminent, they might seize the moment to renew "their suspended machinations." Madison left the letter unsigned and sent it to Dayton in New Jersey.[54]

Dayton never came forward. In 1808 he probably heard nothing aside from the same vague blusters as Henry but had written his zealous warning to repair his tattered reputation after the Burr debacle. In 1809, he backpedaled, claiming the conspirators no longer posed a threat. Finally, when pressed in 1812, he denied even writing the anonymous letter. Like Henry, he had no names. Madison still owned a stash of almost worthless information. Decades of distrust and uncertainty had conditioned partisans to interpret acrimony as conspiracy, dissent as disloyalty.[55]

Eden

On the morning of April 14, 1812, Henry passed near the head of Paris's Tuileries Gardens toward an opulent chateau situated on the northwest corner of the Place de la Concorde. Henry was probably shown to the drawing room, which boasted an elegant fireplace of white marble topped by a large, framed mirror. Tall windows allowed sunlight to slide past outdoor columns and light the room. He met the real Count de Crillon.[56]

Before Henry left the United States, he had lent Soubiran $6,000, and the con artist repaid him with pay orders on Parisian associates and stock in a French bank. Soubiran provided him with letters of introduction to some of his friends in France. When Henry arrived in Paris, he learned that Soubiran had scammed him. The impostor had given him fake pay orders, bogus stocks, and a deed to an imaginary estate.[57]

Henry showed Soubiran's papers to Crillon, who confirmed what Henry had begun to fear since his final days in the United States. Soubiran

FIGURE 12.1 The Hôtel de Crillon (building on the *left*), 1830, on the northwest corner of the Place de la Concorde. Assuming Henry was shown to the drawing room, he would have entered the left wing, on the corner of the Place and Rue Boissy d'Anglas. Courtesy Bibliothèque Nationale de France.

was a fraud. It was not just a misunderstanding; no other Crillon of nobility lived in France or Spain. The addressees for the pay orders and letters of introduction didn't exist. Soubiran had double-crossed Henry even more than the Irishman realized. Knowing that Henry planned to abscond to France after the deal, Soubiran denounced him to French authorities. Henry would arrive as a British agent, "sent to commit the most frightful crime." He likely wanted more praise from people who could help him obtain a pardon from Napoleon. Just as likely, he wanted Henry arrested before he discovered Soubiran's duplicity.[58]

Irate, Henry left Crillon's chateau and wrote Monroe about Soubiran's subterfuge. An equally irate Crillon visited the US minister Barlow and asked for help to apprehend Soubiran. He wanted Monroe to "undeceive" Sérurier and would pay 100 guineas to catch the man using his name.[59]

Madison and Monroe received the warnings too late to change course even had they been inclined to do it. Soubiran departed the United States on May 28. To punctuate his deviousness, he scammed 70,000 livres off the French consul just before he left. Word soon spread that the Frenchman had been a con artist, confirmed when the real Count de Crillon wrote to contacts in the United States about the impostor. "So much for the associate of Mr. Henry, the acquaintance of Governor Gerry and President Madison," one newspaper sneered. Even had he learned Soubiran's true identity earlier, Madison likely would have released Henry's letters to Congress, knowing as he did that they were authentic.[60]

Soubiran grew bitter as his and Henry's fates diverged. The moment he landed back in France in 1812, French police apprehended him and seized his effects. He somehow fled but shipwrecked in Gibraltar and then sailed to Britain. After swindling some Englishmen, he was arrested and languished in Tothill Fields prison until his extradition to France after Napoleon's downfall. Between 1816 and 1820, he turned useful to France, as officials employed his unique skills at con artistry to sniff out Bonapartist plots against Louis XVIII. Then, as if the universe taunted him with parallels to Henry, his government offered only meager compensation for his service. Meanwhile, Henry retired in France with his daughters, living in wealth and high circles in Paris until his death in 1853, two years before Soubiran's.[61]

Throughout the fiasco, Madison never believed he ceded the moral high ground, for, like many partisans, he thought his opponents monopolized partisanship. Madison agreed with his brother-in-law John Jackson's lament "that nothing can conquer the inveterate hostility of the opposition." Jackson moaned to Madison, "the damning proofs of british perfidy furnished by the documents you communicated to Congress have failed to unite them with the friends of our Country." He mourned that Federalist criticism proved "that Great Britain with much justice counts upon a party amongst us." Jackson implied what Jefferson had articulated a year earlier, when he refused to call Republicans a party: "Republicans are the nation. Their opponents are but a faction." A rich, British-backed faction, to be sure, but a faction, nonetheless. Republicans were Americans; Federalists were partisans.[62]

Madison concurred and could scarcely believe that "the incurable spirit of opposition to the will of the Majority . . . seems to have gained strength" at a time when it should have evaporated. The opposition would "sacrifice every duty of a Citizen, to the fury of the partizan." He viewed the release of the Henry documents as a crusade against irredeemable partisanship rather than a manifestation of his own bias.[63]

Committed to his course, Madison needed to convince the nation that Henry had disclosed information worth having, if not about Federalists then at least about Britain. Republicans rallied to the banner. The British minister Foster grumbled that the Madison administration campaigned for reelection by fomenting "that spirit of hostility to England on which they rose to power." Even he admitted, though, that the documents "made too apparent" that James Craig had employed Henry in "unwarrantable schemes for eventually and in case of war assisting to dismember the Union." He heard rumors about gleeful French officials who supposed "that if this event does not produce a war nothing will."[64]

Republicans condemned Britain even if they couldn't convict Federalists. Ten days after Madison revealed the papers, a congressional committee admitted that they lacked evidence of criminal conduct by any American. Even so, they denounced the British government for "pursuing measures to divide these States, and to involve our citizens in all the guilt of treason, and the horrors of a civil war."[65]

In the following months, Republicans shot resolutions to Madison berating Britain's depravity and cheering for war. As one group of petitioners put it: "We have seen a serpent, in the shape of a spy, stealing to our firesides and altars, and attempting to sting us in the very heart of our Union." Another used the same imagery: "a gloting, civilised British spy is found like the Serpent in Eden, tempting our weakness with untried changes and with all the wileness of his nature beguiling us to our perdition." To bruise the serpent's head, they called for "a prompt vigorous and open war."[66]

The Message

In the afternoon of June 1, 1812, the Senate and House of Representatives cleared their respective galleries of onlookers and closed their doors. They had just received a confidential written message from the president to be read on the floor of each chamber. Madison listed a litany of British iniquities stretching back decades. "We behold, in fine," he concluded, "on the side of Great Britain a state of war against the United States; and on the side of the United States, a state of peace towards Great Britain." The listeners couldn't mistake the president's meaning: He wanted them to declare war. Congress obliged on June 17. Madison declared a state of hostilities two days later.[67]

Had Madison waited until August, he would have learned that the British government had repealed their orders in council six days after Congress authorized war. However tepid the British measure may have been, it might have delayed war while Madison gauged the government's sincerity, maybe even until Napoleon's downfall in 1814. Madison could have boasted that his economic coercion had succeeded and averted hostilities. Once Congress declared war, though, Madison would settle for nothing less than a renunciation of impressment. He prepared to fight.[68]

In his 2,800-word message, Madison spent only about sixty-two on the John Henry episode: "A secret agent . . . was employed in intrigues, having for their object, a subversion of our Government, and a dismemberment of our happy union." Direct but brief, the statement seemed a subtle admission that the controversy had caused outsized ire that spring, a grievance worth mentioning but not belaboring.[69]

Madison relegated the fracas to its proper place as a secondary issue, but it culminated a decades-long cycle that landed Americans on the precipice of war. Foreign meddling bred political distrust, political distrust reinforced partisanship, and partisanship encouraged foreign meddling. On their own, foreign powers or disloyal citizens posed manageable problems, but the fear of each magnified the danger of the other. Blind to their own partisanship, Federalists and Republicans fed the cycle. It spiraled until Madison plunged the nation into war to eradicate what he viewed as a foreign threat emboldened by internal enemies.[70]

EPILOGUE

───◦◦◦───

The Fall of Washington

LATE IN THE EVENING OF August 24, 1814, British Rear-Admiral George Cockburn found and grabbed an account book. The slim volume hardly seemed like a trophy worthy of Britain's war effort against the United States. It bore an unremarkable marble-patterned cover and brown leather spine. A makeshift label of green Morocco leather was pasted on the front, with modest gold lettering that read "PRESIDENT OF THE U. STATES." However prosaic, the book symbolized British triumph.[1]

The commander held the volume in Madison's small chamber in the abandoned US Capitol. Madison had fled the city hours earlier with other residents. Cockburn decided to keep the book, tucking it away as a memento of the time he stood master of the president's office. He would later inscribe a note on the inside cover: "Taken in President's room in the Capitol; at the destruction of that building by the British, on the Capture of Washington 24th: August 1814." He slipped out of the room, and flames soon swallowed the building.[2]

The American war effort had sputtered from the start, not least because the senior commander, Henry Dearborn, wasted time scrutinizing an imagined Federalist rebellion in New England. US forces bungled an invasion of Canada. Impressive naval victories eased some pressure in 1813, and Harrison's troops killed Tecumseh, breaking the Indian–British confederacy in the Ohio Valley. Elsewhere, progress faltered. In 1814, Napoleon's defeat freed up British troops to shift toward offensive warfare.

Cockburn resolved to punish Americans and burn their capital. By the evening of August 24, 1814, his soldiers had routed everyone on the path to Washington and entered the capital almost without resistance. British troops burned public buildings, including the executive mansion, where commanders toasted the Prince Regent with Madison's wine and ate the president's dinner before they torched the place.[3]

British propagandists celebrated the burning with some of their favorite barbs about Madison as Napoleon's junior partner. Illustrator Charles Williams caricatured Madison and a cabinet member deserting the burning city, toting "Correspondence with Boney" and "Boney's Instructions." One American bystander supposes Madison will hightail it "to Elba to his bosom friend," Napoleon. George Cruikshank illustrated "John Bull making a *Capital* bonfire & Mr. Madison running away by the light of it," making a pun out of the eighteenth-century slang word "capital," meaning excellent. Madison flees Washington's flames while Napoleon invites his "Friend Madass . . . to come & live quietly with" him in exile on Elba.

FIGURE E.1 The Fall of Washington—or Maddy in full flight, 1814, by Charles Williams. Madison and perhaps Secretary of War John Armstrong escape Washington carrying plans to conquer Canada and subdue England, along with "Correspondence with Boney" and "Instructions from Boney." Madison complains that he must flee his celebratory dinner he had planned for the stand of Washington. One American suspects that Madison will join "his bosom friend" Napoleon on Elba. Other Americans look on while British sailors ridicule Madison's flight. Courtesy Library of Congress.

FIGURE E.2 John Bull making a Capital bonfire & Mr. Madison running away by the light of it!! 1814, by George Cruikshank. Cruikshank depicts Madison fleeing Washington with other Americans while British troops burn the city. The image portrays Napoleon inviting Madison into exile on Elba. In the background, soldiers eat the dinner Madison had ordered to celebrate the expected defense of the city. Courtesy Bodleian Library.

Cruikshank evoked imagery and epithets he and others had used throughout the war. After Canada repelled a US invasion in 1812, he had illustrated an apoplectic Madison flanked by the devil and Napoleon, pleading for their help while Americans beg Britain for reconciliation. He titled it, "A sketch for the REGENTS speech on MAD-ASS-SON'S insanity." Another British satirist wrote a fictional letter from Madison to Napoleon:

> Every thing's in confusion and going to waste,
> In short to the devil we're all off post haste.
> This in anguish of heart I am now forc'd to say,
> Can you not give me some little help on my way;
> O say, ere despair bears him off from the earth,
> Can you not give your Maddy in Elba some birth?[4]

Madison had in fact pledged to avoid a French alliance, but he failed to reassure Federalists. They agreed with British critics that Napoleon clutched the president, as one Federalist newspaper put it, in "the fangs of his influence." They cheered Napoleon's downfall, convinced it meant peace

A sketch for the REGENTS speech on MAD-ASS-SON'S insanity.

FIGURE E.3 A sketch for the Regents speech on Mad-ass-son's insanity, 1812, by George Cruikshank. Cruikshank drew this image in December 1812, depicting an angel announcing critical British-Canadian victories. Madison complains to the devil and Napoleon and pleads for their help. Napoleon complains of his own hardships and promises that the devil will help them, while the devil plans to "carry them to Hell to Cure their Chilblains." Americans beg for reconciliation with Britain, who carries a banner in Latin that translates as "No one attacks me with impunity." Courtesy Library of Congress.

with Great Britain. Napoleon's exile "will make Mr. Madison as pacific as his master was humble," one reveled. "He will not abdicate his throne, but he will abandon his war." A more acerbic group of Federalists toasted with a smirk, "May James Madison and Thomas Jefferson be permitted to visit the island of Elba and never return."[5]

At their most vitriolic, Federalists exposed themselves to accusations of treasonous opposition to the war, calling to withhold militia and other resources. "The Union has long since virtually dissolved," one New Englander insisted, "and it is full time that this part of the Disunited States should take care of themselves." One attributed America's failed Canadian invasion to "the Almighty Will." British commanders compelled some parts of New England to declare neutrality in the conflict. Federalist Massachusetts governor Caleb Strong tried to negotiate a secret peace with Canada. Leading Federalists met at the Hartford Convention to coordinate resistance to the administration. They flirted with secession, stopping just shy of it. Madison sent an agent to Hartford to reconnoiter the secret proceedings—an unwelcome distraction from prosecuting a war.[6]

Some Republicans interpreted any opposition to the war as treason to the nation. They condemned detractors, in the words of one Republican group in Massachusetts, as "the Hydra of opposition" that reared "its envenomed heads in every direction." Such were "fit only to be *Slaves*." Baltimore Republicans demolished a Federalist press during a party-line riot that involved muskets and a cannon, leaving one Republican and one Federalist dead. The war with Britain threatened to plunge the nation into civil war.[7]

Still unable to distinguish political opponents from foreign foes, Americans perpetuated their distrust until Cockburn's fires devoured their capital. They all shared the same fear as a writer in the *American Mercury*: "The moment the enemy finds he can neutralize one political party, or one section of the country, he has obtained the secret that will prove the ruin of the whole." Unable to agree on a common enemy, however, they branded each other apostates and possible traitors.[8]

During the war, a pseudonymous Federalist called "Refederator"—possibly John Lowell Jr.—highlighted Madison's part in fomenting the political turmoil of the day in an open letter to the president. History furnished no stronger examples of partisan hostility than Madison and Jefferson, he claimed, not even the "feuds and divisions" of ancient Greece or "*party dominion*" of ancient Rome. An early American would have struggled to find anyone more conversant than Madison with feuds and divisions from the Classical world. He had once studied them to devise a constitution that could withstand the lethal combination of party malice and foreign intrusion. Almost three decades later, his enemies accused him of driving those divisions and waved the Henry documents as key evidence of his corruption. Refederator savored the irony that Madison had paid $50,000 to prove nothing more than his own factionalism and New England fidelity.[9]

Despite the seeming disparity between the Madison of the Constitutional Convention and the Madison of the Henry-Soubiran scandal, his core values had changed little over the decades. He labored throughout his career to maintain the integrity of a republican union against foreign meddling, but he also struggled to discern his own role in sustaining such meddling. At each stage of his career, from the American Revolution, through the Mississippi River debates, into the 1790s, and to his executive leadership, he dreaded that a dangerous contingent of Americans threatened his vision for the nation. He believed that that vision stemmed from dispassionate study rather than self-interested partisanship. To combat his opponents, he embraced the conduct he despised in them, morphing his ideological values into partisan loyalty in a way that invited foreign manipulation. Madison hadn't transformed from a philosopher-statesman into a partisan politician after the 1780s. The identities had been in tension since his earliest political involvement—tension perpetuated by the hazy line between principles and partisanship.

Most Americans joined Madison in believing that they acted with lofty purpose and their opponents with base prejudice. Advocating the Hartford Convention, Refederator propounded a theory of state sovereignty that made Madison and Jefferson's Virginia and Kentucky Resolutions seem tame by comparison. The Constitution was nothing more than a treaty between sovereign states, he declared. He even hinted that Massachusetts retained the right to war against the United States. He thanked Madison for authoring the Virginia Resolution, thereby prescribing the remedy to New England's suffering. He admitted that New England might consider disunion at the approaching convention. "The States are already separated—the bond of Union is already broken—broken by you."[10]

Madison rejoined that individuals like Refederator might seduce "deluded partizans" and other New Englanders to cooperate with Britain to win power and revolt. In the Hartford Convention and New England resistance, Madison thought he saw the fruition of his decades-long fears for the union. Fractious New Englanders gave Britain the "sole inducement" to continue the war. Party plagues might surrender the sovereignty of the entire nation.[11]

In the 1780s, Madison had wondered if the republic could overcome the calamitous cycle of domestic strife and foreign encroachment; in 1812, he waged a war that almost proved that it could not. As Refederator lamented in a rare moment of introspection, "We are wrangling on the edge of a precipice—and so firmly grasped, that both parties may go over together."[12]

At critical moments, Republicans and Federalists withdrew from the cliffside. Madison moved with "delicacy," collecting intelligence on the Hartford Convention without suppressing First Amendment rights, still a civil libertarian at heart. His caution annoyed such Republicans as Mathew Carey, who saw "a conspiracy of the most treasonable kind" and wanted a stronger response. Federalists at the Hartford Convention retreated from Refederator's most militant proposals.[13]

In early 1815, Americans eked out a draw in the war against Britain, but the burning of Washington warned them how close they had stood to defeat. Days before flames scorched the city, State Department clerk Stephen Pleasonton removed the Declaration of Independence, the Constitution, state papers of the revolutionary era, and correspondence of George Washington (including his letter resigning his commission) from the capital. In a fitting metaphor, partisan rancor and foreign meddling started a war that nearly left the founding charters in ashes. Americans arrived at the crisis not because of their political differences, but because they confused opposition with corruption, dissent with disloyalty.[14]

Americans celebrated the peace as a victory, and a surge of national pride gripped the country. During the war, "Uncle Sam" emerged as a symbol of the US government, most often depicted by Federalists as a bumbling incompetent unable to prosecute the conflict. After the war, though, some corners adopted the icon to represent the proud conqueror of the British John Bull. Alongside now-forgotten "Brother Jonathan," Uncle Sam gradually replaced the delicate Columbia as the most prominent caricature of the United States. One cartoon depicted Madison as Brother Jonathan giving John Bull a bloody nose and black eyes. In 1823, President James Monroe declared the Americas off-limits to European recolonization. Americans began to discard their perception of the nation as a tender maiden and replace it with an image of virile vigor. The process culminated by the end of the nineteenth century with now-familiar depictions of a steel-willed Uncle Sam. The newfound confidence belied the icon's precarious origins and the way foreign meddling combined with partisan conflict to almost shatter the vulnerable republic.[15]

The War of 1812 revealed the fortitude and the fragility of US institutions, a precarious balance that lingers to this day. Convinced of their nation's frailty, early Americans saw subversives everywhere, especially among those with differing political views. A healthy awareness of the nation's weaknesses eroded into a dread of its imminent collapse that facilitated rather than prevented foreign meddling. As Americans grapple with that history, they may take heart from the nation's early resilience and caution from its near catastrophe, confident in its durability but mindful of its delicacy.

Madison left a complicated legacy as a fierce adversary of foreign meddling and determined champion of political debate—but also as a partisan operative who facilitated the first by inflaming the second. Americans of Madison's day realized that because elections effectively allowed the legal overthrow of their leaders, republics make fertile ground for foreign tampering. By positing sovereignty in the people, with free presses and

UNCLE SAM, TO THE PATRONIZERS OF THE
IDIOT.

FIGURE E.4 An Early Image of Uncle Sam. *Idiot, or Invisible Rambler* (Boston, MA), March 28, 1818. The publishers used the same cartoon to caricature several objects of jest. The earliest imagery of Uncle Sam came from Federalists, who derided him as incompetent to prosecute the misguided war against Britain. By the end of the nineteenth century, however, bolder images of Uncle Sam replaced the more common representation of the United States as a delicate woman.

free elections, they blurred traditional lines between dissidence and subversion. Foreign powers leveraged that ambiguity to manipulate US domestic politics, exploiting freedom of debate and dissent to sow distrust and reap chaos.

The dilemma has outlasted the decades of the early republic, emerging at periods when suspicion runs high and fear deep. Between 1915 and 1917, British agents tried to urge Americans into World War I while German operatives tried to strengthen the anti-war contingent. The Germans organized propaganda campaigns and sabotage missions to hamper US support for Britain. They paid lobbyists to disrupt the munitions trade, spread pro-German messages through German-American media, and escalated

FIGURE E.5 Detail of America Guided by Wisdom, 1815, by Benjamin Tanner. This image shows the United States symbolized by a woman who sits next to the Roman goddess Minerva, with Ceres and Mercury in the background. The United States is depicted as confident but delicate and succored by deities and the reassuring presence of George Washington. Over the next century, such depictions of the United States as demure and vulnerable would be replaced by Uncle Sam as strong and assertive. Courtesy Library of Congress.

to planting bombs on bridges and US ships carrying munitions. Less flagrant and more effective, the British used sophisticated covert or circuitous networks to publicize anti-German content. When those networks produced evidence that Germany had offered to help Mexico reconquer part of the United States, some anti-war Americans dismissed the evidence as a British lie. In 1917 and 1918, British agents prodded Congress and President Woodrow Wilson to enact laws that curbed free speech and dissent, fearful that some Americans might aid or embolden Germany. One British agent essentially took credit for the imperious 1917 Espionage Act.[16]

In 1968, accusations circulated that Republican presidential candidate Richard Nixon and South Vietnamese officials colluded to scuttle peace talks with North Vietnam and get Nixon elected. Nixon believed successful diplomacy would hurt his election chances in a close race with Democratic vice president Hubert Humphrey. Nixon sent to South Vietnam a secret

FIGURE E.6 A Boxing Match, Or Another Bloody Nose for John Bull, 1813, by William Charles. A bloodied King George III pleads for mercy from "Brother Jonathan," depicted as Madison. During the War of 1812, Americans began to adopt virile images such as Brother Jonathan and then more commonly Uncle Sam as caricatures of the United States. Courtesy Library of Congress.

envoy, who convinced its diplomats to ditch the negotiations. Democratic president Lyndon Johnson decried the alleged interference as "treason."[17]

Until 2016, though, no moments really matched the toxic mix of partisanship and foreign meddling that the early republic produced. The Civil War tore at the seams of American democracy, but, aside from some concerns about British diplomacy with the South, the divisions had little to do with foreign relations. During World War I, pro- and anti-war factions never split along Democrat/Republican lines. Wilson confused dissent with disloyalty, but the war was not the product of decades-long fears of subversion by foreign powers and their domestic partners. In 1968, Americans lived in the last gasp of what historians call the "liberal consensus"—a two-decade period after World War II marked by moderate partisanship and broadly shared values. Despite salivating that "it would rock the world if it were said he [South Vietnamese President Nguyen Van Thieu] were conniving with the Republicans," Johnson never outed Nixon in public. In fact, Johnson preferred a Nixon victory. He left the decision to Humphrey whether to expose Nixon, and Humphrey refused. He worried that without smoking-gun evidence the allegations would destabilize the nation—a quibble that would have hardly stopped more virulent partisans of Madison's era.[18]

It would take a stronger strain of partisan hostility to reintroduce the pernicious cycle that existed in James Madison's America—the sort of hostility that began to emerge in the decades before the 2016 presidential election. In 1980, Republican Ronald Reagan defeated incumbent Democratic president Jimmy Carter, inaugurating a new chapter of partisan politics with a campaign that provoked cries of foreign collusion. During the campaign, the nation learned that Iranian revolutionaries held Americans hostage. In 1991, a former member of the Carter administration alleged that Reagan's campaign team had promised the Iranians an arms deal if they held the hostages until the election concluded, weakening Carter's reelection chances. Reagan's critics dusted off the Logan Act to assess possible violations. In 1992, House and Senate panels convened to investigate.[19]

Enough goodwill remained for the Democrat-controlled panels to conclude that no credible evidence implicated Reagan, but the accusations boded ill for the coming era of party alignment. The period produced the 1998 impeachment of President Bill Clinton and a fraught 2000 presidential campaign, decided by a handful of votes in Florida and a controversial Supreme Court decision. During Democrat Barack Obama's presidency, a small but vocal group, including future Republican President Donald Trump, claimed that Obama was foreign-born. Elections made wild swings from Obama and Democrats' explosive victories in 2008 to the "shellacking" (to use Obama's phrase) that Democrats received in the 2010 midterms.[20]

Polarization and distrust increased until the 2016 campaign witnessed foreign meddling on a scale not seen since Madison's time. That year, Russia worked to "sow discord in the U.S. political system," according to Special Council Robert Mueller, who investigated President Donald Trump for possible collusion with the Kremlin during the campaign. Mueller found insufficient evidence to charge Trump or his campaign officials with any crimes of conspiracy, but partisan rancor steamed ahead. Trump and his allies demanded that the Justice Department "investigate the investigators," casting him as the victim of a political prosecution. In 2019, shadow diplomats assured Trump, on the avowal of foreign agents, that Ukrainian officials held incriminating information on Hunter Biden, the son of Trump's leading Democratic opponent in the 2020 presidential campaign. Trump withheld military aid to Ukraine, allegedly to pressure officials there to investigate the Bidens, or at least to announce an investigation to embarrass his rival. Trump's opponents accused him of misusing public funds for his own political benefit, and the House of Representatives impeached him.[21]

Announcing the articles of impeachment, Democratic House Speaker Nancy Pelosi invoked Madison to denounce Trump. She declared, "James Madison, the architect of the Constitution, warned that a president might betray his trust to foreign powers which might prove fatal to the republic." She spoke apparently unaware of the irony that Madison's own opponents had once accused him of misusing public funds to acquire dirt on his rivals from foreign nationals to aid his election.[22]

Forged in partisan conflict, the United States remains vulnerable to foreign powers that aggravate political discord. Foreign meddling—perceived and actual—continues to stem from and increase party hostility and polarization. Madison didn't intend to resolve those problems with less partisanship. "An extinction of parties," he warned in *Federalist* no. 50, "implies . . . an absolute extinction of liberty." Instead, he had hoped to erect a constitutional structure that could embrace political acrimony without surrendering American democracy to foreign intrigues.[23]

That structure never worked as he intended. He envisioned a multitude of smaller factions—none of which could win a majority—rather than two major, organized parties. That system would not have eradicated foreign meddling, but it might have deterred political polarization when foreign meddling occurred, debilitating a key part of the cycle. Instead, Madison helped design a system that unintentionally incentivized two major parties vying for the majority then became a critical player in perpetuating it.

His early theories may show a path out of the cycle. Amid their distress for their fragile republic, early Americans rarely acknowledged that democracies can be uniquely resistant to foreign manipulation. In monarchies of the *ancien régime*, an agent might bribe, flatter, or win the ear of the right minister and shift the international policies of the court. It was easier to coax a few officials than half a nation. Democracy can prove unwieldy for foreign agents, but a polarized two-party system divides the electorate, making it easier for foreign powers to pit one side against another. A multi-party system could help restore democracy's inherent advantages against foreign meddling.

Madison believed that a republic couldn't depend on the better angels of the people's nature to protect it. It needed to neutralize the worst impulses of the leaders and the people. Madison viewed a multiplicity of factions as vital to that end. When people lacked "better motives," their "rival interests" could counter each other; the more rival interests the better. Rather than count on Americans to jettison factionalism, Madison believed that the governing structure needed to make factions an asset instead of a liability. In recent decades, political researchers have recommended voting reforms, such as ranked-choice voting, that could weaken the two-party "duopoly," encourage the rise of other parties, and result in something closer to what Madison imagined.[24]

In his final years, Madison penned a memorandum entitled "Advice to My Country," which remained unread until after his death in 1836. "The advice nearest to my heart and deepest in my convictions is that the Union of the States be cherished and perpetuated. Let the open enemy to it be regarded as a Pandora with her box opened; and the disguised one, as the Serpent creeping with his deadly wiles into Paradise." Madison died unsure but hopeful about the fate of his country. Unable to escape the vices of a partisan-riven age, he summoned the very specters he feared, feeding the division that encouraged foreign meddling. Through the decades, though, he aspired to protect a vulnerable democracy and sustain a strong nation. Madison's fears and vices persist, but so does his hope.[25]

NOTES

Abbreviations

AAE	Archives du Ministère des Affaires Étrangères, Paris
AHN	Archivo Historico Nacional (Madrid, Spain)
AP	*The Adams Papers Digital Edition*, ed. Sara Martin. Charlottesville: University of Virginia Press, Rotunda.
ASP-FR	*American State Papers: Foreign Relations* from *American State Papers: Documents, Legislative and Executive, of the Congress of the United States.* 38 vols.; Washington, D.C., 1832-61.
ASP-IA	*American State Papers: Indian Affairs* from *American State Papers: Documents, Legislative and Executive, of the Congress of the United States.* 38 vols.; Washington, D.C., 1832-61.
CFM	Frederick J. Turner, ed., "Correspondence of French Ministers to the United States, 1791–1797," in *Annual Report of the American Historical Association for the Year 1903.* Vol. 2 (Washington, 1904).
DGM	*The Diaries of Gouverneur Morris Digital Edition*, ed. Melanie Randolph Miller. Charlottesville: University of Virginia Press, Rotunda.
DHFFC	*The Documentary History of the First Federal Congress of the United States, March 4, 1789–March 3, 1791: Digital Edition*, ed. Charlene Bangs Bickford, Kenneth R. Bowling, William C. diGiacomantonio, and Helen E. Veit. Charlottesville: University of Virginia Press, Rotunda.
DHRC	*The Documentary History of the Ratification of the Constitution Digital Edition*, ed. John P. Kaminski, Gaspare J. Saladino, Richard Leffler, Charles H. Schoenleber and Margaret A. Hogan. Charlottesville: University of Virginia Press, Rotunda.

DLC   Library of Congress
  JMP   James Madison Papers
  TJP   Thomas Jefferson Papers
DNA   National Archives and Records Administration
  IM   Instructions to Ministers, RG 59
  DL   Domestic Letters, RG 59
  ML   Miscellaneous Letters, RG 59
  DD   Diplomatic Dispatches, RG 59
MNE   Ministério dos Negócios Estrangeiros, Arquivo Nacional da Torre do
            Tombo.
NA-UK   National Archives, (Surrey, United Kingdom).
  FO   Foreign Office
PAH   *The Papers of Alexander Hamilton Digital Edition*, ed. Harold C. Syrett.
            Charlottesville: University of Virginia Press, Rotunda.
PCPPAB   Mary Jo Kline and Joanne Wood Ryan, eds., *Political Correspondence
            and Public Papers of Aaron Burr* 2 vols. Princeton: Princeton University
            Press, 1983.
PDM   *The Papers of Dolley Madison Digital Edition*, ed. Holly C. Shulman.
            Charlottesville: University of Virginia Press, Rotunda.
PGW-D   *Papers of George Washington: Diaries of George Washington* from *The
            Papers of George Washington Digital Edition*. Charlottesville: University
            of Virginia Press, Rotunda.
PGW-PS   *Papers of George Washington: Presidential Series* from *The Papers of
            George Washington Digital Edition*. Charlottesville: University of
            Virginia Press, Rotunda.
PGW-RW   *Papers of George Washington: Revolutionary War Series* from *The Papers
            of George Washington Digital Edition*. Charlottesville: University of
            Virginia Press, Rotunda.
PJJ   *The Selected Papers of John Jay Digital Edition*, Elizabeth M. Nuxoll, ed-
            itor. Charlottesville: University of Virginia Press, Rotunda.
PJM   *The Papers of John Marshall Digital Edition*, Charles Hobson, editor.
            Charlottesville: University of Virginia Press, Rotunda.
PJM-CS   *Papers of James Madison: Congressional Series* from *The Papers of
            James Madison Digital Edition*, J. C. A. Stagg, editor. Charlottesville:
            University of Virginia Press, Rotunda.
PJM-PS   *Papers of James Madison: Presidential Series* from *The Papers of James
            Madison Digital Edition*, J. C. A. Stagg, editor. Charlottesville:
            University of Virginia Press, Rotunda.
PJM-SS   *Papers of James Madison: Secretary of State Series* from *The Papers of
            James Madison Digital Edition*, J. C. A. Stagg, editor. Charlottesville:
            University of Virginia Press, Rotunda.
PJMon   *The Papers of James Monroe Digital Edition*, Daniel Preston and Robert
            Karachuk, eds. Charlottesville: University of Virginia Press, Rotunda.
PREPS   *The Papers of the Revolutionary Era Pinckney Statesmen Digital Edition*,
            ed. Constance B. Schulz. Charlottesville: University of Virginia Press,
            Rotunda.

PTJ-MS   *The Papers of Thomas Jefferson: Main Series* from *The Papers of Thomas Jefferson Digital Edition*, ed. James P. McClure and J. Jefferson Looney. Charlottesville: University of Virginia Press, Rotunda.

PTJ-RS   *The Papers of Thomas Jefferson: Retirement Series* from *The Papers of Thomas Jefferson Digital Edition*, ed. James P. McClure and J. Jefferson Looney. Charlottesville: University of Virginia Press, Rotunda.

Introduction

1. *Annals of Congress*, House of Representatives, 12th Cong., 1st Sess., 1220–24; Adams, "Count Edward de Crillon," 51–69; Morison, "Henry-Crillon Affair," 208–209; Cruikshank, *Political Adventures*, 145; James Craig to John Henry, February 6, 1809, ASP-FR, 3:546–547.
2. *Annals of Congress*, House of Representatives, 12th Cong., 1st Sess., 1220–24; Adams, "Count Edward de Crillon," 58–59, 67–69.
3. Taylor, *Civil War*, 22–24; Perkins, *Prologue to War*, 369; Morison, "Henry-Crillon Affair," 208–209; Cruikshank, *Political Adventures*.
4. Adams, "Count Edward de Crillon," 60–64.
5. Adams, "Count Edward de Crillon," 60–64.
6. Morison, "Henry-Crillon Affair," 213–15; Adams, "Count Edward de Crillon," 58–59.
7. Morison, "Henry-Crillon Affair," 213–15; Madison, "To Congress," June 1, 1812, PJM-PS, 4:436
8. *Poulson's American Daily Advertiser*, June 30, 1813; Inhabitants of Richmond, Manchester, and Vicinity to Madison, May 30, 1812, in PJM-PS, 4:429–30; Citizens of the First Congressional District of Pennsylvania to the People of the United States," enclosed in William Jones to Madison, May 22, 1812, in PJM-PS, 4:410.
9. Benjamin Rush to John Adams, June 13, 1808, in Butterfield, *Letters of Benjamin Rush*, 2:967 ("trunk," "muscles"); Kerber, *Women of the Republic*, xii, 40, 223, 234, 266–267.
10. Calloway, *Scratch of a Pen*, 3–18; Silver, *Our Savage Neighbors*, xvii–xxvi; Mortimer, "Before Domestic Dependent Nationhood," 185–195.
11. Paine, *Common Sense*, 24 ("it").
12. *Federalist* no. 2, Rossiter, *Federalist Papers*, 32 ("people").
13. Madison, "Popular Election of the First Branch of the Legislature," June 6, 1787 in PJM-CS, 10:33 ("divided"); Freeman, *Affairs of Honor*; 1–10; Wood, *Radicalism*, 95–109, esp. 95 ("any thing"); Taylor, *American Revolutions*, 353–393.
14. DuVal, *Independence Lost*, 223–269, 339; PJM-CS, 11:240n1; PTJ-MS, 19:469–470.
15. *Federalist* no. 10, Rossiter, *Federalist Papers*, 71–79, esp. 73 ("liberty").
16. Freeman, *Affairs of Honor*, 9–10.
17. For party development and political culture in early America, see Hofstadter, *Idea of a Party System*, 1–39; Freeman, *Affairs of Honor*, 1–10; Sharp, *American Politics*, 1–14.

18. Feldman, *Three Lives*, 395–405; Cheney, *James Madison*, 257–261; Sharp, *American Politics*, 121.

19. Sharp, *American Politics*, 151; Berkin, *Sovereign People*, 151–200; "An Act in addition to the act, entitled 'An act for the punishment of certain crimes against the United States,'" July 14, 1798, *Statutes at Large*: 1:596–597.

20. James Madison, *Report of 1800*, in PJM-CS, 17:336–337 ("people").

21. Thomas McKean, speech before the Pennsylvania Ratifying Convention, November 28, 1787, in DHRC ("supreme"); Morgan, *Inventing the People*; Bailyn, *Ideological Origins*, 227–228; Wood, *Radicalism*, 169; José Corrêa da Serra to Tomás Antônio Vilanova Portugal, January 2, 1819, MNE ("dependent administrators").

22. Carlos Martínez de Yrujo to Madison, October 3, 1804 in PJM-SS, 8:118; Yrujo to Turreau, February 11, 1806, legajo 5541, AHN ("true"); Madison, "Case of the Marquis de Casa Yrujo, Envoy Extraordinary and Minister Plenipotentiary of His Catholic Majesty to the United States" enclosed in Madison to James Monroe, January 30, 1807, IM, vol. 5, DNA.

23. Taylor, *American Revolutions*, 367 ("when").

24. "Report of Erick Bollmann's Communication," January 24, 1807, in PJM-SS, 13:310–317; Stewart, *American Emperor*, 117–120, 139; Lewis, *Burr Conspiracy*, 201–203; Coxe to Madison, ca. January 26 and November 4, 1807, both in JMP, DLC.

25. Nichols, *Red Gentlemen*, 10–11; Taylor, *Civil War*, 125–127.

26. Taylor, *Civil War*, 125–127.

27. Wheelan, *Mr. Adams's Last Crusade*, 23; Berkin, *Sovereign People*, 81–150; Sharp, *American Politics*, 121–122, 151–152; Narrett, *Adventurism and Empire*, 237–241.

Chapter 1

1. Burton, "Haldimand Papers," 174–183; Rau, "Chêne Family in Detroit," 9–13; Butts, *Simon Girty*, 11–34; Kelsay, *Joseph Brant*, 311; Keeler, *Old Fort Sandoski*, 401–402.

2. Burton, "Haldimand Papers," 174–183; Taylor, *Divided Ground*, 22–28.

3. Burton, "Haldimand Papers," 177.

4. Kelsay, *Joseph Brant*, 484.

5. Calloway, *Scratch of a Pen*, 92–100.

6. Jasanoff, *Liberty's Exiles*, 38; MacDonald, "Caught between Two Fires," 67–87; DuVal, *Independence Lost*, 90–100, 185, 238–240; Calloway, *Indian World*, 215–234; Ephraim Douglass to Benjamin Lincoln, August 18, 1783, Letters and Reports from Maj. Gen. Benjamin Lincoln, vol. 3, Papers of the Continental Congress, DNA; Kelsay, *Joseph Brant*, 345; Nichols, *Red Gentlemen*, 1.

7. Burton, "Haldimand Papers," 176–177 ("manly"); Jasanoff, *Liberty's Exiles*, 189–191; Thomas Brown to Guy Carleton, April 26, 1783, Headquarters Papers of the British Army in America, NA-UK ("Englishman," "our").

8. Taylor, *Divided Ground*, 46–49; Jasanoff, *Liberty's Exiles*, 189–194.

9. Burton, "Haldimand Papers," 179 ("we"); Jasanoff, *Liberty's Exiles*, 194.

10. Taylor, *American Revolutions*, 338 ("diplomatic").

11. Feldman, *Three Lives*, 50; McCoy, *Last of the Fathers*, 26; Louis-Guillaume Otto, "Liste des Membres et Officiers du Congrés," 1788, in Farrand, *Records of the Federal Convention*, 3:237 ("this").

12. Adair, "James Madison's Autobiography," 197; Ketcham, *James Madison*, 20.

13. Reeder, "Lines of Separation," 267–272 ("squabbled," "diabolical").

14. Madison to Bradford, July 1, 1774, PJM-CS, 1:114–116, esp. 114 ("war blood"); Holton, *Forced Founders*, 3–38.

15. Madison to Bradford, July 1, 1774, PJM-CS, 1:114–116; Holton, *Forced Founders*, 41–45; Walsh, "Black Cotted Raskolls," 32; O'Neil, "Notes on Sister Mary Theonella Hite and Her Family," 97–98.

16. Cheney, *James Madison*, 55; *Virginia Gazette*, January 28, 1775; Madison to William Bradford, July 28, 1775, in PJM-CS, 1:161, 162n10; Otto Lohrenz, "Reverend John Wingate," 43–47.

17. Madison to William Bradford, August 23, 1774, November 26, 1774, and January 20, 1775 ("sinister," "honest"), Bradford to Madison, January 4, 1775, PJM-CS, 1:121, 130, 132, 135; Mekeel, "Relation of the Quakers to the American Revolution," 3–12.

18. Taylor, *Internal Enemy*, 22–24; Madison to William Bradford, June 19, 1775, in PJM-CS, 1:153 ("if"); also see Madison to William Bradford, November 26, 1774, in PJM-CS, 1:129–130.

19. "Certificate of Election of James Madison Jr., and William Moore, April 25, 1776, in PJM-CS, 1:165n2; Adair, "James Madison's Autobiography," 199; Cheney, *James Madison*, 55–58.

20. *Proceedings of the convention*, 7 ("inimical), 12 ("unfriendly and dangerous"), 15.

21. Broadwater, *George Mason*, 81–87; "Declaration of Rights and Form of Government of Virginia," May 16–June 29, 1776, in PJM-CS1:170–175, 179nn5–10; Adair, "James Madison's Autobiography," 199; Cheney, *James Madison*, 64; Muñoz, *God and the Founders*, 32–34; Muñoz, *Religious Liberty*, 455–456.

22. "Declaration of Rights and Form of Government of Virginia," May 16–June 29, 1776, in PJM-CS, 1:170–175, 179nn5–10.

23. Broadwater, *George Mason*, 80, 84; Cheney, *James Madison*, 58–59. The final version of the Declaration of Rights did not contain any exceptions to religious freedom. The convention likely scrapped any exceptions as a compromise between those who wanted broader authority to regulate religion and those who wanted the exception narrower, as Madison wrote it. By not enumerating exceptions, the body purposely left the question unanswered (*Proceedings of the convention*, 43).

24. Feldman, *Three Lives*, 28–30; Adair, "James Madison's Autobiography," 199–200.

25. "Session of Virginia Council of State," January 14, 1778, in PJM-CS, 1:214–215.

26. Ferreiro, *Brothers at Arms*, 146–150; "Session of Virginia Council of State," January 14, 1778, in PJM-CS, 1:216 ("alarming Accounts").

27. "Session of Virginia Council of State," February 27, 1778, in PJM-CS, 1:230–231; Patrick Henry in Council to Henry Laurens, June 18, 1778, in PJM-CS, 1:245; "Session of Virginia Council of State, December 23, 1778," in PJM-CS, 1:278 ("ill-armed"); Patrick Henry in Council to Virginia Delegates in Congress, January 20, 1778, in PJM-CS, 1:219–221, esp. 221.

28. Burstein and Isenberg, *Madison and Jefferson*, 29; Madison to William Bradford, August 23, 1774, in PJM-CS, 1:120 ("perfidious").

29. Mildred Edwards Whitmire, "A Man and His Land: The Story of Jacob and Frances Madison Hite and the Cherokees," *Magazine of the Jefferson County Historical Society* 44 (1978), 42–45.

30. George Rogers Clark to Patrick Henry, April 29, 1779, in James, *George Rogers Clark Papers*, 172–173 ("there"); Calloway, *Indian World*, 244; Silver, *Our Savage Neighbors*, 227–260.

31. Taylor, *American Revolutions*, 257–258; Nash, *Unknown American Revolution*, 350–351.

32. Taylor, *American Revolutions*, 257–258; Nash, *Unknown American Revolution*, 350–351; Burstein and Isenberg, *Madison and Jefferson*, 64–65, 68–71, esp. 70 ("scalp-buyer"); Wallace, *Jefferson and the Indians*, 29 ("wretches"), 66–67.

33. "Order of Virginia Council of State Placing Henry Hamilton and Others in Irons," June 16, 1779, in PJM-CS, 1:288–291, esp. 289 ("standing"); Burstein and Isenberg, *Madison and Jefferson*, 70–71.

34. "From the Journal of the Council," January 12, 1778, Patrick Henry to Bernardo de Gálvez, January 14, 1778, Patrick Henry to Edward Hand, January 15, 1778, and Patrick Henry to George Rogers Clark, January 15, 1778, all in McIlwaine, *Official Letters*, 1:227–230; Conde de Aranda to Marques de Grimaldi, January 13, 1777, Legajo 3884, AHN; Diego Navarro to José de Gálvez, June 13, 1778, Legajo 3884, AHN.

35. Kellogg, *Frontier Retreat*, 82–94.

36. Butler, *History of the Commonwealth of Kentucky*, 102–104; Kellogg, *Frontier Retreat*, 82–94.

37. "Extract of a Letter from Col. Clarke, dated Falls of Ohio, Oct. 9, 1779," *New-York Gazette, and Weekly Mercury*, December 20, 1779; Thomas Jefferson to Bernardo Gálvez, January 29, 1780, in PTJ-MS, 27:688; Patrick Henry to George Rogers Clark, January 15, 1778, in McIlwaine, *Official Letters*, 1:230 ("greatest").

38. Kellogg, *Frontier Retreat*, 93–94; Nash, *Unknown American Revolution*, 351–353, esp. 353; George Rogers Clark to Jonathan Clark, January 16, 1780, in James, *George Rogers Clark Papers*, 382–383 ("depredations," "four").

39. Inman, "A Dark and Bloody Ground," 267–268; Andrew Rainsford and others to George Germain, July 12, 1779, CO 5/81, NA-UK; Herbert, "To Treat with All Nations," 28–29.

40. Andrew Rainsford and others to George Germain, July 12, 1779, CO 5/81, NA-UK; George Rogers Clark to John Todd Jr., March 1780, in James, *George Rogers Clark Papers*, 404 ("English," "prove").

41. Pittman, *Present State of the European Settlements*, 10–12; DuVal, *Independence Lost*, 13–14, 96; Narrett, *Adventurism and Empire*, 16.

42. Pittman, *Present State of the European Settlements*, 10–12; *Plan of the city and suburbs of New Orleans*, 1815, DLC; Huber, *New Orleans*, 30–31; Saravia, *Bernardo de Gálvez*, 9.

43. DuVal, *Independence Lost*, 15–16 ("artful," forked," "we").

44. Ferreiro, *Brothers at Arms*, 50–53; DuVal, *Independence Lost*, 239–240.

45. DuVal, *Independence Lost*, 161; Bernardo de Gálvez to José de Gálvez, May 12, 1777, and September 2, 1778, Legajo 3884bis., AHN; Saravia, *Bernardo de Gálvez*, 57–61; George Germain to John Stuart, December 2, 1778, CO 5/79, NA-UK; White, *Middle Ground*, 100–101.

46. DuVal, *Independence Lost*, 161.

47. John Campbell to George Germain, February 12, 1780, CO 5/597, NA-UK ("extraordinary," "present"); Alexander Cameron to George Germain, July 18, 1780, CO 5/81, NA-UK.

48. Patrick Henry to Bernardo de Gálvez, January 14, 1778, in McIlwaine, *Official Letters*, 1:227–229; Gould, *Among the Powers of the Earth*, 122–123.

49. Ruigómez, *Gobierno Español*, 250 ("they").

50. Ruigómez, *Gobierno Español*, 250–251 ("protection," "fatal").

51. Leal, "España sostiene financieramente al Congreso," in *Recovered Memories, Memorias Recobradas*, 157n18; Campillo, *Relaciones Diplomaticas*, xi–xiv; French, "Spain and the Birth of the American Republic," 188–190; Rappleye, *Robert Morris*, 160, 206–208; Diego Joseph Navarro to George Washington, March 11, 1778, in PGW-RW, 14:146.

52. French, "Spain and the Birth of the American Republic," 189–190; McCadden, "Juan de Miralles," 365; George Washington to Conrad-Alexandre Gérard, May 1, 1779, in PGW-RW, 20:281n.

53. McCadden, "Juan de Miralles," 363–364; Campillo, *Relaciones Diplomaticas*, xi–xv.

54. James Lovell to John Adams, September 14, 1779, in AP ("villains"); Richard Henry Lee to John Adams, October 8, 1779, in AP; Juan de Miralles to George Washington, November 29, 1779, PGW-RW, 486–489.

55. Madison to Joseph Jones, November 25, 1780, in PJM-CS, 2:202–203 ("will," "unanimity").

56. Murphy, *Charles Gravier*, 3, 261–279; Ruigómez, *Gobierno Español*, 257–259; Taylor, *American Revolutions*, 175–209.

57. Mingo Homaw, Poymau Tauhau, and Tuskau Pautassau to Isaac Shelby, May 22, 1779, CO 5/81, NA-UK ("surprised").

58. Murphy, *Charles Gravier*, 234; Ruigómez, *Gobierno Español*, 127, 145–146 ("sufficient"); John Jay to Samuel Huntington, March 3, 1780, in PJJ, 2:50 ("France").

59. Ferreiro, *Brothers at Arms*, 161–162, 253–254; "Motion on Navigation of Mississippi," February 1, 1781, in PJM-CS, 2:302–303.

60. John Randolph to Thomas Jefferson, October 25, 1779, in PTJ-MS, 3:116 ("France"); Jefferson, "Notes of Proceedings in the Continental Congress," June 7–August 1, 1776, in PTJ-MS, 1:310 ("partition").

61. Vergennes to Benjamin Franklin, 19 November 1781," *Founders Online*, National Archives, https://founders.archives.gov/documents/Franklin/

01-36-02-0048 (accessed April 5, 2023); Hale and Hale Jr., *Franklin in France*, 2:2; Wharton, *Revolutionary Diplomatic Correspondence*, 1:495; Ferreiro, *Brothers at Arms*, 273.

62. Benjamin Franklin to Vergennes, 20 November 1781, *Founders Online*, National Archives, https://founders.archives.gov/documents/Franklin/01-36-02-0052 (accessed April 5, 2023).

63. Taylor, *American Revolutions*, 305–306 ("keep"); Ferreiro, *Brothers at Arms*, 302–303.

64. Madison to Edmund Pendleton, March 19, 1782 ("arts") and to Edmund Randolph, May 7, 1782, in PJM-CS, 4:106; Gerard to Congress, March 17, 1779, in Wharton, *Revolutionary Diplomatic Correspondence*, 3:85–86 ("domestic"); Taylor, *American Revolutions*, 306; "Motion on Instructions on Treaty of Commerce," June 29, 1781, in PJM-CS, 3:168–169.

65. Reverend James Madison to Madison, September 18, 1782, in PJM-CS, 5:137 ("dolus"), 138nn4–5; Brant, *James Madison*, 2:256 ("deceive," "all"); Virginia Delegates to Benjamin Harrison, May 7, 1782, in PJM-CS, 4:214 ("scrupulous," "vigorous").

66. PJM-CS, 5:xv.

67. PJM-CS, 5:xv; "Comments on Instructions to Peace Commissioners," August 2 and 8, 1782, in PJM-CS, 5:14–15, 33–36; "Comments on Instructions to John Jay," August 6, 1782, in PJM-CS, 5:23–25; "Comments on Edmund Randolph's 'Facts and Observations,'" August 16, 1782, in PJM-CS, 5:56–57; "Report on Peace Negotiations," October 4, 1782, in PJM-CS, 5:180–182; Brant, *James Madison*, 2:257.

68. Taylor, *American Revolutions*, 306–308; John Jay to Robert R. Livingston, September 18, 1782, in PJJ, 3:154 ("under"); Brant, *James Madison*, 2:261; "The Rayneval and Vaughan Missions to England," PJJ, 3:95–99.

69. "The Rayneval and Vaughan Missions to England," PJJ, 3:97.

70. "The Rayneval and Vaughan Missions to England," PJJ, 3:97 ("cut"); John Jay to Gouverneur Morris, October 13, 1782, in PPJ-MS, 3:195 ("had").

71. Taylor, *American Revolutions*, 306.

72. Madison, "Notes on Debates," December 24, 1782, in PJM-CS, 5:441–442 ("sensible," "more").

73. John Thaxter to John Adams, September 18, 1783, in AP; Diary of John Quincy Adams, November 12, 1779, n. 2, in AP; Zachariah Loreilhe to John Adams, September 24, 1783, in AP; PJM-CS, 7: xvii, xxvii.

74. Brant, *James Madison*, 2:269–271; Madison to Edmund Randolph, September 13, 1783, in PJM-CS, 7:314; PJM-CS, 7:xvii; Madison to Thomas Jefferson, September 20, 1783, in PJM-CS, 7:353 ("impotence").

75. Madison to Thomas Jefferson, September 20, 1783, in PJM-CS, 7:353 ("object," "reduced").

76. Brant, *James Madison*, 2:293.

77. PJM-CS, 7:xvii; Brant, *James Madison*, 2:291–300; Madison to Edmund Randolph, February 25, 1783, in PJM-CS, 6:287 ("dissolution").

78. Feldman, *Three Lives*, 38–43; Madison to Edmund Randolph, June 17, 1783, in PJM-CS, 7:159 ("paroxism").

79. Madison to Edmund Randolph, May 20, 1783, in PJM-CS, 7:60–61 ("instrusion").

80. Kelsay, *Joseph Brant*, 346; Taylor, *Civil War*, 25.

81. Burton, "Haldimand Papers," 179 ("laid," "just").

82. Feldman, *Three Lives*, 40 ("present").

83. Madison to Thomas Jefferson, December 10, 1783, in PJM-CS, 7:401–402, esp. 401 ("proper").

Chapter 2

1. Madison to Thomas Jefferson, December 10, 1783, in PJM-CS, 7:401–403; Alexander McGillivray to Arturo O'Neill, December 5, 1783, in Caughey, *McGillivray*, 63–64; Pope, *Tour*, 48; Milfort, *Memoirs*, 22 ("small"); Saunt, *New Order*, 70–71.

2. Waselkov, *Conquering Spirit*, 39; DuVal, *Independence Lost*, 27–29; Langley, "Tribal Identity," 231–234; Calloway, *Indian World*, 347; Pope, *Tour*, 48 ("delicate"); Saunt, *New Order*, 67–69; DuVal, *Independence Lost*, 296–297.

3. Arturo O'Neill to José de Ezpeleta, October 19, 1783, in Caughey, *McGillivray*, 62–63; Whitaker, *Spanish-American Frontier*, 49–50; Gould, *Among the Powers*, 122–123; Narrett, *Adventurism*, 110–111, 128; Weber, *Spanish Frontier*, 204–206.

4. Dowd, *Spirited Resistance*, 93–95; Francisco Cruzat to Esteban Miró, August 23, 1784, in Kinnaird, *Spain in the Mississippi Valley*, 117 ("plague").

5. Madison to Thomas Jefferson, December 10, 1783, in PJM-CS, 7:401–403, 403n1; Alexander McGillivray to Arturo O'Neill, December 5, 1783, in Caughey, *McGillivray*, 63–64.

6. Alexander McGillivray to Arturo O'Neill, January 1, 1783, in Caughey, *McGillivray*, 64–66, esp. 65 ("out"); Alexander McGillivray to Esteban Miró, March 28, 1784, in Caughey, *McGillivray*, 73–74, esp. 74 ("great," "distracted"); Alexander McGillivray to Arturo O'Neill, February 5, 1784, in Caughey, *McGillivray*, 69–70, esp. 70 ("settle").

7. Saunt, *New Order*, 75, 75–76n34; ASP-FR, 1:278–179; Whitaker, *Spanish-American Frontier*, 60–61; "Copia del Discurso Preliminar sobre Indios que el Governador de San Agustin de la Florida Cita en su Representacion, November 16, 1786," in Campillo, *Relaciones Diplomaticas*, 446–449; Benjamin Hawkins and others to Charles Thomson, November 17, 1785, in DHFFC ("dangerous").

8. Madison to Thomas Jefferson, February 11, 1784, in PJM-CS, 7:418–419; Madison to Thomas Jefferson, March 16, 1784, in PJM-CS, 8:11 ("winter").

9. Madison to Thomas Jefferson, March 16, 1784, in PJM-CS, 8:11; Jefferson to Madison, May 25, 1784, in PJM-CS, 8:42–44 and 44n2; Jefferson to Madison, November 11, 1784, in PJM-CS, 8:130–131.

10. Madison to Thomas Jefferson, March 16, 1784, in PJM-CS, 8:11; Madison to Jefferson, April 25, 1784, in PJM-CS, 21; "Resolutions to Strengthen Powers

of Congress," May 19, 1784, in PJM-CS, 8:38–39; Madison to Jefferson, April 25, 1784, in PJM-CS, 8:21 ("impotency").

11. Madison to Jefferson, September 7, 1784, in PJM-CS, 113 ("ramble"); Madison to James Madison Sr., September 6, 1784, in PJM-CS, 8:112; Brant, *James Madison*, 2:325–326, esp. 326 ("most"); Madison to James Madison, Sr., September 6, 1784, in PJM-CS, 112.

12. Calloway, *Indian World*, 301–303 ("dependants").

13. Brant, *James Madison*, 2:16, 324–325.

14. *Providence Gazette*, August 14, 1784; Whitaker, *Spanish-American Frontier*, 65; Otero, "American Mission," 68–70; McCoy, *Elusive Republic*, 123–124; Madison especially hoped that western traders would help shift US commerce from Britain to France, which he viewed as beneficial to southern states (Öhman, "Mississippi," 44–45).

15. Van Cleve, *We Have Not a Government*, 142 ("driven," "stand," "touch").

16. Madison to Jefferson, September 7, 1784 in PJM-CS, 8:113–114 ("ideas," "actual").

17. Madison to Jefferson, August 20, 1784, in PJM-CS, 8:104–106 ("impolitic," "sow," "depend," "complexity"). Madison enclosed this letter he had written earlier within his September 7 letter and mailed them together; Madison to Jefferson, March 18, 1786, in PJM-CS, 8:503.

18. Madison to Jefferson, September 15, 1784, in PJM-CS, 8:115.

19. Brant, *James Madison*, 2:330; Barbé-Marbois, *Our Revolutionary Forefathers*, 184 ("everything"), 186.

20. Madison to Jefferson, October 11, 1784, in PJM-CS, 8:116; Brant, *James Madison*, 2:331; Zenzen, *Fort Stanwix*, 17; Calloway, *Indian World*, 301–302.

21. Calloway, *Indian World*, 302 ("two"); Madison to Jefferson, October 11 and 17, 1784, in PJM-CS, 8:116–118, 118–121, esp. 120 ("eclipsed"); Madison to James Monroe, November 27, 1784, in PJM-CS, 8:156 ("violated").

22. Madison to Jefferson, October 11 and 17, 1784, in PJM-CS, 8:116–118, 118–121, esp. 117 ("are"); Brant, *James Madison*, 2:334.

23. John Mercer to Madison, November 12, 1784, in PJM-CS, 8:134–135 ("intrigues," "settled," "internal," "discordant"); Madison to James Monroe, November 14, 1784, in PJM-CS, 8:136 ("spurring"); James Monroe to Madison, 15 November 1784, in PJM-CS, 8:142; Mercer to Madison, November 26, 1784, in PJM-CS, 8:152 ("long").

24. Richard Henry Lee to Madison, November 26, 1784, in PJM-CS, 8:151; Madison to Lee, December 25, 1784, in PJM-CS, 8:201 ("union," "perpetuity").

25. Madison to Lafayette, March 20, 1784, in PJM-CS, 8:254.

26. John Jay to Diego de Gardoqui, October 4, 1785, in PJJ, 4:195–196; John Jay to Sarah Livingston Jay, January 2, 1785, in PJJ, 4:2; John Jay to James Duane, September 30, 1785, in PJJ, 4:194; Kline, "Sarah Livingston Jay," 166; Stahr, *John Jay*, 223; Gardoqui to Floridablanca, August 27, 1784, in Campillo, *Relaciones Diplomaticas*, xxxv ("dominates," "blindly," "nothing," "with," "lavishments," "secure").

27. Campillo, *Relaciones Diplomaticas*, xxiv; Ferreiro, *Brothers at Arms*, 40–41, 44, 303.

28. Van Cleve, *We Have Not a Government*, 165; Diego de Garoqui to Conde de Floridablanca, December 6, 1787, Estado, Legajo 3893, AHN; Diego de Gardoqui to Conde de Floridablanca, August 27, 1784 and May 12, 1787, both in Campillo, *Relaciones Diplomaticas*, xxxv ("there," "good wines"), 518 ("he"); John Jay to Diego de Gardoqui, October 4, 1785 and March 1, 1786, in PJJ, 4:195–196 ("public"), 304–305; John Jay to Charles Thomson, March 3, 1786, in PJJ, 4:305–306, 306n2.

29. Diego de Gardoqui to Conde de Floridablanca, June 30, 1785, in Campillo, *Relaciones Diplomaticas*, 488–489; Campillo, *Relaciones Diplomaticas*, xxxvi, xlv; Lydon, *Fish and Flour*, 238–240; Reeder, *Smugglers, Pirates, and Patriots*, 69–70, 87–92; Whitaker, *Spanish-American Frontier*, 74; Van Cleve, *We Have Not a Government*, 166 ("entire").

30. Van Cleve, *We Have Not a Government*, 166; Campillo, *Relaciones Diplomaticas*, lii, 1; James Monroe to Madison, May 31, 1786, in PJM-CS, 9:69 ("from").

31. Whitaker, *Spanish-American Frontier*, 76; Campillo, *Relaciones Diplomaticas*, li, liii ("infinity").

32. Madison to Jefferson, August 12, 1786, in PJM-CS, 9:96 ("foment," "seize," "court," "betrayed"); Madison to Jefferson, August 20, 1785, in PJM-CS, 8:344 ("want," "breach").

33. "Notes on Debates," March 13, 1787, in PJM-CS, 9:309; Gardoqui to Floridablanca, June 30, 1785, in Campillo, *Relaciones Diplomaticas*, 486–487 ("first," "finest"); Otero, "American Mission," 278; Homberger, *Mrs. Astor's New York*, 68–69; Valdivielso, *Diego de Gardoqui*, 119–120; Smith, *City of New York*, 19; Gardoqui to George Washington, July 24, 1789, in PGW-PS, 3:300n1; Gardoqui to Floridablanca, May 12, 1787, in Campillo, *Relaciones Diplomaticas*, 374.

34. "Notes on Debates," March 13, 1787, in PJM-CS, 9:309–310 ("Spain," "make").

35. "Notes on Debates," March 13, 1787, in PJM-CS, 9:310 ("hinted," "would").

36. Barksdale, *Lost State*, 147 ("consider," "win"); Solano, *Conspiración Española*, 223–224.

37. Barksdale, *Lost State*, 3–4; Jefferson to Richard Henry Lee, July 12, 1785, in PTJ-MS, 8:287 ("states," "every").

38. Barksdale, *Lost State*, 146–147; Narrett, *Adventurism*, 167.

39. Barksdale, *Lost State*, 146; Esteban Miró to Marqués de Sonora, June 28, 1786 and enclosures/copies, Estado, Legajo 3887, AHN; DuVal, *Independence Lost*, 310–311, 315–316; Van Cleve, *We Have Not a Government*, 149; Narrett, *Adventurism*, 126–127; Solano, *Conspiración Española*, 57.

40. Diego de Gardoqui to Conde de Floridablanca, May 12, 1787, in Campillo, *Relaciones Diplomaticas*, 378 ("every"); Diego de Gardoqui to Conde de Floridablanca, October 28, 1786, Estado, Legajo 3893, AHN.

41. Barksdale, *Lost State*, 147; Gardoqui to Floridablanca, May 12, 1787, in Campillo, *Relaciones Diplomaticas*, 376.

42. "Notes on Debates," March 13 and 29, 1787, in PJM-CS, 9:311 ("inflexibility"), 338 ("which").

43. "Notes on Debates," March 29, 1787, in PJM-CS, 9:338, 339n10; Gardoqui to Floridablanca, May 12, 1787, in Campillo, *Relaciones Diplomaticas*, 517–519 ("enemy," "France's"); Campillo, *Relaciones Diplomaticas*, lvii; Madison to Jefferson, March 29, 1787, in PJM-CS, 9:320.

44. James Monroe to James Madison, May 31, 1786, in PJM-CS, 9:72n5 ("France"); Van Cleve, *We Have Not a Government*, 1 ("we").

45. "Notes on Debates," March 29, 1787, in PJM-CS, 9:339 ("some").

46. "Notes on Debates," March 30, 1787, in PJM-CS, 9:341; "Negotiations with Gardoqui Reach an Impasse," in PJJ, 4:364–378; Jefferson to Madison, June 20, 1787, in PJM-CS, 10:64–65; "Notes on Debates," April 25 and 26, 1787, in PJM-CS, 9:404–407.

47. Madison to Jefferson, March 19, 1787, in PJM-CS, 9:318–320 ("foment," "British," "harmony," "intemperance").

48. Madison to Jefferson, March 19, 1787, in PJM-CS, 9:318–320.

49. Madison to Monroe, October 5, 1786, in PJM-CS, 9:140–141; "Vices of the Political System of the United States," April 1787, in PJM-CS, 9:356–357; Madison to James Madison, Sr., April 1, 1787, in PJM-CS, 9:359 ("mortal," "general").

50. Madison to Eliza House Trist, February 10, 1787, in PJM-CS, 9:259.

51. Madison to Monroe, August 7, 1785, in PJM-CS, 8:333–335 ("perfect," "must"); Klarman, *Framers' Coup*, 20.

52. Madison to Monroe, August 7, 1785, in PJM-CS, 8:334–335 ("harmony," "fœderal," "can").

53. Feldman, *Three Lives*, 76–77; Cheney, *James Madison*, 117–118; Madison to Monroe, September 11, 1786, in PJM-CS, 9:121–122.

54. Cutterham, *Gentlemen Revolutionaries*, 9–18; Brant, *James Madison*, 2:188.

55. Feldman, *Three Lives*, 76–80; "Address of the Annapolis Convention," September 14, 1786, in PAH, 3:688 ("defects"); Madison to Jefferson, August 12, 1786, in PJM-CS, 9:96; Cheney, *James Madison*, 118–119.

56. *Federalist* no. 19, Rossiter, *Federalist Papers*, 126, 128–129; Madison, "Notes on Ancient and Modern Confederacies," April–June 1786, PJM-CS, 9:3–24, esp. 8 ("seduced," "dissensions"), 17 ("tampering"), 18.

57. "Report on Books for Congress," January 23, 1783, in PJM-CS, 6:76; Temple Stanyan, *The Graecian History: From the End of the Peloponnesian War, to the Death of Philip of Macedon* (2 vols., London, 1739), 2:231–270, esp. 267 ("fomented"), 269 ("artifice," ("zeal").

58. "Notes on Ancient and Modern Confederacies," April–June, 1786, in PJM-CS, 9:6–7 ("she").

59. Madison to George Washington, December 9, 1785, in PJM-CS, 8:439 ("imitate"); Madison to Jefferson, March 18, 1786, in PJM-CS, 8:503 ("danger," "fit").

60. Klarman, *Framers' Coup*, 88–94; Madison to George Muter, January 7, 1787, in PJM-CS, 9:231 ("adversaries").

61. Madison to Jefferson, March 19, 1787, in PJM-CS, 9:318 ("every"), 322n2; Madison to Jefferson, October 17, 1788, in PJM-CS, 11:299 ("direct"); Read, *Power versus Liberty*, 25–30.

62. Madison, "Memorial and Remonstrance," ca. June 20, 1785, in PJM-CS, 8:302–303 ("majority"); Madison to Washington, April 16, 1787, in PJM-CS, 9:383–384; "Popular Election of the First Branch of the Legislature," June 6, 1787, in PJM-CS, 10:32–34, 34n2; Madison to Jefferson, October 24, 1787, in PJM-CS, 205–220. For Madison's gradual articulation of these ideas, especially on the broad extent of republics, see Bilder, *Madison's Hand*, 70–74.

63. Gardoqui to Floridablanca, May 12, 1787, in Campillo, *Relaciones Diplomaticas*, 378–379 ("frankly," "disunity"), 512 ("there"); Gardoqui didn't mention names of those he met with, but Rufus King may have been among them. King had favored relinquishing the Mississippi claims and apparently had met Gardoqui confidentially in the past to discuss the treaty. Campillo, *Relaciones Diplomaticas*, l; Van Cleve, *We Have Not a Government*, 166–167.

64. Madison to William Irvine, May 5, 1787, in PJM-CS, 9:409; Madison to Jefferson, May 15, 1787, in PJM-CS, 9:415; "The Virginia Plan," May 29, 1787, in PJM-CS, 10:12–18; Klarman, *Framers' Coup*, 137–138.

65. "Reply to the New Jersey Plan," June 19, 1787, in PJM-CS, 10:59 ("secure"); "Revisionary Power of the Executive and the Judiciary," June 6, 1787, in PJM-CS, 10:35; "Rule of Representation in the Legislature," July 5, 1787, in PJM-CS, 10:93 ("rash"); "Method of Appointing the Executive," July 25, 1787, in PJM-CS, 10:115–116; "Impeachment of the Executive," July 20, 1787, in PJM-CS, 10:108; "Citizenship Qualifications for Senators," August 9, 1787, in PJM-CS, 10:141; Bilder, *Madison's Hand*, 90, 104, 106; Klarman, *Framers' Coup*, 193–194, 197–199, esp. 199 ("if"). During the ratification process, some Rhode Island Antifederalists made the argument that they could refuse to join the union, offer European powers freeports, and count on those nations for support if the United States tried to abridge their sovereignty (Klarman, *Framers' Coup*, 519).

66. Klarman, *Framers' Coup*, 126–256; Madison to Edmund Pendleton, September 20, 1787, in PJM-CS, 10:171 ("proper").

67. Madison to Jefferson, October 24, 1787, in PJM-CS, 10:215; Maier, *Ratification*, 47 ("corrupt"), 92–93.

68. Gardoqui to Floridablanca, April 18, 1788, in Campillo, *Relaciones Diplomaticas*, 532 ("disgust"); Klarman, *Frames' Coup*, 389; Perkins, *Annals of the West*, 313–314.

69. Miró and Navarro to Váldes, September 25, 1787, in Solano, *Conspiración Española*, 203; Hay, "Charles Williamson and the Burr Conspiracy," 184; Linklater, *Artist in Treason*, 1–11, 15–16, 52, 69–70; Narrett, "Geopolitics and Intrigue," 101, 106.

70. Solano, *Conspiración Española*, 42; Shepherd, "Wilkinson and the Beginnings of the Spanish Conspiracy," 498–499 ("distinct," "real"); Miró

and Navarro to Váldes, September 25, 1787, in Solano, *Conspiración Española*, 209–210; Narrett, *Adventurism and Empire*, 166–167, 170.

71. Miró and Navarro to Váldes, September 25, 1787, in Solano, *Conspiración Española*, 210–211 ("precarious").

72. McGillivray to O'Neill, April 25, 1788, in Caughey, *McGillivray*, 178–179 ("were").

73. Wilkinson to Miró, May 15, 1787, in Solano, *Conspiración Española*, 221–222 ("distract," retranslated into English from a Spanish translation of Wilkinson's original letter in English); Campillo, *Relaciones Diplomaticas*, lxii.

74. Shepherd, "Wilkinson and the Beginnings of the Spanish Conspiracy," 499; Campillo, *Relaciones Diplomaticas*, lxii, ("unites," "fearsome"), lxix ("depends").

75. Madison to Washington, November 18, 1787, in PJM-CS, 10:253; Madison to Madison, Sr., September 30, 1787, in PJM-CS, 10:178; Maier, *Ratification*, 83–85.

76. Maier, *Ratification*, 83–85; *Federalist* no. 4, 6, 7, and 19, Rossiter, *Federalist Papers*, 44 ("three," "poor"), 48 ("violent"), 57, 60 ("become"), 128 ("anarchy").

77. *Federalist* no. 10, Rossiter, *Federalist Papers*, 71–79, esp. 72 ("some").

78. *Federalist* no. 14, Rossiter, *Federalist Papers*, 94 ("bulwark"), 98 ("strength").

79. *Federalist* nos. 18–20, Rossiter, *Federalist Papers*, 118–134, esp. 120 ("internal," "fresh," "secretly"), 123 ("dissensions," "by"), 133 ("surrounding," "nourish," "always").

80. *Federalist* no. 41, Rossiter, *Federalist Papers*, 252 ("security").

81. "*The Federalist* Number 63," March 1, 1788, in PJM-CS, 10:544–550; Klarman, *Framers' Coup*, 463–465; Washington to Madison, October 10, 1787, in PJM-CS, 10:190 ("more").

82. Madison to Eliza House Trist, March 25, 1788, in PJM-CS, 11:5 ("absurd," "harangue"); Klarman, *Framers' Coup*, 464–465.

83. Burstein and Isenberg, *Madison and Jefferson*, 148; Klarman, *Framers' Coup*, 460–461; Jefferson to Madison, December 8, 1784, in PJM-CS, 8:178 ("pray").

84. "Weaknesses of the Confederation," June 7, 1788, in PJM-CS, 11:92; DHRC, 9:910, 910n6, 992 ("internal"), 1029–1030; "The Virginia Convention," June 2–27, 1788, in PJM-CS, 11:72–76.

85. Madison to [Hamilton,] King, and Washington, June 25, 1788, in PJM-CS, 11:177–178; Hamilton to Madison, June 27, 1788, in PJM-CS, 11:183; Madison to Hamilton, June 30, 1788, in PJM-CS, 11:184; Madison to Hamilton, June 27, 1788, in PJM-CS, 11:181–182; Madison to Randolph, July 16, 1788, in PJM-CS, 11:187–188; "The Mississippi Question," June 13, 1788, in PJM-CS, 11:137–139.

86. Solano, *Conspiración Española*, 60; Narrett, *Adventurism and Empire*, 165–166; Gardoqui to Floridablanca, July 25, 1787, in Brown, *Political Beginnings*, 146–148 ("artfully"); Perkins, *Annals of the West*, 313–314; Watlington, *Partisan Spirit*, 160–165.

87. "Threat of Disunion in the West," in PTJ-MS, 19:470n122 ("interesting"); Madison to Butler, October 11, 1834, JMP, DLC ("mischievously"); Madison to Jefferson, August 23, 1788, in PJM-CS, 11:239 ("disgust," "seduce").

88. Brown to Madison, August 26, 1788, in PJM-CS, 11: 242–243; Madison to Brown, September 26, 1788, in PJM-CS, 11:266–267 ("political," "hazardous"); Gardoqui to Esteban Miró, October 2, 1788, Estado, Legajo 3894, AHN; Narrett, *Adventurism*, 166; John Brown to Gardoqui, January 15, 1789, Estado, Legajo 3894 (apartado 5, no. 316), AHN. While Brown was wavering in September, he sent Gardoqui news that Kentuckians seemed ready for independence before writing him on December 17 that their plans wouldn't work. He wrote as though he still favored the plan for independence, but his correspondence with Madison suggests that he vacillated and was trying to save face with Gardoqui after giving him such strong assurances in person (Brown to Gardoqui, September 15, 1788, Estado, Legajo 3894, AHN; "Traduccion de los Extractos del Diario de la Convencion celebrada en Danville el 28 de Julio de 1788," Estado, Legajo 3894; Gardoqui to Floridablanca, November 22, 1788, Estado, Legajo 3894, AHN; Brown to Gardoqui, December 17, 1788 [misdated by Gardoqui in his translation as 1789], Estado, Legajo 3894 (apartado 6), AHN; John Brown to Gardoqui, January 15, 1789, Estado, Legajo 3894 (apartado 5, no. 316), AHN). Brown did remain supportive of a plan to establish a settlement in Spanish territory on the banks of the Mississippi (John Brown to Gardoqui, January 15, 1789, Estado, Legajo 3894, AHN; "Traduccion de la Peticion presentada a Don Diego de Gardoqui por los sugetos cuios nombres aparecen al pie," Estado, Legajo 3894 (apartado 5, no. 316), AHN; Narrett, "Geopolitics and Intrigue," 144–145n94).

89. Barksdale, *Lost State*, 152; Narrett, *Adventurism*, 166–167; Gardoqui to Floridablanca, April 18, 1788, in Campillo, *Relaciones Diplomaticas*, 536; John Sevier to Gardoqui, September 12 (two letters), 1788, Estado, Legajo 3894.

90. Gardoqui to Floridablanca, April 18, 1788, in Campillo, *Relaciones Diplomaticas*, 533–534; Narrett, *Adventurism*, 167.

91. Narrett, *Adventurism*, 167, 169; Solano, *Conspiración Española*, 79, 144n28, 323–325; Barksdale, *Lost State*, 160; DuVal, *Independence Lost*, 320. North Carolina did not ratify the US Constitution until November 1789, but the process toward ratification had commenced in November 1788, and by the spring of 1789, it seemed only a matter of time before a second state ratifying convention acceded (Klarman, *Framers' Coup*, 515–516).

92. Madison to Randolph, November 23, 1788, in PJM-CS, 11:363; Madison to Washington, December 2, 1788, in PJM-CS, 11:377; "Madison's Election to the First Federal Congress," in PJM-CS, 11:302–304.

93. Madison to Washington, March 8, 1789, in PJM-CS, 12:6, 6n3; Narrett, *Adventurism*, 172.

94. Madison to Randolph, March 1, 1789, in PJM-CS, 11:453 ("contentions").

Chapter 3

1. *Courier de Boston*, April 30, 1789; Comte de Moustier Diary, April 24, 1789, in DHFFC ("infinite"); *Daily Advertiser*, April 24, 1789; George Washington Diary, April 23, 1789, in PGW–D, 5:447–448; Bordewich, *First Congress*, 44–45.

2. Bordewich, *First Congress*, 45; *Daily Advertiser*, April 24, 1789; *New-York Packet*, April 24, 1789; Gardoqui to Floridablanca, April 24, 1789, in Campillo, *Relaciones Diplomaticas*, 542–544; Waldstreicher, *In the Midst of Perpetual Fetes*, 118–121.

3. Comte de Moustier, Diary, April 24, 1789 and Elias Boudinot to William Bradford, Jr., April 24, 1789, both in DHFFC.

4. Gardoqui to Floridablanca, April 24, 1789, in Campillo, *Relaciones Diplomaticas*, 544; Elias Boudinot to Hannah Boudinot, April 24, 1789, in DHFFC; Moustier to Washington, October 5, 1788, in PGW-PS, 1:37n.

5. Moustier to Montmorin, April 7, 1789, in DHFFC ("here").

6. Moustier to Montmorin, March 20 ("how") and April 7 ("language," "this"), 1789, in DHFFC.

7. Moustier, "Description of the Inauguration," April 30, 1789, in DHFFC ("most"); Madison to Jefferson, May 23, 1789, in DHFFC.

8. Elkins and McKitrick, *Age of Federalism*, 18–26, 46–50; Taylor, *American Revolutions*, 395–398.

9. Taylor, *American Revolutions*, 415.

10. Moustier to Montmorin, April 7, 1789 ("ground"), Moustier to Jacques Necker, May 12, 1789 ("infant"), and Moustier to Montmorin, June 9, 1789 ("epoch," "disquieting," "dangerous"), all in DHFFC; Reuter, "Petty Spy," 476.

11. Victor Marie du Pont de Nemours to Éleuthère Iréné du Pon de Nemours, May 15, 1789, in DHFFC; Chervinsky, *Cabinet*, 145; Moustier to Montmorin, June 9, 1789, in DHFFC; Madison to Jefferson, December 8, 1788, in PJM-CS, 11:383 ("unsocial").

12. "Address of the President to Congress," April 30, 1789, in PJM-CS, 12:120–121; Madison to Jefferson, May 27, 1789, in PJM-CS, 12:185; Leibiger, *Founding Friendship*, 109–110.

13. Victor Marie du Pont de Nemours to Éleuthère Iréné du Pon de Nemours, May 15, 1789, in DHFFC ("everyone," "rise"); Madison to Jefferson, May 23 ("Moustier") and 27, 1789, in PJM-CS, 12:183, 186; Moustier to Montmorin, June 9, 1789, in DHFFC ("representative").

14. Madison to Jefferson, May 27, 1789, in PJM-CS, 12:186 ("commercial"); "Conversation with George Beckwith," October 1789, in PAH, 5:484; "Import and Tonnage Duties," April 8, 1789, in PJM-CS, 12:64–66; "Memorandum for George Washington," ca. October 8, 1789, in PJM-CS, 12:433–434.

15. Madison to Monroe, August 7, 1785, in PJM-CS, 8:334; "Import Duties," April 25, 1789, in PJM-CS, 12:110; Madison to Jefferson, June 30, 1789, in PJM-CS, 12:269–270 ("essential," "superfluities"); McCoy, *Elusive Republic*, 137–145; Madison to Jefferson, May 27, 1789, in PJM-CS, 12:268–270;

Dorchester to Grenville, September 25, 1790, in Brymner, *Report on Canadian Archives*, 257 ("real").

16. "George Beckwith: Conversation with Different Persons," n.d., 1789, in DHFFC ("all"); Moustier to Montmorin, June 29, 1789, in DHFFC ("French," "propitious").

17. Madison to Jefferson, June 30, 1789, in PJM-CS, 12:269–270; Boyd, *Number 7*, 26; "Conversation with George Beckwith," October 1789, in PAH, 5:484 ("promote").

18. Moustier to Montmorin, September 17, 1789, in DHFFC (quotations).

19. "Thomas Jefferson's Explanations of the Three Volumes Bound in Marbled Paper," in PTJ-RS, 12:425 ("most"); PAH, 4:192 ("in").

20. Lefkowitz, *Indispensable Men*, 147–148; Armitage, "Foreword," xii; Nelson, *Royalist Revolution*, 5–7; Arcenas, "Defending an Energetic Executive," 168 ("feeble").

21. Schwarz, "Great Divergence," 423; Cost, *Price of Greatness*, 117–120.

22. Moustier to Montmorin, October 3, 1789, in DHFFC; Jefferson to Madison, August 28, 1789, in PJM-CS, 12:362 ("moved").

23. Boyd, *Number 7*, 27 ("greatly" and "republican").

24. George Washington Diary, October 8, 1789, in PGW–D, 5:456; Madison to Henry Lee, October 4, 1789, in PJM-CS, 12:427; Jefferson to William Short, October 7, 1789, in PTJ-MS, 15:508–509.

25. George Washington Diary, October 8, 1789, in PGW–D, 5:456 ("superior"); Brookhiser, *Gentleman Revolutionary*; Mintz, "Gouverneur Morris," 651–652; "Memorandum for George Washington," ca. October 8, 1789, in PJM-CS, 12:433–434.

26. Madison to Jefferson, June 30, 1789, in PJM-CS, 12:268–270.

27. George Washington Diary, October 7, 1789, in PGW–D, 5:455; Madison to Jefferson, June 30, 1789, in PJM-CS, 12:269–270; Boyd, *Number 7*, 26.

28. George Washington Diary, October 8, 1789, in PGW–D, 5:456; "Memorandum for George Washington," ca. October 8, 1789, in PJM-CS, 12:433–434; Reuter, "Petty Spy," 480.

29. Madison to Jefferson, October 8, 1787 [1789], in PJM-CS, 12:433 (quotations).

30. Jefferson to William Short, October 7, 1789, in PTJ-MS, 15:508–509; Meacham, *Thomas Jefferson*, 232; Madison to Washington, January 4, 1790, in PJM-CS, 12:466–467; Gordon-Reed, *Hemingses*, 389, 397, 445; Madison to Jefferson, October 8, 1787 [1789], in PJM-CS, 12:433.

31. Reuter, "Petty Spy," 471–472, 479.

32. Taylor, *Civil War*, 34–35 ("there"); Reuter, "Petty Spy," 480.

33. Bemis, *Jay's Treaty*, 43–44.

34. Reuter, "Petty Spy," 491; Boyd, *Number 7*, 21 ("undeviating"); "George Beckwith: *Conversations with Different Persons*," n.d. 1789, in DHFFC ("eleve," "enlightened").

35. Boyd, *Number 7*, 23; Brymner, *Report on Canadian Archives*, 239.

36. Boyd, *Number 7*, 25.

37. "Conversation with George Beckwith," October 1789, in PAH, 5:482.
38. "Conversation with George Beckwith," October 1789, in PAH, 5:482–490.
39. "Conversation with George Beckwith," October 1789, in PAH, 5:488.
40. "Conversation with George Beckwith," October 1789, in PAH, 5:488.
41. "Conversation with George Beckwith," October 1789, in PAH, 5:489; Ketcham, *James Madison*, 305.
42. Madison to Jefferson, June 30, 1789 in PJM-CS, 12:268–270, esp. 269 ("British"); "Conversation with George Beckwith," October 1789, in PAH, 5:482.
43. Boyd, *Number 7*, 26.
44. Boyd, *Number 7*, 30–32.
45. Madison to Randolph, March 21, 1790, in PJM-CS, 13:110; Jefferson to Thomas Mann Randolph, March 28, 1790, in PTJ-MS, 16:278.
46. "Conversation with George Beckwith," March 22–April 1790, in PAH, 26:526–534; George Beckwith to William Lord Grenville, April 7, 1790, in DHFFC ("cultivate").
47. Reuter, "Petty Spy," 484–485; Hamilton to Washington, July 8, 1790, in PGW-PS, 6:24–31; Dorchester to Beckwith, June 27, 1790, two letters, in Brymner, *Report on Canadian Archives*, 143–144; Boyd, *Number 7*, 36–38.
48. Boyd, *Number 7*, 45–46.
49. George Washington Diary, July 8, 1790, in PGW-D, 6:87–88.
50. Hamilton to Washington, July 8, 1790, in PGW-PS, 6:24–31; Boyd, *Number 7*, 39–47.
51. Jefferson to Morris, August 12, 1790, in PTJ-MS, 17:127–128; Boyd, *Number 7*, xiii, 48–53; "The Federalist No. 70," March 15, 1788, in PAH, 4:599 ("unity").
52. Feldman, *Three Lives*, 292–293.
53. Burstein and Isenberg, *Madison and Jefferson*, 215; Madison to Hamilton, November 19, 1789, in PJM-CS, 12:449–451; PJM-CS, 13:xvii; Ellis, *Founding Brothers*, 56–57.
54. Burstein and Isenberg, *Madison and Jefferson*, 214–215.
55. PJM-CS, 13:xviii.
56. Burstein and Isenberg, *Madison and Jefferson*, 214–216, 221; Ellis, *Founding Brothers*, 57–58.
57. Madison to Monroe, July 24 [25?], 1790, in PJM-CS, 13:282 ("spirit").
58. PJM-CS, 13:xxi; Madison to Pendleton, January 2, 1791, in PJM-CS, 13:344 ("you"); Burstein and Isenberg, *Madison and Jefferson*, 221 ("monied").
59. Burstein and Isenberg, *Madison and Jefferson*, 222.
60. Rutland, *James Madison*, 96–97; "The Bank Bill," February 2, 1791, in PJM-CS, 13:372–381.
61. "The Bank Bill," February 2, 1791, in PJM-CS, 13:374–379.
62. Rutland, *James Madison*, 97.
63. Madison to Jefferson, May 1, 1791, in PJM-CS, 14:16 ("partizans").
64. Madison to Jefferson, March 13, 1791, in PJM-CS, 13:404–405; Jefferson to Madison, March 13, 1791, in PJM-CS, 13:405–406; Sheehan, *Mind of James Madison*, ix–x; Ketcham, *James Madison*, 323.

65. Jefferson to Madison, March 13, 1791, in PJM-CS, 13:405 ("take"); Reuter, "Petty Spy," 485; Boyd, *Number 7*, 35–37.

66. Calloway, *Indian World*, 380–384; "Memorandum to Thomas Jefferson," ca. April 18, 1791, in PJM-CS, 14:7–9.

67. "Memorandum to Thomas Jefferson," ca. April 18, 1791, in PJM-CS, 14:7–9.

68. "Unofficial Diplomacy on Indian Affairs," in PTJ-MS, 20:106–141.

69. "Unofficial Diplomacy on Indian Affairs," in PTJ-MS, 20:106–141.

70. "Unofficial Diplomacy on Indian Affairs," in PTJ-MS, 20:112; Calloway, *Indian World*, 387–388.

71. Calloway, *Victory with No Name*, 90–92; Calloway, *Indian World*, 390–391.

72. Calloway, *Victory with No Name*, 115–128; Calloway, *Indian World*, 391–392; Hogeland, *Autumn of the Black Snake*, 114–117.

73. Beckwith to John Simcoe, December 19, 1791, in Cruikshank, *Correspondence of Simcoe*, 1:94; Taylor, *Civil War*, 36, 45–47.

74. Simcoe to Henry Dundas, December 7, 1791, in Cruikshank, *Correspondence of Simcoe*, 1:88; Taylor, *Civil War*, 49; Stevenson to Simcoe, January 7, 1792, in Cruikshank, *Correspondence of Simcoe*, 1:100–101; Stevenson to Nepean, January 11, 1792, in Cruikshank, *Correspondence of Simcoe*, 1:102.

75. "Memorandum of Consultation on Indian Policy," March 9, 1792, in PTJ-MS, 23:240; George Hammond to Simcoe, November 27, 1792, in Cruikshank, *Correspondence of Simcoe*, 1:268.

76. Stevenson to Simcoe, May 8, 1792, in Cruikshank, *Correspondence of Simcoe*, 1:155–156.

77. Stevenson to Simcoe, May 8, 1792, in Cruikshank, *Correspondence of Simcoe*, 1:155–156.

78. Simcoe to Clarke, August 20, 1792, in Cruikshank, *Correspondence of Simcoe*, 1:201 ("determined").

79. "Unofficial Diplomacy on Indian Affairs," in PTJ-MS, 20:140 ("such").

80. "Memorandum on a Discussion of the President's Retirement," May 5, 1792, in PJM-CS, 14:299–303; Chervinsky, "Thomas Jefferson's Cabinet," https://www.whitehousehistory.org/thomas-jeffersons-cabinet (accessed October 27, 2020).

81. "Memorandum on a Discussion of the President's Retirement," May 5, 1792, in PJM-CS, 14:299–303.

82. "Memorandum on a Discussion of the President's Retirement," May 5, 1792, in PJM-CS, 14:299–303

83. "Memorandum on a Discussion of the President's Retirement," May 5, 1792, in PJM-CS, 14:299–303

84. Washington to Hamilton, August 26, 1792, in PGW-PS, 11:39 ("mutual"); Washington to Jefferson, PGW-PS, 11:30 ("our," "weight").

85. Jefferson to Washington, September 9, 1792, in PGW-PS, 11:104; Hamilton to Washington, September 9, 1792, in PGW-PS, 11:92–93; "The Origins of Freneau's *National Gazette*," July 25, 1791, in PJM-CS, 14:56–57; Stewart, *Opposition Press*, 7–9.

86. Hamilton to Washington, September 9, 1792, in PGW-PS, 11:92–93 ("formed"); "Catallus No. 1," September 15, 1792 and "Catallus No. 2," September 19, 1792, in PAH, 12:379–384, 393–401.
87. "A Candid State of Parties," September 22, 1792, in PJM-CS, 14:370–372.
88. Feldman, *Three Lives*, 350 ("checks"); Chervinsky, *Cabinet*, 181–182.
89. "A Candid State of Parties," September 22, 1792, in PJM-CS, 14:372 ("republican"); Feldman, *Three Lives*, 327 ("British").
90. "Thomas Jefferson's Conversation with Washington," October 1, 1792, in PGW-PS, 11:182–185.
91. Freeman, *Washington*, 605–611.
92. Boyd, *Number 7*, 83–84 ("his").

Chapter 4
1. *Mirrour*, December 16, 1793.
2. Chervinsky, *Cabinet*, 96–97, esp. 97 ("superior"); Maier, *American Scripture*, 112 ("wrong"); Walzer, *Regicide and Revolution*, 1–2.
3. Maier, *American Scripture*, 100–101, 107–108, 122 ("courtiers"), 123; "Pacificus No. VI," July 17, 1793, in PAH, 15:101 ("melancholy"); Hamilton to _____, May 18, 1793, in PAH, 14:475.
4. Madison to Jefferson, April 12, 1793, in PJM-CS, 15:7 ("spurious," "bloodthirstyness," and "ought").
5. Madison to George Nicholas, March 15, 1793, in PJM-CS, 14:472 ("symptoms").
6. Madison to George Nicholas, March 15, 1793, in PJM-CS, 14:472 ("most").
7. Rapport, *Napoleonic Wars*, 24–26.
8. Mitchell, *Alexander Hamilton*, 230 ("vanity"); Jusserand, "La Jeunesse du Citoyen Genet," 243–245; Ammon, *Genet Mission*, 1–4; Blackwell, "Citizen Genet," 75–79; Berkin, *Sovereign People*, 88 ("insane").
9. Ammon, *Genet Mission*, 144; Ternant to Minister of Foreign Affairs, November 13, 1792, in CFM, 164–165.
10. *City Gazette*, April 9, 1793; Berkin, *Sovereign People*, 92; Ammon, *Genet Mission*, vii; Genet to Lebrun, April 16, 1793, in CFM, 211–213.
11. DeConde, *Entangling Alliance*, 200; Genet to Lebrun, April 16, 1793, in CFM, 211–213.
12. Furstenberg, *When the United States Spoke French*, 302–303.
13. Deconde, *Entangling Alliance*, 201–202; *City Gazette*, May 4, 1793; John Steele to Hamilton, April 30, 1793, in PAH, 14:359.
14. Deconde, *Entangling Alliance*, 202–207; Moats, *Navigating Neutrality*, 20 ("highway").
15. Chervinsky, *Cabinet*, 197–205.
16. *Dunlap's American Daily Advertiser*, May 21, 1793; *Connecticut Journal*, May 22, 1793 ("flocked"); Ammon, *Genet Mission*, 55; Genet to Lebrun, May 18, 1793, in CFM, 214215 ("triumph").
17. Genet to Lebrun, May 18, 1793, in CFM, 214 ("destroyed"); Genet to Lebrun, October 7, 1793, in CFM, 245 ("cold").

18. "Supplement Aux Instructions Données au Citoyen Genet, Ministre Plénipotentiaire de la Republique Française Prés des Etats Unis de l'Amerique," in CFM, 207 ("English"), 210 ("zealous"), 215nd.

19. Genet to Lebrun, May 31, 1793, in CFM, 216 ("voice").

20. Genet to Lebrun, August 2, 1793, in CFM, 235 ("vox").

21. Chervinsky, *Cabinet*, 196–205.

22. Jefferson to Madison, May 19, 1793, in PJM-CS, 15:19 ("confederacy").

23. Madison to Jefferson, June 13, 1793, in PJM-CS, 15:29 ("monarchical"); Combs, *Jay Treaty*, 108.

24. Stewart, *Opposition Press*, 11–13; Adelman, *Revolutionary Networks*, 194–196; Pasley, *Tyranny of Printers*, 78 ("partisan").

25. Jefferson to Madison, June 9, 1791, in PJM-CS, 15:27; Chervinksky, *Cabinet*, 226; Stewart, *Opposition Press*, 147–148; *National Gazette*, June 8, 1793 ("opiate"); Slaughter, *Whiskey Rebellion*, 156 ("infamously," "horrid," "gambling").

26. Jefferson to Madison, June 9, 1793, in PJM-CS, 15:27 ("I am," "rags"); Madison to Jefferson, June 19, 1793, in PJM-CS, 15, 33–34 ("every").

27. Genet to Jefferson, June 8, 1793, in ASP-FR, 1:151 ("confirmed").

28. Hardie, *Philadelphia Directory, 1793*, 51; Alexander Dallas, "To the Public," *General Advertiser*, December 10, 1793.

29. Alexander Dallas, "To the Public," *General Advertiser*, December 10, 1793.

30. Jefferson to Monroe, June 28, 1793, in PTJ-MS, 26:393; "Memorandum of a Conversation with Edmond Charles Genet," in PTJ-MS, 26:466; Furstenburg, *When the United States Spoke French*, 307–312; "Notes of Cabinet Meeting and Conversations with Edmond Charles Genet," July 5, 1793, in PTJ-MS, 26:438.

31. Holloway, *Hamilton versus Jefferson*, 256–257;

32. Jefferson to Madison, July 7, 1793, in PJM-CS, 15:43 ("never," "take").

33. "Reasons for the Opinion of the Secretary of the Treasury and the Secretary at War Respecting the Brigantine Little Sarah," July 8, 1793, in PAH, 15:75–76 ("evidence," "fatal").

34. Madison to Jefferson, July 18, 1793, in PJM-CS, 15:44; "Pacificus No. VI," July 17, 1793, PAH, 15:106 ("insidious," "patronage," "caresses").

35. "Pacificus No. VI," July 17, 1793, PAH, 15:106 ("foreign").

36. Madison to Jefferson, July 18, 1793, in PJM-CS, 15:44–45; Madison to Jefferson, July 30, 1793, in PJM-CS, 15:48 ("grating").

37. "No Jacobin No. I," July 31, 1793, in PAH, 15:145; "No Jacobin No. V," August 14, 1793, in PAH, 15:244 ("popular intrigue"); "No Jacobin No. VII," August 23, 1793, in PAH, 15:268–269; Kelly and Lovell, "Thomas Jefferson," 145.

38. Broadwater, "Madison, Hamilton, and the Neutrality Proclamation," 171–192; Ketcham, *James Madison*, 346.

39. Holloway and Wilson, *Political Writings*, 445.

40. Chervinsky, *Cabinet*, 197; Jefferson to Madison, August 3, 1793, in PJM-CS, 15:50 ("sink"); Ammon, *Genet Mission*, 101–105.

41. Ammon, *Genet Mission*, 102 (quotations).

42. Ammon, *Genet Mission*, 101–106; "Notes of a Conversation with George Washington," August 6, 1793, in PTJ-MS, 26:628.

43. "Introductory Note: Hamilton to Rufus King, August 13, 1793," in PAH, 15:233; *Journal*, August 10, 1793; *Diary*, August 7, 1793 ("who"); "Resolutions on Franco-American Relations," in PJM-CS, 15:76–78; Citizens of Richmond to George Washington, August 17, 1793, in PGW-PS, 13:483 ("any").

44. Madison to Jefferson, September 2, 1793, in PJM-CS, 15:92; Jefferson to Madison, August 11, 1793, in PJM-CS, 15:54; Jefferson to Madison, August 11, 1793, second letter, in PJM-CS, 15:57 ("absolutely"), 59n1; Jefferson to Madison, August 3, 1793, in PJM-CS, 15:50; Madison to Jefferson, August 11, 1793, in PJM-CS, 15:52.

45. Madison to Jefferson, August 27, 1793, in PJM-CS, 15:75; "Resolutions on Franco-American Relations," ca. August 27, 1793, in PJM-CS, 15:76–80.

46. "Resolutions on Franco-American Relations," ca. August 27, 1793, in PJM-CS, 15:77–80, esp. 77 ("imprudence" and "highly").

47. Madison to Monroe, September 15, 1793, in PJM-CS, 15:110–111 ("conduct").

48. Sheridan, "Recall of Edmond Charles Genet," 480–482, esp. 480 ("head").

49. Madison to Jefferson, March 2, 1794, in PJM-CS, 15:270–271.

50. Sheridan, "Recall of Edmond Charles Genet," 483–487; "Madison in the Third Congress," December 2, 1793–March 3, 1795, in PJM-CS, 15:146–147.

51. "Madison in the Third Congress," December 2, 1793–March 3, 1795, in PJM-CS, 15:146; Cheney, *James Madison*, 246; *Columbian Centinel*, February 19, 1794 ("most"), March 1, 1794 ("close"); *New-Hampshire Gazette*, February 22, 1794.

52. John Adams to Jefferson, June 30, 1813, in PTJ-RS, 6:254 ("terrorism").

53. Slaughter, *Whiskey Rebellion*, 109–124; Chervinsky, *Cabinet*, 236.

54. Slaughter, *Whiskey Rebellion*, 155–156, 159–160; Baron de Carondelet to Simcoe, January 2, 1794, in Cruikshank, *Correspondence of Simcoe*, 2:129130; Turner, *Correspondence of Clark and Genet*, 943; Calloway, *Indian World*, 438; José de Jáudenes to Duque de la Alcudia, August 10, 1794, Legajo 3895bis., AHN ("Great Britain," "easy"); Griffin, *American Leviathan*, 234 ("renounce").

55. Edmund Randolph to George Washington, March 15, 1794, in PGW-PS, 15:385n1 ("laboured"); John Jay to George Washington, July 21, 1794, in PGW-PS, 16:399.

56. Simcoe to John Wentworth, November 11, 1793, in Cruikshank, *Correspondence of Simcoe*, 2:105 is one of many examples in Simcoe's correspondence tracking Wayne's movements; Calloway, *Indian World*, 438–439; Taylor, *Divided Ground*, 287–288.

57. George Washington Diary, September 30, 1794, in PGW–D, 6:178–179 ("pleasing").

58. Slaughter, *Whiskey Rebellion*, 195 ("center"); Chervinsky, *Cabinet*, 254; Gould, *Among the Powers of the Earth*, 135.

59. Chervinsky, *Cabinet*, 261.

60. Link, *Democratic-Republican Societies*, 144, 145n94; Foner, *Democratic-Republican Societies*, 23 ("impure"); Washington to Henry Lee, August

26, 1794, in PGW-PS, 16:602 ("father"); Washington to Daniel Morgan, October 8, 1794, in PGW-PS, 17:40 ("diabolical leader"); Washington to Burgess Ball, September 25, 1794, in PGW-PS, 16:723.

61. Furstenberg, *When the United States Spoke French*, 315–316 ("knew"); Randolph, *Vindication*, 15.

62. Chervinsky, *Cabinet*, 288; Gould, *Among the Powers of the Earth*, 135; José de Jáudenes to Duque de la Alcudia, October 31, 1794, Legajo 3895bis., AHN; "Copia de una Carta reservada al Ministro de Su Magestad Catolica en Philadelphia por la Comitiva Secreta de Correspondencia del Oueste," October 13, 1794, Legajo 3895bis., AHN.

63. *Journal of the House*, November 19, 1794, 3rd Cong. 2nd Sess., 33–37.

64. "House Address to the President," November 27, 1794, in PJM-CS, 15:391; Madison to Jefferson, November 30, 1794, in PJM-CS, 15:396 ("attack").

65. *Journal of the House*, November 19, 1794, 3rd Cong. 2nd Sess., 34 ("certain"); Madison to Monroe, December 4, 1794, in PJM-CS, 15:406 ("greatest").

66. Madison to Monroe, December 4, 1794, in PJM-CS, 15:406 ("the game"); Madison to Jefferson, November 30, 1794, in PJM-CS, 15:397–398 ("opposition," "most," "liberties").

Chapter 5

1. Jean Antoine Joseph Fauchet to minister of foreign affairs, June 5, 1794, in CFM, 378.

2. Jean Antoine Joseph Fauchet to minister of foreign affairs, May 5, 1794, and June 5, 1794, in CFM, 330, 378; Furstenberg, *When the United States Spoke French*, 1–2, 68–69; Earl, "Talleyrand in Philadelphia," 282–298.

3. Wilson and Fiske, *Appletons' Cyclopaedia*, 2:421; Furstenberg, *When the United States Spoke French*, 1–8, 177.

4. Samuel Vaughan Jr. to Madison, February 14, 1794, two letters, in PJM-CS, 258–259; Furstenberg, *When the United States Spoke French*, 67, 69; Madison to the minister of the interior of the French Republic, April 1793, in PJM-CS, 15:4 ("triumphs").

5. Jean Antoine Joseph Fauchet to minister of foreign affairs, June 5, 1794, in CFM, 378; Furstenberg, *When the United States Spoke French*, 1–8, 140.

6. Furstenberg, *When the United States Spoke French*, 141; Earl, "Talleyrand in Philadelphia," 282.

7. Edmund Randolph to Washington, February 23, 1794, in PGW-PS, 15:265–266, 66n2.

8. Fauchet to minister of foreign affairs, June 4 and 5, 1794, in CFM, 373, 378–379; Abigail Adams to John Adams, November 13, 1780 n2, in AP; Antoine de la Forest to Comte de Montmorin, September 28, 1787 n1, in DHRC.

9. Wilson, *Friendly Relations*, 3–5.

10. Wilson, *Friendly Relations*, 6.

11. Wilson, *Friendly Relations*, 6–7, 12 ("wanton"); Gould, *Among the Powers of the Earth*, 135

12.   Bartholomew Dandridge to James Madison, March 31, 1795, in PJM-CS, 15:505; George Washington Diary, October 8, 1789, in PGW–D, 5:456. There is no record of the dinner other than Washington's invitation, but the evidence suggests that the Madisons must have accepted. Their family had recently recovered from illness, so health would not have prevented them from attending. However familiar Madison was with Washington, one simply did not turn down invitations to dine with the eminent president. The Madisons had sufficiently recent, close contact with Washington's household before their departure that Dolley could report to Washington's niece in Virginia that the president and Martha Washington "were perfectly well" (Madison to Jefferson, March 23, 1795, in PJM-CS, 15:494; Harriot Washington to George Washington, April 24, 1795, in PGW-PS, 18:83).

13.   Bartholomew Dandridge to James Madison, March 31, 1795, in PJM-CS, 15:505 ("family").

14.   Brant, *James Madison*, 3:406–410; Allgor, *Queen of America*, 95 ("great"); Dolley Payne Todd Madison to Elizabeth (Eliza) Collins Lee, s.d., in PDM ("darling"); Catherine Coles to Dolley Payne Todd, June 1, 1794, in PJM-CS, 15:342 ("night").

15.   Brant, *James Madison*, 3:403–410.

16.   Ammon, *James Monroe*, 112–114; Ketcham, *James Madison*, 380–383.

17.   Madison to Monroe, February 15, 1795, in PJM-CS, 15:473 ("betrayed"); Sharp, *American Politics*, 115–116.

18.   Feldman, *Three Lives*, 394; Madison to Jefferson, March 23, 1795, in PJM-CS, 15:493–494.

19.   Estes, *Jay Treaty Debate*, 24–25; Van Cleve, *We Have Not a Government*, 12; Elkins and McKitrick, *Age of Federalism*, 408–409; Calloway, *Indian World*, 438–439.

20.   DeConde, *Entangling Alliance*, 107–108.

21.   Madison to Monroe, March 11, 1795, in PJM-CS, 15:487; Madison to Jefferson, March 23, 1795, in PJM-CS, 15:493 ("inpenetrable"); Randolph, *Vindication*, 28; Estes, *Jay Treaty Debate*, 27–29; Elkins and McKitrick, *Age of Federalism*, 409–417; Öhman, "Mississippi Question," 46–47.

22.   Madison to Monroe, March 26, 1795, in PJM-CS, 15:496 ("as much"); Madison to Robert R. Livingston, February 8, 1795, in PJM-CS, 15:468–469; James Madison, "Political Observations," April 20, 1795, in PJM-CS, 15:527–528; Estes, *Jay Treaty Debate*, 27; Feldman, *Three Lives*, 396.

23.   Madison to William Branch Giles, April 3, 1795, in PJM-CS, 15:505; Leibiger, *Founding Friendship*, 197–222. Washington couldn't have shown Madison the treaty even if he wanted. The single copy he received from Jay remained concealed tight in the hands of Secretary of State Randolph, the only other person in America who knew its contents (Miller, *Treaties*, 2:267–268; Randolph, *Vindication*, 28).

24.   Alden, *George Washington*, 278 ("kick"); Wilson, *Friendly Relations*, 16–17; Tagg, *Benjamin Franklin Bache*, 249; Oliver Wolcott to Laura Collin

Wolcott, July 26, 1795, in Gibbs, *Memoirs*, 1:218; Edmund Randolph to George Washington, July 27, 1795, in PGW-PS, 18:436. The crowd went to the new French minister's house on the corner of Twelfth and High Streets then to British consul Phineas Bond's house before proceeding to Hammond's.

25. Cheney, *James Madison*, 255.

26. Pierce Butler to Madison, June 12, 17, 24, 26, 1795, in PJM-CS, 16:14–16, 23–25; Jefferson to Madison, July 13, 1795, in PJM-CS, 16:37.

27. Madison to Livingston, August 10, 1795, in PJM-CS, 16:47 ("foreign," "his"); Madison to Jefferson, June 14, 1795, in PJM-CS, 16:19–20.

28. Sharp, *American Politics*, 118; Reardon, *Edmund Randolph*, 296; Freeman, *Washington*, 666.

29. Madison to Monroe, December 20, 1795, in PJM-CS, 16:168; Freeman, *Washington*, 666; Pierre-Auguste Adet to the Committee on Public Safety, July 6, 1795, in CFM, 744–745; Waldstreicher, *Midst of Perpetual Fetes*, 138 ("best").

30. Freeman, *Washington*, 666–667.

31. Reardon, *Edmund Randolph*, 139; Feldman, *Three Lives*, 28, 94–95; Chervinsky, *Cabinet*, 67–75.

32. Reardon, *Edmund Randolph*, 121150.

33. Reardon, *Edmund Randolph*, 150; Jefferson to Madison, August 11, 1793, in PJM-CS, 15:57 ("poorest"); George Nicholas to Madison, February 9, 1794, in PJM-CS, 15:256 ("I").

34. Freeman, *Washington*, 667–668; Randolph, *Vindication*, 29–32.

35. Randolph, *Vindication*, 31–32; "Sixth and Arch Streets, Philadelphia, May 1794–October 1796," *Buildings of the Department of State, Office of the Historian*, https://history.state.gov/departmenthistory/buildings/section16 (accessed June 22, 2021).

36. Randolph, *Vindication*, 31–32.

37. Hammond to Grenville, July 27, 1795, FO 5/9, NA-UK; Randolph to Washington, July 27, 1795, in PGW-PS, 18:436–437; Randolph to Washington, July 31, 1795, in PGW-PS, 18:486.

38. Hammond to Grenville, July 27, 1795, FO 5/9, NA-UK ("take").

39. Hammond to Grenville, July 27, 1795, FO 5/9, NA-UK ("character").

40. Chervinsky, *Cabinet*, 271–272, 276, 291–292; Madison to Monroe, December 20, 1795, in PJM-CS, 16:168; Gibbs, *Memoirs*, 1:232.

41. Grenville to Hammond, November 20, 1795, in Mayo, *Instructions to the British Ministers*, 71–72, 75.

42. Gibbs, *Memoirs*, 1:232.

43. Conway, *Omitted Chapters*, 298–299.

44. Grenville to Hammond, May 9 and June 5, 1795 ("well disposed"), in Mayo, *Instructions to the British Ministers*, 83, 85.

45. Fauchet to Commissioner of Foreign Relations, October 31, 1794, in CFM, 444 ("precieuses"); Brant, "Edmund Randolph," 193; *Dictionnaire de l'Académie Françoise*, 1:286.

46. Brant, "Edmund Randolph," 187.

47. Number 6 suggested that Randolph wanted the French government to advance money to a few unnamed individuals who could help prove British involvement in the Whiskey Rebellion. The merchants needed "sufficient funds" to shield them from "English persecution." Fauchet and Randolph each gave plausible but not unassailable explanations about the request (Fauchet to commissioner of foreign relations, September 5, 1794, in CFM, 411–418; Brant, "Edmund Randolph," 187). Fauchet to commissioner of foreign relations, October 31, 1794, in CFM, 451 ("Mr.").

48. Brant, "Edmund Randolph," 183n5.

49. Brant, "Edmund Randolph," 194n17; Randolph, *Vindication*, 51–52; Brant makes a strong case that Hammond possessed Number 6, but he presents weak evidence for his claim that Hammond would have shared it with Wolcott and Pickering. Hammond had no incentive to share potentially exculpatory material with Wolcott, who, however great his enmity with Randolph, might have felt duty-bound to share it with Washington. Wolcott and Pickering likely told the truth when they claimed not to possess Number 6.

50. Gibbs, *Memoirs*, 232–233; Oliver Wolcott to Alexander Hamilton, November 16, 1795, in Gibbs, *Memoirs*, 265 ("French").

51. Washington to Randolph, August 20, 1795 in PGW-PS, 18:571–572; Gibbs, *Memoirs*, 233; Clarfield, *Timothy Pickering and the American Republic*, 164, 216; Wills, *Negro President*, 20–21; Reardon, *Edmund Randolph*, 306–307; Pickering and Upham, *Life of Timothy Pickering*, 3:217; Brant, "Edmund Randolph," 193–195.

52. Timothy Pickering to George Washington, July 31, 1795, in PGW-PS, 18:481 ("special"); Reardon, *Edmund Randolph*, 461n15; Pickering and Upham, *Life of Timothy Pickering*, 3:217.

53. Pickering and Upham, *Life of Timothy Pickering*, 3:217 ("what").

54. Pickering and Upham, *Life of Timothy Pickering*, 3:217–218 ("that").

55. Pickering and Upham, *Life of Timothy Pickering*, 3:217–218. Pickering wrote his account in 1826. Records closer to the period in question corroborate many of the details he provides, and his reconstruction of the events is incredibly lucid, though not perfect, in many respects. But in 1795 and thereafter, Wolcott claimed to have delivered the dispatch and its translation to Washington that evening, rather than Pickering. Irving Brant views the contradiction as evidence that Pickering's account is "fanciful," while others, such as the editors of the *Papers of Alexander Hamilton*, conclude that Wolcott and Pickering both likely visited Washington that night (Brant, "Edmund Randolph," 185n7; Alexander Hamilton to Oliver Wolcott, July 30, 1795, in PAH, 18:528n1).

56. Smith, *American Honor*, 175; Clarfield, *Timothy Pickering and the American Republic*, 159.

57. Reardon, *Edmund Randolph*, 461n16; Washington to Randolph, July 22, 1795, in PGW-PS, 18:403–404.

58. Randolph, *Vindication*, 54 ("unutterable"); Pickering and Upham, *Life of Timothy Pickering*, 3:218; Garry Wills defends Pickering's actions in this episode by claiming that Pickering had no need to persuade Washington to sign the treaty, because the president had already decided to sign it (Wills, *Negro President*, 34). That argument ignores Washington's apparent determination to *wait* to sign it until he resolved the provisions order issue, a determination that the best evidence suggests was shaken due to his new distrust of Randolph. While Pickering and Wolcott may not have intentionally twisted facts to oust Randolph, they hardly operated in good faith. Wills also curiously cites a source that he claims argues that Washington cared *less* about Randolph's position on the Jay Treaty than his revelations to Fauchet of inter-cabinet disputes, something his cited source does not argue (*Negro President*, 34 and 240n4).

59. Pickering and Upham, *Life of Timothy Pickering*, 3:218 ("I").

60. Freeman, *George Washington*, 7:290n117 ("clear").

61. Randolph, *Vindication*, 1.

62. Randolph, *Vindication*, 1 ("Mr.").

63. Randolph, *Vindication*, 6–7; Wolcott to John Marshall, June 9, 1806, in Gibbs, *Memoirs*, 245.

64. Randolph, *Vindication*, 7 ("would"); Chervinsky, *Cabinet*, 296.

65. Randolph, *Vindication*, 56 ("Mr.").

66. Pierce Butler to Madison, August 21, 1795, in PJM-CS, 16:54 ("vile").

67. Fauchet to commissioner of foreign relations, October 31, 1794, in CFM, 452; Randolph, *Vindication*, 54–55; Lowe, "Political Thought," 1–13; Freeman, *Affairs of Honor*.

68. Fauchet to commissioner of foreign relations, October 31, 1794, in CFM, 451 ("whom").

69. George Washington to Alexander Hamilton, August 3, 1795, in PAH, 19:85–86; Madison to Henry Tazewell, September 25, 1795, in PJM-CS, 16:94 ("collision"); John Beckley, September 10, 1795 in PJM-CS, 16:85; Robert R. Livingston to Madison, November 16, 1795, in PJM-CS, 16:126 ("any").

70. Edmund Randolph to Madison, November 1, 1795, in PJM-CS, 16:117; Madison to Jefferson, November 8, 1795, in PJM-CS, 16:121 ("malice").

71. Randolph, *Vindication*; Madison to Monroe, January 26, 1796, in PJM-CS, 16:204 ("his"); Elkins and McKitrick, *Age of Federalism*, 426; Bonsteel Tachau, "George Washington," 34.

72. Cobbett, *A New-Year's Gift*; Madison to Jefferson, January 10, 1796, in PJM-CS, 16:182 ("sufficient," "satirical"); *American Mercury*, July 10, 1797 ("May").

73. Madison to Monroe, December 20, 1795, in PJM-CS, 16:169; Cobbett, *A New-Year's Gift*, 42, 43 ("proof"); Edmund Randolph to Madison, November 1, 1795, in PJM-CS, 16:117 ("president").

74. Madison to Jefferson, February 7, 1796, in PJM-CS, 16:215 ("official"); "Notes of a Conversation with George Washington," August 6, 1793, in PTJ-MS, 26:628; Madison to Jefferson, September 2, 1793, in PJM-CS, 15:94.

75. Jefferson to Madison, September 24, 1795, in PJM-CS, 16:89.

76.   "Draft of the Petition to the General Assembly of the Commonwealth of Virginia," ca. September 1795, in PJM-CS, 16:70 ("ostensible"); "The Defence No. 1," July 22, 1795, in PAH, 18:479–480.

77.   Estes, "Art of Presidential Leadership," 127; Joseph Jones to Madison, October 29, 1795, in PJM-CS, 16:114 ("violent").

78.   Madison to Jefferson, February 29, 1796, in PJM-CS, 16:238 ("very").

79.   Leibiger, *Founding Friendship*, 205–206.

80.   Leibiger, *Founding Friendship*, 206–207.

81.   Leibiger, *Founding Friendship*, 209–210 ("stronger"), 259n30;

82.   Feldman, *Three Lives*, 406.

83.   "Farewell Address," September 19, 1796, in PGW-PS, 20:714 ("against"); Leibiger, *Founding Friendship*, 211–212.

84.   Leibiger, *Founding Friendship*, 209–213, esp. 213 ("snares").

85.   Washington to William Heath, May 20, 1797, in PGW-RS, 1:149 ("advocate").

86.   Washington to Gouverneur Morris, December 22, 1795, in PGW-PS, 19:281 ("peace," "factious"); Washington to Marquis de Lafayette, December 25, 1798, in PGW-RS, 3:283–284 ("it").

87.   John Adams to Abigail Adams, December 20, 1796, in AP; Furstenberg, *When the United States Spoke French*, 343 ("sojourn").

88.   John Adams to Abigail Adams, December 20, 1796, in AP ("bitter"); Conlin, "American Mission," 491; Furstenberg, *When the United States Spoke French*, 346–348; Mary Stead Pinckney to Alice DeLancey Izard, December 18–19, 1796, in PREPS; Randolph, *Vindication*, 9–11.

89.   Furstenberg, *When the United States Spoke French*, 350–353; Johnson, *Diplomacy in Black and White*, 51; Charles-Maurice de Talleyrand, "Essay on Fauchet's dispatch," [ca. August–September 1795], Alexander Hamilton Papers, DLC; Earl, "Talleyrand in America," 296; Mary Stead Pinkneey to Alice DeLancey Izard, December 18–19, 1796, in PREPS; Stinchcombe, "Talleyrand and the American Negotiations," 577–578; "Friday 5 May [1797]," in DGM.

90.   Furstenberg, *When the United States Spoke French*, 349; Madison to Jefferson, May 1, 1796, in PJM-CS, 16:343; DeConde, *Entangling Alliance*, 446.

Chapter 6

1.   Collot, *Voyage dans L'Amérique Septentrionale*, 2:35–39; James McHenry to Governor St. Clair, May 1796, in Smith, *The St. Clair Papers*, 2:395–396; Cruzat, "General Collot's Reconnoitering Trip," 304; The dugout canoe was large enough to fit at least eight men (Collot, *Voyage dans L'Amérique Septentrionale*, 2:6).

2.   James McHenry to Governor St. Clair, May 1796, in Smith, *The St. Clair Papers*, 2:395–396; Collot, *Voyage dans L'Amérique Septentrionale*, 2:35–39.

3.   Collot, *Voyage dans L'Amérique Septentrionale*, 2:35–39.

4.   Collot, *Voyage dans L'Amérique Septentrionale*, 2:35–39; The casse-tête was sometimes conflated with the tomahawk, but the English translation of

Collot's writings, which Collot oversaw, rendered the word "club" in this portion (Collot, *Journey in North America*, iii).

5. Collot, *Voyage dans L'Amérique Septentrionale*, 2:35–39.

6. Collot, *Voyage dans L'Amérique Septentrionale*, 2:35–39.

7. Collot, *Voyage dans L'Amérique Septentrionale*, 2:35–39, 54 ("true").

8. Bemis, *Pinckney's Treaty*, 226–279; Kuethe and Andrien, *Spanish Atlantic World*, 343; Johnson, *Diplomacy in Black and White*, 51; Kyte, "Spy on the Western Waters," 430; Echeverria, "General Collot's Plan," 512–514.

9. Pierre-Auguste Adet to Minister of Foreign Relations, June 21, 1796, in CFM, 929; Narrett, *Adventurism and Empire*, 234–235; Echeverria, "General Collot's Plan," 514–515.

10. Pierre-Auguste Adet to the Committee on Public Safety, July 6 and 26, 1795, in CFM, 744–745, 756.

11. Pierre-Auguste Adet to Minister of Foreign Relations, June 21, 1796, in CFM, 930 ("deprive"); Echeverria, "General Collot's Plan," 517 ("try").

12. Madison to Monroe, September 29, 1796, in PJM-CS, 16:404 ("his"); Madison to Monroe, February 26, 1796, in PJM-CS, 16:232–233.

13. Jefferson to Madison, December 17, 1796, in PJM-CS, 16:431; Malone, *Jefferson and the Ordeal of Liberty*, 274–275. One Jefferson biographer has claimed on weak evidence that Jefferson wanted to be president more than he let on (Meacham, *Thomas Jefferson*, 301). As Jefferson's closest confidant, though, Madison worried that Jefferson would refuse the candidacy to stay at Monticello. Jefferson's protests about the position seem to have been sincere.

14. "Rethinking the Electoral College Debate," 2527–2529.

15. Madison to Monroe, September 29, 1796, in PJM-CS, 16:404; Madison to Monroe, May 14, 1796, in PJM-CS, 16:358; Madison to Jefferson, December 5, 1796, in PJM-CS, 16:422; Ackerman and Fontana, "Jefferson Counts Himself into the Presidency," 563.

16. Conlin, "American Mission," 509.

17. Conlin, "American Mission," 490–491; DeConde, *Entangling Alliance*, 424; Koekkoek, *Citizenship Experiment*, 129; CFM, 728n2.

18. Adet to Committee of Public Safety, July 3, 1795, in CFM, 742 ("any"); Hamilton to Oliver Wolcott, June 26, 1795, in PAH, 18:390–392n2; Henry Tazewell to Jefferson, July 1, 1795 in PTJ-MS, 28:399–400n; Conlin, "American Mission," 495.

19. "Relations with France," PAH, 19:527; Adet to Minister of Foreign Relations, March 24, 1796, in CFM, 881–882; Madison to Monroe, May 14, 1796, in PJM-CS, 16:358 ("Adet").

20. "Projet d'instructions pour le Citoyen Mangourit—Chargé d'affaires de la Republique près les Etats Unis," August 6, 1796, in CFM, 937.

21. Adet to Minister of Foreign Relations, June 9, 1796, in CFM, 921 ("men"); Adet to Minister of Foreign Relations, September 24, 1796, in CFM, 948 ("abandon," "they").

22. Adet to Minister of Foreign Relations, September 24, 1796, in CFM, 948.

23. Adet to Minister of Foreign Relations, November 22, 1796, in CFM, 972; Malone, *Jefferson and the Ordeal of Liberty*, 286; *Aurora General Advertiser*, October 31, 1796; Adet to Minister of Foreign Relations, September 24, 1796, in CFM, 948. The French decree proclaimed that they would treat neutral vessels in the same manner the neutral nation suffered its vessels to be treated by Britain. For the United States, that practically meant seizure of US vessels carrying wartime contraband to Britain.

24. Conlin, "American Mission," 507–508 ("let"); Malone, *Jefferson and the Ordeal of Liberty*, 286–287.

25. Conlin, "American Mission," 509 (strokes); Malone, *Jefferson and the Ordeal of Liberty*, 287–288; for Pennsylvania returns, see "Pennsylvania 1796 Electoral College," *A New Nation Votes: American Election Returns 1787–1825*, https://elections.lib.tufts.edu/catalog/cv43nz221 (accessed September 8, 2021).

26. Abigail Adams to John Quincy Adams, November 11, 1796, in AP ("arts"); Gannon, "Escaping," 416 ("than"); Conlin, "American Mission," 509 ("sooner"); John Adams to John Quincy Adams, November 11, 1796, in AP ("thrown"); Chauncey Goodrich to Oliver Wolcott, Sr., December 17, 1796, in Gibbs, *Memoirs*, 413.

27. Madison to Jefferson, December 5, 1796, in PJM-CS, 16:422 ("Adet's," "electioneering").

28. Madison to James Madison Sr., December 25, 1796, in PJM-CS, 16:436 ("Mr. Adams").

29. "Inaugural Address of John Adams," March 4, 1797, at *The Avalon Project: Documents in Law, History, and Diplomacy*, https://avalon.law.yale.edu/18th_century/adams.asp (accessed February 3, 2022).

30. Collot, *Voyage dans L'Amérique Septentrionale*, 2:129–131, 158–163, esp. 129 (surrounded); Baron de Carondelet to Manuel de Godoy, November 1, 1796, with enclosures and November 11, 1796, Legajo 3900, AHN; Marquis de Casa Yrujo to Manuel de Godoy, January 16, 1797, Estado, Legajo 3896bis, AHN.

31. Baron de Carondelet to Manuel de Godoy, November 1 and 11, 1796 ("demolish"), Legajo 3900, AHN; Collot, *Voyage dans L'Amérique Septentrionale*, 157–168 ("sworn").

32. Collot, *Voyage dans L'Amérique Septentrionale*, 88–89; CFM, 990–991nA.

33. Narrett, *Adventurism and Empire*, 238; Clarfield, *Timothy Pickering and American Diplomacy*, 120–121. Evidence suggests Blount may have once looked to France and Genet for the same purposes, supporting Genet's mission to invade and seize Spanish territory (Campbell, "French Intrigue," 787).

34. Clarfield, *Timothy Pickering and American Diplomacy*, 131–132; Narrett, *Adventurism and Empire*, 237–240.

35. Collot, *Voyage dans L'Amérique Septentrionale*, 2:162–165.

36. Wharton, *Social Life*, xiii; Kyte, "Spy on the Western Waters," 440; Adet to Minister of Foreign Relations, February 24, 1797, in CFM, 990–992 and

990–991nA; Victor Collot to Carlos Martínez de Yrujo, March 1, 9 and April 15, 1797, in Turner, "Documents on the Blount Conspiracy," 577–582, 585–587; Collot, *Voyage dans L'Amérique Septentrionale*, 2:87.

37.   Clarfield, *Timothy Pickering and American Diplomacy*, 124–125.

38.   Joseph Philippe Letombe to Charles-François Delacroix, July 18, 1797, in CFM, 1050; Campbell, "French Intrigue," 789; *Annals of Congress*, Senate, 5th. Cong., 2d. Sess., 2349–2350.

39.   Clarfield, *Timothy Pickering and American Diplomacy*, 132–133; Robert Liston to Lord Grenville, July 8, 1797, in Turner, "Documents on the Blount Conspiracy," 593.

40.   "Signora Catoni" [Sarah McKean] to Dolley Madison, August 3, 1797, in PJM-CS, 17:38 ("behaving"); Benjamin Bache, "To Aristides, Mr. Fenno, or any of their friends," *Aurora General Advertiser*, August 22, 1797 ("collusive").

41.   *Gazette of the United States*, July 15 and 17, 1797; Clarfield, *Timothy Pickering and American Diplomacy*, 136–138; "Signora Catoni" [Sarah McKean] to Dolley Madison, August 3, 1797, in PJM-CS, 17:38 ("some").

42.   "Notes on a Conversation with John Adams and George Washington," [after October 1797], in PTJ-MS, 29:551–553.

43.   "Notes on Conversations with John Adams and George Washington" [after October 1797], in PTJ-MS, 29:551–553; John Adams to Abigail Adams, January 14, 1797, in AP.

44.   "Notes of a Conversation with George Washington," August 6, 1793, in PTJ-MS, 26:628; Madison to Jefferson, September 2, 1793, in PJM-CS, 15:94; Ammon, *James Monroe*, 112–114; "Notes on a Conversation with John Adams and George Washington" [after October 1797], in PTJ-MS, 29:551–553; Berkin, *Sovereign People*, 164.

45.   John Dawson to Madison, August 13, 1797, in PJM-CS, 17:42; John Dawson to Madison, September 7, 1797, in PJM-CS, 17:44; Madison to Jefferson, December 25, 1797, in PJM-CS, 17:63 ("Liston's").

46.   Madison to Jefferson, February 12, 1798, in PJM-CS, 17:78 ("misdemeanours"); Elkins and McKitrick, *Age of Federalism*, 643–655.

47.   Paul, *Without Precedent*, 108–109.

48.   Paul, *Without Precedent*, 117, 125–126; Smith, *John Marshall*, 200; Berkin, *Sovereign People*, 172.

49.   Paul, *Without Precedent*, 125–126; Stinchcombe, "Talleyrand and the American Negotiations," 584; "Paris Journal," October 18–19, in PJM; Stinchcombe, "Talleyrand and the American Negotiations," 575–590.

50.   "Paris Journal," October 18–19, in PJM.

51.   Berkin, *Sovereign People*, 173–185; Elkins and McKitrick, *Age of Federalism*, 571–578.

52.   Berkin, *Sovereign People*, 188–193.

53.   Berkin, *Sovereign People*, 191–192; Madison to Jefferson, April 15, 1798, in PJM-CS, 17:113 ("more"); Madison to Jefferson, April 22, 1798, in PJM-CS, 17:118; Madison to Jefferson, April 29, 1798, in PJM-CS, 17:122 ("libel").

Unaware that the negotiations had failed completely, Madison worried that the publication would harm them, but he was upset about the publication regardless of the status of the negotiations.

54. Abigail Adams to Mary Smith Cranch, April 13, 1798, and n4, in AP ("common," "we").

55. Stinchcombe, "Talleyrand and the American Negotiations," 582–583; even Adet, who mourned Jefferson's defeat, conceded that France might not always be able to count on the Virginian. "Jefferson loves us because he hates Britain," he assessed, more fairly than Jefferson's political rivals. The new vice president might turn on France if it ever became more dangerous than its enemy (Adet to Minister of Foreign Relations, December 15 and 31, 1796, in CFM, 978, 983 ["Jefferson"]) and 983nA.

56. Madison to Jefferson, April 15, 1798, in PJM-CS, 17:113 ("depravity," "unparalleled"); Berkin, *Sovereign People*, 172–173.

57. Deconde, *Quasi-war*; Fehlings, "America's First Limited War," 101–143; Henry Tazewell to Madison, July 12, 1798, in PJM-CS, 17:164n4. Fehlings's title is a misnomer for the Quasi-War, as the nation had fought other undeclared, limited wars against Native nations before the Quasi-War.

58. Moreau, *Voyage aux Etats-Unis de l'Amérique*, 256–257; Niemcewicz, *Under Their Vine*, 33.

59. Furstenberg, *When the United States Spoke French*, 355–359, 373–374 ("only"); Madison to Edmund Pendleton, October 15, 1782, in PJM-CS, 5:198n14; Gouverneur Morris diary, Sunday, April 28, 1799, in DGM ("rash"); Moreau spelled Flamand with the variant "Flamin" in his account, certainly the same person listed both as "James Flaming" and "James Flamand" in the 1797 and 1798 Philadelphia directories, respectively, and referenced as "Flamand" in writing by Létombe (Philippe de Létombe to Jefferson, February 28, 1801, in PTJ-MS, 33:96–99); For one example of the likelihood of Volney's acquaintance with Kościuszko, see Jefferson to Volney, March 17, 1801, in PTJ-MS, 341–342nn describing a small dinner in March 1798 attended by Volney and Kościuszko's close Polish friend and boarding companion Julian Niemcewicz. Some Federalists assumed Kościuszko was in league with Volney ("Communications," *Gazette of the United States* (Philadelphia, PA), November 6, 1798).

60. "Communications," *Gazette of the United States* (Philadelphia, PA), November 6, 1798.

61. Moreau, *Voyage aux Etats-Unis de l'Amérique*, 256–257; Haiman, *Kosciuszko*, 83; Storozynkski, *Peasant Prince*, 1–19, 207–210, 219; *Federal Gazette*, September 11, 1797; Ferreiro, *Brothers at Arms*, 124–126, 158–159; Pula, "Mr. Jefferson's Secret Agent," 7; *Herald*, August 2, 1797; Evans, *Memoir of Thaddeus Kosciuszko*, 45.

62. Niemcewicz, *Under Their Vine*, 19; Moreau, *Voyage aux Etats-Unis de l'Amérique*, 256–257; Haiman, *Kosciuszko*, 83; *Philadelphia Gazette, and Universal Daily Advertiser*, August 19, 1797; *Federal Gazette*, April 8, 1797; *Bee* (New London, CT), September 6, 1797.

63. Storozynkski, *Peasant Prince*, 239, 328n1; Haiman, *Kościuszko*, 83; Pawlickiego, *Pamiętniki Józefa Drzewieckiego*, 152 ("unwitting"); Fiszerowa, *Pamiętnik o Kościuszce*, 9–10; Alexander, "Jefferson and Kosciuszko," 91–92.

64. Philippe Joseph Létombe to Charles François Delacroix, August 20, 1797, in CFM, 1068–1069 ("only"); Sokol and Kissane, *Polish Biographical Dictionary*, 200–201; Storozynkski, *Peasant Prince*, 234.

65. Jefferson to Tadeusz Kosciuszko, June 18, 1798, in PTJ-MS, 30:416.

66. Pawlickiego, *Pamiętniki Józefa Drzewieckiego*, 152.

67. Pula, "Mr. Jefferson's Secret Agent," 15–16.

68. Jefferson to Tadeusz Kościuszko, May 30, 1798, in PTJ-MS, 30:376–377; Kusielewicz and Krzyzanowski, "Julian Ursyn Niemcewicz's American Diary," 95–96; Storozynkski, *Peasant Prince*, 236–238; Haiman, *Kosciuszko*, 79–80.

69. Jefferson to Julian Ursin Niemcewicz, June 1, 1798, in PTJ-MS, 30:383; Julian Ursin Niemcewicz to Jefferson, May 27, 1798, in PTJ-MS, 30:369–372 ("overwhelmed"); Niemcewicz, *Under Their Vine*, 66–67, 84–85.

70. Niemcewicz, *Under Their Vine*, 212; Julian Ursin Niemcewicz to Jefferson, September 3, 1798, in PTJ-MS, 30:506–508; *Aurora General Advertiser*, August 25, 1798.

71. Haiman, *Kosciuszko*, 83; *Gazette nationale ou le Moniteur universel*, July 8, 1798 ("lived").

72. Haiman, *Kosciuszko*, 83; "Communications," *Gazette of the United States*, November 6, 1798 (quotations).

73. Niemcewicz, *Under Their Vine*, 56–58 ("madness," "volley").

74. Niemcewicz, *Under Their Vine*, 58 ("we").

75. Niemcewicz, *Under Their Vine*, 58 ("your").

76. "Certificate for George Logan," June 4, 1798, in PTJ-MS, 30, 386–387; "Communication," *Gazette of the United States*, June 18, 1798; *Porcupine's Gazette*, June 18, 1798; Jefferson to Madison, June 21, 1798, in PJM-CS, 17:155 ("extravagance").

77. "Communications," *Gazette of the United States*, November 6, 1798; Fehlings, "Storm on the Constitution," 72–73; *Porcupine's Gazette*, November 8, 1798 ("mutilated"); Philadelphiensis, "Reflections on a late publication by Doctor Logan," *Gazette of the United States*, January 8, 1799 ("hired"); *South-Carolina State-Gazette*, February 23, 1799.

78. Pula, "Mr. Jefferson's Secret Agent," 19–24; Haiman, *Kosciuszko*, 85–86; Nathaniel Cutting to Thomas Jefferson, August 27, 1798, in PTJ-MS, 30:499; Berkin, *Sovereign People*, 198.

79. Berkin, *Sovereign People*, 194–197; Tolles, "Unofficial Ambassador," 22–23 ("why").

80. Berkin, *Sovereign People*, 194–198; Tolles, "Unofficial Ambassador," 22–23.

81. Madison to Jefferson, June 10, 1798, in PJM-CS, 17:150 ("tragicomedy"); Madison to Jefferson, ca. February 18, 1798, in PJM-CS, 17:82; John Adams to Abigail Adams, January 14, 1797, in AP ("political").

82. Echeverria, "General Collot's Plan," 512, 514–515; Furstenberg, *When the United States Spoke French*, 375; *Philadelphia Gazette & Universal Daily*

Advertiser, July 3, 1797; One writer, likely the French consul at Charleston, South Carolina, Victor Marie DuPont de Nemours, tried to quiet fears about Collot's expedition and convince Americans it was harmless (*City Gazette*, April 22, 1797).

83.   Harvey, "Tools of Foreign Influence," 542; "French Influence, Still Triumphant," *Columbian Centinel* (Boston, MA), July 19, 1797; See also "French Influence Demonstrated," *Columbian Centinel* (Boston, MA), August 9, 1797.

84.   William Wilcocks, "The Contrast," *New-York Gazette & General Advertiser*, May 3, 1798.

85.   Jefferson to Madison, April 26, 1798, in PJM-CS, 17:120 ("but"); Fehlings, "Storm on the Constitution," 72–108; Kyte, "Detention of General Collot," 628–630; Madison to Jefferson, May 20, 1798, in PJM-CS, 17:134 ("monster"); Taylor, *Civil War*, 83–88; "An Act concerning Aliens," June 25, 1798, "An Act supplementary to and to amend the act, intituled 'An act to establish an uniform rule of naturalization; and to repeal the act heretofore passed on that subject,'" June 18, 1798, "An Act in addition to the act, entitled 'An act for the punishment of certain crimes against the United States,'" July 14, 1798, all in *Statutes at Large*: 1:566–569, 570–572, 596–597 ("scandalous"); Stewart, *Opposition Press*, 466.

86.   John Adams to Beriah Phipps, June 11, 1798, in AP; Freeman, "Explaining the Unexplainable," 39–41.

87.   Madison to Jefferson, May 13, 1798, in PJM-CS, 17:130 ("management," "perhaps"); Rule of Representation in the First Branch of the Legislature," June 29, 1787, in PJM-CS, 10:87 ("means").

88.   Henry Tazewell to Jefferson, July 5, 1798, in PTJ-MS, 30:442 ("he"); "Virginia Resolutions: Editorial Note," PJM-CS, 17:186.

89.   "Virginia Resolutions: Editorial Note," PJM-CS, 17:186–187; Madison to Jefferson, April 29, 1798, in PJM-CS, 17:122–123; Jefferson to Madison, November 17, 1798, in PJM-CS, 17:175; Madison to Monroe, December 11, 1798, in PJM-CS, 17:184; Ketcham, *James Madison*, 395.

90.   Ketcham, *James Madison*, 395; Cheney, *James Madison*, 276.

91.   Ketcham, *James Madison*, 396 ("void"); Jefferson to Madison, November 17, 1798, in PJM-CS, 17:175; Feldman, *Three Lives*, 417–420; Nicholas P. Trist Memoranda, September 27, 1834 in Farrand, *Records of the Federal Convention*, 3:533–534.

92.   Feldman, *Three Lives*, 419–420; "Virginia Resolutions," December 21, 1798, in PJM-CS, 17:189 ("warm," "interpose"); Ketcham, *James Madison*, 396–397; Cheney, *James Madison*, 277.

93.   "Virginia Resolutions," December 21, 1798, in PJM-CS, 17:189 ("palpable," "criminal").

94.   Madison to Jefferson, January 12, 1799, in PJM-CS, 17:206–207;

95.   "Foreign Influence," January 23, 1799, in PJM-CS, 17:216–217.

96.   "Foreign Influence," January 23, 1799, in PJM-CS, 17:216–218, esp. 216 ("Great," "misery").

97. "Foreign Influence," January 23, 1799, in PJM-CS, 17:219 ("foreign"); Pasley, *Tyranny of Printers*, 105–106, 126.

98. "Foreign Influence," January 23, 1799, in PJM-CS, 17:219 ("foreign," "tainted"); Potter, "William Cobbett in North America," 4–28.

99. "Political Reflections," February 23, 1799, in PJM-CS, 17:237–242.

100. Jefferson to Philip Mazzei, April 24, 1796, in PTJ-MS, 29:82 ("harlot"); Marraro, "Four Versions," 22–23 ("subserviency," "more").

101. Furstenberg, *When the United States Spoke French*, 375 ("Collot"); Kyte, "Detention of General Collot," 630; Smith, "Enforcement," 93.

102. Smith, "Enforcement," 86; Pasley, *Tyranny of Printers*, 125, 129; Stewart, *Opposition Press*, 467–472.

Chapter 7

1. Edward Thornton to Madison, March 17, 1802, in PJM-SS, 3:43 ("passion"); Jefferson to Madison, August 13, 1801, in PJM-SS, 2:41 ("heroine"); "Chess," *Thomas Jefferson Encyclopedia*, https://www.monticello.org/site/research-and-collections/chess (accessed October 8, 2021); Jefferson to Madison, August 13, 1801, in PJM-SS, 2:41 ("heroine"); Gordon-Reed and Onuf, *Most Blessed*, 98–99; Anna Payne to Dolley Madison, May 1804, in Cutts, *Memoirs and Letters*, 39–40; Jefferson to Madison, August 13, 1801, in PJM-SS, 2:41. Jefferson's description of Payne as a "chess heroine" reveals his respect for her talents.

2. Bird, "Reassessing," 519–551; Hamilton to Theodore Sedgwick, February 2, 1799 in PAH, 22:452 ("conspiracy"); Jefferson to Madison, August 23, 1799, in PJM-CS, 17:258; Jefferson to Wilson Cary Nicholas, September 5, 1799, in PTJ-MS, 31:179.

3. Jefferson to Wilson Cary Nicholas, September 5, 1799, in PTJ-MS, 31:179; "Report of 1800: Editorial Note," in PJM-CS, 17:304.

4. Jefferson to Madison, January 16, 1799, in PJM-CS, 17:210 ("sin"); Cheney, *James Madison*, 282. It is unknown when Dolley arrived. George Watson listed a charge on January 22 for "3 Days Bord for Self and Lady," the only time the account for board specified Dolley, suggesting she may have arrived as late as January 19. Another line item lists "2 Dinners for Ladys" on December 10, though it is unclear what that means (Account with George Watson, January 23, 1800, in PJM-CS, 17:358–359).

5. "The Report of 1800: Editorial Note," in PJM-CS, 17:304–305; Madison to Jefferson, December 29, 1799, in PJM-CS, 17:297.

6. "The Report of 1800: Editorial Note," in PJM-CS, 17:306–350, esp. 316 ("pave"); Read, *Power versus Liberty*, 25–30.

7. "The Report of 1800: Editorial Note," in PJM-CS, 17:327–329, 342.

8. "The Report of 1800: Editorial Note," in PJM-CS, 17:327–329, 336–337 ("people"), 342.

9. Charles Pinckney to Madison, May 16, 1799, in PJM-CS, 17:250–251.

10. "The Election of 1800," in PJM-CS, 17:415–416; Madison to Jefferson, January 18, 1800, in PJM-CS, 17:357; Brant, *James Madison*, 4:13–14.

11. Ketcham, *James Madison*, 403–404.
12. Waldstreicher, *Slavery's Constitution*, 57–105; Wilentz, *No Property in Man*, 61–62.
13. Klarman, *Framers' Coup*, 270–272; George Hammond, "A brief Sketch of the actual General Politicks of this Country as referring to its Internal Concerns," 1793, in Wilson, *Friendly Relations*, 10; Jean-Baptiste Petry to le Maréchal de Castries Charleston, November 16, 1787, in DHRC; Amar, "Some Thoughts on the Electoral College," 470; Waldstreicher, *Slavery's Constitution*, 89; Wilentz, *No Property*, 70–71; Wills, *Negro President*, 11; "Method of Appointing the Executive," July 19, 1787, in PJM-CS, 10:107–108; "Method of Appointing the Executive," July 25, 1787, in PJM-CS, 10:116–117. For a refutation of his own earlier arguments about the centrality of slavery to the creation of the Electoral College, see Wilentz's preface to the paperback edition, *No Property*, x, 70. In an illuminating essay, Michael L. Rosin shows that the absence of the Three-Fifths clause would not have inherently prevented Jefferson's election as president in 1800 as some have concluded (Rosin, "Three-Fifths Rule," 159–227). That does not change the fact, however, that the presence of the Three-Fifths clause did facilitate his election as the electoral system stood in 1800.
14. Bradburn, "Clamor," 566–567; *Report of 1800*, PJM-CS, 17:306.
15. Chervinsky, "Political Practices," 227; Cheney, *James Madison*, 278–279 ("regal"), 287; Peskin, "Conspiratorial Anglophobia," 652–653; Sharp, *American Politics*, 210–213.
16. Alexander Hamilton to John Adams, August 1, 1800, in PAH, 25:51, 52n2 ("English"); Narrett, *Adventurism and Empire*, 249–251; Lycan, "Hamilton's Florida Policy," 153–155.
17. Jefferson to Madison, March 4, 1800, in PJM-CS, 17:369; Isenberg, *Fallen Founder*, 1, 129–130, 138–141.
18. Baker, "Attack," 558–559; Freeman, *Affairs of Honor*, 227–228.
19. Murphy, "Very Convenient Instrument," 233–266.
20. John Dawson to Madison, May 4, 1800, in PJM-CS, 17:386; John Nicholas to Madison, November 28, 1800, in PJM-CS, 17:439–440, 441n2; Baker, "Attack," 559; Madison to Monroe, ca. October 21, 1800, in PJM-CS, 17:426.
21. Ketcham, *James Madison*, 405.
22. Gouverneur Morris diary, February 11, 1801, in DGM; Dickey, *Empire of Mud*, 1–25; Feldman, *Three Lives*, 444; Ketcham, *James Madison*, 408.
23. *Journal of the Senate*, 6th Cong. 2nd Sess., 124–125; Bushong, *Glenn Brown's History*, 95–101; Meacham, *Thomas Jefferson*, 348.
24. *Journal of the Senate*, 6th Cong. 2nd Sess., 124–125.
25. *Journal of the Senate*, 6th Cong. 2nd Sess., 124–125, 799; Ferling, *Adams vs. Jefferson*, 142–143.
26. Jefferson to Madison, December 19, 1800, in PJM-CS, 17:444; *Daily Advertiser*, February 9, 1801; *Philadelphia Gazette & Daily Advertiser*, January 30, 1801; *Gazette of the United States*, January 12, 1801; "On the Election of the President," *National Intelligencer*, January 7, 1801; *Impartial Register*, January

5, 1801; John Adams to Elbridge Gerry, February 7, 1801, in Adams, *Works of John Adams*, 9:97–98.

27. John Beckley to Jefferson, February 27, 1801, in PTJ-MS, 33:84 ("tempestuous"); John Adams to Joseph Ward, February 4, 1801, in Adams, *Works of John Adams*, 9:97 ("clouds"); John Adams to Elbridge Gerry, February 7, 1801, in Adams, *Works of John Adams*, 9:98 ("tempestuous sea"); Jefferson to Madison, December 19, 1800, in PJM-CS, 17:444 ("storms").

28. Tench Coxe to Jefferson, January 10, 1801, in PTJ-MS, 32:425 ("unfriendly"); Tench Coxe, *Strictures upon the letter imputed to Mr. Jefferson, addressed to Mr. Mazzei* (June 1800), 6 ("English"); Peskin, "Conspiratorial Anglophobia," 652–653; *Aurora General Advertiser*, July 24, 1799 ("secret").

29. *Federal Gazette*, February 16, 1801 ("Septemberize").

30. Jefferson to Madison, February 18, 1801, in PJM-CS, 17:467 ("certainty"); Abigail Adams to Thomas Boylston Adams, February 14, 1801, in AP; John Dawson to Madison, February 12, 1801, in PJM-CS, 17:465 ("I"); Elizabeth Smith Shaw Peabody to Abigail Adams, December 15, 1800, in *The Adams Papers Digital Edition* ("heaven").

31. *Washington Federalist*, February 6, 1801 ("Burr," "foreign"); John Marshall to Edward Carrington, December 28, 1800, in PJM ("undue").

32. Hamilton to Gouverneur Morris, December 24, 1800," in PAH, 25:272 ("listen,"); Hamilton to James Ross, December 29, 1800 in PAH, 25:281 ("no"); Jefferson to Madison, February 18, 1801, in PJM-CS, 17:467 ("zealous").

33. Baker, "Attack," 553–598; Freeman, *Affairs of Honor*, 247–248; Ketcham, *James Madison*, 405.

34. Gouverneur Morris diary, February 13, 1801, in DGM ("still"); Abigail Adams to John Adams, February 13, 1801, *Adams Papers Digital Edition*; *Journal of the House*, February 13, 1801, 6th Cong. 2nd Sess., 803; Abigail Adams to Thomas Boylston Adams, February 14, 1801, in *Adams Papers Digital Edition* ("Game").

35. Baker, "Attack," 555n2; Freeman, *Affairs of Honor*, 200; Jefferson to John Dickinson, March 6, 1801, in PTJ-MS, 33:196 ("storm").

36. Monroe to Jefferson, March 3, 1801, in PTJ-MS, 33:127 ("desperate").

37. *Times; and District of Columbia Daily Advertiser*, November 29, 1800; Sloan and McKean, *Great Decision*, 90; Smith, *First Forty Years*, 10; *Federal Gazette*, November 28, 1800; Meacham, *Thomas Jefferson*, 357.

38. "First Inaugural Address," March 4, 1801, in PTJ-MS, 33:134.

39. "First Inaugural Address," March 4, 1801, in PTJ-MS, 33:150 ("honest");

40. Mikaberidze, *Napoleonic Wars*, xii, 105–107; Elkins and McKitrick, *Age of Federalism*, 677–678.

41. Elkins and McKitrick, *Age of Federalism*, 680 ("rejoiced"); Cogliano, *Emperor of Liberty*, 4 ("cold-blooded").

42. Sharp, *American Politics*, 210–213; Elkins and McKitrick, *Age of Federalism*, 662–690; Mikaberidze, *Napoleonic Wars*, 115–118.

43. Elkins and McKitrick, *Age of Federalism*, 680–681, 687; Rohrs, "Federalist Party," 246.

44. Elkins and McKitrick, *Age of Federalism*, 687; Rohrs, "Federalist Party," 252–253.

45. "First Inaugural Address," March 4, 1801, in PTJ-MS, 33:149–150 ("we," "exterminating").

46. Leralta, *Madrid*, 2:157; World Heritage Convention, UNESCO, "Aranjuez Cultural Landscape," https://whc.unesco.org/uploads/nominations/1044. pdf (accessed July 5, 2022); Domingo de Aguirre, *Topografía del Real Sitio de Aranjuez*.

47. Lucien Bonaparte to Charles Maurice de Talleyrand, March 21, 1801 (30 Ventôse l'an IX), Espagne, AAE; "Convenio original celebrado con Francia para la cesión del Ducado de Parma, fechado en Aranjuez el 21 de marzo de 1801," Tratados internacionales suscritos por España, AHN; Bush, *Louisiana Purchase*, 33; Mikaberidze, *Napoleonic Wars*, 130–131.

48. Mikaberidze, *Napoleonic Wars*, 130–136; Dubois, *Avengers*.

49. Dubois, *Avengers*, 225, 304; Mikaberidze, *Napoleonic Wars*, 130–136; Johnson, *Diplomacy in Black and White*; Brown, *Toussaint's Clause*, 138; Girard, "Leclerc Expedition," https://doi.org/10.1093/acrefore/9780199366 439.013.743 (accessed February 9, 2022).

50. Weber, *Spanish Frontier*, 212; Pietri, *Lucien Bonaparte*, 153, 159; Cogliano, *Emperor of Liberty*, 185–186; DeConde, *Quasi-War*, 256; Jacobs, *Rogue Diplomats*, 81–82; Barbé-Marbois, *Histoire de la Louisiane*, 188–189; Elkins and McKitrick, *Age of Federalism*, 662–663. Though it bore the official date of September 30, 1800, the provisional Treaty of Mortefontaine, which ended the Quasi-War, was signed at 2:00 A.M. on October 1, 1800, the same day the preliminary Treaty of San Ildefonso was signed between Spain and France; Carnot, *Reply*, 46 ("which").

51. David Humphreys to Madison, March 23, 1801, in PJM-SS, 1:36 ("affords"); "Convenio original celebrado con Francia para la cesión del Ducado de Parma," March 21, 1801, Tratados internacionales suscritos por España, AHN. Earlier that spring, rumors maintained that the cession of Louisiana would come in exchange for conferring the kingship of Etruria on the *infante* Duke of Parma (Rufus King to Madison, March 29, 1801, in PJM-SS, 1:55).

52. Madison to Jefferson, February 28, 1801, in PJM-CS, 17:475; "Madison and the Hiatus at the State Department," March 4–May 2, 1801, in PJM-SS, 1:1–2.

53. Feldman, *Three Lives*, 445–446; Cheney, *James Madison*, 306–307; Smith, *First Forty Years*, 29.

54. Madison to William Thornton, April 24, 1801, in PJM-SS, 1:112–113; Feldman, *Three Lives*, 444–446; Burke, *Homes of the Department of State*, 29–31; "Estimate for the Service of the Year 1806," December 10, 1805, in PJM-SS, 10:645.

55. Ketcham, *James Madison*, 409–410; "First Inaugural Address," March 4, 1801, in PTJ-MS, 33:134; Feldman, *Three Lives*, 447; Smith, *First Forty Years*, 29.

56. Ketcham, *James Madison*, 425; Lewis, "Strongest Government," 222–224; "First Inaugural Address," March 4, 1801, in PTJ-MS, 33:149 ("I").

57. Jefferson to Pierre Samuel Du Pont de Nemours, April 25, 1802 in PTJ-MS, 37:333 ("embryo").

58. Madison to Alexander Hamilton, May 26, 1801, in PJM-SS, 1:228–229 and 29n2; Alexander Hamilton to Harrison Gray Otis, January 26, 1799, in PAH, 22:440–441.

59. Madison to Monroe, June 1, 1801, in PJM-SS, 1:245; Madison to Robert Livingston and Monroe, March 2, 1803, in PJM-SS, 4:366; Madison to Charles Pinckney, June 9, 1801, in PJM-SS, 1:275–276, 279n4; Madison to Wilson Cary Nicholas, July 10, 1801 in PJM-SS, 1:394.

60. Madison to Rufus King, July 24, 1801, in PJM-SS, 1:470; Madison to Wilson Cary Nicholas, July 10, 1801, in PJM-SS, 1:394; Madison to Robert R. Livingston, July 11, 1801, in PJM-SS, 1:402–404.

61. Ketcham, *James Madison*, 415; Jefferson to Pierre Samuel Du Pont de Nemours, May 5, 1802, in PTJ-MS, 37:418 ("it").

62. Madison to Robert R. Livingston, July 11, 1801, in PJM-SS, 1:402–404; Bowman, "Pichon," 263 ("austere"); Louis-André Pichon to Charles-Maurice de Talleyrand, July 22, 1801, 53:169–172, AAE ("daily"); Ketcham, *James Madison*, 415.

63. Louis-André Pichon to Charles-Maurice de Talleyrand, July 22, 1801, 53:172, AAE ("all").

64. Louis-André Pichon to Charles-Maurice de Talleyrand, July 22, 1801, 53:173, AAE ("some").

65. Madison to Robert R. Livingston, September 28, 1801, in PJM-SS, 2:144.

66. Robert R. Livingston to Madison, March 14, 1802, in PJM-SS, 3:26 ("fact"); Elkins and McKitrick, *Age of Federalism*, 680; Dangerfield, *Chancellor*, 314–315, 324; Robert R. Livingston to Madison, February 26, 1802, in PJM-SS, 2:493; Napoleon Bonaparte to Charles-Maurice de Talleyrand, July 4, 1802, in Lentz, *Napoléon Bonaparte: Correspondance générale*, 3:1017 (document 6992) ("first").

67. Dangerfield, *Chancellor*, 320; Robert R. Livingston to Madison, December 31, 1801, in PJM-SS, 2:359 ("it," "Jacobin").

68. Robert R. Livingston to Madison, December 31, 1801, in PJM-SS, 2:359n2; Robert R. Livingston to Madison, January 13, 1802, in PJM-SS, 2:389; Robert R. Livingston to Madison, March 14, 1802, in PJM-SS, 3:26; Robert R. Livingston to Madison, March 22, 1802, in PJM-SS, 3:61.

69. Mikaberidze, *Napoleonic Wars*, 133–136.

70. Robert R. Livingston to Madison, December 31, 1801, in PJM-SS, 2:360nn1–2; Ketcham, *James Madison*, 416.

71. Öhman, "Mississippi Question," 48; Cogliano, *Emperor of Liberty*, 191; Madison to Rufus King, January 29, 1803, in PJM-SS, 4:290–291.

72. Robert R. Livingston to Madison, November 10, 1802, in PJM-SS, 4:110–111 ("attempt"); Robert R. Livingston to Madison, January 24, 1803, in PJM-SS, 4:278; Monroe to Madison, March 7, 1803, in PJM-SS, 4:396

("opportunity"); Daniel Clark to Madison, April 27, 1803, in PJM-SS, 4:553 ("measure").

73. Jefferson to Madison, March 22, 1803, in PJM-SS, 4:444; Toulmin to Madison, April 5, 1803, in PJM-SS, 4:478 ("crack'd"), 480n3; Seitzinger, "Conducting Foreign Relations," 3.

74. Madison to Robert R. Livingston and Monroe, March 2, 1803, in PJM-SS, 4:366 ("separate"); Taylor, *American Republics*, 69–70 ("French").

75. *City Gazette*, June 24, 1802 ("hostilities," "acts"); Madison to Robert R. Livingston and Monroe, March 2, 1803, in PJM-SS, 4:366–367.

76. *American Citizen*, April 1, 1802; *New-York Herald*, April 3, 1802; *Columbian Centinel*, January 1, 1803.

77. Theriault, "Party Politics during the Louisiana Purchase," 302–303; *Spectator*, March 12, 1803 ("timid"); "Preface," PJM-SS, 4:xxviii; *Connecticut Courant*, March 9, 1803 ("must"); *Columbian Centinel*, March 12, 1803 ("made"); *Columbian Centinel*, March 16, 1803; *Morning Chronicle*, December 15, 1802; Mikaberidze, *Napoleonic Wars*, 140–141; Robert R. Livingston to Madison, November 14, 1802, in PJM-SS, 4:121; Christopher Gore to Madison, October 20, 1802, in PJM-SS, 4:33, 34n1.

78. Brown, *Address to the Government*, 43–44 ("their"), 49, 55–56; Cole, "Brockden Brown," 254, 256.

79. *Chronicle Express*, January 13, 1803; Madison to Robert R. Livingston and Monroe, April 18, 1803, in PJM-SS, 4:528–530; Madison to Robert R. Livingston, March 16, 1802, in PJM-SS, 3:38; Brant, *James Madison*, 4:128–129.

80. Monroe to Madison, March 7, 1803, in PJM-SS, 4:396.

81. Barbé-Marbois, *Histoire de la Louisiane*, 285, 286–287 ("I," "they"), 297; Brant, *James Madison*, 4:124–125.

82. Mikaberidze, *Napoleonic Wars*, 134–135, 139, 140–144.

83. Mikaberidze, *Napoleonic Wars*, 135; Gleijeses, *America's Road to Empire*, 58 ("three"); Jacobs, *Rogue Diplomats*, 99 ("laugh"); Dangerfield, *Chancellor*, 369–370.

84. Mikaberidze, *Napoleonic Wars*, 148–157; Brant, *James Madison*, 4:124–125.

85. Barbé-Marbois, *Histoire de la Louisiane*, 287, 297–298; Brant, *James Madison*, 4:124–125; Jacobs, *Rogue Diplomats*, 102–103.

86. Barbé-Marbois, *Histoire de la Louisiane*, 297–300 ("time"); Roberts, *Napoleon*, 282, 470–471.

87. Jacobs, *Rogue Diplomats*, 104–109, esp. 109 ("most"); Robert R. Livingston to Madison, April 11, 1803, in PJM-SS, 4:500–502; Robert R. Livingston to JM, April 13, 1803, in PJM-SS, 4:511–515.

88. Dangerfield, *Chancellor*, 362–369; Jacobs, *Rogue Diplomats*, 108; "Memorandum of the Negotiations for the Cession of Louisiana," May 1, 1803, in PJMon.

89. "Memorandum of the Negotiations for the Cession of Louisiana," May 1, 1803, in PJMon; Gouverneur Morris diary, September 14, 1789, DGM; Landon, *Annales du Musée*, 5–7; *St. George's Chronicle, and Grenada Gazette*,

May 5, 1810; Theodore Child, "The Story of the Paris Salon, 1673–1884," *Frank Leslie's Popular Monthly* 23 (January to June 1887), 108–111; St. John, *Louvre*, 304; Johnson, *Napoleon*, 40–41, 87–88.

90. *Encyclopædia Britannica*, 17:81; Rowell, *Paris*, 1–2 ("Paris"); Monroe to Madison, May 14, 1803, in PJM-SS, 4:614 ("great").

91. Gordon-Reed, *Hemingses of Monticello*, 12.

92. Taylor, *American Republics*, 1.

93. For the conversation, see "Memorandum of the Negotiations for the Cession of Louisiana," May 1, 1803, in PJMon.

94. Barbé-Marbois, *Histoire de la Louisiane*, 300 ("perhaps," "confederations," "present").

95. Madison to Monroe, May 1, 1803, in PJM-SS, 4:563 ("admiration"); Madison to Monroe and Livingston, July 29, 1803, in PJM-SS, 5:238.

96. Lewis, *Problem of Neighborhood*, 24–26; Onuf, *Jefferson's Empire*, 118–119; Kastor, *Nation's Crucible*, 39–40; Mikaberidze, *Napoleonic Wars*, 137; Monroe to Madison, May 14, 1803, in PJM-SS, 4:610; Jefferson to Joseph Priestley, January 29, 1804, in PTJ-MS, 42:368; Brant, *James Madison*, 4:116 ("very"). Robert Livingston had negotiated for land west of the Mississippi and above the Arkansas River prior to France's offer of the entire colony, but Madison did not include that region of Louisiana in the instructions he sent with Monroe (Livingston to Madison, April 17, 1803, in PJM-SS, 4:525; Madison to Livingston and Monroe, July 29, 1803, in PJM-SS, 5:238–239). Madison and Jefferson both affirmed to French associates that they believed that rapid migration west of the Mississippi at that time would harm the United States (Brant, *James Madison*, 4:116–117, 133–134; Jefferson to Pierre Samuel Du Pont de Nemours, in PTJ, 37:418). There is little reason to question their sincerity. Monroe wrote a defensive letter to Madison, explaining his decision to exceed his instructions and purchase the entire territory. He suggested that the land could be held vacant indefinitely, suggesting that he knew Madison and Jefferson's concerns were real (Monroe to Madison, May 14, 1803, in PTJ-MS, 418). Madison rejoiced in the Louisiana Purchase less because of the land it acquired than because it kept the French off the continent without risking liberty by raising an army, was cheaper than a war to secure New Orleans, would keep the nation from fraying in the West, and gave the United States "exclusive jurisdiction of the Mississippi," which averted "much perplexity and collision" (Madison to Monroe, July 30, 1803, in PJM-SS, 5:248).

97. Kastor, *Nation's Crucible*, 42; Heidenreich, "U.S. National Security and Party Politics," 370–371; Jefferson to Monroe, November 24, 1801, in PTJ-MS, 35:719; Jefferson to Pierre Samuel Du Pont de Nemours, May 5, 1802 in PTJ-MS, 37:418; Taylor, *American Republics*, 70–71; Jefferson to Livingston, April 18, 1802, in PTJ-MS, 37:264 ("our"); Jefferson to Nicholson, May 13, 1803, in PTJ-MS, 40:371 ("foreign").

98. Cogliano, *Emperor of Liberty*, 172–173; Ketcham, *James Madison*, 422; Jefferson to Thomas Mann Randolph, July 5, 1803, in PTJ-MS, 40:661 ("removes").

99. Madison to Monroe, July 30, 1803, in PJM-SS, 5:248; Jefferson to George W. Erving, July 10, 1803, in PTJ-MS, 40:712 ("coup").
100. Theriault, "Party Politics during the Louisiana Purchase," 308–310; Heidenreich, "U.S. National Security and Party Politics," 382–385 ("mean," "I," "exultation").
101. Gannon, "Escaping," 422–424; Thierault, "Party Politics during the Louisiana Purchase," 310–311; "Review of Mr. Jefferson's Administration," *Columbian Centinel*, September 29, 1804.
102. "To Thomas Paine, Esquire," *Hive*, August 7, 1804; "Party Names," *Portsmouth Oracle*, September 15, 1804; Gannon, "Escaping," 424–426 ("four").
103. Jefferson to George W. Erving, July 10, 1803, in PTJ-MS, 40:711 ("this"); Thomas Paine to Jefferson, August 2, 1803, in PTJ-MS, 41:139n ("who"); Jefferson to John Breckenridge, November 24, 1803, in PTJ-MS, 42:37 ("bloody").
104. Gannon, "Escaping," 425–441, esp. 441 ("cease").

Chapter 8

1. *Aurora General Advertiser*, September 21, 1804.
2. "Enclosure: Statement Regarding a Conversation with Carlos Martínez de Irujo," in PTJ-MS, 44:357–358 ("exchanged").
3. "Enclosure: Statement Regarding a Conversation with Carlos Martínez de Irujo," in PTJ-MS, 44:357–358.
4. "Enclosure: Statement Regarding a Conversation with Carlos Martínez de Irujo," in PTJ-MS, 44:357–358.
5. Robinson, *Philadelphia Directory, 1805*; *Gazette of the United States*, May 8, 1802; *Poulson's American Daily Advertiser*, July 8, 1803; Sarah (Sally) McKean Maria Theresa Martínez de Yrujo to Dolley Madison, May 11, 1804, in PDM; Jozé Rademaker to Antônio de Araujo de Azevedo, March 16, 1806, Rademaker letterbook, Livro 411, MNE ("very"); Sarah (Sally) McKean Maria Theresa Martínez de Yrujo to Dolley Madison, September 3, [1796?], in PDM.
6. Beerman, "Spanish Envoy to the United States," 447; Brant, *James Madison*, 4:323; Yrujo to Pedro Cevallos, January 25, 1804, Estado, legajo 3892bis., AHN ("by," "state," "public"); Yrujo to Cevallos, May 5, 1804, Estado, legajo 3892bis., AHN ("intrigues").
7. Enclosure: Statement Regarding a Conversation with Carlos Martínez de Irujo," in PTJ-MS, 44:358 ("accosted," "you"); Ward, "Jackson, William."
8. Yrujo to Madison, September 4 and 27, 1803, in PJM-SS, 5:378, 464; Stagg, *Borderlines*, 42; Kastor, *Nation's Crucible*, 42; Daniel Clark to Madison, December 3, 1803, in PJM-SS, 6:139, 139n5; Charles Pinckney to Madison, December 12, 1803, in PJM-SS, 6:161–162;
9. Stagg, *Borderlines*, 42; Brant, *James Madison*, 4:141–159; McMichael, *Atlantic Loyalties*, 54–60.
10. Kastor, *Nation's Crucible*, 4–6, 41–52, 70–71; Melville, "John Carroll and Louisiana," 400–401 ("silence"); Reeder, "Lines of Separation," 287–297; "Preface," PJM-SS, 7:xxvi; McMichael, *Atlantic Loyalties*, 62–63, 67–75.

11. William C. C. Claiborne to Madison, January 19, 1805, in PJM-SS, 8:488 ("people").

12. McMichael, *Atlantic Loyalties*, 26–27, 67–70.

13. Kastor, *Nation's Crucible*, 66–70; Kessell, "To Stop Captain Merry," 127–129.

14. McMichael, *Atlantic Loyalties*, 69–70 ("great"); Madison to William C. C. Claiborne, August 28, 1804, in PJM-SS, 7: 643 ("in").

15. "An Act for laying and collecting duties on imports and tonnage within the territories ceded to the United States," February 24, 1804, *Statutes at Large*, 2:254.

16. Madison to Livingston, March 31, 1804, in PJM-SS, 6:636; Yrujo to Madison, March 7, 1804, in PJM-SS, 6:557–562, esp. 558 ("one"); Yrujo to Cevallos, August 6 and September 13, 1805, legajo 5541, AHN ("altercation"); Madison to Monroe, March 5, 1804, in PJM, 6:548 ("remonstrated"); Madison to Charles Pinckney, April 10, 1804, in PJM-SS, 7:29; Yrujo to Madison, May 10, 1804, in PJM-SS, 7:205.

17. Yrujo to Madison, March 7, 1804, in PJM-SS, 6:559; Madison to Pinckney, April 10, 1804, in PJM-SS, 7:29–30 ("insulting," "ill," "intemperance"); Madison to Yrujo, March 19, 1804, in PJM-SS, 6:604–605; Yrujo to Cevallos, May 5, 1804, Estado, Legajo 3892bis, AHN; Yrujo to Cevallos, September 13, 1805, legajo 5541, AHN; Yrujo to Madison, May 10, 1804, in PJM-SS, 7:205; Madison to Jefferson, April 24, 1804, in PJM-SS, 104; Stagg, *Borderlines*, 42.

18. Madison to Jefferson, August 28, 1804, in PJM-SS, 7:645 ("passions"); "Preface," PJM-SS, 7:xxv–xxvi; Brant, *James Madison*, 4:208–209.

19. Yrujo to Cevallos, October 29, 1804, legajo 5541, AHN ("newspapers").

20. "Enclosure: Statement Regarding a Conversation with Carlos Martínez de Irujo," in PTJ-MS, 44:358 ("you").

21. Ward, "Jackson, William"; Prince, *Federalists and the Origins of the U.S. Civil Service*, 304n13; David Jackson, Jr. to Thomas Jefferson, February 10, 1804, in PTJ-MS, 42:445; "Enclosure: Statement Regarding a Conversation with Carlos Martínez de Irujo," in PTJ-MS, 44:358 ("political," "useful"); Yrujo to Pedro Cevallos, October 29, 1804, legajo 5541, AHN.

22. "Enclosure: Statement Regarding a Conversation with Carlos Martínez de Irujo," in PTJ-MS, 44:358.

23. "Enclosure: Statement Regarding a Conversation with Carlos Martínez de Irujo," in PTJ-MS, 44:358 ("stifled," "restrained," "suppressed"); Yrujo to Pedro Cevallos, October 29, 1804, legajo 5541, AHN.

24. "Enclosure: Statement Regarding a Conversation with Carlos Martínez de Irujo," in PTJ-MS, 44:357–359.

25. Yrujo to Jefferson, September 7, 1804, in PTJ-MS, 44:356; Jefferson to Yrujo, September 15, 1804, in PTJ-MS, 44:397–398; Yrujo to Cevallos, October 29, 1804, legajo 5541, AHN; Yrujo to Cevallos, February 11, 1806, legajo 5541, AHN; Jefferson to Madison, September 25, 1804, in PJM-SS, 8:88.

26. Yrujo to Cevallos, February 11, 1806, legajo 5541, AHN; *Freeman's Journal and Philadelphia Daily Advertiser*, September 21, 1804 republished in *American Citizen*, September 25, 1804.

27. Relf's *Philadelphia Gazette* essays republished in *United States' Gazette*, September 15, 17, 19 ("aggravated," "peevish"), 1804; Brant, *James Madison*, 4:209–212, 502n15.

28. *Freeman's Journal and Philadelphia Daily Advertiser*, September 21, 1804 republished in *American Citizen*, September 25, 1804; *American Citizen*, September 19, 1804 ("Spanish"); *Aurora General Advertiser*, September 18, 1804; Tench Coxe to Madison, September 21, 1806, in PJM-SS, 8:73 ("foreign"); Wagner to Madison, September 23, 1804, in PJM-SS, 8:82–83.

29. *Freeman's Journal and Philadelphia Daily Advertiser*, September 21, 1804, republished in *American Citizen*, September 25, 1804 ("calculated"); Jacob Wagner to Madison, September 21, 1804, in PJM-SS, 8:73–74.

30. Yrujo to Cevallos, October 29, 1804, legajo 5541, AHN ("what"); *Daily Advertiser*, September 24, 1804 ("shocking"); *Republican Watch-Tower*, September 26, 1804 ("every").

31. *Washington Federalist*, September 26, 1804 ("another"); *Courier of New Hampshire*, October 3, 1804.

32. Yrujo to Cevallos, October 29, 1804, legajo 5541, AHN ("miserable," "peacefully," "world").

33. Yrujo to Madison, October 3, 1804, in PJM-SS, 8:114–119.

34. Yrujo to Madison, October 3, 1804, in PJM-SS, 8:114–119.

35. Yrujo to Madison, October 3 and 7, 1806, in PJM-SS, 8:114–119, 134; Yrujo to Cevallos, September 13, 1805, legajo 5541, AHN (quotations).

36. Madison to Monroe, October 26, 1804, in PJM-SS, 8:218-225 ("appeal").

37. Yrujo to Madison, October 3, 1804, in PJM-SS, 8:118; Yrujo to Cevallos, September 13, 1805, legajo 5541, AHN ("greatly").

38. Yrujo to Cevallos, September 13, 1805, legajo 5541, AHN ("in").

39. Madison to Monroe, October 26, 1804, in PJM-SS, 8:224; Charles Pinckney and James Monroe to Cevallos, April 13, 1805, legajo 5541, AHN; Charles Pinckney to Madison, April 8, 1804, in PJM-SS, 7:16; Seitzinger, "Conducting Foreign Relations," 3.

40. Charles Pinckney and James Monroe to Cevallos, April 13 ("whole") and 25, 1805, legajo 5541, AHN; Cevallos to Pinckney and Monroe, April 16, 1805, legajo 5541, AHN; Cevallos to Yrujo, April 18, 1805, legajo 5541, AHN; Monroe to Madison, April 16, 1805, in PJM-SS, 9:249–251; Madison to Monroe, January 30, 1807, enclosure, in PJM-SS, 13:344–363.

41. Cevallos to Yrujo, April 18 ("minister," "government"), May 11, and May 21, 1805, legajo 5541, AHN; Yrujo to Cevallos, February 11, 1806, legajo 5541, AHN; Yrujo to Cevallos, August 6, 1805, legajo 5541, AHN ("there").

42. Yrujo to Cevallos, February 11, 1806, legajo 5541, AHN; "Preface," in PJM-SS, 10:xxv; Dolley Madison to Anna Payne Cutts, June 4, 1805, in PDM; Madison to Jefferson, July 22, 1805, in PJM-SS, 10:98–99; Dolley Madison to Anna Payne Cutts, July 31, 1805, in PDM ("not"); Robinson, *Philadelphia Directory, 1805*.

43. Yrujo to Cevallos, February 11, 1806, legajo 5541, AHN ("with").

44. Madison to Alexander Dallas, November 20, 1805, in PJM-SS, 10:564.

45. Madison to Alexander Dallas, November 20, 1805, in PJM-SS, 10:564 ("continue").

46. Yrujo to Cevallos, February 11, 1806, legajo 5541, AHN ("tone").

47. Madison to Yrujo, January 15, 1806 in PJM-SS, 11:185–186; Yrujo to Cevallos, February 11, 1806, legajo 5541, AHN; Mugridge, "Augustus Foster and His Book," 349; Lucy Payne Washington Todd to Anna Payne Cutts, January 14, 1812, in PDM; Clark, *Life and Letters of Dolly Madison*, 77–78; *Historical Directory of the District of Columbia*, 57–58; Brant, *James Madison*, 4:266–268.

48. Brant, *James Madison*, 4:266–268; Dolley Madison to James Madison, November 4, 1805, in PJM-SS, 10:495; Plumer, *Plumer's Memorandum*, 205, 208 ("his"), 345 ("unfeeling"), 390 ("heart"); Lucy Payne Washington Todd to Anna Payne Cutts, January 14, 1812, in PDM; Clark, *Life and Letters of Dolly Madison*, 77–78; Dolley Madison to Anna Payne Cutts, June 4, 1805, in PDM.

49. Brant, *James Madison*, 4:266–277 ("does"); Yrujo to Cevallos, February 11, 1806, legajo 5541, AHN; Brant, *James Madison*, 4:267; Yrujo to Madison, October 7, 1804, in PJM-SS, 8:134; *Washington Federalist*, October 24, 1804; *Rutland Herald*, January 10, 1807.

50. Sloan and McKean, *Great Decision*, 90; Plumer, *Plumer's Memorandum*, 333–334; Janson, *Stranger in America*, 218 (quotations). According to some rumors, Yrujo tried to excite the Tunisian ambassador's anger against the government while they lodged together at Stelle's (*Enquirer*, April 29, 1806; Madison to William Duane, November 21, 1808, DL, DNA).

51. Plumer, *Plumer's Memorandum*, 393; John Quincy Adams to Abigail Smith Adams, January 25, 1806, Adams Papers, MHS ("usual").

52. Yrujo to Cevallos, February 11, 1806, legajo 5541, AHN; Madison to Yrujo, January 15, 1806 in PJM-SS, 11:185–186; Plumer, *Plumer's Memorandum*, 383; Yrujo to Cevallos, March 10, 1806, legajo 5541, AHN.

53. Yrujo to Madison, January 16, 1806 in PJM-SS, 11:196–198; Yrujo to Cevallos, February 11, 1806, legajo 5541, AHN ("insulting," "even").

54. *Report of 1800*, PJM-CS, 17:319 ("not").

55. Yrujo to Cevallos, August 6, 1805 ("insist") and February 11, 1806 (Yrujo's appeal to the US Constitution), both in legajo 5541, AHN.

56. Yrujo to Cevallos, March 10, 1806 ("persecuted") and September 13, 1805 ("all" and "in a country"), both in legajo 5541, AHN.

57. Yrujo to Madison, December 6, 1805, in PJM-SS, 10:621–626; Yrujo to Cevallos, February 11, 1806, legajo 5541, AHN ("open," "machinations").

58. Yrujo to Cevallos, February 11, 1806, legajo 5541, AHN ("whomever"); Yrujo to the diplomatic corps, January 21, 1806, legajo 5541, AHN.

59. Yrujo to Cevallos, February 11, 1806, legajo 5541, AHN ("infinity"); *Aurora General Advertiser*, January 29, 1806 ("in").

60. Yrujo to Cevallos, February 11, 1806, legajo 5541, AHN; *United States' Gazette*, February 6, 1806 ("we").

61. Yrujo to Louis-Marie Turreau de Garambouville, ca. January 21, 1806, legajo 5541, AHN; Yrujo to Cevallos, February 14, 1806, legajo 5541, AHN; *United*

States' Gazette, February 14, 1806. After weeks passed without seeing the correspondence in the newspapers, Yrujo likely dismissed his caution and took additional steps to prompt the publication in the *United States' Gazette*. If he did, he concealed his actions from Cevallos. By the time it was published in February 1806, Yrujo had returned to Philadelphia, home of the *United States' Gazette* (Yrujo to Cevallos, February 11, 1806, legajo 5541, AHN); *United States' Gazette*, February 14, 1806 ("golden").

62.   Plumer, *Plumer's Memorandum*, 379–380; "An Act making provision for defraying any extraordinary expenses attending the intercourse between the United States and foreign nations," February 13, 1806, *Statutes at Large*, 2:349–350; Risjord, *Jefferson's America*, 357–358; Carson, "Ground Called Quiddism," 86; Yrujo to Cevallos, February 11, 1806, legajo 5541, AHN ("guerrilla"); *Washington Federalist*, February 12, 1806.

63.   Brant, *James Madison*, 4:390–392; Risjord, *Jefferson's America*, 357–358; Egan, "United States, France, and West Florida," 229–240, esp. 234 ("l'argent").

64.   Egan, "United States, France, and West Florida," 235, 237–340.

65.   Carson, "Ground Called Quiddism," 83, 86; "Plumer, *Plumer's Memorandum*, 383 ("France"); 396 ("haste"), 409–410, 427 ("president"); Baldwin, *Life and Letters of Simeon Baldwin*, 452 ("going"). Plumer's suspicions of French spies probably included Yrujo, who was accused of acting as a "priviledged" spy for France ("Mr. Randolph's Speech," *New-York Gazette & General Advertiser*, March 25, 1806; Plumer, *Plumer's Memorandum*, 448).

66.   *Connecticut Courant*, April 30, 1806 ("national"); John Quincy Adams to John Adams, February 11, 1806, in Ford, *Writings of John Quincy Adams*, 3:134–135 ("nothing," "unqualified").

67.   John Adams to John Quincy Adams, December 23, 1805, Adams Papers, MHS ("if," "sale"); John Adams to François Adriaan Van der Kemp, April 30, 1806, John Adams Letters, Historical Society of Pennsylvania ("shoelickers"); Shaw, *Sallust*, 244, 244n201.

68.   *Repertory*, May 6, 1806 ("money"); "The House that George Built," *Commercial Advertiser*, June 27, 1806 (parody).

69.   Carson, "Ground Called Quiddism," 71–92.

70.   Carson, "Ground Called Quiddism," 83–84 ("we," "public").

71.   Carson, "Ground Called Quiddism," 77, 81, 86–87. Jefferson did submit Monroe's negative view to the Senate (Monroe to Madison, October 18, 1805, in PJM-SS, 10:441–447 and 47n; Plumer, *Plumer's Memorandum*, 380).

72.   Carson, "Ground Called Quiddism," 84 ("cunning"), 87 ("if").

73.   "Mr. Randolph's Speech," *New-York Gazette & General Advertiser*, March 25, 1806.

74.   *Diaries of John Quincy Adams*, February 15, 1806; Yrujo to Cevallos, April 14, 1806, legajo 5541, AHN; Nagel, *John Quincy Adams, 125*.

75.   *Diaries of John Quincy Adams*, February 15, 1806. Nagel, *John Quincy Adams*, 143; Mann, "Slavery exacts an impossible price," 106; Plumer, *Plumer's Memorandum, 448 ("abuse")*.

76. *Diaries of John Quincy Adams*, February 15, 1806; *Washington Federalist*, February 12, 1806; *Moore, The Madisons, 184*.
77. *Diaries of John Quincy Adams*, February 15, 1806.
78. Yrujo to Turreau, February 11, 1806, legajo 5541, AHN ("American"); *Report of 1800*, in PJM-CS, 17:336–337 ("the people"); Yrujo to Cevallos, September 13, 1805, legajo 5541, AHN ("true").
79. Yrujo to Cevallos, September 13, 1805, and October 29, 1804, legajo 5541, AHN; Yrujo to Madison, October 3, 1804, in PJM-SS, 8:118; Pedro Cevallos to Moses Young, June 2, 1806, legajo 5541, AHN.
80. *Journal of the Senate*, 9th Cong., 1st sess., 54–55; John Quincy Adams to Abigail Smith Adams, March 14, 1806, Adams Papers, MHS; *Diaries of John Quincy Adams*, February 18, 1806; *Plumer, Plumer's Memorandum*, 447–448; Jefferson to Madison, October 11, 1805, in PJM-SS, 10:421; Jefferson, cabinet meeting notes, July 19, 1806, TJP, DLC; Yrujo to Cevallos, April 14, 1806, legajo 5541, AHN.
81. Yrujo to Cevallos, March 10, 1806, legajo 5541, AHN ("notorious").
82. Miranda, *Archivo del General Miranda*, 17:283–287, esp. 284 ("pleasure"); Madison to Rufus King, December 4, 1805, in PJM-SS, 10:614–615; Francisco de Miranda to Madison, December 10, 1805, in PJM-SS, 10:646; "Account of State Department Salaries," December 31, 1806, in PJM-SS, 13:216.
83. Miranda, *Archivo del General Miranda*, 17:287;
84. Racine, *Francisco de Miranda*, 158; Iserov, "Francisco de Miranda"; Rufus King to Madison, November 25, 1806 and Benjamin Rush to Madison, December 3, 1806, in PJM-SS, 10:583–584, 613; Schakenbach, "Schemers," 267–268; Brant, *James Madison*, 4:325–326.
85. Miranda, *Archivo del General Miranda*, 17:287–288.
86. Miranda, *Archivo del General Miranda*, 17:287–289 ("private"); Madison to John Armstrong, March 15, 1806, in PJM-SS, 11:394 ("incumbent").
87. Miranda, *Archivo del General Miranda*, 17:289–290. According to one letter of Miranda's, Madison invited him to dinner to continue the conversation on December 17, and Miranda decided to attend. If he did attend, however, nothing happened worth mentioning in his journal entry for that day (17:292, 296–297).
88. Reeder, *Smugglers, Pirates, and Patriots*, 114–117.
89. Miranda, *Archivo del General Miranda*, 17:296–297 ("their"); Iserov, "Francisco de Miranda;" Schakenbach, "Schemers," 267.
90. Robertson, *Francisco de Miranda*, 369–370; Yrujo to Turreau, February 4, 1806, legajo 5541, AHN; Yrujo to Cevallos, February 11, 1806, legajo 5541, AHN; Yrujo to Cevallos, February 11, 1806, legajo 5541, AHN.
91. Yrujo to Turreau, February 4, 1806, legajo 5541, AHN.
92. Yrujo to Turreau, March 10, 1806, legajo 5541, AHN; Yrujo to Cevallos, March 10, 1806, legajo 5541, AHN; Jefferson to Madison, October 11, 1805, in PJM-SS, 10:421; Madison to Jefferson, October 16, 1805, in PJM-SS, 10:431; Jefferson, cabinet meeting notes, November 12, 1805, TJP, DLC; *National Intelligencer*, November 27, 1806; Rufus King to Madison, November 25, 1805,

in PJM-SS, 10:583–584; Madison to Rufus King, December 4, 1805 in PJM-SS, 10:614.

93. Yrujo to Turreau, February 4 and March 10, 1806, legajo 5541, AHN; "Serious Questions to Mr. Madison," *Philadelphia Gazette*, February 19, 1806, republished in *United States' Gazette*, February 20, 1806; *New-York Evening Post*, February 21, 1806; *National Aegis*, March 12, 1806. For more on Yrujo's authorship of accounts of the Madison–Miranda meetings, see Gerard Cazeaux to Talleyrand, November 1806, AAE.

94. *Enquirer*, February 28, 1806 ("every"); *Aurora General Advertiser*, February 19, 1806 ("take"); *National Intelligencer*, February 26, 1806 ("deadly"); *Republican Advocate*, March 7, 1806 ("his"). The *National Intelligencer* didn't use Yrujo's name, but strongly implied that he was the author.

95. Gerard Cazeaux to Talleyrand, November 1806, AAE.

96. Shakenbach, "Schemers," 268, 280–281; Brant, *James Madison*, 4:335–337.

97. Robertson, *Francisco de Miranda*, 373–374; Egan, "United States, France, and West Florida," 248–249.

98. Pasley, *Tyranny of Printers*, 35.

99. Madison, "Case of the Marquis de Casa Yrujo, Envoy Extraordinary and Minister Plenipotentiary of His Catholic Majesty to the United States," enclosed in Madison to James Monroe, January 30, 1807, in PJM-SS, 13:344–363; Madison to George Erving, January 20, 1807, IM. The copy of the document Madison enclosed to Erving is no longer extant.

100. Madison, "Case of the Marquis de Casa Yrujo."

101. Madison, "Case of the Marquis de Casa Yrujo."

102. Madison to Monroe, May 22, 1807, IM, vol. 6, DNA.

Chapter 9

1. Adams, *History of the United States*, 3:261–262. Despite all that has been written about the Burr conspiracy, Adams's work remains the strongest scholarship on its international and diplomatic components, with McCaleb's *Aaron Burr Conspiracy* an important work as well.

2. McCaleb, *Aaron Burr Conspiracy*, xiii–xv; Isenberg, *Fallen Founder*, 302–303.

3. For summaries of the evidentiary problems and historiographical discussion of the episode, see Lewis, *Burr Conspiracy*, 1–14. For some of the most salient works, see Isenberg, *Fallen Founder*; Melton, *Aaron Burr*; McCaleb, *Aaron Burr Conspiracy*; Newmyer, *Treason Trial*; Jenkinson, *Aaron Burr*; Todd, *True Aaron Burr*; Linklater, *Artist in Treason*; Jefferson to Joseph Priestley, January 29, 1804, in PTJ-MS, 42:368.

4. Lewis, *Burr Conspiracy*, 114.

5. *Morning Chronicle*, August 9, 1804; Anthony Merry to Lord Harrowby, August 6, 1804 (three letters), FO 5/42, NA-UK.

6. Hay, "Charles Williamson and the Burr Conspiracy," 175–177.

7. Hay, "Charles Williamson and the Burr Conspiracy," 175–185; Melton, *Aaron Burr*, 59.

8. Anthony Merry to Lord Harrowby, August 6, 1804, FO 5/42, NA-UK.

9. Meacham, *Thomas Jefferson*, 398; Merry to Lord Hawkesbury, March 13, 1804, FO 5/41, NA-UK; Isenberg, *Fallen Founder*, 590–592; Brant, *James Madison*, 4:160–176.

10. Isenberg, *Fallen Founder*, 290–292; Mohl, "Britain and the Aaron Burr Conspiracy," 391–398.

11. Isenberg, *Fallen Founder*, 280 ("known").

12. Isenberg, *Fallen Founder*, 272–279.

13. Anthony Merry to Lord Harrowby, March 29, 1805, FO 5/45, NA-UK.

14. McCaleb, *Aaron Burr Conspiracy*, 25–28, 42–47; Newmyer, *Treason Trial*, 26–27; Isenberg, *Fallen Founder*, 302.

15. McCaleb, *Aaron Burr Conspiracy*, 25–41; Isenberg, *Fallen Founder*, 292–294, 302.

16. *United States' Gazette*, July 27, 1805 ("form").

17. McCaleb, *Aaron Burr Conspiracy*, 37–41; Melton, *Aaron Burr*, 68.

18. Adams, *History of the United States*, 3:219, 233–234; Vile, *Men Who Made the Constitution*, 45–48; Isenberg, *Fallen Founder*, 282.

19. Isenberg, *Fallen Founder*, 302; Adams, *History of the United States*, 3:233–235; McCaleb, *Aaron Burr Conspiracy*, 52–54.

20. Isenberg, *Fallen Founder*, 299, 302–303; Cox, "Western Reaction," 78–79; "Report of Erick Bollmann's Communication," January 24, 1807, in PJM-SS, 13:310–317; Stewart, *American Emperor*, 118–120.

21. Adams, *History of the United States*, 3:236–239; McCaleb, *Aaron Burr Conspiracy*, 56–58; Anthony Merry to Lord Mulgrave, November 25, 1805, in PCPPAB, 2:943–944; Isenberg, *Fallen Founder*, 302. Dayton proved his good will by divulging what he knew about Jefferson and Madison's talks with Miranda. In fact, Yrujo based his newspaper attacks against Madison on Dayton's information (Adams, *History of the United States*, 3:192–194; Robertson, *Francisco de Miranda*, 366).

22. Plumer, *Plumer's Memorandum*, 436, 517; *Aurora General Advertiser*, December 27, 1806; "Report of Erick Bollmann's Communication," January 24, 1807, in PJM-SS, 13:310–317.

23. McCaleb, *Aaron Burr Conspiracy*, 57 ("Spain"); Isenberg, *Fallen Founder*, 302–303; Melton, *Aaron Burr*, 98–99; Narrett, "Geopolitics and Intrigue," 125–126.

24. Joseph Hamilton Daveiss to Thomas Jefferson, January 10, 1806, TJP, DLC; Isenberg, *Fallen Founder*, 289.

25. Linklater, *Artist in Treason*, 164–176, 199–201; Isenberg, *Fallen Founder*, 288–289.

26. Linklater, *Artist in Treason*, 206–213, 218–219; PCPPAB, 2:978.

27. Lewis, *Burr Conspiracy*, 202; Isenberg, *Fallen Founder*, 289–290; Linklater, *Artist in Treason*, 230–237.

28. Linklater, *Artist in Treason*, 214–217, 221–222, 229 ("you"), 233, 236.

29. Linklater, *Artist in Treason*, 236.

30. Smith, "Kadohadacho Indians," 180–181 ("remarkably"); Perttula, *Caddo Nation*, 39–41; Kastor, *Nation's Crucible*, 68–70; Isenberg, *Fallen Founder*, 311; Territorio del Misisipy," August 18, 1806, Estado, Legajo 5543, AHN.

31. Isenberg, *Fallen Founder*, 311; Lewis, *Burr Conspiracy*, 369–370; Newmyer, *Treason Trial*, 32.

32. PCPPAB, 2:974; Lewis, *Burr Conspiracy*, 171; Linklater, *Artist in Treason*, 245.

33. PCPPAB, 2:973–974; Linklater, *Artist in Treason*, 245–246; Melton, *Aaron Burr*, 119–121; Lewis, *Burr Conspiracy*, 170–171, 173; Isenberg, *Fallen Founder*, 312.

34. Lewis, *Burr Conspiracy*, 170, 173, 202–206. Even if Burr did not pen the letter, he almost certainly dictated it or oversaw its writing, making it his letter.

35. Melton, *Aaron Burr*, 119–120 (quotations); Lewis, *Burr Conspiracy*, 204.

36. PCPPAB, 2:976–978; Linklater, *Artist in Treason*, 248–249.

37. Lewis, *Burr Conspiracy*, 205; Isenberg, *Fallen Founder*, 312–313; Newmyer, *Treason Trial*, 31.

38. Melton, *Aaron Burr*, 123.

39. PCPPAB, 2:976–977.

40. PCPPAB, 2:977 ("deep"), 981; Melton, *Aaron Burr*, 124–125; Newmyer, *Treason Trial*, 32; Lewis, *Burr Conspiracy*, 172–173.

41. William C. C. Claiborne to Madison, November 25, 1806, in PJM-SS, 13:90; "Étienne Lemaire," *Thomas Jefferson Encyclopedia*; Chervinsky, "Thomas Jefferson's Cabinet"; "Inventory of the President's House," February 19, 1809, TJP, DLC; James Wilkinson to Thomas Jefferson, November 6, 1805, TJP, DLC.

42. "Record of Cabinet Meetings," March 5, 1806–February 25, 1809, TJP, DLC; James Wilkinson to Jefferson, October 21, 1806, Burr Conspiracy Collection, DLC ("prime").

43. PCPPAB, 2:978; "Record of Cabinet Meetings," March 5, 1806–February 25, 1809, TJP, DLC ("what"); Linklater, *Artist in Treason*, 238–239.

44. Lewis, *Burr Conspiracy*, 170, 173, 180–181; Linklater, *Artist in Treason*, 238–239; Newmyer, *Treason Trial*, 31–35, esp. 35 ("scoundrels").

45. Newmyer, *Treason Trial*, 31–33, esp. 31 ("guilt"); Lewis, *Burr Conspiracy*, 91–108.

46. "Substance of a communication made on the 23ᵈ. [24] of Janʸ. 1807 by Doctor Bollman to the President," January 24, 1807, TJP, DLC.

47. Newmyer, *Treason Trial*, 38; "Deposition of James Wilkinson," December 26, 1806, in PJM-SS, 13:196–202; "Report of Erick Bollmann's Communication," January 24, 1807, in PJM-SS, 13:310–317.

48. "Special Message to Congress on the Burr Conspiracy," January 22, 1807; Lewis, *Burr Conspiracy*, 116.

49. "Report of Erick Bollmann's Communication," January 24, 1807, in PJM-SS, 13:310–317.

50. "Substance of a communication made on the 23ᵈ. [24] of Janʸ. 1807 by Doctor Bollman to the President," January 24, 1807, TJP, DLC.

51. "Report of Erick Bollmann's Communication," January 24, 1807, in PJM-SS, 13:314 ("deadly").

52. "Report of Erick Bollmann's Communication," January 24, 1807, in PJM-SS, 13:310–317.

53. "Report of Erick Bollmann's Communication," January 24, 1807, in PJM-SS, 13:310–317.

54. Madison to George W. Erving, January 20, 1807, in PJM-SS, 13:289 ("perfidious"); Madison to Monroe, January 30, 1807, in PJM-SS, 13:343 ("entered"). As Burr's alleged conspiracy unfolded, newspapers reported on earlier Spanish intrigues, such as Gardoqui's communication with Brown, and Madison enclosed some of those reports in his correspondence with Erving and Monroe. He didn't mention his personal involvement in the talks between Brown and Gardoqui.

55. Madison to Monroe, January 30, 1807, in PJM-SS, 13:343 ("Burr").

56. Madison to Monroe, January 30, 1807, in PJM-SS, 13:343 ("pretty," "handful"); Lewis, "Strongest Government," 223 ("great"); William C. C. Claiborne to Madison, February 28, 1807, in PJM-SS, 13:457n1; Madison to Lewis Ford, March 23, 1807, in PJM-SS, 13:527.

57. Tench Coxe to Madison, ca. January 23, 1807, in PJM-SS, 13:307 ("confederated").

58. Tench Coxe to Madison, ca. January 23, 1807, in PJM-SS, 13:306–308 (quotations).

59. Tench Coxe to Madison, ca. January 11, 1807, in PJM-SS, 13:262 ("antirepublican").

60. Tench Coxe to Madison, ca. February 3–7, 1807, in PJM-SS, 13:387 ("subconfederate," "with," "your"); Tench Coxe to Madison, March 2, 1807, in PJM-SS, 13:460–461 ("they," "illegitimate," "under").

61. Lewis, Burr Conspiracy, 71–73, 76–77; Morris B. Belknap to Timo E. Danielson, October 11, 1806, enclosed in William Eaton to Madison, October 27, 1806, in PJM-SS, 12:406–407 ("fever").

62. Philadelphia Poulson's American Daily Advertiser, January 24, 1807 ("secret"); Weekly Inspector, January 31, 1807 ("leave," "trust");

63. New-York Evening Post, January 2, 1807.

64. People's Friend, January 14, 1807 ("proclamation").

65. Public Advertiser, January 16 ("open," "Liston," "plan," "hired") and February 4, 1807; James Sullivan to Thomas Jefferson, August 2, 1807, TJP, DLC ("miserable"); Bee (Hudson, NY), January 13, 1807 ("leading," "but").

66. Public Advertiser, February 5, 1807 (quotations).

67. Middlesex Gazette, February 6, 1807 (quotations).

68. Weekly Inspector, January 31, 1807. Newspapers often referred to the Marquis de Casa Yrujo simply as the "Marquis."

69. United States' Gazette, May 23, 1807 ("I"); Voltaire, Epitre à l'auteur, 2 ("if").

70. Francis Scott Key and William H. Dorsey to Madison, January 26, 1807, in PJM-SS, 13:329; Newmyer, Treason Trial, 46–49.

71. Newmyer, *Treason Trial*, 48–49; Lewis, *Burr Conspiracy*, 93 ("honor"); Paul, *Without Precedent*, 286.

72. Newmyer, *Treason Trial*, 49–51; *U.S. v. Bollman*, 24 F. Cas. 1189 (CCDC 1807), 14,622 ("instructions").

73. Paul, *Without Precedent*, 12–13, 255–258; Newmyer, *Treason Trial*, 59 ("solid"); "Preface," PJM-SS, 2:xxviii; Jefferson to William Johnson, June 12, 1823, in Pollak, "Marbury v. Madison," 5n10 ("gratuitous," "perversion").

74. Newmyer, *Treason Trial*, 58–64.

75. Madison to William Thornton, April 24, 1801, in PJM-SS, 1:113n1; Dayton to Madison, August 5, 1807, Princeton University; Lewis, *Burr Conspiracy*, 298, 148–162.

76. Dayton to Madison, August 5, 1807, Princeton University.

77. Dayton to Madison, August 5, 1807, Princeton University ("wretched"); Dayton to Jefferson, August 6, 1807, TJP, DLC; Madison to Dayton, August 18, 1807, JMP, DLC; Jefferson to Dayton, August 17, 1807, TJP, DLC; Madison to Jefferson, August 16 (two letters), 1807, TJP, DLC; Madison to Jefferson, August 19, 1807, TJP, DLC; Jefferson to Madison, August 20, 1807, JMP, DLC.

78. Newmyer, *Treason Trial*, 1, 11–12; Jefferson to George Hay, September 7, 1807, TJP, DLC ("heap"); Paul, *Without Precedent*, 287; Jefferson to William Branch Giles, April 20, 1807, TJP, DLC; Jefferson to James Bowdoin, April 2, 1807, TJP, DLC; Jefferson to Marquis de Lafayette, May 26, 1807, TJP, DLC ("federal").

79. Jefferson to George Morgan, March 26, 1807, TJP, DLC ("federalists appear"); Jefferson to James Bowdoin, April 2, 1807, TJP, DLC ("the fact"); Thomas Jefferson to William Branch Giles, April 20, 1807, TJP, DLC ("federalists too," "overturn," "rid").

80. Coxe to Madison, June 30, 1807, JMP, DLC ("main"); Taylor to Madison, July 19, 1807, JMP, DLC; Joshua Hatheway, "Federalism Unmasked," *American Citizen*, May 4, 1807; Backus, "Early Bar of Oneida County," 323–324.

81. Lewis, *Burr Conspiracy*, 372–373; *United States' Gazette*, June 26, 1807 ("for"); *New-York Evening Post*, May 14, 1807 ("yet").

82. Newmyer, *Treason Trial*, 3, 9, 68, 154–155, 169–170; John Cleves Symmes to Madison, November 19, 1807, Letters of Application and Recommendation, RG 59, DNA ("furnished"); Jefferson to George Hay, September 4, 1807, Papers on Thomas Jefferson, DLC ("become"); Jefferson to Madison, May 25, 1810, in PJM-PS, 2:357 ("twistifications").

83. Newmyer, *Treason Trial*, 158–159; *Federalist* no. 43, Rossiter, *Federalist Papers*, 269 ("new-fangled").

Chapter 10

1. Tucker and Reuter, *Injured Honor*, 1–17; Taylor, *Civil War*, 101.

2. Perkins, *Prologue to War*, 141–142.

3. Cray, "Remembering the USS Chesapeake," 453–454 ("I"); Perkins, *Prologue to War*, 142; Tucker and Reuter, *Injured Honor*, 6–9, 16; Guyatt, *Hated Cage*,

165; Reeder, *Smugglers, Pirates, and Patriots*, 193; Frykman, *Bloody Flag*, 130 ("thirteen"); Coats, "1797 Mutinies," 134 (also "thirteen").

4. Tucker and Reuter, *Injured Honor*, 6–9; Perkins, *Prologue to War*, 141–142.

5. Tucker and Reuter, *Injured Honor*, 15–16; Cray, "Remembering the USS Chesapeake," 453–454, 465; Taylor, *Civil War*, 101–102; Tracy, *Naval Chronicle*, 4:59.

6. Tucker and Reuter, *Injured Honor*, 9; Reeder, "Britain, France, and the Road to War," 140; Stagg, *War of 1812*, 28; Taylor, *Civil War*, 102–103. Guyatt; *Hated Cage*, 46–48; Madison to George Steptoe Washington, December 7, 1807, in Barnard, *Dorothy Payne, Quakeress*, 91–93.

7. Taylor, *Civil War*, 102–103, 105; Reeder, "Britain, France, and the Road to War," 140; Perkins, *Prologue to War*, 88–89; Stagg, *War of 1812*, 28–29; Guyatt, *Hated Cage*, 46–48.

8. Brant, *James Madison*, 4:381; Cheney, *James Madison*, 342; Perkins, *Prologue to War*, 144; Madison to Jefferson, June 29, 1807, TJP, DLC; Draft of a Proclamation, July 2, 1807, TJP, DLC.

9. DeWitt Clinton to Madison, April 26, 1807, in PJM-SS, 12:507n1; Perkins, *Prologue to War*, 106–108; Monroe to Madison, April 20, 1807, DD, Great Britain, vol. 12, DNA; Madison to Jefferson, June 29, 1807, TJP, DLC ("uncontrouled," "even"). Jefferson had written that Pierce's murder "remains unpunished" (Draft of a Proclamation, July 2, 1807, TJP, DLC). Madison's change added the recent finality of the decision that came from the acquittal. Jefferson scrapped any specific mention of Pierce in the final draft ("A Proclamation," *National Intelligencer*, July 3, 1807); Madison implied that Britain's failure to control its officers threatened "all the existing relations between the two nations" (Madison to Jefferson, June 29, 1807, TJP, DLC).

10. Brant, *James Madison*, 4:381–382; "A Proclamation," *National Intelligencer Extra*, July 2, 1807, in FO 5/52, NA-UK; Madison to Jefferson, June 29, 1807, TJP, DLC; Draft of a Proclamation, July 2, 1807, TJP, DLC.

11. Jay to Madison, July 4, 1807, ML, DNA.

12. Jay to Madison, July 4, 1807, ML, DNA.

13. David Erskine to George Canning, July 2, 1807, FO 5/52, NA-UK ("indignation"); Tench Coxe to Madison, July 2, 1807, JMP, DLC; *United States' Gazette*, July 22, 1807; Perkins, *Prologue to War*, 143 ("probability").

14. Sylvanus Bourne to Madison, January 18, 1807, in PJM-SS, 13:287–288; Perkins, *Prologue to War*, 78–84; Madison, *An examination of the British doctrine, which subjects to capture a neutral trade, not open in time of peace* (n.p. [1806]) and in PJM-SS, 11:36–162.

15. Stagg, *War of 1812*, 27–28; Perkins, *Prologue to War*, 105–107, 147–148; Mikaberidze, *Napoleonic Wars*, 230; Hill, *Napoleon's Troublesome Americans*, 29–30.

16. Coxe to Madison, June 30, 1807, JMP, DLC ("criminal," "discretion," "decrease"); Jay to Madison, July 4, 1807, ML, DNA.

17. Madison to Monroe, July 6, 1807, JMP, Rives Collection, DLC ("abolishing"); Hickey, "Monroe-Pinkney Treaty," 65–88; Madison to James

Monroe and William Pinkney, May 17, 1806, in PJM-SS, 11:578; Monroe and Pinkney to Madison, January 3, 1807, in PJM-SS, 13:227–245; Taylor, *Civil War*, 111.

18. Madison to Monroe, July 6, 1807, JMP, Rives Collection, DLC ("outrage").

19. Thomas Barclay to David Erskine, February 2, 1807, in Rives, *Selections*, 259–261; "Politics for Farmers no. VII," reprinted in *Salem Register*, February 26, 1807; *Aurora General Advertiser*, September 26, 1807 ("warmly," "swears").

20. *Aurora General Advertiser*, July 2, 1807 ("hostility," "wrongs"); Coxe to Madison, July 1, 1807, JMP, DLC; *Democratic Press*, July 1, 1807 ("enemies").

21. Coxe to Madison, July 1, 1807, JMP, DLC ("carry," "federalists," "negative"); Coxe to Madison, July 4, 1807, JMP, DLC.

22. James Sullivan to Jefferson, August 2, 1807, TJP, DLC ("again," "change");

23. *Repertory*, July 3 and 17, 1807; *Weekly Inspector*, July 4, 1807; Perkins, *Prologue to War*, 88–89.

24. Cray, "Remembering the USS Chesapeake," 464–465 ("colored"); Guyatt, *Hated Cage*, 55–57, esp. 56 ("mulatto"); Thomas Newton to Madison, January 13, 1807, in PJM-SS, 13:270–271.

25. Daniel Brent to Upton Bruce, July 1, 1807, DL, DNA; Daniel Brent to Madison, September 10, 1807, JMP, DLC; Tucker and Reuter, *Injured Honor*, 113–114.

26. *People's Friend*, July 1, 1807 ("he," "then").

27. John Page to Jefferson, July 12, 1807, TJP, DLC ("bent," "support"); With the "choice spirits" phrase, Page ridiculed the cipher letter line that referred to Burr's potential army as "choice spirits" (Lewis, *Burr Conspiracy*, 174).

28. Cray, "Remembering the USS Chesapeake," 453–454, 465; Taylor, *Civil War*, 101–102; Tracy, *Naval Chronicle*, 4:59–60 ("contemptuous").

29. Erskine to Madison, September 14, 1807, Notes from Foreign Legations—Great Britain, vol. 4, RG 59, DNA ("upon"); Madison to William Pinkney, October 21, 1807, Pinkney Papers, Princeton University; Brant, *James Madison*, 4:387; Madison to Jefferson, September 18, 1807, TJP, DLC. Erskine believed Ratford's true name was Thomas Wilson and that he changed it to Ratford aboard the *Chesapeake*. Actually, Ratford was his name, and he changed it to John Wilson (Tucker and Reuter, *Injured Honor*, 15).

30. Madison to Erskine, October 9, 1807, Notes to Foreign Ministers and Consuls, RG 59, DNA ("aggravated"); *National Intelligencer*, October 7, 1807; Madison to Jefferson, September 20, 1807, TJP, DLC.

31. Madison to Jefferson, September 20, 1807, TJP, DLC ("probably," "radical"); Brant, *James Madison*, 4:391.

32. Brant, *James Madison*, 4:387–388; "British Proclamation," October 16, 1807, in ASP-FR, 3:25–26; Stagg, *War of 1812*, 30.

33. Brant, *James Madison*, 4:374, 393–394; John Armstrong to Madison, September 24, 1807 and Claude Ambroise Régnier, September 18, 1807, both in DD, France, vol. 10, DNA.

34. Brant, *James Madison*, 4:393–394, 397–398; Taylor, *Civil War*, 116; Madison to Monroe, August 7, 1785, in PJM-CS, 8:334 ("retaliating," "harmony");

"Import Duties," April 25, 1789, in PJM-CS, 12:109–110; Cheney, *James Madison*, 343; Madison to Monroe and Pinkney, December 20, 1806, in PJM-SS, 13:169–170.

35. Brant, *James Madison*, 4:393–394; Ketcham, *James Madison*, 456; Draft of a message to Congress, [December 17, 1807], TJP, DLC; ASP-FR, 3:25.

36. *National Intelligencer*, December 23 ("habitual"), 25, and 28, 1807.

37. *New-York Evening Post*, December 26, 1807; Perkins, *Prologue to War*, 153–156, esp. 155.

38. Brant, *James Madison*, 4:395 ("Jefferson"); Pickering to Rufus King, January 2, 1808, in King, *Life and Correspondence of Rufus King*, 5:46 ("as only").

39. [Madison,] "Embargo," *National Intelligencer*, December 23 ("impartial") and 25 ("general"), 1807; Hill, *Napoleon's Troublesome Americans*, 37; Perkins, *Prologue to War*, 157; Taylor, *Civil War*, 117–118.

40. Samuel Taggart to John Taylor, December 22, 1807, in Haynes and Reynolds, "Letters of Samuel Taggart," 223–225, esp. 223 ("my").

41. John Armstrong to Madison, October 9 and 15, 1807, both in DD, France, vol. 10, DNA; ASP-FR, 3:25–26; Adams, *History of the United States*, 4:171–172; *American Citizen*, December 29, 1807. Between late November and mid-December, Madison received a mass of information from Britain and France, some of which Jefferson submitted to Congress before the embargo, much of which he did not. On November 30, Madison received word from Armstrong that France would extend its blockade to the United States, but Armstrong was unsure whether French warships would enforce the measure. In that letter, Armstrong mistranslated some parts of a message from a French official (Armstrong to Madison, September 24, 1807, and Claude Ambroise Régnier to Armstrong, September 18, 1807, both in DD, France, vol. 10, DNA). On December 5, Madison received duplicate dispatches (which arrived before the originals) from Monroe and Pinkney dated October 10, 1807, that related to the negotiations over a settlement of the *Chesapeake* affair (Monroe and Pinkney to Madison, October 10, 1807, DD, Great Britain, vol. 12, DNA; ASP-FR, 3:24; *American Citizen*, December 26, 1807; *New-York Gazette & General Advertiser*, December 11, 1807). On that same day, Madison received Monroe and Pinkney's dispatch of October 22, 1807, which accompanied the duplicate of October 10. The letter explained the royal proclamation of October 16, 1807, and enclosed a copy of it from a London newspaper. Jefferson submitted a newspaper copy of the proclamation with his embargo message, but he withheld the cover letter until later in March 1808 (Monroe and Pinkney to Madison, October 22, 1807, RG 46, 10B–B1, DNA). In mid-December, Madison received the October 9 and 15, 1807, dispatches from Armstrong, which Jefferson withheld from Congress, but the president submitted several enclosures from those letters (see n45). Jefferson had unofficial information about Britain's order in council of November 11 that required ships sailing for Europe to pass through Britain and pay a duty, but without official notice, Madison suggested he scrap mention of it from his message (Adams, *History of the United States*, 4:168–172). For a variety of reasons, then, Jefferson decided

to submit minimal supporting documents with his embargo message, one
that pertained to Britain and three to France, and none of them contained the
opinions of the diplomats about the measures.

42. Compare versions of the message in *American Citizen*, December 26,
1807 and ASP-FR, 3:25; *Hampshire Federalist*, January 7, 1808; Pickering
to Rufus King, January 2, 1808, in King, *Life and Correspondence of Rufus
King*, 5:46 ("contained"); Armstrong to Champagny, September 24, 1807,
and Champagny to Armstrong, October 7, 1807 ("common," "support"),
DD, France, vol. 10, DNA. The administration did eventually release the
Armstrong–Champagny correspondence (*National Intelligencer*, March 30,
1808). When it came out, critics did use it in the ways Jefferson probably
feared they would (*New-York Gazette & General Advertiser*, April 2, 1808).

43. *Connecticut Herald*, January 5, 1808; *Commercial Advertiser*, January 11, 1808;
Pickering to Rufus King, January 2, 1808, in King, *Life and Correspondence
of Rufus King*, 5:46; Samuel Taggart to John Taylor, December 22, 1807, in
Proceedings of the American Antiquarian Society 33 (1923), 224–225.

44. *New-York Evening Post*, December 22, 1807 ("of course"); *United States'
Gazette*, December 26, 1807 ("is it").

45. Pickering to Rufus King, January 2, 1808, in King, *Life and Correspondence
of Rufus King*, 5:46; *Commercial Advertiser*, January 11, 1808 ("my");
Cunningham, "Who Were the Quids?" 262–263, 263n41; Samuel Taggart to
John Taylor, December 22, 1807, in *Proceedings of the American Antiquarian
Society*, 33 (1923), 225–226; Morgan Lewis to Madison, January 9, 1808, JMP,
DLC ("sacrifice").

46. *Connecticut Herald*, January 5, 1808 and *Albany Gazette*, January 4, 1808
("letters"); *United States' Gazette*, December 26, 1807 ("what"); *New-York
Evening Post*, December 29, 1807; *Commercial Advertiser*, January 11, 1808
("perhaps"); *Political Atlas*, January 23, 1808 ("we").

47. *American Citizen*, December 29 ("disgraceful") and 30 ("throwing"), 1807,
and January 4, 1808. The *American Citizen* supported George Clinton for the
1808 presidential contest and later declared that "the external commerce of
the U. States will be annihilated" if Madison were elected (*American Citizen*,
May 30, 1808); *United States' Gazette*, December 30, 1807; *Connecticut
Herald*, January 5, 1808 ("leading"); *Repertory*, January 5, 1808; *Providence
Gazette*, January 9, 1808; *Portsmouth Oracle*, January 9, 1808.

48. Brant, *James Madison*, 4:443; Clarfield, *Timothy Pickering and the American
Republic*, 234–235; *A Letter from the Hon. Timothy Pickering . . .* Hartford,
CT, 1808; *Boston Commercial Gazette*, March 10, 1808; *Salem Gazette*, March
11, 1808 ("why"); *Enquirer*, March 29, 1808.

49. *Diaries of John Quincy Adams*, March 15, 1808; Perkins, *Prologue to War*,
158–159; John Adams to John Quincy Adams, January 17, 1808, Adams
Papers, MHS.

50. *Diaries of John Quincy Adams*, March 4, 12, 15, 1808; James Sulley to James
Madison, May 21, 1812, in PJM-PS, 4:407n1; *New-England Palladium*,
September 11, 1807.

51. *New-England Palladium*, August 21 and September 11, 1807 ("very," "drive," "Americans"); *Newburyport Gazette*, September 14, 1807; Isaac Brock to Francis Gore, September 21, 1807, in Cruikshank, "Some Unpublished Letters," 23.

52. Taylor, *Civil War*, 114–115; Bonnault, "Napoleon et le Canada," 39, 41n52.

53. Parker, "Secret Reports," 72 ("offended," "bring").

54. *Political Observatory*, December 29, 1807; *Eastern Argus* (Portland, ME), February 18, 1808; *Alexandria, Daily Advertiser*, March 3, 1808; *L'Oracle and Daily Advertiser*, March 5, 1808; *Norfolk Repository*, March 8, 1808; *Repertory*, March 8, 1808; *New-York Evening Post*, March 14, 1808; *New-England Palladium*, December 18, 1807; John Adams to John Quincy Adams, January 17, 1808, Adams Papers, MHS ("Moreau").

55. *Diaries of John Quincy Adams*, March 15, 1808; *Enquirer*, July 24, 1807; Gouverneur Morris diary, November 10, 1807 n74, in DGM; Le Hir, *French Immigrants*, 164; Arthur Campbell to Madison, July 11 and August 1807, JMP, DLC.

56. *Diaries of John Quincy Adams*, March 4 ("merely") and 12, 1807; *Annals of Congress*, Senate, 10th Cong., 2nd sess., 122–123 ("this").

57. Mayo-Bobee, "Understanding the Essex Junto," 624–625, 632–633; James Sullivan to Madison, April 12, 1808, JMP, DLC ("from"); James Sullivan to Jefferson, April 5, 1808, TJP, DLC ("deep").

58. Clarfield, *Timothy Pickering and the American Republic*, 236–237; Brant, *James Madison*, 4:416.

59. Brant, *James Madison*, 4:405–406, 415.

60. Clarfield, *Timothy Pickering and the American Republic*, 236–237 ("operate," "fewer"); Buel, *America on the Brink*, 42.

61. Jefferson to Levi Lincoln, March 23, 1808, in Washington, *Writings of Thomas Jefferson*, 5:264–265 ("effectually"); Clarfield, *Timothy Pickering and the American Republic*, 237; Brant, *James Madison*, 4:443–446, esp. 446 ("those"); ASP-FR, 3:80–220, 242–250.

62. Levi Lincoln to Jefferson, April 7, 1808, TJP, DLC ("Pickering's," "eradicate," "british").

63. *Diaries of John Quincy Adams*, March 16, 1807; John Quincy Adams to Abigail Smith Adams, April 20, 1808, in Ford, *Writings of John Quincy Adams*, 3:232–235; Adams, *A letter to the Hon. Harrison Gray Otis*.

64. Adams, *Letter*, 8 ("French emperor"), 10 ("pretences," "servitude"), 22 ("lash").

65. James Sullivan to Madison, April 12, 1808, JMP, DLC ("countenances," "letter," "endure").

66. George Prevost to John Howe, April 1808 and John Howe to George Prevost, May 5, 1808, both in Parker, "Secret Reports," 76, 77–78.

67. Sabine, *Biographical Sketches*, 1:548–550; John Howe to George Prevost, May 31, 1808, in Parker, "Secret Reports," 84 ("when").

68. John Howe to George Prevost, May 5, 1808, in Parker, "Secret Reports," 78.

69. Cotton, *Boston Directory*, 3; John Howe to George Prevost, May 5, 1808, in Parker, "Secret Reports," 77–78.

70. John Howe to George Prevost, May 5, 1808, in Parker, "Secret Reports," 78 ("great"); Cotton, *Boston Directory*, 3 ("most"), 163.

71. Reeder, *Smugglers, Pirates, and Patriots*, 133–144, esp. 144 ("what").

72. John Howe to George Prevost, May 5, 1808, in Parker, "Secret Reports," 79 ("wealth," "suffering," "you," "they," "very").

73. John Howe to George Prevost, May 5, 1808 and June 7, 1808, in Parker, "Secret Reports," 79–82, 87–88, 90–91 ("assure").

74. John Howe to George Prevost, May 5 and 31, 1808, and August 5, 1808, all in Parker, "Secret Reports," 81 ("real"), 83–85 ("readiness"), 102.

75. Some sources attribute the drawing to George Cruikshank (who would have been sixteen years old at the time), but the handwriting matches that of the father, Isaac. The artistic style is also closer to Isaac than George.

76. John Page to Thomas Jefferson, July 12, 1807, TJP, DLC; John Howe to George Prevost, June 7, 1808, in Parker, "Secret Reports," 87–88 ("manifest," "prevent").

77. Adams, "History of the United States," 4:201–203; Kelly and Lovell, "Thomas Jefferson," 153–155.

78. Perkins, *Prologue to War*, 166 ("great"); Hill, *Napoleon's Troublesome Americans*, 37, 44–45; *Mercantile Advertiser*, July 29, 1808; *Providence Gazette* (Rhode Island), August 27, 1808 ("evident").

79. John Howe to George Prevost, June 7, 1808, in Park, "Secret Reports," 87 ("nearly").

80. Ketcham, *James Madison*, 465–466; 474–475; Reeder, *Smugglers, Pirates, and Patriots*, 152; Perkins, *Prologue to War*, 226–233.

81. Ketcham, *James Madison*, 474–475; First Inaugural Address, March 4, 1809, in PJM-PS, 1:16–17 ("foreign").

82. Madison to William Pinkney, December 5, 1808, and January 3, 1809, Pinkney Papers, Princeton University ("ready"); Abigail Adams to Abigail Adams Smith, November 3, 1808, in Forbes, "Abigail Adams," 149 ("ride," "if," "the").

Chapter 11

1. Jortner, *Gods of Prophetstown*, 3–4 ("common"), 97–98; Edmunds, *Shawnee Prophet*, 28–34; Cave, *Prophets of the Great Spirit*, 63–64.

2. Edmunds, *Shawnee Prophet*, 28–29, 32–34; Jortner, *Gods of Prophetstown*, 97–98.

3. Edmunds, *Shawnee Prophet*, 34; Cozzens, *Tecumseh and the Prophet*, 155–156.

4. Johnson and Wilentz, *Kingdom of Matthias*, 6; Scully, *Religion and the Making of Nat Turner's Virginia*, 3–4; Dowd, *Spirited Resistance*, 37, 125–126; Jortner, *Gods of Prophetstown*, 4–5, 30, 110–111; Smith, *First Great Awakening*, 262; Lee, *Masters of the Middle Waters*, 131; Cave, "Delaware Prophet Neolin," 100, 109; Edmunds, *Shawnee Prophet*, 34–39; Cave, *Prophets of the Great Spirit*, 5–6, 16, 65–69.

5. Dowd, *Spirited Resistance*, xi–xiv, 131–136; Edmunds, *Shawnee Prophet*, 34–39, 92–93.

6. Jortner, *Gods of Prophetstown*, 138, 150–151; Edmunds, *Shawnee Prophet*, 60–63; Goltz, "Tecumseh," 124–125.

7. James W. Stevens to Madison, March 2, 1809, in PJM-PS, 1:6–7 ("early," "let"); Taylor, *Civil War*, 17, 136–140.

8. James W. Stevens to Madison, March 2, 1809, in PJM-PS, 1:9 ("decidedly").

9. William H. Harrison to Henry Dearborn, July 11, 1807, in Burton, *Manuscripts*, 135 ("I").

10. Whitmire, "Man and His Land," 42–45; Silver, *Our Savage Neighbors*, 227260; Burstein and Isenberg, *Madison and Jefferson*, 68–71, esp. 70 ("scalp-buyer"); Madison to Jefferson, June 2, 1780, in PJM-CS, 2:37 ("savages are making").

11. Nichols, *Red Gentlemen*, 93; Calloway, *Indian World*, 302, 323–325, 355, 484; Jortner, *Gods of Prophetstown*, 53; Constitution text cited from https://www.archives.gov/founding-docs/constitution-transcript (accessed September 15, 2022).

12. *The Federalist*, no. 38, January 12, 1788, in PJM-CS, 10:370–371 ("mine," "furnish"); Madison to George Nicholas, May 17, 1788, in PJM-CS, 11:49–50; Petition to the General Assembly of the Commonwealth of Virginia, October 12, 1795, in PJM-CS, 16:96–97 ("both"); see also Jay's Treaty, April 15, 1796, in PJM-CS, 16:316–317.

13. George Washington to John Jay, August 30, 1794, in PGW-PS, 16:614 ("all"); Calloway, *Indian World*, 444–445.

14. Calloway, *Indian World*, 444–445; Taylor, *Civil War*, 55–56; Dowd, *Spirited Resistance*, 131–132.

15. Allen, "Federalists and the West," 315–317, esp. 315 ("little"); Cayton, "Radicals in the 'Western World,'" 77–96; Calloway, *Pen and Ink Witchcraft*, 107.

16. McCoy, *Elusive Republic*, 120–122, 185–208.

17. McCoy, *Elusive Republic*, 118–123, 140–142; Madison and "Americanus," April–May 1816, PJM-PS, 10:360–364.

18. Onuf, *Jefferson's Empire*, 47–51; Calloway, *Pen and Ink Witchcraft*, 114–116; Madison to James Monroe and William Pinkney, May 30, 1806, in PJM-SS, 11:625 ("abolish"); Madison and "Americanus," April–May 1816, PJM-PS, 10:360–364.

19. Madison and "Americanus," April–May 1816, PJM-PS, 10:360–364, esp. 361 ("disinclination"); "Thomas Jefferson Second Inaugural Address," March 4, 1805, *The Avalon Project: Documents in Law, History, and Diplomacy*, https://avalon.law.yale.edu/19th_century/jefinau2.asp ("sanctimonious"); Memorandum to Thomas Jefferson, February 8, 1805, in PJM-SS, 9:21 ("blind"); Madison to Hubbard Taylor, October 11, 1791, in PJM-CS, 14:78 ("true").

20. Sadosky, *Revolutionary Negotiations*, 194–195; Onuf, *Jefferson's Empire*, 47–49; Madison to James Monroe and William Pinkney, May 30, 1806, in PJM-SS, 11:625 ("Indian"); Stanley Griswold to Madison, December 21, 1805, in PJM-SS, 10:673–674; Madison to Monroe and Pinkney, July 11, 1806, in PJM-SS, 12:101; Taylor, *Civil War*, 126. In his May 30 letter to Monroe and Pinkney, Madison described the United States as the "nation to which they [Indians]

belong," revealing Native Americans' ambiguous status as foreign sovereigns or domestic dependents.

21. Latimer, *1812*, 25; Taylor, *Civil War*, 125–126; Goltz, "Tecumseh," 109–111, 117.

22. Cave, *Prophets of the Great Spirit*, 92–95; Jortner, *Gods of Prophetstown*, 133; Dowd, *Spirited Resistance*, 143; Taylor, *Divided Ground*, 293–94.

23. Jortner, *Gods of Prophetstown*, 138 ("sacred," "fool," "not"); Edmunds, *Shawnee Prophet*, 62.

24. Edmunds, *Shawnee Prophet*, 67–70; Dowd, *Spirited Resistance*, 143; Cave, *Prophets of the Great Spirit*, 97; Jortner, *Gods of Prophetstown*, 141–153; Edmunds, *Shawnee Prophet*, 68.

25. Edmunds, *Shawnee Prophet*, 69–70; Jortner, *Gods of Prophetstown*, 141, 148–153.

26. Edmunds, *Shawnee Prophet*, 69–71 ("watch," "if"); Jortner, *Gods of Prophetstown*, 144.

27. Edmunds, *Shawnee Prophet*, 68.

28. Goltz, "Tecumseh," 109–119; Muir, *Early Political and Military History of Burford*, 1:181–182; Latimer, *1812*, 25.

29. Edmunds, *Shawnee Prophet*, 70–71.

30. Goltz, "Tecumseh," 111–113, 122–123; Edmunds, *Shawnee Prophet*, 70–71.

31. Jortner, *Gods of Prophetstown*, 151 ("I have heard"); William Henry Harrison to Henry Dearborn, September 1, 1808, in Esarey, *Governors Messages and Letters*, 1:302 ("I was not"); Edmunds, *Shawnee Prophet*, 74 ("never").

32. Thomas Kirker to Jefferson, October 8, 1807, Daniel Parker Papers, Historical Society of Pennsylvania; Jefferson to Thomas Worthington, April 24, 1808, TJP, DLC; Worthington to Jefferson, June 12, 1808, TJP, DLC; Jefferson to Henry Dearborn, August 12, 1807 ("scoundrel") and August 2, 1808 ("preference"), both in TJP, DLC; Dowd, *Spirited Resistance*, 114, 131–134; Calloway, *Pen and Ink Witchcraft*, 116.

33. First Inaugural Address, March 4, 1809, in PJM-PS, 1:17 ("carry"); Chiefs and Sachems of the Wyandot Nation to Madison, February 5, 1812, in PJM-PS, 4:165–166 ("pretence"); Latimer, *1812*, 25 ("discontent," "ascribe").

34. William Eustis to William Henry Harrison, July 15, 1809, in ASP-IA, 1:761 ("practicable").

35. Calloway, *Pen and Ink Witchcraft*, 115–116; "A Treaty between the United States of America and the tribes of Indians called the Delawares, Pattawatamies, Miamies, and Eel River Miamies," September 30, 1809, in ASP-IA, 1:761; Ratified Indian Treaty 57: Delaware, Potawatomi, Miami, and Eel River—Fort Wayne, September 30, 1809, Indian Treaties, Record Group 11 (General Records of the United States Government, DNA.; Edmunds, *Shawnee Prophet*, 80.

36. William McIntosh to Madison, September 3, 1810, in PJM-PS, 2:523.

37. John Smith to Madison, September 7, 1810, in PJM-PS, 2:533 ("Scotch"); Madison to Hobohoilthle, November 6, 1809, in PJM-PS, 2:54 ("line").

38. Madison to Hobohoilthle, November 6, 1809, in PJM-PS, 2:54 ("look"); White, *Middle Ground*, 84–85.

39. Waselkov, *Conquering Spirit*, 76–78; William Henry Harrison to William Eustis, August 6, 1811, in Esarey, *Governors Messages and Letters*, 1:544 ("held").

40. Edmunds, *Shawnee Prophet*, 81–84, 92–93; Waselkov, *Conquering Spirit*, 76–77; Mortimer, "Before Domestic Dependent Nationhood," 192.

41. Waselkov, *Conquering Spirit*, 77–79; Sadosky, *Revolutionary Negotiations*, 196; Nichols, *Red Gentlemen*, 198; Hobohoilthle to Madison, October 24, 1810, in PJM-PS, 2:592–593 ("there").

42. Cave, *Prophets of the Great Spirit*, 111–112; Edmunds, *Shawnee Prophet*, 83, 93, 96–98; Waselkov, *Conquering Spirit*, 78.

43. Harrison to William Eustis June 26, 1810 (enclosed in Eustis to Madison, July 12, 1810), in PJM-PS, 2:411 ("inspired"); Harrison to Eustis, July 4, 1810 (enclosed in John Smith to Madison, July 19, 1810), in PJM-PS, 2:428 and Esarey, *Governors Messages and Letter*, 440 ("mere"); Harrison to Eustis, July 25, 1810 (enclosed in John Smith to Madison, August 8, 1810), in PJM-PS, 2:470 ("most"); William Henry Harrison, Annual Message, November 12, 1810, in Esarey, *Governors Messages and Letters*, 1:490 ("Prophet").

44. Inhabitants of Knox County, Indiana Territory to Madison, July 31, 1811, in PJM-PS, 3:397 ("we"); *Weekly Aurora*, November 12, 1811 ("both").

45. Madison to Albert Gallatin, August 10, 1811, in PJM-PS, 3:411; Madison to Monroe, August 23, 1811, in PJM-PS, 3:427–428; Madison to Richard Cutts, August 24, 1811, in PJM-PS, 3:429 ("delightfully"); Madison to William Eustis, August 24, 1811, in PJM-PS, 3:429; Meeting of Citizens of the Indiana Territory to Madison, November 4, 1810, n.1, in PJM-PS, 3:2n1; William Eustis to Madison, August 21, 1811, in PJM-PS, 3:426–427; Jortner, *Gods of Prophetstown*, 180–183, esp. 183 ("general").

46. William Henry Harrison to William Eustis, August 7, 1811, in Esarey, *Governors Messages and Letters*, 548–551, esp. 548–549 ("time"), enclosed in Eustis to Madison, August 21, 1811, in PJM-PS, 3:426–427. Harrison claimed that the intelligence about the British came from a Potawatomi chief. Either the chief or Harrison probably misinterpreted the gifting of arms and ammunition as a call to use them, since the British continued cautious war preparations while wishing to avoid confrontation.

47. Madison to William Eustis, August 24, 1811, in PJM-PS, 3:429 ("needless"); Edmunds, *Shawnee Prophet*, 105–108; Cave, *Prophets of the Great Spirit*, 109 ("he").

48. Jortner, *Gods of Prophetstown*, 192–195; Edmunds, *Shawnee Prophet*, 106–109; William Henry Harrison to Charles Scott, December 13, 1811, in Clanin and Dorrel, *Papers of William Henry Harrison*, 5:147.

49. Edmunds, *Shawnee Prophet*, 109–112; Jortner, *Gods of Prophetstown*, 193–194; Cave, *Prophets of the Great Spirit*, 119–120.

50. Edmunds, *Shawnee Prophet*, 111–112; William Henry Harrison to Charles Scott, December 13, 1811, in Clanin and Dorrel, *Papers of William Henry Harrison*, 5:146–155; John Tipton Journal, Tippecanoe expedition, 1811, John

Tipton Papers, Rare Books and Manuscripts, Indiana State Library at https://
indianamemory.contentdm.oclc.org/digital/collection/p1819coll11/id/102
(accessed October 7, 2022).

51. William Henry Harrison to Charles Scott, December 13, 1811, in Clanin and
Dorrel, *Papers of William Henry Harrison*, 5:146–155 ("night").

52. Edmunds, *Shawnee Prophet*, 113; John Tipton Journal, Tippecanoe
expedition, 1811, John Tipton Papers, Rare Books and Manuscripts, Indiana
State Library at https://indianamemory.contentdm.oclc.org/digital/col
lection/p1819coll11/id/102 (accessed October 7, 2022); Jortner, *Gods of
Prophetstown*, 195; Feldman, *Three Lives*, 534–535.

53. Jortner, *Gods of Prophetstown*, 195; Edmunds, *Shawnee Prophet*, 113–115; Cave,
Prophets of the Great Spirit, 123–128.

54. Madison to Congress, December 18, 1811, in PJM-PS, 4:73–74 ("dauntless");
William Henry Harrison to Charles Scott, December 13, 1811, in Clanin
and Dorrel, *Papers of William Henry Harrison*, 5:146–147; Jortner, *Gods of
Prophetstown*, 191–192.

55. *Commercial Advertiser*, November 27, 1811 ("ability"); *Federal Republican*,
November 28 and December 2 ("enormous"), 1811; Monroe to Madison,
August 4, 1812, in PJM-PS, 115n3; "Indian Hostilities," *Washingtonian*,
December 30, 1811 ("Mr. Madison").

56. William Henry Harrison to Charles Scott, December 13, 1811, in Clanin
and Dorrel, *Papers of William Henry Harrison*, 5:147; Latimer, *1812*, 29
("Anglo-Savage War," "British savages"); "Indian Hostilities," *Weekly Aurora*,
December 10, 1811; *Reporter*, December 10, 1811 ("blood"); William Jones
to Madison, May 22, 1812, in PJM-PS, 4:410 ("tomahawk"); Cheney, *James
Madison*, 374; Taylor, *Internal Enemy*, 121 ("half-Indian").

57. Hill, "Savannah Riots," 499–510; Hill, *Napoleon's Troublesome Americans*,
175–176; "Indian Hostilities," *Washingtonian*, December 30, 1811 ("bloody");
"The Riot at Savannah," *Weekly Aurora*, December 10, 1811 ("lets").

58. *Rhode-Island Republican*, March 18, 1812 ("angels"); "Republican Address to
the Electors of Massachusetts," *American Advocate*, March 24, 1812; Ebenezer
Sage to Madison, February 8, 1812, in PJM-PS, 4:173 ("strike"); Peskin,
"Conspiratorial Anglophobia," 656; David Fay to Madison, February 20, 1812,
in PJM-PS, 4:211–212.

59. Ketcham, *James Madison*, 427–428, 518; Madison to Congress, June 11, 1812,
in PJM-PS, 4:470–471n1 ("subordinate").

60. Madison to Congress, June 11, 1812, in PJM-PS, 4:470–477n1.

Chapter 12

1. *Annals of Congress*, House of Representatives, 12th Cong., 1st Sess., 1220–
1224; Sullivan, *Familiar Letters*, 292; Cruikshank, *Political Adventures*, 1,
85; Soubiran to the Duke de Rovigo, February 10, 1812, in Adams, "Count
Edward de Crillon," 66.

2. *Annals of Congress*, House of Representatives, 12th Cong., 1st Sess., 1221;
Cruikshank, *Political Adventures*, 68.

3. *Annals of Congress*, House of Representatives, 12th Cong., 1st Sess., 1221–1222 ("what").

4. *Annals of Congress*, House of Representatives, 12th Cong., 1st Sess., 1221–1222; Morison, "Henry–Crillon Affair," 210; "Memoir of Soubiran," ca. 1813 and Soubiran to Henry, July 1814, both in Adams, "Count Edward de Crillon," 58 ("our"), 67.

5. Saint-Allais, *Nobiliaire Universel de France*, 10:263–264; Adams, "Count Edward de Crillon," 53; Morison, "Henry–Crillon Affair," 211–212; Cruikshank, *Political Adventures*, 145.

6. Adams, "Count Edward de Crillon," 51–69; Morison, "Henry–Crillon Affair," 211–212; Cruikshank, *Political Adventures*, 102–103.

7. *Annals of Congress*, House of Representatives, 12th Cong., 1st Sess., 1221–1222; Cruikshank, *Political Adventures*, 72, 113, 146; "Memoir of Soubiran," ca. 1813 and Soubiran to Henry, July 1814, both in Adams, "Count Edward de Crillon," 58–59, 67–69, esp. 67 ("hiding"); Saint-Allais, *Nobiliaire Universel de France*, 10:261–262; Elbridge Gerry to Madison, January 2, 1812, in PJM-PS, 4:116–117.

8. "Memoir of Soubiran," ca. 1813, in Adams, "Count Edward de Crillon," 58–59 ("loaded"); Cruikshank, *Political Adventures*, 113.

9. "Memoir of Soubiran," ca. 1813 and Sérurier to the Duke de Bassano, February 8, 1812, both in Adams, "Count Edward de Crillon," 58–61; Morison, "Henry–Crillon Affair," 215–221; Wertheimer, "Self-Abstracting Letters of War," 329.

10. "Memoir of Soubiran," ca. 1813 and Sérurier to the Duke de Bassano, February 8, 1812, both in Adams, "Count Edward de Crillon," 58 ("treasure"), 60 ("produce").

11. Cruikshank, *Political Adventures*, 1–2.

12. Cruikshank, *Political Adventures*, 5 ("Democrats"), 9 ("good," "wretched").

13. Morison, "Henry–Crillon Affair," 209–211; Cruikshank, *Political Adventures*, 18–22, esp. 22 ("will," "awake").

14. Cruikshank, *Political Adventures*, 23, 32 ("northern").

15. Herman Ryland to John Henry, January 26, 1809, in ASP-FR, 3:546; John Henry to Herman Ryland, January 31, 1809, in ASP-FR, 3:547.

16. James Craig to John Henry, February 6, 1809, in ASP-FR, 3:546 ("make").

17. John Henry to James Craig, March 7, 1809, in ASP-FR, 3:549 ("federal," "freely," "giddy," "inconsistently").

18. John Henry to James Craig, March 13, 1809, in ASP-FR, 3:550 ("revolution"); John Henry to James Craig, May 5, 1809, in ASP-FR, 3:551–552.

19. Stagg, *War of 1812*, 34–35; John Henry to James Craig, April 26, 1809, in ASP-FR, 3:551; John Henry to James Craig, May 5, 1809, in ASP-FR, 3:551–552 ("seems").

20. Stagg, *War of 1812*, 34–35; John Henry to James Craig, May 25, 1809, in ASP-FR, 3:552 ("temporary"); John Henry to James Craig, June 12, 1809, in ASP-FR, 3:552.

21. Cruikshank, *Political Adventures*, 62–65, esp. 62 ("injure"), 63 ("French"), 65.

22. Cruikshank, *Political Adventures*, 41, 66–72; "Memoir of Soubiran," ca. 1813, in Adams, "Count Edward de Crillon," 58.

23. Soubiran to Henry, July 1814, in Adams, "Count Edward de Crillon," 67; Cruikshank, *Political Adventures*, 72, 132–133, 135.

24. Prefect of the Department of the Gers to the Duke de Richelieu, March 1, 1816, and Soubiran to the Vice Grand Elector Sieyès, February 12, 1812, both in Adams, "Count Edward de Crillon," 54, 65; Léoutre, *Lectoure par la Carte Postale*, 8–10; Cruikshank, *Political Adventures*, 135 ("always"); Elbridge Gerry to Madison, January 2, 1812, in PJM-PS, 4:117n1; Puech, "Aventurier Gascon," 14–17, 21–24; *Hereford Journal*, June 17, 1812.

25. "Memoir of Soubiran," ca. 1813, in Adams, "Count Edward de Crillon," 55–60, esp. 58 ("his"); Saint-Hilaire, *L'Art de payer ses dettes*; Vause, *In the Red*, 13, 193, 294n9.

26. Prefect of the Department of the Gers to the Duke de Richelieu, March 1, 1816, and Soubiran to the Vice Grand Elector Sieyès, February 12, 1812, both in Adams, "Count Edward de Crillon," 54 ("intriguer," "Spain," "roles"), 65 ("obliged").

27. Puech, "Aventurier Gascon," 17; "Memoir of Soubiran," ca. 1813 and Sérurier to the Duke de Bassano, February 8, 1812, both in Adams, "Count Edward de Crillon," 57–58, 61.

28. "Memoir of Soubiran," ca. 1813, in Adams, "Count Edward de Crillon," 58–59, 67; *New-England Palladium*, December 24, 1811.

29. Sérurier to the Duke de Bassano, February 8, 1812, in Adams, "Count Edward de Crillon," 60–61 ("letter"); *Newburyport Herald*, April 9, 1811; Bacon-Foster, "Story of Kalorama," 106; Morison, "Henry–Crillon Affair," 212–213.

30. Sérurier to the Duke de Bassano, February 18, 1812, and Soubiran to the Duke de Rovigo, February 10, 1812, both in Adams, "Count Edward de Crillon," 61–63 ("romance"), 66 ("English"); Stagg, *War of 1812*, 38.

31. Sérurier to the Duke de Bassano, February 18, 1812, in Adams, "Count Edward de Crillon," 62–63; Elbridge Gerry to Madison, January 2, 1812, in PJM-PS, 4:116. In a subsequent letter, Gerry clarified to Madison that "Crillon" was "an entire stranger" to him (Elbridge Gerry to Madison, January 3, 1812, in PJM-PS, 4:118).

32. Morison, "Henry–Crillon Affair," 213; Cruikshank, *Political Adventures*, 77; *Annals of Congress*, House of Representatives, 12th Cong., 1st Sess., 1223; Sullivan, *Familiar Letters*, 294–295.

33. Morison, "Henry–Crillon Affair," 213; Stagg, *War of 1812*, 34–43, esp. 36 ("unhinged"); Wertheimer, "Self-Abstracting Letters of War," 316–317.

34. Sullivan, *Familiar Letters*, 295–296; "Biography," *New-York Evening Post*, March 16, 1812. As it turned out, Massachusetts held a form of popular vote for president in 1812 ("A resolve for districting the Commonwealth for the purpose of choosing electors of the President and Vice-President," October 21, 1812, DLC).

35. Morison, "Henry–Crillon Affair," 213–214; Sérurier to Duke de Bassano, February 18, 1812, in Adams, "Count Edward de Crillon," 62–63; Officer, "Dollar–Sterling Mint Parity and Exchange Rates, 1791–1834," *Journal of Economic History* 43 (September 1983), 592.

36. Sérurier to Duke de Bassano, February 18, 1812, in Adams, "Count Edward de Crillon," 62–63; Morison, "Henry–Crillon Affair," 213–214; Cruikshank, *Political Adventures*, 79–80, 135–137.

37. Sérurier to Duke de Bassano, February 18, 1812, in Adams, "Count Edward de Crillon," 62–63; *Liverpool Mercury*, June 19, 1812; *New-York Evening Post*, March 16, 1812.

38. PJM-SS, 12:xxvii; Morison, "Henry–Crillon Affair," 214–215.

39. Cruikshank, *Political Adventures*, 115–117 ("you," "make"); Morison, "Henry–Crillon Affair," 216–217.

40. Sérurier to the Duke de Bassano, February 18, 1812, in Adams, "Count Edward de Crillon," 62; Morison, "Henry–Crillon Affair," 214–216, 221–222.

41. Cruikshank, *Political Adventures*, 137 ("without"); Soubiran to Henry, July 1814, in Adams, "Count Edward de Crillon," 68.

42. Cruikshank, *Political Adventures*, 116; John Henry to James Monroe, February 20, 1812, in ASP-FR, 3:545 ("unanimity," "melt").

43. John Henry to James Monroe, February 20, 1812, in ASP-FR, 3:545; Cruikshank, *Political Adventures*, 88 ("extinguish").

44. Madison to the Senate and House of Representatives, March 9, 1812, in ASP-FR, 3:545 ("they," "intrigues").

45. Cruikshank, *Political Adventures*, 121 ("such").

46. Madison to Jefferson, March 9, 1812, and Madison to John G. Jackson, March 9, 1812, both in PJM-PS, 4:236–237 ("discovery").

47. Quincy, *Life of Josiah Quincy*, 251 ("individual"); "Private Correspondence for the Commercial Advertiser," *Commercial Advertiser*, March 16, 1812 ("Henry's"); Morison, "Henry–Crillon Affair," 222n35; Cruikshank, *Political Adventures*, 137–138; John Henry to Edward J. Coale, February 27, 1812, in *Facts Relative to John Henry and His Negotiation*; Henry Dearborn to Madison, March 21, 1812, in PJM-PS, 4:258n1.

48. "Private Correspondence for the Commercial Advertiser," *Commercial Advertiser*, March 16, 1812; Cruikshank, *Political Adventures*, 124 ("no"); Morison, "Henry–Crillon Affair," 222n35 ("I"); "Biography," *New-York Evening Post*, March 16, 1812; Quincy, *Life of Josiah Quincy*, 251 ("arts").

49. "Private Correspondence for the Commercial Advertiser," *Commercial Advertiser*, March 16, 1812; *Alexandria Gazette*, March 14, 1812; *New-York Evening Post*, March 16, 1812 ("what"); "A Whisper," *New-York Gazette & General Advertiser*, March 17, 1812; *Long-Island Star* (Brooklyn, NY), March 18, 1812 ("proof"); Quincy, *Josiah Quincy*, 251–252; "Money Obtained from the Treasury," *Poulson's American Daily Advertiser*, March 18, 1812, and June 30, 1813 ("Frenchman"). They hardly needed to overplay their hand; even the most measured censures looked bad for Madison, such as that leveled in

a pamphlet, *Facts Relative to John Henry and His Negotiation* (Washington? 1812?).

50. Albert Gallatin to Thomas Jefferson, March 10, 1812, in PTJ-RS, 4:547 ("discoveries"); Johnson, "Suspense was Hell," 253n31; Jefferson to Madison, March 26, 1812, in PJM-PS, 4:263 ("prostrates").

51. Cruikshank, *Political Adventures*, 137–138 ("obvious").

52. Morison, "Henry–Crillon Affair," 223–224; Cruikshank, *Political Adventures*, 136 ("reclaim," "punish").

53. Madison to Jonathan Dayton, March 17, 1812, in PJM-PS, 4:249–250; Jonathan Dayton to Madison, December 9, 1808, Princeton University ("if," "there"); Jonathan Dayton to Madison, May 29, 1809, in PJM-PS, 1:210 ("completely").

54. Madison to Jonathan Dayton, March 17, 1812, in PJM-PS, 4:249–250 ("moment," "British," "domestic," "their"); Jonathan Dayton to Madison, May 29, 1809, in PJM-PS, 1:211n1; Jonathan Dayton to Madison, March 21, 1812, in PJM-PS, 4:257–258.

55. Jonathan Dayton to Madison, May 29, 1809, in PJM-PS, 1:211, 211n1; Jonathan Dayton to Madison, March 21, 1812, in PJM-PS, 4:257–258.

56. Cruikshank, *Political Adventures*, 146; Lambeau, "Rapport Présenté, 3194–3196; "François-Félix-Dorothée de Balbe-Berton," *Nobiliaire Universel de France* (Paris, 1817), 10:263–264.

57. Cruikshank, *Political Adventures*, 145–146.

58. Cruikshank, *Political Adventures*, 113, 146; Soubiran to the Vice Grand Elector Sieyès, February 5, 1812 and Soubiran to the Duke de Rovigo, February 10, 1812, both in Adams, "Count Edward de Crillon," 64–66.

59. Cruikshank, *Political Adventures*, 146–147 ("undeceive").

60. Cruikshank, *Political Adventures*, 153; *Spectator*, May 30, 1812 ("so much").

61. "Memoir of Soubiran," ca. July 1813, Soubiran to Henry, July 1814, Prefect of the Department of the Gers to the Duke de Richelieu, March 1, 1816, all in Adams, "Count Edward de Crillon," 54–55, 58–59, 67–69; Cruikshank, *Political Adventures*, 189–191; Morison, "Henry-Crillon Affair," 227–230; Puech, "Aventurier Gascon," 110–117, 123.

62. John G. Jackson to Madison, March 30, 1812, in PJM-PS, 4:273–274 ("nothing," "great"); Jefferson to William Duane, March 28, 1811, in PTJ-RS, 3:508 ("republicans").

63. Madison to John G. Jackson, May 17, 1812, in PJM-PS, 4:391–392 ("incurable," "sacrifice").

64. Cruikshank, *Political Adventures*, 123 ("made," "unwarrantable"), 127–128 ("if," "spirit").

65. Madison to the Senate, March 12, 1812, in PJM-PS, 4:246n1 ("pursuing").

66. Andrew Brown and Others to Madison, May 9, 1812, in PJM-PS, 4:371–372; Inhabitants of Richmond, Manchester, and Vicinity to Madison, May 30, 1812, in PJM-PS, 4:429–430 ("we"); Citizens of the First Congressional District of Pennsylvania to the People of the United States," enclosed in William Jones to Madison, May 22, 1812, in PJM-PS, 4:410 ("gloting," "prompt").

67. *Journal of the Senate*, 12th Cong., 1st Sess., 139; *Journal of the House*, 12th Cong., 1st Sess., 359; Madison to Congress, June 1, 1812, in PJM-PS, 4:437 ("we"); Stagg, *War of 1812*, 18–20, 46–47.

68. Feldman, *Three Lives*, 540–542; Stagg, *War of 1812*, 139–140.

69. Madison to Congress, June 1, 1812, in PJM-PS, 4:432–439.

70. Buel, *America on the Brink*, 154.

Epilogue

1. Latimer, *1812*, 316–318; Powell, *Books of a New Nation*, 18–19; a digital image of the account book is available at *An Account of the Receipts and Expenditures of the United States for the Year 1810* (Washington, 1812), at https://www.loc.gov/resource/rbc0001.2013gen56773/?st=gallery (accessed December 7, 2022).

2. Vogel, *Through the Perilous Fight*, 172; Latimer, *1812*, 313, 316–318; Powell, *Books of a New Nation*, 18–19; *Account of the Receipts*.

3. Taylor, *Civil War*, 180, 413; Stagg, *War of 1812*, 91–108; Buel, *America on the Brink*, 208–209; Latimer, *1812*, 311–319.

4. "Madison to Buonaparte," *Leicester Journal*, August 26, 1814.

5. Madison to Congress, June 1, 1812, in PJM-PS, 4:437; *Repertory*, January 4, 1814 ("fangs"); Buel, *America on the Brink*, 204–205; *Boston Daily Advertiser*, June 17, 1814 ("will"); *Albany Register*, August 5, 1814 ("may").

6. Ketcham, *James Madison*, 536–538, esp. 537 ("union"), 544–545; Taylor, *Civil War*, 175–185, 415–416; *Boston Daily Advertiser*, June 17, 1814 ("almighty").

7. Republican Citizens of Berkshire County, Massachusetts, July 4, 1812, in PJM-PS, 4:558 ("hydra," "envenomed," "fit"); Taylor, *Civil War*, 177–179.

8. *American Mercury*, September 20, 1814 ("moment").

9. "To the President of the United States, on the subject of the New-England Convention," Nos. I and VI, both in *Repertory*, November 14 and 19, 1814; Morison, "Our Most Unpopular War," 51n14.

10. "To the President of the United States, on the subject of the New-England Convention No. III," *Repertory*, November 16, 1814; No. IV, *Repertory*, November 18, 1814.

11. Madison to Wilson Cary Nicholas, November 26, 1814, in PJM-PS, 8:401–402 ("deluded," "sole").

12. "To the President of the United States, on the subject of the New-England Convention No. X," *Repertory*, November 24, 1814 ("we").

13. Feldman, *Three Lives*, 598–600 ("delicacy," "conspiracy"); Taylor, *Civil War*, 415–416.

14. Stephen Pleasonton to William H. Winder, August 7, 1848, in Ingraham, *Sketch*, 47–49; Latimer, *1812*, 317.

15. For samples of the emergence and evolution of "Uncle Sam," see *Bennington News-Letter*, December 23, 1812; *Salem Gazette*, April 30, 1813; *New-England Palladium*, October 8, 1813; *Columbian Centinel*, October 9, 1813; *Washingtonian*, February 14, 1814; *Delaware Gazette and State Journal*, May 5, 1814; *Gazette*, November 14, 1814; *Essex Register*, January 28, 1815;

"Frederick Augustus Fidfaddy," *The Adventures of Uncle Sam*; "John Bull's Epistle," *Vermont Republican*, December 4, 1815; *American Telegraph*, June 19, 1816; "Uncle Sam," *Albany Gazette*, August 11, 1817; "A Dialogue Between Uncle Sam and John Bull," *Massachusetts Spy*, November 27, 1816; "Marine News Extra," *Vermont Republican*, March 3, 1817; *New-England Galaxy* (Boston, MA), January 9, 1818; *American Advocate*, January 2, 1819; see also, Morgan, *American Icon*, 63; Kerber, *Women of the Republic*, xii, 40, 223, 234, 266–267.

16. Luff, "Anxiety of Influence," 756–785; Boghardt, *Zimmermann Telegram*, 177, 257–261.

17. Milne, "1968 Paris Peace Negotiations," 593–595; Johns, *Price of Loyalty*, 123–125 ("treason"); Goudsouzian, *Men and the Moment*, 136–138. Historian Luke Nichter has questioned the evidence of Nixon's collusion, but the historical consensus remains that he oversaw the secret talks with Saigon to sabotage the negotiations (Nichter, *Year That Broke Politics*, 202–212).

18. Foreman, *World on Fire*; Jones, *Union in Peril*; Dubrulle, "Civil War Diplomacy," 209–222; Boghardt, *Zimmermann Telegram*, 148–150; Cunningham, *American Politics*, 91–125; Milne, "1968 Paris Peace Negotiations," 594–595; Johns, *Price of Loyalty*, 124.

19. Brands, *Reagan*, 231–237.

20. Brands, *Reagan*, 233–234; *The "October Surprise" Allegations and the Circumstances Surrounding the Release of the American Hostages Held in Iran* (Washington: US Government Printing Office, 1992), 114–115; *Joint Report of the Task Force to Investigate Certain Allegations Concerning the Holding of American Hostages by Iran in 1980* (Washington: US Government Printing Office, 1993), 1–3; Liz Halloran, "Obama Humbled by Election 'Shellacking,'" November 3, 2010, *NPR*, https://www.npr.org/2010/11/03/131046118/obama-humbled-by-election-shellacking (accessed September 25, 2023).

21. Robert S. Mueller, III, *Report on the Investigation into Russian Interference in the 2016 Presidential Election* (Washington, DC, 2019), 4, 9, https://www.justice.gov/archives/sco/file/1373816/download (accessed April 21, 2021) ("sow"); Toluse Olorunnipa, "'Investigate the Investigators' Is New Trump Rallying Cry to Counter Mueller Report," May 9, 2019, *Washington Post*, https://www.washingtonpost.com/politics/investigate-the-investigators-is-new-trump-rallying-cry-to-counter-mueller-report/2019/05/04/9319b520-6db6-11e9-be3a-33217240a539_story.html (accessed April 21, 2021); Simon Shuster, "U.S. Sanctions Giuliani's Sources of Biden Dirt, Labels Them Part of a Russia-Linked 'Influence Network,'" January 11, 2021, *Time*, https://time.com/5928781/u-s-sanctions-giulianis-sources-of-biden-dirt-labels-them-part-of-a-russia-linked-influence-network/ (accessed April 21, 2021); "Trump Impeachment: The Short, Medium and Long Story," February 2020, *BBC News*, https://www.bbc.com/news/world-us-canada-49800181 (accessed April 21, 2021).

22. "Read Nancy Pelosi's Remarks on Articles of Impeachment," December 5, 2019, *New York Times*, https://www.nytimes.com/2019/12/05/us/politics/pelosi-impeachment-trump.html (accessed September 16, 2023).

23. *Federalist* no. 50, Rossiter, *Federalist Papers*, 317 ("extinction," "implies").

24. *Federalist* nos. 10 and 51, Rossiter, *Federalist Papers*, 72–79, 318–319 ("better," "rival"); Gehl and Porter, *Politics Industry*, 143–168; Drutman, *Breaking the Two-Party Doom Loop*, 177–192.

25. Ketcham, *Selected Writings*, 362 ("advice").

BIBLIOGRAPHY

"Chess." *Thomas Jefferson Encyclopedia*. https://www.monticello.org/site/research-and-collections/chess.

"Étienne Lemaire." *Thomas Jefferson Encyclopedia*. https://www.monticello.org/site/research-and-collections/etienne-lemaire.

"Frederick Augustus Fidfaddy." *The Adventures of Uncle Sam in Search After His Lost Honor*. Middletown, 1816.

"Inaugural Address of John Adams," March 4, 1797, at *The Avalon Project: Documents in Law, History, and Diplomacy*. https://avalon.law.yale.edu/18th_century/adams.asp.

"Pennsylvania 1796 Electoral College." *A New Nation Votes: American Election Returns 1787–1825*. https://elections.lib.tufts.edu/catalog/cv43nz221.

"Rethinking the Electoral College Debate: The Framers, Federalism, and One Person, One Vote." *Harvard Law Review* 114 (June 2001): 2526–2549.

"Sixth and Arch Streets, Philadelphia, May 1794–October 1796." *Buildings of the Department of State, Office of the Historian*, https://history.state.gov/department history/buildings/section16.

"Special Message to Congress on the Burr Conspiracy," January 22, 1807, at *Presidential Speeches*. UVA Miller Center. https://millercenter.org/the-preside ncy/presidential-speeches/january-22-1807-special-message-congress-burr-con spiracy.

"Thomas Jefferson Second Inaugural Address," March 4, 1805, *The Avalon Project: Documents in Law, History, and Diplomacy*. https://avalon.law.yale.edu/19th_century/jefinau2.asp.

Ackerman, Bruce and David Fontana, "Thomas Jefferson Counts Himself into the Presidency." *Virginia Law Review* 90 (2004): 551–643.

Adair, Douglass. "James Madison's Autobiography." *William and Mary Quarterly* 2 (April 1945): 191–209.

Adams, Charles Francis, ed. *The Works of John Adams, Second President of the United States*. 10 vols. Boston, 1850–1856.

Adams, Henry. "Count Edward de Crillon." *American Historical Review* 1 (October 1895): 51–69.

Adams, Henry. *History of the United States of America*. 9 vols. New York, 1889–1891.

Adams, John Quincy. *A letter to the Hon. Harrison Gray Otis, a member of the Senate of Massachusetts, on the present state of our national affairs; with remarks upon Mr. T. Pickering's Letter, to the governor of the commonwealth* (Salem, 1808).

Adelman, Joseph M. *Revolutionary Networks: The Business and Politics of Printing the News, 1763–1789*. Baltimore: Johns Hopkins University Press, 2019.

Aguirre, Domingo de. *Topografía del Real Sitio de Aranjuez*. s.n. 1775.

Alden, John R. *George Washington: A Biography*. Baton Rouge: Louisiana State University Press, 1984.

Alexander, Edward P. "Jefferson and Kosciuszko: Friends of Liberty and of Man." *Pennsylvania Magazine of History and Biography* 92 (January 1968): 87–103.

Allen, Michael. "The Federalists and the West, 1783–1803." *Western Pennsylvania Historical Magazine* 61 (October 1978): 315–332.

Allgor, Catherine, ed. *The Queen of America: Mary Cutts's Life of Dolley Madison*. Charlottesville: University of Virginia Press, 2012.

Amar, Akhil Reed. "Some Thoughts on the Electoral College." *Ohio Northern University Law Review* 33 (2007): 467–480.

Ammon, Harry. *James Monroe: The Quest for National Identity*. Charlottesville: University Press of Virginia, 1990.

Ammon, Harry. *The Genet Mission*. New York: W. W. Norton, 1973.

An account of the receipts and expenditures of the United States for the year 1810. Washington, 1812.

Arcenas, Claire Rydell. "Defending an Energetic Executive: Theory and Practice in *The Federalist*," in *Political Thought and the Origins of the American Presidency*, edited by Ben Lowe, 165–186. Gainesville: University Press of Florida, 2021.

Armitage, David. "Foreword," in *Political Thought and the Origins of the American Presidency*, edited by Ben Lowe, xi–xiv. Gainesville: University Press of Florida, 2021.

Backus, Oswald P. "The Early Bar of Oneida County." *Proceedings of the New York State Historical Association* 14 (1915): 312–332.

Bacon-Foster, Corra. "The Story of Kalorama." *Records of the Columbia Historical Society, Washington, D.C.* 13 (1910): 98–118.

Baker, Thomas N. "'An Attack Well Directed': Aaron Burr Intrigues for the Presidency." *Journal of the Early Republic* 31 (Winter 2011): 553–598.

Baldwin, Simeon E. *Life and Letters of Simeon Baldwin*. New Haven: Tuttle, Morehouse & Taylor, 1919.

Barbé-Marbois, Francois. *Histoire d la Louisiane et de la Cession de Cette Colonie par la France aux États-Unis de l'Amérique Septentrionale*. Paris, 1829.

Barbé-Marbois, Francois. *Our Revolutionary Forefathers: The Letters of François, Marquis de Barbé-Marbois, during his residence in the United States as Secretary of the French Legation, 1779–1785*, edited by E. P. Chase. Freeport, NY: Books for Libraries Press, 1969.

Barksdale, Kevin T. *The Lost State of Franklin: America's First Secession*. Lexington, University Press of Kentucky, 2008.

Barnard, Ella Kent. *Dorothy Payne, Quakeress: A Side-Light upon the Career of "Dolly" Madison*. Philadelphia: Ferris & Leach, 1909.

Baylin, Bernard. *The Ideological Origins of the American Revolution*. Fiftieth anniversary edition. Cambridge, MA: Belknap Press of Harvard University Press, 2017.

Beerman, Eric. "Spanish Envoy to the United States (1769–1809): Marques de Casa Irujo and His Philadelphia Wife Sally McKean." *Americas* 37 (April 1981): 445–456.

Bemis, Samuel Flagg. *Jay's Treaty: A Study in Commerce and Diplomacy*. New York: Macmillan, 1923.

Bemis, Samuel Flagg. *Pinckney's Treaty: A Study of America's Advantage from Europe's Distress, 1783–1800*. Baltimore: Johns Hopkins University Press, 1926.

Berkin, Carol. *A Sovereign People: The Crises of the 1790s and the Birth of American Nationalism*. New York: Basic Books, 2017.

Bilder, Mary Sarah. *Madison's Hand: Revising the Constitutional Convention*. Cambridge, MA: Harvard University Press, 2015.

Bird, Wendell. "Reassessing Responses to the Virginia and Kentucky Resolutions: New Evidence from the Tennessee and Georgia Resolutions and from Other States." *Journal of the Early Republic* 35 (Winter 2015): 519–551.

Blackwell, William L. "Citizen Genet and the Revolution in Russia, 1789–1792." *French Historical Studies* 3 (Spring 1963): 72–92.

Boghardt, Thomas. *The Zimmermann Telegram: Intelligence, Diplomacy, and America's Entry in World War I*. Annapolis: Naval Institute Press, 2012.

Bonnault, Claude de. "Napoleon et le Canada." *Revista de Historia de América* 41 (June 1956): 31–56.

Bonsteel Tachau, Mary K. "George Washington and the Reputation of Edmund Randolph." *Journal of American History* 73 (June 1986): 15–34.

Bordewich, Fergus M. *The First Congress: How James Madison, George Washington, and a Group of Extraordinary Men Invented the Government*. New York: Simon & Schuster, 2016.

Bowman, Albert H. "Pichon, the United States, and Louisiana." *Diplomatic History* 1 (Summer 1977): 257–70.

Boyd, Julian P. *Number 7: Alexander Hamilton's Secret Attempts to Control American Foreign Policy*. Princeton: Princeton University Press, 1964.

Bradburn, Douglas. "A Clamor in the Public Mind: Opposition to the Alien and Sedition Acts." *William and Mary Quarterly* 65 (July 2008): 565–600.

Brands, H. W. *Reagan: The Life*. New York: Anchor Books, 2015.

Brant, Irving. "Edmund Randolph, Not Guilty!" *William and Mary Quarterly* 7 (April 1950): 179–198.

Brant, Irving. *James Madison*. 4 vols. Indianapolis: Bobbs-Merrill, 1941–1961.

Broadwater, Jeff. "Madison, Hamilton, and the Neutrality Proclamation of 1793: Debating Presidential Power and Foreign Affairs." *The Historian* 83 (2021): 171–192.

Broadwater, Jeff. *George Mason: Forgotten Founder*. Chapel Hill: University of North Carolina Press, 2006.

Brookhiser, Richard. *Gentleman Revolutionary: Gouverneur Morris—the Rake Who Wrote the Constitution*. New York: Free Press, 2003.

Brown, Charles Brockden. *An Address to the Government of the United States, on the Cession of Louisiana to the French*. Philadelphia, 1803.

Brown, Gordon S. *Toussaint's Clause: The Founding Fathers and the Haitian Revolution*. Jackson: University of Mississippi Press, 2005.

Brown, John Mason. *The Political Beginnings of Kentucky*. Louisville, 1889.

Brymner, Douglas. *Report on Canadian Archives, 1890*. Ottawa, 1891.

Buel, Richard. *American on the Brink: How the Political Struggle Over the War of 1812 Almost Destroyed the Young Republic*. New York: Palgrave Macmillan, 2005.

Burke, Lee H. *Homes of the Department of State, 1774–1976: The Buildings Occupied by the Department of State and Its Predecessors*. Washington: Historical Office, Bureau of Public Affairs, Department of State, 1977.

Burstein, Andrew and Nancy Isenberg. *Madison and Jefferson*. New York: Random House, 2010.

Burton, M. Agnes, ed. *Manuscripts from the Burton Historical Collection*. Detroit, 1916–1918.

Burton, M. Agnes, ed.. "Haldimand Papers." *Michigan Historical Collections: Collections and Researches Made by the Pioneer and Historical Society of the State of Michigan* 20 (1892; reprint 1912):1–296.

Bush, Robert D. *The Louisiana Purchase: A Global Context*. New York: Routledge, 2014.

Bushong, William, ed. *Glenn Brown's History of the United States Capitol*. Washington, DC: Government Printing Office, 1998.

Butler, Mann. *A History of the Commonwealth of Kentucky*. 2nd ed. Cincinnati, 1836.

Butts, Edward. *Simon Girty: Wilderness Warrior*. Toronto, Canada: Dundurn, 2012.

Butterfield, L. H., ed. *Letters of Benjamin Rush*. 2 vols.; Princeton: Princeton University Press, 1951.

Calloway, Colin G. *Pen and Ink Witchcraft: Treaties and Treaty Making in American Indian History*. New York: Oxford University Press, 2013.

Calloway, Colin G. *The Indian World of George Washington: The First President, the First Americans, and the Birth of the Nation*. New York: Oxford University Press, 2018.

Calloway, Colin G. *The Scratch of a Pen: 1763 and the Transformation of North America*. New York: Oxford University Press, 2006.

Calloway, Colin G. *The Victory with No Name: The Native American Defeat of the First American Army*. New York: Oxford University Press, 2015.

Campbell, Wesley J. "The French Intrigue of James Cole Mountflorence." *William and Mary Quarterly* 65 (October 2008): 779–796.

Campillo, Miguel Gómez del. *Relaciones Diplomaticas Entre España y los Estados Unidos.* 2 vols. Madrid: Consejo Superior de Investigaciones Cientificas, 1944.

Carnot, Lazare. *Reply of L. N. M. Carnot, citizen of France to the Report made on the Conspiracy of the 18th Fructidor, 5th year, by J. Ch. Bailleul, in the name of the Select Committee.* 3rd ed. London, 1799.

Carson, David A. "That Ground Called Quiddism: John Randolph's War with the Jefferson Administration." *Journal of American Studies* 20 (April 1986): 71–92.

Caughey, John Walton. *McGillivray of the Creeks.* Norman: University of Oklahoma Press, 1938.

Cave, Alfred A. "The Delaware Prophet Neolin: A Reappraisal." *Ethnohistory* 46 (Spring 1999): 265–290.

Cave, Alfred A. *Prophets of the Great Spirit: Native American Revitalization Movements in Eastern North America.* Lincoln: University of Nebraska Press, 2006.

Cayton, Andrew R. L. "Radicals in the 'Western World': The Federalist Conquest of Trans-Appalachian North America," in Doron Ben-Atar and Barbara B. Oberg, *Federalists Reconsidered,* 77–96. Charlotteville: University Press of Virginia, 1998.

Cheney, Lynne. *James Madison: A Life Reconsidered.* New York: Viking, 2014.

Chervinsky, Lindsay M. *The Cabinet: George Washington and the Creation of an American Institution.* Cambridge, MA: Belknap Press of Harvard University Press, 2020.

Chervinsky, Linday M. "The Political Practices of the First Presidents: The Cabinet and the Executive Branch," in *Political Thought and the Origins of the American Presidency,* edited by Ben Lowe, 217–242. Gainesville: University Press of Florida, 2021.

Chervinsky, Lindsay M. "Thomas Jefferson's Cabinet." *White House Historical Association.* https://www.whitehousehistory.org/thomas-jeffersons-cabinet.

Child, Theodore. "The Story of the Paris Salon, 1673–1884." *Frank Leslie's Popular Monthly* 23 (January 1887):107–111.

Clanin, Douglas E. and Ruth Dorrel. *The Papers of William Henry Harrison, 1800–1815.* 10 microfilm reels. Indianapolis: Indiana Historical Society, 1999.

Clarfield, Gerard H. *Timothy Pickering and American Diplomacy, 1795–1800.* Columbia: University of Missouri Press, 1969.

Clarfield, Gerard H. *Timothy Pickering and the American Republic.* Pittsburgh: University of Pittsburgh Press, 1980.

Clark, Allen C. *Life and Letters of Dolly Madison.* Washington: W. F. Roberts, 1914.

Coats, Ann Veronica. "The 1797 Mutinies in the Channel Fleet: A Foreign-Inspired Revolutionary Movement?" in *The Naval Mutinies of 1797: Unity and Perseverance,* edited by Ann Veronica Coats and Philip MacDougall, 120–141. Woodbridge, UK: Boydell Press, 2011.

Cobbett, William. *A New-Year's Gift to the Democrats.* Philadelphia, 1796.

Cogliano, Francis D. *Emperor of Liberty: Thomas Jefferson's Foreign Policy.* New Haven: Yale University Press, 2014.

Cole, Charles C., Jr. "Brockden Brown and the Jefferson Administration." *Pennsylvania Magazine of History and Biography* 72 (July 1948): 253–263.

Collot, Georges-Henri-Victor. *A Journey in North America*. 3 vols. Paris, 1826.

Collot, Georges-Henri-Victor. *Voyage dans l'Amérique Septentrionale*. 3 vols. Paris, 1826.

Combs, Jerald A. *The Jay Treaty: A Political Background of the Founding Fathers*. Berkeley: University of California Press, 1970.

Conlin, Michael F. "The American Mission of Citizen Pierre-Auguste Adet: Revolutionary Chemistry and Diplomacy in the Early Republic." *Pennsylvania Magazine of History and Biography* 124 (October 2000): 489–520.

Conway, Moncure Daniel. *Omitted Chapters of History Disclosed in the Life and Papers of Edmund Randolph*. New York, 1888.

Cost, Jay. *The Price of Greatness: Alexander Hamilton, James Madison, and the Creation of American Oligarchy*. New York: Basic Books, 2018.

Cotton, Edward. *Boston Directory*. Boston, 1807.

Cox, Isaac Joslin. "Western Reaction to the Burr Conspiracy," in *Transactions of the Illinois State Historical Society for the Year 1928*, 73–100. Springfield: Philips Bros., 1928.

Coxe, Tench. *Strictures upon the letter imputed to Mr. Jefferson, addressed to Mr. Mazzei*. s.n. 1800.

Cozzens, Peter. *Tecumseh and the Prophet: The Shawnee Brother Who Defied a Nation*. New York: Knopf, 2020.

Cray, Robert E., Jr. "Remembering the USS Chesapeake: The Politics of Maritime Death and Impressment." *Journal of the Early Republic* 25 (Fall 2005): 445–474.

Cruikshank, E. A. "Some Unpublished Letters from General Brock." *Ontario Historical Society, Papers and Records* 13 (1915): 8–23.

Cruikshank, E. A. *The Correspondence of Lieut. Governor John Graves Simcoe*. 5 vols. Toronto: Ontario Historical Society, 1923.

Cruikshank, E. A. *The Political Adventures of John Henry: The Record of An International Imbroglio*. Toronto: Macmillan, 1936.

Cruzat, Heloise Hulse. "General Collot's Reconnoitering Trip Down the Mississippi and His Arrest in New Orleans in 1796, by Order of the Baron de Carondelet." *Louisiana Historical Quarterly* 1 (1918): 303–320.

Cunningham, Noble E. "Who Were the Quids?" *Mississippi Valley Historical Review* 50 (September 1963): 252–263.

Cutterham, Tom. *Gentlemen Revolutionaries: Power and Justice in the New American Republic*. Princeton: Princeton University Press, 2017.

Cutts, Lucia Beverly, ed. *Memoirs and Letters of Dolly Madison*. Boston, 1887.

Dangerfield, George. *Chancellor Robert R. Livingston of New York, 1746–1813*. New York: Harcourt, 1960.

DeConde, Alexander. *Entangling Alliance: Politics & Diplomacy under George Washington*. Durham: Duke University Press, 1958.

DeConde, Alexander. *The Quasi-War: The Politics and Diplomacy of the Undeclared War with France, 1979–1801*. New York: Charles Scribner's Sons, 1966.

Dickey, Jeff. *Empire of Mud: The Secret History of Washington, D.C.* Guilford, CT: Lyons Press, 2014.

Dictionnaire de l'Académie Françoise. 5th ed. 2 vols. Paris, 1798.

Dowd, Gregory Evans. *A Spirited Resistance: The North American Indian Struggle for Unity, 1745–1815*. Baltimore: Johns Hopkins University Press, 1992.

Drutman, Lee. *Breaking the Two-Party Doom Loop: The Case for Multiparty Democracy in America*. New York: Oxford University Press, 2020.

Dubois, Laurent. *Avengers of the New World: The Story of the Haitian Revolution*. Cambridge, MA: Belknap Press of Harvard University Press, 2004.

Dubrulle, Hugh. "Civil War Diplomacy," in Tyson Reeder, *Routledge History of U.S. Foreign Relations*, 185–198. New York: Routledge, 2022.

DuVal, Kathleen. *Independence Lost: Lives on the Edge of the American Revolution*. New York: Random House, 2015.

Earl III, John L. "Talleyrand in Philadelphia, 1794–1796." *Pennsylvania Magazine of History and Biography* 91 (July 1967): 282–298.

Echeverria, Durand, trans. "General Collot's Plan for Rennaissance of the Ohio and Mississippi Valley, 1796." *William and Mary Quarterly* 9 (October 1952): 512–520.

Edmunds, David R. *The Shawnee Prophet*. Lincoln: University of Nebraska Press, 1983.

Egan, Clifford L. "The United States, France, and West Florida, 1803–1807." *Florida Historical Quarterly* 47 (January 1969): 227–252.

Elkins, Stanley M. and Eric L. McKitrick. *The Age of Federalism*. New York: Oxford University Press, 1993.

Ellis, Joseph J. *Founding Brothers: The Revolutionary Generation*. New York: Knopf, 2000.

Encyclopædia Britannica, 7th ed., 22 vols.; Edinburgh, 1842.

Esarey, Logan. *Governors Messages and Letters: Messages and Letters of William Henry Harrison*. 2 vols; Indianapolis: Indiana Historical Commission, 1922.

Estes, Todd. "The Art of Presidential Leadership: George Washington and the Jay Treaty." *Virginia Magazine of History and Biography* 109 (2001): 127–158.

Estes, Todd. *The Jay Treaty Debate, Public Opinion, and the Evolution of the Early American Political Culture*. Amherst: University of Massachusetts Press, 2006.

Evans, Anthony Walton White. *Memoir of Thaddeus Kosciuszko: Poland's Hero and Patriot*. New York, 1883.

Facts Relative to John Henry and His Negotiation. [Washington? 1812?].

Farrand, Max. *The Records of the Federal Convention of 1787*. 3 vols. New Haven: Yale University Press, 1911.

Fehlings, Gregory E. "America's First Limited War." *Naval War College Review* 53 (Summer 2000): 101–143.

Fehlings, Gregory E. "Storm on the Constitution: The First Deportation Law." *Tulsa Journal of Comparative and International Law* 10 (2002): 63–114.

Feldman, Noah. *The Three Lives of James Madison: Genius, Partisan, President*. New York: Random House, 2017.

Ferling, John. *Adams vs. Jefferson: The Tumultuous Election of 1800*. New York: Oxford University Press, 2004.

Ferreiro, Larrie D. *Brothers at Arms: American Independence and the Men of France and Spain Who Saved It*. New York: Vintage, 2016.

Fiszerowa, Wirydianna. *Pamiętnik o Kościuszce Wirydjanny z Radolińskich Kwileckiej-Fiszerowej*. Edited by Adam Mieczysław Skałkowski. Warsaw, 1934.

Foner, Philip S., ed. *The Democratic-Republican Societies, 1790–1800: A Documentary Sourcebook of Constitutions, Declarations, Addresses, Resolutions, and Toasts*. Westport, CT: Greenwood Press, 1976.

Forbes, Allyn B. ed. "Abigail Adams, Commentator." *Proceedings of the Massachusetts Historical Society* 66 (October 1936–May 1941): 126–153.

Ford, Worthington Chauncey. *Writings of John Quincy Adams*. 7 vols. New York: Macmillan, 1913–1917.

Foreman, Amanda. *A World on Fire: Britain's Crucial Role in the American Civil War*. New York: Random House, 2010.

Freeman, Douglas Southall. *Washington*, abridged edition by Richard Harwell. New York: Charles Scribner's Sons, 1968.

Freeman, Joanne B. "Explaining the Unexplainable: The Cultural Context of the Sedition Act," in *The Democratic Experiment: New Directions in American Political History*, edited by Meg Jacobs, William J. Novak, and Julian E. Zelizer, 20–49. Princeton: Princeton University Press, 2003.

Freeman, Joanne B. *Affairs of Honor: National Politics in the New Republic*. New Haven: Yale University Press, 2001.

French, Gregg. "Spain and the Birth of the American Republic: Establishing Lasting Bonds of Kinship in the Revolutionary Era," in *Spain and the American Revolution: New Approaches and Perspectives*, edited by Gabriel Paquette and Gonzalo M. Quintero Saravia, 184–196. New York: Routledge, 2019.

Frykman, Niklas. *The Bloody Flag: Mutiny in the Age of Atlantic Revolution*. Berkeley: University of California Press, 2020.

Furstenberg, François. *When the United States Spoke French: Five Refugees Who Shaped a Nation*. New York: Penguin, 2014.

Gannon, Kevin M. "Escaping 'Mr. Jefferson's Plan of Destruction': New England Federalists and the Idea of a Northern Confederacy, 1803–1804." *Journal of the Early Republic* 21, no. 3 (Autumn 2001): 413–443.

Gehl, Katherine M. and Michael E. Porter. *The Politics Industry: How Political Innovation Can Break Partisan Gridlock and Save Our Democracy*. Cambridge, MA: Harvard Business Review Press, 2020.

Gibbs, George. *Memoirs of the Administrations of Washington and John Adams*. 2 vols. New York, 1846.

Girard, Philippe. "The Leclerc Expedition to Saint-Domingue and the Independence of Haiti, 1802–1804." *Oxford Research Encyclopedia: Latin American History* (May 2019). https://doi.org/10.1093/acrefore/9780199366439.013.743.

Gleijeses, Piero. *America's Road to Empire: Foreign Policy from Independence to World War One*. New York: Bloomsbury, 2022.

Goltz, Herbert Charles. "Tecumseh, The Prophet and the Rise of the Northwest Indian Confederation." PhD diss., University of Western Ontario, 1973.

Gordon-Reed, Annette and Peter S. Onuf. *"Most Blessed of the Patriarchs": Thomas Jefferson and the Empire of the Imagination*. New York: Liveright, 2016.

Gordon-Reed, Annette and Peter S. Onuf. *The Hemingses of Monticello: An American Family*. New York: W. W. Norton, 2008.

Goudsouzian, Aram. *The Men and the Moment: The Election of 1968 and the Rise of Partisan Politics in America*. Chapel Hill: University of North Carolina Press, 2019.

Gould, Eliga H. *Among the Powers of the Earth: The American Revolution and the Making of the New World Empire*. Cambridge, MA: Harvard University Press, 2012.

Griffin, Patrick. *American Leviathan: Empire, Nation, and Revolutionary Frontier*. New York: Hill and Wang, 2007.

Guyatt, Nicholas. *The Hated Cage: An American Tragedy in Britain's Most Terrifying Prison*. New York: Basic Books, 2022.

Haiman, Miecislaus. *Kosciuszko: Leader and Exile*. New York: Polish Institute of Arts and Sciences in America, 1946.

Hale, Edward E. and Edward E. Hale Jr. *Franklin in France*. 2 vols. Boston, 1888.

Hardie, James. *The Philadelphia Directory, 1793*. Philadelphia, 1793.

Harvey, Sean P. "Tools of Foreign Influence: Albert Gallatin, Geneva, and Federalist Nativism before the Alien and Sedition Acts." *Journal of the Early Republic* 41 (Winter 2021): 523–551.

Hay, Thomas Robson. "Charles Williamson and the Burr Conspiracy." *Journal of Southern History* 2 (May 1936): 175–210.

Haynes, George Henry and Mary Robinson Reynolds. "Letters of Samuel Taggart, Representative in Congress, 1803–1814." *Proceedings of the American Antiquarian Society* 33 (1923): 113–226.

Heidenreich, Donald E. Jr. "U.S. National Security and Party Politics: The Consensus on Louisiana, 1789–1803." *Arkansas Historical Quarterly* 62 (Winter 2003): 370–385.

Herbert, Jason. "'To Treat with All Nations': Invoking Authority in the Chickasaw Nation, 1783–1795." *Ohio Valley History* 18 (Spring 2018): 27–44.

Hickey, Donald R. "The Monroe-Pinkney Treaty of 1806: A Reappraisal." *William and Mary Quarterly* 44 (January 1987): 65–88.

Hill, Peter P. "The Savannah Riots: A Burning Issue in Franco-American Hostility, 1811–1812." *Georgia Historical Quarterly* 88 (Winter 2004): 499–510.

Hill, Peter P. *Napoleon's Troublesome Americans: Franco-American Relations, 1804–1815*. Dulles: Potomac Books, 2005.

Historical Directory of the District of Columbia. Washington: State Historic Committee, Daughters of the American Revolution, 1922.

Hofstadter, Richard. *The Idea of a Party System: The Rise of Legitimate Opposition in the United States, 1780–1840*. Berkeley: University of California Press, 1969.

Hogeland, William. *Autumn of the Black Snake: The Creation of the U.S. Army and the Invasion That Opened the West*. New York: Farrar, Straus and Giroux, 2017.

Holloway, Carson and Bradford P. Wilson, eds. *The Political Writings of Alexander Hamilton*. New York: Cambridge University Press, 2017.

Holloway, Carson and Bradford P. Wilson, eds. *Hamilton versus Jefferson in the Washington Administration: Completing the Founding or Betraying the Founding?* New York: Cambridge University Press, 2015.

Holton, Woody. *Forced Founders: Indians, Debtors, Slaves, and the Making of the American Revolution in Virginia.* Chapel Hill: University of North Carolina Press, 1999.

Homberger, Eric. *Mrs. Astor's New York: Money and Social Power in a Gilded Age.* New Haven: Yale University Press, 2002.

Huber, Leonard Victor. *New Orleans: A Pictorial History from the Earliest Times to the Present Day.* Crown, 1971; Gretna, LA: Pelican, 1991.

Ingraham, Edward Duncan. *A Sketch of the Events Which Preceded the Capture of Washington by the British, on the Twenty-Fourth of August, 1814.* Philadelphia, 1849.

Inman, Natalie. "'A Dark and Bloody Ground': American Indian Responses to Expansion during the American Revolution." *Tennessee Historical Quarterly* 70 (Winter 2011): 258–275.

Isenberg, Nancy. *Fallen Founder: The Life of Aaron Burr.* New York: Viking, 2007.

Iserov, Andrey. "Francisco de Miranda." *Oxford Research Encyclopedia: Latin American History* (August 2019). https://doi.org/10.1093/acrefore/9780199366 439.013.745.

Jacobs, Seth. *Rogue Diplomats: The Proud Tradition of Disobedience in American Foreign Policy.* New York: Cambridge University Press, 2020.

James, James Alton, ed. *George Rogers Clark Papers, 1771–1781.* Springfield, IL: Trustees of the Illinois State Historical Library, 1912.

Janson, Charles William. *The Stranger in America.* London, 1807.

Jasanoff, Maya. *Liberty's Exiles: American Loyalists in the Revolutionary World.* New York: Vintage, 2011.

Jenkinson, Isaac. *Aaron Burr: His Person and Political Relations with Thomas Jefferson and Alexander Hamilton.* Richmond, IN: M. Cullaton, 1902.

Johns, Andrew L. *The Price of Loyalty: Hubert Humphrey's Vietnam Conflict.* New York: Rowman & Littlefield, 2020.

Johnson, Leland R. "The Suspense Was Hell: The Senate Vote for War in 1812." *Indiana Magazine of History* 65 (December 1969): 247–267.

Johnson, Paul E. and Sean Wilentz. *The Kingdom of Matthias.* New York: Oxford University Press, 1994.

Johnson, Paul. *Napoleon.* New York: Viking, 2002.

Johnson, Ronald Angelo. *Diplomacy in Black and White: John Adams, Toussaint Louverture, and Their Atlantic World Alliance.* Athens: University of Georgia Press, 2014.

Jones, Howard. *Union in Peril: The Crisis of British Intervention in the Civil War.* Chapel Hill: University of North Carolina Press, 1992.

Jortner, Adam. *The Gods of Prophetstown: The Battle of Tippecanoe and the Holy War for the American Frontier.* New York: Oxford University Press, 2012.

Jusserand, J. J. "La Jeunesse de Citoyen Genet." *Revue d'histoire diplomatique* 44 (1930): 237–268.

Kastor, Peter J. *The Nation's Crucible: The Louisiana Purchase and the Creation of America*. New Haven: Yale University Press, 2004.

Keeler, Lucy Elliot. *Old Fort Sandoski of 1745 and the "Sandusky Country,"* reprinted from *Ohio Archaeological and Historical Society Publications* 17 (October 1908): 357–430.

Kellogg, Louise Phelps. *Frontier Retreat on the Upper Ohio, 1779–1781*. Madison: Wisconsin Historical Society, 1917.

Kelly, James C. and B. S. Lovell. "Thomas Jefferson: His Friends and Foes." *Virginia Magazine of History and Biography* 101 (January 1993): 133–157.

Kelsay, Isabel Thompson. *Joseph Brant, 1743–1807: Man of Two Worlds*. Syracuse: Syracuse University Press, 1984.

Kerber, Linda K. *Women of the Republic: Intellect and Ideology in Revolutionary America*. Chapel Hill: University of North Carolina Press, 1980.

Kessell, John L. "To Stop Captain Merry: Spanish Efforts to Intercept Lewis and Clark." *New Mexico Historical Review* 81 (2006): 125–140.

Ketcham, Ralph. *James Madison: A Biography*. Charlottesville: University of Virginia Press, 1990.

Ketcham, Ralph. *Selected Writings of James Madison*. Indianapolis: Hackett, 2006.

King, Charles R., ed. *The Life and Correspondence of Rufus King: Comprising His Letters, Private and Official, His Public Documents, and His Speeches*. 6 vols. New York, 1894–1900.

Kinnaird, Lawrence. *Spain in the Mississippi Valley, 1765–1794*. Washington, DC: Government Printing Office, 1949.

Klarman, Michael J. *The Framers' Coup: The Making of the United States Constitution*. New York: Oxford University Press, 2016.

Kline, Mary-Jo. "Sarah Livingston Jay (1756–1802): A Republican Lady in Spain," in *Spain and the American Revolution: New Approaches and Perspectives*, edited by Gabriel Paquette and Gonzalo M. Quintero Saravia, 159–170. New York: Routledge, 2019.

Koekkoek, René. *The Citizenship Experiment: Contesting the Limits of Civic Equality and Participation in the Age of Revolutions*. Boston: Brill, 2020.

Kuethe, Allen J. and Kenneth J. Andrien. *The Spanish Atlantic World in the Eighteenth Century: War and the Bourbon Reforms, 1713–1796*. New York: Cambridge University Press, 2014.

Kusielewicz, Eugene and Ludwik Krzyzanowski. "Julian Ursyn Niemcewicz's American Diary." *Polish Review* 3 (Summer 1958): 83–115.

Kyte, George William. "A Spy on the Western Waters: The Military Intelligence Mission of General Collot in 1796." *Mississippi Valley Historical Review* 34 (December 1947): 427–442.

Lambeau, Lucien. "Rapport Présenté par M. Lucien Lambeau, au nom de la 1re Sous commission, sur l'hôtel de Crillon, la place de la Concorde et la statue équestre de Louis XV." *Bulletin Municipal Officiel de la Ville de Paris* (September 7, 1905): 3194–3200.

Landon, Charles-Paul. *Annales du Musée e de l'École Moderne des Beaux-arts: Salon de 1808*. vol. 1. Paris, 1808.

Langley, Linda. "The Tribal Identity of Alexander McGillivray: A Review of the Historical and Ethnographic Data." *Journal of the Louisiana Historical Association* 46 (Spring 2005): 231–239.

Latimer, Jon. *1812: War with America.* Cambridge, MA: Belknap Press of Harvard University Press, 2007.

Le Hir, Marie-Pierre. *French Immigrants and Pioneers in the Making of America.* Jefferson, NC: McFarland, 2022.

Leal, Guillermo Calleja. "Spain Financially Sustained the Continental Congress and Its Army During the American Revolutionary War," in *Recovered Memories: Spain, New Orleans and the Support for the American Revolution,* edited by José Manuel Guerrero Acosta,131–66. Iberdrola, 2018.

Lee, Jacob F. *Masters of the Middle Waters: Indian Nations and Colonial Ambitions Along the Mississippi.* Cambridge, MA: Belknap Press of Harvard University Press, 2019.

Lefkowitz, Arthur S. *George Washington's Indispensable Men: The 32 Aides-de-Camp Who Helped Win American Independence.* Mechanicsburg, PA: Stackpole Books, 2003.

Leibiger, Stuart. *Founding Friendship: George Washington, James Madison, and the Creation of the American Republic.* Charlottesville: University of Virginia Press, 2001.

Lentz, Thierry, ed. *Napoléon Bonaparte: Correspondance Générale.* 15 vols. Paris: Fayard, 2004–present.

Léoutre, Pierre. *Lectoure par la Carte Postale.* Norderstedt, Germany: Books on Demand, 2022.

Leralta, Javier. *Madrid: Cuentos, Leyendas, y Anécdotas.* 2 vols. Madrid, Spain: Silex, 2002.

Lewis, James E. Jr. " 'The Strongest Government on Earth' Proves Its Strength: The Jefferson Administration and the Burr Conspiracy," in Joanne B. Freeman and Johann N. Neem, *Jeffersonians in Power: The Rhetoric of Opposition Meets the Realities of Governing,* 222–241. Charlottesville: University of Virginia Press, 2019.

Lewis, James E. Jr. *The Burr Conspiracy: Uncovering the Story of an Early American Crisis.* Princeton: Princeton University Press, 2017.

Lewis, James E. Jr. *The American Union and the Problem of Neighborhood: The United States and the Collapse of the Spanish Empire, 1783–1829.* Chapel Hill: University of North Carolina Press, 1998.

Link, Eugene Perry. *Democratic-Republican Societies, 1790–1800.* New York: Octagon Books, 1973.

Linklater, Andro. *An Artist in Treason: The Extraordinary Double Life of General James Wilkinson.* New York: Walker, 2009.

Lohrenz, Otto. "The Reverend John Wingate: An Economic Casualty of Revolutionary Virginia." *Journal of American Culture* 18 (Winter 1995): 43–49.

Lowe, Ben. "Political Thought and the Intellectual Origins of the American Presidency: Royalism, Executive Power, and the History of Ideas," in *Political Thought and the Origins of the American Presidency,* edited by Ben Lowe, 1–15. Gainesville: University Press of Florida, 2021.

Luff, Jennifer. "The Anxiety of Influence: Foreign Intervention, U.S. Politics, and World War I." *Diplomatic History* 44 (2020): 756–785.

Lycan, Gilbert L. "Alexander Hamilton's Florida Policy." *Florida Historical Quarterly* 50 (October 1971): 143–157.

Lydon, James G. *Fish and Flour for Gold, 1600–1800: Southern Europe in the Colonial Balance of Payments*. Philadelphia: e-published by the Program in Early American Economy and Society, Library Company of Philadelphia, 2008.

MacDonald, James. "Caught Between Two Fires: The Catawba and the Cherokee Choose Sides in the American Revolution," in *North Carolina's Revolutionary Founders*, edited by Jeff Broadwater and Troy L. Kickler, 67–87. Chapel Hill: University of North Carolina Press, 2019.

Maier, Pauline. *American Scripture: Making the Declaration of Independence*. New York: Vintage, 1997.

Maier, Pauline. *Ratification: The People Debate the Constitution, 1787–1788*. New York: Simon & Schuster, 2011.

Malone, Dumas. *Jefferson and the Ordeal of Liberty*. Boston: Little, Brown, 1962.

Mann, Alison T. "Slavery Exacts an Impossible Price: John Quincy Adams and the Dorcas Allen Case, Washington, DC." PhD diss., University of New Hampshire, 2010.

Marraro, Howard R. "The Four Versions of Jefferson's Letter to Mazzei." *William and Mary Quarterly* 22 (January 1942): 18–29.

Mayo, Bernard, ed. *Instructions to the British Ministers to the United States, 1791–1812*. Washington, DC: Government Printing Office, 1941.

Mayo-Bobee, Dinah. "Understanding the Essex Junto: Fear, Dissent, and Propaganda in the Early Republic." *New England Quarterly* 88 (December 2015): 623–656.

McCadden, Helen Matzke. "Juan de Miralles and the American Revolution." *The Americas* 29 (January 1973): 359–375.

McCaleb, Walter Flavius. *The Aaron Burr Conspiracy and A New Light on Aaron Burr*. Expanded ed. 1936. New York: Argosy-Antiquarian, reprint 1966.

McCoy, Drew R. *The Elusive Republic: Political Economy in Jeffersonian America*. Chapel Hill: University of North Carolina Press, 1980.

McCoy, Drew R. *The Last of the Fathers: James Madison and the Republican Legacy*. Cambridge: Cambridge University Press, 1989.

McIlwaine, Henry Read, ed. *Official Letters of the Governors of the State of Virginia*. 3 vols. Richmond, 1926.

McMichael, F. Andrew. *Atlantic Loyalties: Americans in Spanish West Florida, 1785–1810*. Athens: University of Georgia Press, 2008.

Meacham, Jon. *Thomas Jefferson: The Art of Power*. New York: Random House, 2012.

Mekeel, Arthur J. "The Relation of the Quakers to the American Revolution." *Quaker History* 65 (Spring 1976): 3–18.

Melton, Buckner F. *Aaron Burr: Conspiracy to Treason*. New York: Wiley, 2002.

Melville, Annabelle M. "John Carroll and Louisiana, 1803–1815." *Catholic Historical Review* 64 (July 1978): 398–440.

Mikaberidze, Alexander. *The Napoleonic Wars: A Global History*. New York: Oxford University Press, 2020.

Milfort, Louis. *Memoirs or a Quick Glance at My Various Travels and My Sojourn in the Creek Nation*. Kennesaw, GA: Continental Book, 1959.

Miller, Hunter, ed. *Treaties and Other International Acts of the United States of America*. 8 vols. Washington: Government Printing Office, 1931–48.

Milne, David. "The 1968 Paris Peace Negotiations: A Two Level Game?" *Review of International Studies*, 2 (April 2011): 577–599.

Mintz, Max M. "Gouverneur Morris, George Washington's War Hawk." *Virginia Quarterly Review* 79 (Autumn 2003): 651–661.

Miranda, Francisco de. *Archivo del General Miranda*. Edited by Vicente Dávil. 24 vols.; Havana: Editorial Lex, 1950.

Mitchell, Broadus. *Alexander Hamilton: The National Adventure, 1788–1804*. New York: Macmillan, 1962.

Moats, Sandra. *Navigating Neutrality: Early American Governance in the Turbulent Atlantic*. Charlottesville: University of Virginia Press, 2021.

Mohl, Raymond. "Britain and the Aaron Burr Conspiracy." *History Today* 21 (June 1971): 391–398.

Moore, Virginia. *The Madisons: A Biography*. New York: McGraw-Hill, 1979.

Moreau de Saint-Méry. *Voyage aux Etats-Unis de l'Amérique*, edited by Stewart L. Mims. New Haven: Yale University Press, 1913.

Morgan, Edmund S. *Inventing the People: The Rise of Popular Sovereignty in England and America*. New York: Norton, 1988.

Morgan, Winifred. *An American Icon: Brother Jonathan and American Identity*. Newark: University of Delaware Press, 1988.

Morison, Samuel Eliot. "Our Most Unpopular War." *Proceedings of the Massachusetts Historical Society* 80 (1968): 38–54.

Morison, Samuel Eliot. "The Henry-Crillon Affair of 1812." *Proceedings of the Massachusetts Historical Society* 69 (October 1947–May 1950): 207–231.

Mortimer, Loren Michael. "Before Domestic Dependent Nationhood: Entanglements of Indigenous Diplomacy and U.S. Foreign Policy," in Tyson Reeder, *Routledge History of U.S. Foreign Relations*, 185–198. New York: Routledge, 2022.

Mugridge, Donald H. "Augustus Foster and His Book." *Records of the Columbia Historical Society, Washington, D.C.* 53/56 (1953/1956): 327–352.

Muir, R. Cuthbertson. *The Early Political and Military History of Burford*. Quebec: La Cie d'Imprimerie Commerciale, 1913.

Muñoz, Vincent Phillip. *God and the Founders: Madison, Washington, and Jefferson*. New York: Cambridge University Press, 2009.

Muñoz, Vincent Phillip. *Religious Liberty and the American Supreme Court: The Essential Cases and Documents*. New York: Rowman & Littlefield, 2013.

Murphy, Brian Phillips. "'A Very Convenient Instrument': The Manhattan Company, Aaron Burr, and the Election of 1800." *William and Mary Quarterly* 65 (April 2008): 233–266.

Murphy, Orville T. *Charles Gravier, Comte de Vergennes: French Diplomacy in the Age of Revolution, 1719–1787*. Albany: State University of New York Press, 1982.

Nagel, Paul C. *John Quincy Adams: A Public Life, A Private Life.* New York: Knopf, 1997.

Narrett, David. "Geopolitics and Intrigue: James Wilkinson, the Spanish Borderlands, and Mexican Independence." *William and Mary Quarterly* 69 (January 2012): 101–146.

Narrett, David. *Adventurism and Empire: The Struggle for Mastery in the Louisiana-Florida Borderlands, 1762–1803.* Chapel Hill: University of North Carolina Press, 2015.

Nash, Gary B. *The Unknown American Revolution: The Unruly Birth of Democracy and the Struggle to Create America.* New York: Penguin, 2005.

Nelson, Eric. *The Royalist Revolution: Monarchy and the American Founding.* Cambridge, MA: Belknap Press of Harvard University Press, 2014.

Newmyer, R. Kent. *The Treason Trial of Aaron Burr: Law, Politics, and the Character Wars of the New Nation.* New York: Cambridge University Press, 2012.

Nichols, David Andrew. *Red Gentlemen and White Savages: Indians, Federalists, and the Search for Order on the American Frontier.* Charlottesville: University of Virginia Press, 2008.

Nichter, Luke A. *The Year That Broke Politics: Collusion and Chaos in the Presidential Election of 1968.* New Haven: Yale University Press, 2023.

Niemcewicz, Julian Ursyn. *Under Their Vine and Fig Tree: Travels Through America in 1797–1799, 1805, with Some Further Account of Life in New Jersey.* Edited and translated by Metchie J. E. Budka. Elizabeth, NJ: Grassmann, 1965.

O'Neil, Scannell. "Notes on Sister Mary Theonella Hite and Her Family." *St. Louis Catholic Historical Review* 11 (April-July 1920): 97–100.

Officer, Lawrence H. "Dollar–Sterling Mint Parity and Exchange Rates, 1791–1834." *Journal of Economic History* 43 (September 1983): 579–616.

Öhman, Martin. "The Mississippi Question in Jeffersonian Political Economy," in *Jeffersonians in Power: The Rhetoric of Opposition Meets the Realities of Governing*, edited by Joanne B. Freeman and Johann N. Neem, 38–58. Charlottesville: University of Virginia Press, 2019.

Onuf, Peter S. *Jefferson's Empire: The Language of American Nationhood.* Charlottesville: University Press of Virginia, 2000.

Otero, Michael A. "The American Mission of Diego de Gardoqui." Ph.D. diss., University of California, Los Angeles, 1948.

Paine, Thomas. *Common Sense.* Edited by Tony Benn. London: Phoenix Press, 2000.

Parker, David W. "Secret Reports of John Howe, 1808." *American Historical Review* 17 (October 1911): 70–102.

Pasley, Jeffrey L. *"The Tyranny of Printers": Newspaper Politics in the Early American Republic.* Charlottesville: University of Virginia Press, 2001.

Paul, Joel Richard. *Without Precedent: John Marshall and His Times.* New York: Riverhead Books, 2018.

Pawlickiego, Stefana. *Pamiętniki Józefa Drzewieckiego (1772–1852).* Krakow, 1891.

Perkins, Bradford. *Prologue to War: England and the United States, 1805–1812.* Berkeley: University of California Press, 1961.

Perkins, James H. *Annals of the West: Embracing a Concise Account of Principal Events Which Have Occurred in the Western States and Territories.* Cincinnati, 1846.

Perttula, Timothy K. *The Caddo Nation: Archaeological & Ethnohistoric Perspectives.* Austin: University of Texas Press, 1992.

Peskin, Lawrence A. "Conspiratorial Anglophobia and the War of 1812." *Journal of American History* 98 (December 2011): 647–669.

Pickering, Octavius and Charles W. Upham. *The Life of Timothy Pickering.* 4 vols. Boston, 1867–1873.

Pietri, François. *Lucien Bonaparte à Madrid, 1801.* Paris: B. Grasset, 1951.

Pittman, Philip. *The Present State of the European Settlements on the Missisippi* [*sic*]. London, 1770.

Plumer, William. *William Plumer's Memorandum of Proceedings in the United States Senate, 1803–1807.* Edited by Everett Somerville Brown. New York: Macmillan, 1923.

Pollak, Louis H. "Marbury v. Madison: What Did John Marshall Decide and Why?" *Proceedings of the American Philosophical Society* 148 (March 2004): 1–13.

Pope, John. *A Tour Through the Southern and Western Territories of the United States of North-America . . .* New York, 1888.

Potter, J. "William Cobbett in North America." *Bulletin (British Association for American Studies)* 2 (March 1961): 4–28.

Powell, J. H. *The Books of a New Nation: United States Government Publications, 1774–1814.* Philadelphia: University of Pennsylvania Press, 1957.

Prince, Carl E. *The Federalists and the Origins of the U.S. Civil Service.* New York: New York University Press, 1977.

Proceedings of the convention of delegates, held at the capitol in the city of Williamsburg in the colony of Virginia, on Monday the 6th of May 1776. Richmond, 1816.

Puech, Louis. "Un Aventurier Gascon: Paul-Émile Soubiran." *Bulletin de la Société Archéologique du Gers* 8 (1907): 13–37, 101–123.

Pula, James S. "Mr. Jefferson's Secret Agent: Tadeusz Kościuszko and the Rapprochement between France and the United States." *Polish Review* 66 (2021): 5–24.

Quincy, Edmund. *Life of Josiah Quincy of Massachusetts.* Boston, 1868.

Racine, Karen. *Francisco de Miranda: A Transatlantic Life in the Age of Revolution.* Wilmington: Scholarly Resources, 2003.

Randolph, Edmund. *A Vindication of Mr. Randolph's Resignation.* Philadelphia, 1795.

Rappleye, Charles. *Robert Morris: Financier of the American Revolution.* New York: Simon & Schuster, 2011.

Rapport, Mike. *The Napoleonic Wars: A Very Short Introduction.* New York: Oxford University Press, 2013.

Rau, Louise. "The Chêne Family in Detroit." *Burton Historical Collection Leaflet* 9 (September 1930): 3–16.

Read, James H. *Power versus Liberty: Madison, Hamilton, Wilson, and Jefferson.* Charlottesville: University of Virginia Press, 2000.

Reardon, John J. *Edmund Randolph: A Biography.* New York: Macmillan, 1974.

Reeder, Tyson. "Britain, France, and the Road to War," in Tyson Reeder, *The Routledge History of U.S. Foreign Relations*, 133–147. New York: Routledge, 2022.

Reeder, Tyson. "Lines of Separation: James Madison on Religious Liberty and National Security." *Journal of the Early Republic* 41 (Summer 2021): 267–297.

Reeder, Tyson. *Smugglers, Pirates, and Patriots: Free Trade in the Age of Revolution.* Philadelphia: University of Pennsylvania Press, 2019.

Reuter, Frank T. "'Petty Spy' or Effective Diplomat: The Role of George Beckwith." *Journal of the Early Republic* 10 (Winter 1990): 471–492.

Risjord, Norman K. *Jefferson's America, 1760–1815.* 3rd ed. New York: Rowman & Littlefield, 2010.

Rives, George Lockhart. *Selections from the Correspondence of Thomas Barclay, Formerly British Consul-General at New York.* New York, 1894.

Roberts, Andrew. *Napoleon: A Life.* New York: Viking, 2014.

Robertson, William Spence. *Francisco de Miranda and the Revolutionizing of Spanish America.* Washington, DC: Government Printing Office, 1909.

Robinson, James. *Philadelphia Directory, 1805.* Philadelphia, [1805].

Rohrs, Richard C. "The Federalist Party and the Convention of 1800." *Diplomatic History* 12 (Summer 1988): 237–260.

Rosin, Michael L. "The Three-Fifths Rule and the Presidential Elections of 1800 and 1824." *University of St. Thomas Law Journal* 15 (2018): 159–227.

Rossiter, Clinton, ed. *The Federalist Papers.* New York: Penguin Putnam, 1961.

Rowell, Diana. *Paris: The "New Rome" of Napoleon I.* New York: Bloomsbury, 2012.

Ruigómez de Hernández, María Pilar. *El Gobierno Español del Despotismo Ilustrado Ante la Independencia de los Estados Unidos de América.* Madrid: Ministerio de Asuntos Exteriores, 1978.

Rutland, Robert Allen. *James Madison: The Founding Father.* Columbia: University of Missouri Press, 1997.

Sabine, Lorenzo. *Biographical Sketches of Loyalists of the American Revolution, With an Historical Essay.* 2 vols. Boston, 1864.

Sadosky, Leonard J. *Revolutionary Negotiations: Indians, Empires, and Diplomats in the Founding of America.* Charlottesville: University of Virginia Press, 2009.

Saint-Allais, Nicolas Viton de. *Nobiliaire Universel de France, ou Recueil Général des Généalogies Historiques des Maisons Nobles de ce Royaume.* 21 vols. Paris, 1817–1843.

Saint-Hilaire, Émile-Marc. *L'Art de payer ses dettes et de satisfaire ses créanciers sans débourser un sou, enseigné en dix leçons, ou Manuel du droit commercial à l'usage des gens ruinés.* Paris, 1827.

Saravia, Gonzalo M. Quintero. *Bernardo de Gálvez: Spanish Hero of the American Revolution.* Chapel Hill: University of North Carolina Press, 2018.

Saunt, Claudio. *A New Order of Things: Property, Power, and the Transformation of the Creek Indians, 1733–1816.* Cambridge, UK: Cambridge University Press, 1999.

Schakenbach, Lindsay. "Schemers, Dreamers, and a Revolutionary Foreign Policy: New York City in the Era of Second Independence, 1805–1815." *New York History* 94 (Summer/Fall 2013): 267–282.

Schwarz, Michael. "The Great Divergence Reconsidered: Hamilton, Madison, and U.S.-British Relations, 1783–89." *Journal of the Early Republic* 27 (Fall 2007): 407–436.

Scully, Randolph Ferguson. *Religion and the Making of Nat Turner's Virginia: Baptist Community and Conflict, 1740–1840.* Charlottesville: University of Virginia Press, 2008.

Seitzinger, Michael V. "Conducting Foreign Relations Without Authority." *Congressional Research Service* (March 11, 2015). https://sgp.fas.org/crs/misc/RL33265.pdf.

Sharp, James Roger. *American Politics in the Early Republic: The New Nation in Crisis.* New Haven: Yale University Press, 1993.

Shaw, E. H. *Sallust and the Fall of the Republic: Historiography and Intellectual Life at Rome.* Leiden: Brill, 2022.

Sheehan, Colleen A. *The Mind of James Madison.* New York: Cambridge University Press, 2015.

Shepherd, William R. "Wilkinson and the Beginnings of the Spanish Conspiracy." *American Historical Review* 9 (April 1904): 490–506.

Sheridan, Eugene R. "The Recall of Edmond Charles Genet: A Study in Transatlantic Politics and Diplomacy." *Diplomatic History* 18 (Fall 1994): 463–488.

Silver, Peter. *Our Savage Neighbors: How Indian War Transformed Early America.* New York: Norton, 2008.

Slaughter, Thomas P. *The Whiskey Rebellion: Frontier Epilogue to the American Revolution.* New York: Oxford University Press, 1986.

Sloan, Cliff and David McKean. *The Great Decision: Jefferson, Adams, Marshall, and the Battle for the Supreme Court.* New York: Public Affairs, 2009.

Smith, Craig Bruce. *American Honor: The Creation of the Nation's Ideals During the Revolutionary Era.* Chapel Hill: University of North Carolina Press, 2018.

Smith, F. Todd. "The Kadhadacho Indians and the Louisiana-Texas Frontier, 1803–1815." *Southwestern Historical Quarterly* 95 (October 1991): 177–204.

Smith, James Morton. "The Enforcement of the Alien Friends Act of 1798." *Mississippi Valley Historical Review* 41 (June 1954): 85–104.

Smith, Jean Edward. *John Marshall: Definer of a Nation.* New York: Henry Holt, 1996.

Smith, Margaret Bayard. *The First Forty Years of Washington Society.* Edited by Gaillard Hunt. New York: Charles Scribner's Sons, 1906.

Smith, Thomas E. V. *The City of New York in the Year of Washington's Inauguration, 1789.* New York, 1889.

Smith, William Henry. *The St. Clair Papers: The Life and Public Service of Arthur St. Clair.* 2 vols. Cincinnati, 1882.

Smith. John Howard. *The First Great Awakening: Redefining Religion in British America, 1725–1775.* Madison, NJ: Fairleigh Dickinson University Press, 2015.

Sokol, Stanley S. and Sharon F. Mrotek Kissane. *The Polish Biographical Dictionary: Profiles of Nearly 900 Poles Who Have Made Lasting Contributions to World Civilization.* Wauconda, IL: Bolchazy-Carducci, 1992.

Solano Costa, José Navarro Latorre y Fernando. *Conspiración Española? 1787–1789: Contribución al Estudio de las Primeras Relaciones Históricas Entre España y los Estados Unidos de Norteamérica.* Zaragoza, 1949.

St. John, Bayle. *The Louvre or, Biography of a Museum.* London, 1855.

Stagg, J. C. A. *Borderlines in Borderlands: James Madison and the Spanish-American Frontier, 1776–1821.* New Haven: Yale University Press, 2009.

Stagg, J. C. A. *The War of 1812: Conflict for a Continent.* New York: Cambridge University Press, 2012.

Stahr, Walter. *John Jay: Founding Father.* New York: Palgrave Macmillan, 2005.

Stanyan, Temple. *The Graecian History: From the End of the Peloponnesian War, to the Death of Philip of Macedon.* 2 vols. London, 1739.

Stewart, David O. *American Emperor: Aaron Burr's Challenge to Jefferson's America.* New York: Simon & Schuster, 2011.

Stewart, Donald H. *The Opposition Press of the Federalist Period.* Albany: State University of New York Press, 1969.

Stinchcombe, William. "Talleyrand and the American Negotiations of 1797–1798." *Journal of American History* 62 (December 1975): 575–590.

Storozynkski, Alex. *The Peasant Prince: Thaddeus Kosciuszko and the Age of Revolution.* New York: St. Martin's Press, 2009.

Sullivan, William. *Familiar Letters of Public Characters and Public Events; From the Peace of 1783, to the Peace of 1815.* Boston, 1834.

Tagg, James. *Benjamin Franklin Bache and the Philadelphia Aurora.* Philadelphia: University of Pennsylvania Press, 1991.

Taylor, Alan. *American Republics: A Continental History of the United States, 1783–1850.* New York: W. W. Norton, 2021.

Taylor, Alan. *American Revolutions: A Continental History, 1750–1804.* New York: Norton, 2016.

Taylor, Alan. *The Civil War of 1812: American Citizens, British Subjects, Irish Rebels, and Indian Allies.* New York: Knopf, 2010.

Taylor, Alan. *The Divided Ground: Indians, Settlers, and the Northern Borderland of the American Revolution.* New York: Vintage, 2006.

Taylor, Alan. *The Internal Enemy: Slavery and War in Virginia, 1772–1832.* New York: Norton, 2013.

The Diaries of John Quincy Adams: A Digital Collection. Boston: Massachusetts Historical Society. https://www.masshist.org/jqadiaries/php/.

Theriault, Sean M. "Party Politics during the Louisiana Purchase." *Social Science History* 30 (Summer 2006): 293–324.

Todd, Charles Burr. *The True Aaron Burr: A Biographical Sketch.* New York: A. S. Barnes, 1902.

Tolles, Frederick B. "Unofficial Ambassador: George Logan's Mission to France, 1798." *William and Mary Quarterly* 7 (January 1950): 1–25.

Tracy, Nicholas, ed. *The Naval Chronicle: The Contemporary Record of the Royal Navy at War, 1807–1810.* 5 vols. Consolidated ed. London: Stackpole, 1998–1999.

Tucker, Spencer and Frank T. Reuter. *Injured Honor: The Chesapeake-Leopard Affair, June 22, 1807.* Annapolis: Naval Institute Press, 1996.

Turner, Frederick J. "Correspondence of Clark and Genet." *Annual Report of the American Historical Association for the Year 1896*. Washington, 1897.

Turner, Frederick J.. "Documents on the Blount Conspiracy, 1795–1797." *American Historical Review* 10 (April 1905): 574–606.

Valdivielso, Alfonso Carlos Saiz. *Diego de Gardoqui: Esplendor y Penumbra*. Bilbao, 2014.

Van Cleve, George William. *We Have Not a Government: The Articles of Confederation and the Road to the Constitution*. Chicago: University of Chicago Press, 2017.

Vause, Erika. *In the Red and in the Black: Debt, Dishonor, and the Law in France Between Revolutions*. Charlottesville: University of Virginia Press, 2018.

Vile, John R. *The Men Who Made the Constitution: Lives of the Delegates to the Constitutional Convention*. Lanham, MD: Scarecrow Press, 2013.

Vogel, Steve. *Through the Perilous Fight: Six Weeks That Saved the Nation*. New York: Random House, 2013.

Voltaire. *Epitre à l'auteur du nouveau livre: Des trois imposteurs*. s.n., 1769.

Waldstreicher, David. *In the Midst of Perpetual Fetes: The Making of American Nationalism, 1776–1820*. Chapel Hill: Omohundro Institute by University of North Carolina Press, 1997.

Waldstreicher, David. *Slavery's Constitution: From Revolution to Ratification*. New York: Hill and Wang, 2009.

Wallace, Anthony F. C. *Jefferson and the Indians: The Tragic Fate of the First Americans*. Cambridge, MA: Belknap Press of Harvard University Press, 1999.

Walsh, James P. "Black Cotted Raskolls: Anti-Anglican Criticism in Colonial Virginia." *Virginia Magazine of History and Biography* 88 (January 1980): 21–36.

Walzer, Michael. *Regicide and Revolution: Speeches at the Trial of Louis XVI*. New York: Columbia University Press, 1992.

Ward, Harry M. "Jackson, William." *American National Biography*, https://doi.org/10.1093/anb/9780198606697.article.0200193.

Waselkov, Gregory A. *A Conquering Spirit: Fort Mims and the Redstick War of 1813–1814*. Tuscaloosa: University of Alabama Press, 2006.

Washington, H. A., ed. *The Writings of Thomas Jefferson*. 9 vols.; New York, 1853–54.

Watlington, Patricia. *The Partisan Spirit: Kentucky Politics, 1779–1792*. New York: Atheneum, 1972.

Weber, David J. *The Spanish Frontier in North America*. Brief Edition. New Haven: Yale University Press, 2009.

Wertheimer, Eric. "The Self-Abstracting Letters of War: Madison, Henry, and the Executive Author," in *Warring for America: Cultural Contests in the Era of 1812*, edited by *Nicole* Eustace and Fredrika J. Teute, 313–330. Chapel Hill: University of North Carolina Press, 2017.

Wharton, Anne Hollingsworth. *Social Life in the Early Republic*. New York: Lippincott, 1903.

Wharton, Francis, ed., *The Revolutionary Diplomatic Correspondence of the United States*. 6 vols. Washington, 1889.

Wheelan, Joseph. *Mr. Adams's Last Crusade: John Quincy Adams's Extraordinary Post-presidential Life in Congress.* New York: Public Affairs, 2008.

Whitaker, Arthur Preston. *The Spanish-American Frontier, 1783–1795: The Westward Movement and the Spanish Retreat in the Mississippi Valley.* Lincoln: University of Nebraska Press, 1969.

White, Richard. *The Middle Ground: Indians, Empires, and Republics in the Great Lakes Region, 1650–1815.* New York: Cambridge University Press, 1991; 2011.

Whitmire, Mildred Edwards. "A Man and His Land: The Story of Jacob and Frances Madison Hite and the Cherokees." *Magazine of the Jefferson County Historical Society* 44 (1978): 37–55.

Wilentz, Sean. *No Property in Man: Slavery and Antislavery at the Nation's Founding.* Cambridge, MA: Harvard University Press, 2018 (Preface to the paperback edition, 2019).

Wills, Garry. *Negro President: Jefferson and the Slave Power.* Boston: Houghton Mifflin, 2003.

Wilson, Beckles. *Friendly Relations: A Narrative of Britain's Ministers and Ambassadors to America (1791–1930).* 2nd ed. Freeport, NY: Books for Libraries, 1969.

Wilson, James Grant and John Fiske. *Appletons' Cyclopaedia of American Biography.* 6 vols. New York, 1887.

Wood, Gordon S. *The Radicalism of the American Revolution.* New York: Vintage, 1991.

World Heritage Convention, UNESCO "Aranjuez Cultural Landscape." Spain, 2000. https://whc.unesco.org/uploads/nominations/1044.pdf.

Zenzen, Joan M. *Fort Stanwix National Monument: Reconstructing the Past and Partnering for the Future.* Albany: State University of New York Press, 2008.

NEWSPAPERS

Albany Gazette (Albany, NY)

Albany Register (Albany, NY)

Alexandria Gazette (Alexandria, VA)

Alexandria, Daily Advertiser (Alexandria, VA)

American Advocate (Hallwell, ME)

American Citizen (New York, NY)

American Mercury (Hartford, CT)

American Telegraph (Brownsville, PA)

Aurora General Advertiser (Philadelphia, PA)

Bee (Hudson, NY)

Bee (New London, CT)

Bennington News-Letter (Bennington, VT)

Boston Commercial Gazette (Boston, MA)

Boston Daily Advertiser (Boston, MA)

Chronicle Express (New York, NY)

City Gazette (Charleston, SC)

Columbian Centinel (Boston, MA)
Commercial Advertiser (New York, NY)
Connecticut Courant (Hartford, CT)
Connecticut Herald (New Haven, CT)
Connecticut Journal (New Haven, CT)
Courier de Boston (Boston, MA)
Courier of New Hampshire (Concord, NH)
Daily Advertiser (New York, NY)
Delaware Gazette and State Journal (Wilmington, DE)
Democratic Press (Philadelphia, PA)
Diary (New York, NY)
Dunlap's American Daily Advertiser (Philadelphia, PA)
Eastern Argus (Portland, ME)
Enquirer (Richmond, VA)
Essex Register (Salem, MA)
Federal Gazette (Baltimore, MD)
Federal Republican (Baltimore, MD)
Freeman's Journal and Philadelphia Daily Advertiser (Philadelphia, PA)
Gazette (Portland, ME)
Gazette nationale ou le Moniteur universel (Paris, France)
Gazette of the United States (Philadelphia, PA)
General Advertiser (Philadelphia, PA)
Hampshire Federalist (Springfield, MA)
Herald (New York, NY)
Hereford Journal (Hereford, England)
Hive (Northampton, MA)
Impartial Register (Salem, MA)
Journal (New York, NY)
L'Oracle and Daily Advertiser (New York, NY)
Leicester Journal (Leicester, England)
Liverpool Mercury (Liverpool, England)
Long-Island Star (Brooklyn, NY)
Massachusetts Spy (Worcester, MA)
Mercantile Advertiser (New York, NY)
Middlesex Gazette (Middletown, CT)
Mirrour (Concord, NH)
Morning Chronicle (New York, NY)
National Aegis (Worcester, MA)
National Gazette (Philadelphia, PA)
National Intelligencer (Washington, DC)
Newburyport Gazette (Newburyport, MA)
Newburyport Herald (Newburyport, MA)
New-England Galaxy (Boston, MA)
New-England Palladium (Boston, MA)
New-Hampshire Gazette (Portsmouth, NH)

New-York Evening Post (New York, NY)
New-York Gazette & General Advertiser (New York, NY)
New-York Gazette, and Weekly Mercury (New York, NY)
New-York Herald (New York, NY)
New-York Packet (New York, NY)
Norfolk Repository (Dedham, MA)
People's Friend (New York, NY)
Philadelphia Gazette, and Universal Daily Advertiser (Philadelphia, PA)
Political Atlas (Stockbridge, MA)
Political Observatory (Walpole, NH)
Porcupine's Gazette (Philadelphia, PA)
Portsmouth Oracle (Portsmouth, NH)
Poulson's American Daily Advertiser (Philadelphia, PA)
Providence Gazette (Providence, RI)
Public Advertiser (New York, NY)
Repertory (Boston, MA)
Reporter (Lexington, KY)
Republican Advocate (Frederick, MD)
Republican Watch-Tower (New York, NY)
Rhode-Island Republican (Newport, RI)
Rutland Herald (Rutland, VT)
Salem Gazette (Salem, MA)
Salem Register (Salem, MA)
South-Carolina State-Gazette (Charleston, SC)
Spectator (New York, NY)
St. George's Chronicle, and Grenada Gazette (St. George's, Grenada)
Times; and District of Columbia Daily Advertiser (Alexandria, VA)
United States' Gazette (Philadelphia, PA)
Vermont Republican (Windsor, VT)
Virginia Gazette (Williamsburg)
Washington Federalist (Washington, DC)
Washingtonian (Windsor, VT)
Weekly Aurora (Philadelphia, PA)
Weekly Inspector (New York, NY)

INDEX

For the benefit of digital users, indexed terms that span two pages (e.g., 52–53) may, on occasion, appear on only one of those pages.

New York, 12, 21–22, 143, 144, 153, 154
   economy, 72
   and election of 1796, 144
   and election of 1800, 144
   newspapers, 50–51
   and ratification, 50, 52
   relations with Great Britain (*see* Great
      Britain, relations with New York)
   relations with Native Americans, 35,
      36–37, 236
New York Assembly, 133
New York Commercial Advertiser, 231f
New York, NY, 38, 41f, 45, 53, 54–55, 62,
      66, 72, 103–4, 193, 195, 214, 215,
      223–24, 252. *see also* Manhattan
   diplomacy in, 39, 40, 58, 61, 62, 63, 66
   Madison boards in, 45–47, 61
   and Miranda Expedition, 185, 186,
      187
   and ratification, 50
   Washington arrives in, 56–57
Newcastle (New Castle), DE, 130, 131
Newfoundland, 27–28
newspapers, 222, 228
   and Burr Conspiracy, 206
   and foreign meddling, 81, 105, 119,
      120, 123–24, 132, 135–36, 189 (*see
      also* Yrujo, Carlos Martínez de, and
      US newspapers)
   and freedom of the press, 135–36, 137,
      172, 173, 177, 183, 188–90, 273–74
   and political conflict, 74–75, 82–83,
      84, 85–87, 110–11, 112, 119, 123, 133,
      171, 188
   and public opinion, 166, 169, 172,
      177–78, 188, 189
Ney, Michel, 255
Niagara River, 30
Niagara, Canada. *see* Fort Niagara
Nicholas, Wilson, 226
Niemcewicz, Julian Ursyn, 130, 131,
      312n.59
Nixon, Richard, 275–77, 348n.17
Non-Importation Act, 220
Nootka Sound Crisis, 66, 67

North Africa, 175–76
North America, 36, 115f, 119–20, 150, 162,
      197–98, 236
   Britain in, 224–25
   and European geostrategy, 3, 25, 43,
      66, 113, 116–17, 122, 150, 161
   France in, 25, 122, 153, 157, 161–62,
      163–64, 321n.96
North Carolina, 41–42, 54, 295n.91
North Vietnam, 275–76
Northwestern Confederacy, 91, 122
Nova Scotia, 224–25, 226, 228

O'Neill, Arturo, 33–34
Obama, Barack, 277
Ogden, Samuel, 188
Ohio River, 8, 19–20, 21, 35–36, 37, 116,
      209
Ohio River Valley, 11, 19, 71, 90–91, 195,
      199, 238, 267–68
Oneida, 11
Orange County Committee of Safety, 14
Orange County, VA, 14, 15–16, 52, 141,
      142–43
Orleans Territory, 167–69, 201
Oswald, Richard, 28
Otis, Harrison Gray, 228

Page, John, 218–19
Paine, Thomas, 3, 163–64
Pandora, 279
Paris, France, 29, 61, 81, 89, 97, 153, 221,
      251, 255, 260
   chess club in, 140
   diplomacy in, 11–12, 24–25, 26, 28, 43,
      95–96, 124, 125, 129, 131, 132, 155,
      156–58, 159, 173, 222
   Henry in, 262, 263, 264
   reflects Napoleonic power, 159–61
Parliament (Great Britain), 69, 75, 78
Parma, Duke of (Ferdinand I), 318n.51
Patton, Philip, 212–13
Payamataha, 21–22
Payne, Anna, 140
Peace of Paris, 1783, 11–12, 29, 32–33

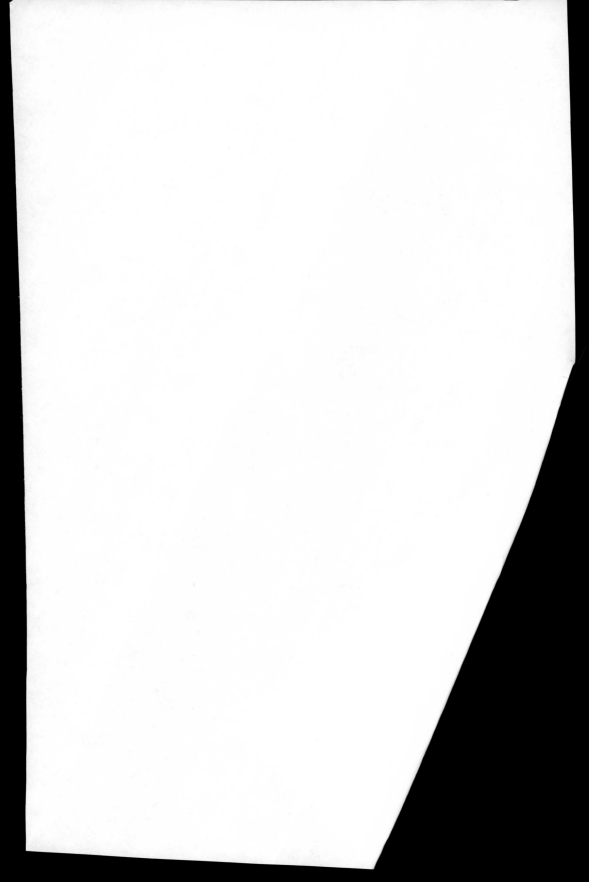